Shattering Empires

The break-up of the Ottoman empire and the disintegration of the Russian empire were watershed events in modern history. The unraveling of these empires was both cause and consequence of World War I and resulted in the deaths of millions. It irrevocably changed the landscape of the Middle East and Eurasia and reverberates to this day in conflicts throughout the Caucasus and Middle East. *Shattering Empires* draws on extensive research in the Ottoman and Russian archives to tell the story of the rivalry and collapse of two great empires. Overturning accounts that portray their clash as one of conflicting nationalisms, this pioneering study argues that geopolitical competition and the emergence of a new global interstate order provide the key to understanding the course of history in the Ottoman–Russian borderlands in the twentieth century. It will appeal to anyone interested in Middle Eastern, Russian, and Eurasian history, international relations, ethnic conflict, and World War I.

MICHAEL A. REYNOLDS is Assistant Professor of Near Eastern Studies at Princeton University.

Shattering Empires

The Clash and Collapse of the Ottoman and Russian Empires, 1908–1918

Michael A. Reynolds

 CAMBRIDGE
UNIVERSITY PRESS

CAMBRIDGE UNIVERSITY PRESS
Cambridge, New York, Melbourne, Madrid, Cape Town, Singapore,
São Paulo, Delhi, Tokyo, Mexico City

Cambridge University Press
The Edinburgh Building, Cambridge CB2 8RU, UK
Published in the United States of America by Cambridge University Press,
New York

www.cambridge.org
Information on this title: www.cambridge.org/9780521149167

First published 2011
4th printing 2011

Printed in the United Kingdom at the University Press, Cambridge

A catalogue record for this publication is available from the British Library

Library of Congress Cataloguing in Publication data
Reynolds, Michael A., 1968–
Shattering empires : the clash and collapse of the Ottoman and Russian
empires, 1908–1918 / Michael A. Reynolds.
    p.   cm.
Includes index.
ISBN 978-0-521-19553-9 (hardback) – ISBN 978-0-521-14916-7 (paperback)
1. Turkey – Foreign relations – Russia.   2. Russia – Foreign relations –
Turkey.   3. Turkey – History – Mehmed V, 1909–1918.   4. Turkey –
History – Revolution, 1909.   5. Russia – History – Nicholas II, 1894–1917.
6. Russia – History – February Revolution, 1917.   7. World War, 1914–1918 –
Turkey.   8. World War, 1914–1918 – Russia.   9. Geopolitics – Caucasus.
10. Geopolitics – Eurasia.   I. Title.
DR479.R9R49   2010
940.3′56 – dc22   2010035477

ISBN 978-0-521-19553-9 Hardback
ISBN 978-0-521-14916-7 Paperback

Contents

Plates

The plates are to be found between pages 166 and 167.

Maps

Note on transliteration and usage

The transliteration of names and places from multiple non-Latin alphabet sources presents numerous irresolvable difficulties. This is particularly true when one is dealing with imperial sources, wherein the language of a document is often unrelated to the native tongue of the subject mentioned therein, thereby raising the real problem of how best to render that subject's name. Names from Ottoman documents are transliterated into their modern Turkish equivalent. English spellings have been retained for Turkish words that already enjoy standard English spellings, such as pasha. Names cited in Russian documents generally are transliterated according to a modified Library of Congress system. Exceptions include well-known figures such as Trotsky (Trotskii) and Yudenich (Iudenich) and prominent place names, such as Yerevan (Erevan). The final Russian soft sign is dropped for place names such as Sevastopol (Sevastopol') and Aleksandropol (Aleksandropol'). Similarly, *dzh* is dropped for the more straightforward *j* in names of Arabic origin and place names: hence, Najmuddin and Ajaria, not Nadzhmuddin and Adzharia. Because Ottoman as well as Russian sources use the term Transcaucasus (*Mavera-yı Kafkasya* and *Zakavkaz'e*), I have chosen to retain it instead of "South Caucasus," a term that has recently come into more popular use.

As a general, but not inviolable, rule, personal names are rendered in the language of the empire with which they were more closely associated, whether by choice or circumstance. Place names are, again generally, selected according to imperial affiliation prior to 1914, and spelled accordingly: Sarikamish, Elisavetpol, and Batumi rather than Sarıkamış, Gence/Gäncä, or Batum. No claims are made with regard to a subject's ethnicity, identity, or presumed political loyalty, or to a territory's proper affiliation. The sole intent is to make the personal and place names accessible to English-speakers.

The reader unfamiliar with Ottoman and Turkish history should be aware that family names were not adopted until 1934. When pertinent, the family name is placed in parentheses upon first mention of an individual, e.g., Halil Bey (Menteşe). The words bey, efendi, and pasha are honorific titles, not last names.

For those readers unfamiliar with Turkish spelling and pronunciation, the following simplified guide may be of use:

C, c	"j" as in "jam"
Ç, ç	"ch" as in "chest"
Ğ, ğ	a soft "g" that generally elongates the preceding vowel
I, ı	a hard "i," something between "i" in "will" and "u" in radium
J, j	similar to the "s" in "treasure"
Ö, ö	same as the German "ö" or the French "eu" as in "seul"
Ş, ş	"sh" as in "should"
Ü, ü	same as the German "ü" or the French "u" as in "lune"

In citations of primary source documents I include two dates. The first is the date found on the document and the second, in brackets, is the conversion to the Gregorian calendar in the form of day, month, and year. The Ottoman empire used three calendars. The dates herein are from the Rumi calendar, which was used for civil matters. The Rumi calendar measured solar years beginning from the *Hijra* and was based on the Julian calendar, which lags thirteen days behind the Gregorian calendar. Hence the Rumi calendar was 584 years and thirteen days behind the Gregorian calendar. In March 1917 the Ottomans eliminated the thirteen-day difference between the Rumi and the Gregorian calendars. Because the Ottoman system for numbering months began not with January but with March, I have written out the names of Ottoman months. Russia used the Julian calendar until 1918 when it switched to the Gregorian. The Transcaucasus made the switch later. For the sake of consistency, I have provided a converted Gregorian date in numerical form, month.day.year, for citations from Ottoman, Russian, and Transcaucasian sources.

Acknowledgments

The advice, assistance, and encouragement of a large number of people made it possible for me to write this book. First are my parents. My father, while he was still alive, instilled in me at a young age the importance of discipline and education. My mother encouraged my sense of adventure and love of travel. Weekend road trips with my Uncle John sparked my interest in history. Karl Crawford impressed upon me the need to study foreign cultures in general and fostered my interest in Russia in particular.

My fascination with the Caucasus began in the world of sport and with the treasured friendship of Avset Asadullaevich Avsetov. He and Suren Petrosovich Bogdasarov will always exemplify the best of the Caucasus to me. Radin Fataliev befriended me when we trained together and remains a trusted confidant and master travel logistician.

Şükrü Hanioğlu introduced me to Ottoman history and has been an invaluable guide, colleague, and friend ever since. Stephen Kotkin was an exemplary teacher and has been a consistent source of sound counsel.

I am profoundly grateful to Stephen Peter Rosen. His support and quiet encouragement were critical to my pursuit of an academic career. The Olin Institute of Harvard University's Weatherhead Center for International Affairs provided an unsurpassed home for research and writing.

Peter Holquist has been a wonderful colleague and friend and a source of inspiration. Robert Crews shared his enthusiasm for the manuscript and his characteristically discerning criticisms and suggestions. Bill Blair read the manuscript carefully and sharpened it. Tsering Wangyal Shawa generously gave his time to prepare the maps.

Portions of this book were presented in Salzburg and Geneva at meetings of the Workshop on Armenian–Turkish Studies. I thank Müge Gökçe, Gerard Libaridian, and Ronald Suny for inviting me to take part and for their intellectual courage and scholarly integrity in initiating the workshop.

Chapters 6, 7 and 8 use material from my article, "Buffers, not Brethren: Young Turk Military Policy in the First World War and the

Myth of Panturanism," *Past and Present*, no. 203 (May 2009), 137–79, and is reprinted with kind permission.

I thank the staffs of the Ottoman Prime Ministerial Archives, Turkish Military History and Strategic Studies archive, Archive of the Foreign Policy of the Russian Empire, State Archive of the Russian Federation, the Russian State Military-Historical Archive, the Russian State Military Archive, the Political Archive of the German Foreign Ministry, the library of Turkey's Grand National Assembly, the Turkish National Library, Ataturk Library, and Russia's State Public Historical Library.

Fellowships and grants from the Smith Richardson Foundation, the International Research and Exchanges Board, the Fulbright Institute of International Education program, the American Research Institute in Turkey, and Princeton's University Committee on Research in the Humanities and Social Sciences made it possible for me to make use of these archives and libraries.

Karen Anderson Howes demonstrated enormous patience in copyediting and improving this book.

Conversations and exchanges with the following directly contributed to this book: Oleg Airepetov, Halit Akarca, Suat Akgül, Mustafa Aksakal, Hizir Amaev, Cemil Aydın, Halil Bal, Robinder Bhatty, Mehmet Darakçıoğlu, Fuat Dündar, Howard Eissenstat, Edward Erickson, Rozaliya Garipova, Ryan Gingeras, Thomas Goltz, Yücel Güçlü, Adeeb Khalid, Hans-Lukas Kieser, Janet Klein, Oleg Kozlov, John LeDonne, Eric Lohr, Hirotake Maeda, Erez Manela, James Meyer, Norihiro Naganawa, Onur Önol, Murat Papşu, Sean Pollock, Musa Qasımlı, Solmaz Rustamova-Tohidi, Joshua Sanborn, Ara Sanjian, Nadia Schadlow, David Schimmelpenninck van der Oye, Norman Stone, and Ahmet Tetik.

The pursuit of scholarship yields unique rewards and demands considerable sacrifice. Yet whereas the rewards are limited mainly to the scholar, the sacrifices are borne disproportionately by those nearby. More than anyone, my beloved wife Olga has had to bear those sacrifices. The love and mirth of my daughters Eva and Yana sustained me through the trying process of writing this book, and to them I dedicate it.

Abbreviations

OTTOMAN ARCHIVAL SOURCES

ATASE   GENELKURMAY ASKERÎ TARİH VE STRATEJİK ETÜT
BAŞKANLIĞI ARŞİVİ
Unless otherwise noted, all citations are from the First World War
Collection (Birinci Dünya Harbi Koleksiyonu).
BDH	Birinci Dünya Harbi
BHK	Balkan Harbi Koleksiyonu

BOA   BAŞBAKANLIK OSMANLI ARŞİVİ
BEO	Bab-ı Âlî Evrak Odası
DH.İD	Dahiliye Nezareti İdarî Kısım
DH.İ.UM	Dahiliye Nezareti İdâre-i Umumiye
DH.KMS	Dahiliye Nezareti Kalem-i Mahsûs Müdüriyeti
DH.MUİ	Dahiliye Nezareti Muhaberat-ı Umumiye İdaresi
DH.ŞFR	Dahiliye Nezareti Şifre Kalemi
DH.SYS	Dahiliye Nezareti Siyasî Kısım
HR.HMŞ.İŞO	Hariciye Nezareti Hukuk Müşavirliği İstişare Odası
MV	Meclis-i Vükelâ Mazbataları

K.	Klasör
D.	Dosya
S.	Sıra
F.	Fihrist
B.	Belge

RUSSIAN ARCHIVAL SOURCES

AVPRI   ARKHIV VNESHNEI POLITIKI ROSSIISKOI IMPERII

GARF   GOSUDARSTVENNYI ARKHIV ROSSIISKII FEDERATSII

RGVA   ROSSIISKII GOSUDARSTVENNYI VOENNYI ARKHIV

RGVIA   ROSSIISKII GOSUDARSTVENNYI VOENNO-ISTORICHESKII
ARKHIV

f.	fond
o.	opis'
d.	delo
l., ll. (pl.)	list', listy (pl.)

GERMAN ARCHIVAL SOURCES

PA-AA   POLITISCHES ARCHIV DES AUSWÄRTIGES AMTES

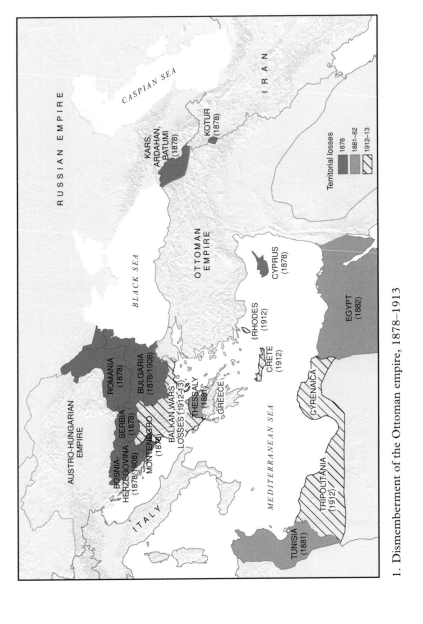

1. Dismemberment of the Ottoman empire, 1878–1913

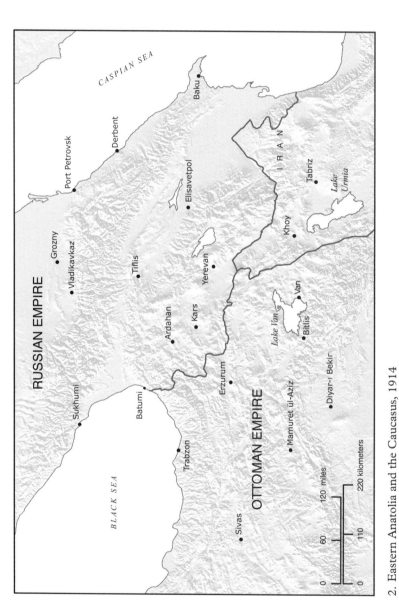

CASPIAN SEA

Baku

Derbent

Port Petrovsk

Elisavetpol

I R A N

Tabriz

Lake
Urmia

Khoy

Grozny

Vladikavkaz

Tiflis

RUSSIAN EMPIRE

Yerevan

Van

Ardahan

Kars

Lake Van

Bitlis

Sukhumi

Erzurum

Batumi

Diyar-ı Bekir

OTTOMAN EMPIRE

Mamuret ül-Aziz

Trabzon

BLACK SEA

Sivas

120 miles

60   110

0   220 kilometers

0

2. Eastern Anatolia and the Caucasus, 1914

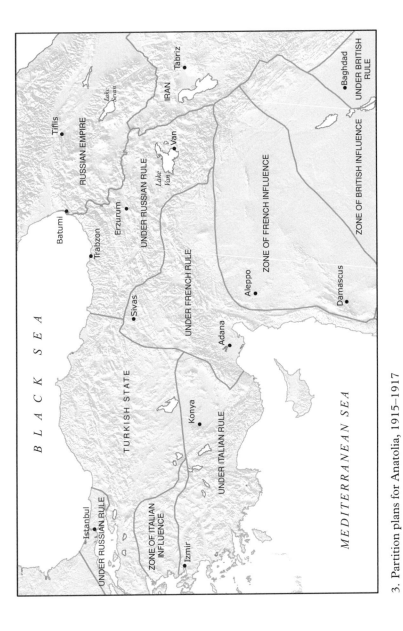

3. Partition plans for Anatolia, 1915–1917

BLACK SEA

MEDITERRANEAN SEA

RUSSIAN EMPIRE

IRAN

Tiflis

Tabriz

Lake Sevan

Batumi

Trabzon

Erzurum

Van

Lake Van

Baghdad

UNDER BRITISH RULE

UNDER RUSSIAN RULE

ZONE OF FRENCH INFLUENCE

ZONE OF BRITISH INFLUENCE

Sivas

UNDER FRENCH RULE

Aleppo

Damascus

TURKISH STATE

Adana

Konya

UNDER ITALIAN RULE

Istanbul

UNDER RUSSIAN RULE

ZONE OF ITALIAN INFLUENCE

Izmir

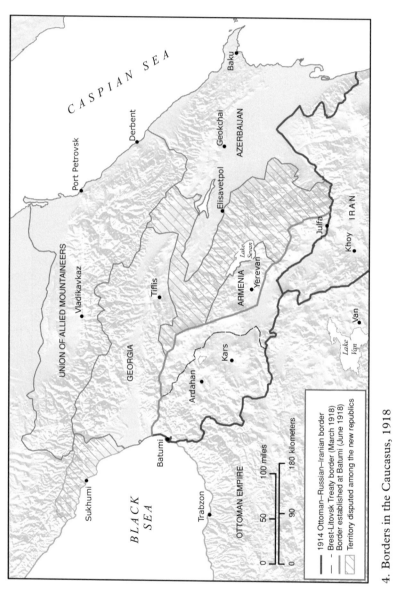

CASPIAN SEA

Baku

Derbent

Geokchai

Elisavetpol

AZERBAIJAN

Port Petrovsk

Julfa

IRAN

Khoy

Lake
Sevan

Yerevan

ARMENIA

Van

Lake
Van

UNION OF ALLIED MOUNTAINEERS

Vladikavkaz

Tiflis

Kars

GEORGIA

Ardahan

Batumi

Sukhumi

BLACK
SEA

Trabzon

OTTOMAN EMPIRE

1914 Ottoman–Russian–Iranian border
Brest-Litovsk Treaty border (March 1918)
Border established at Batumi (June 1918)
Territory disputed among the new republics

100 miles
50
0

180 kilometers
90
0

4. Borders in the Caucasus, 1918

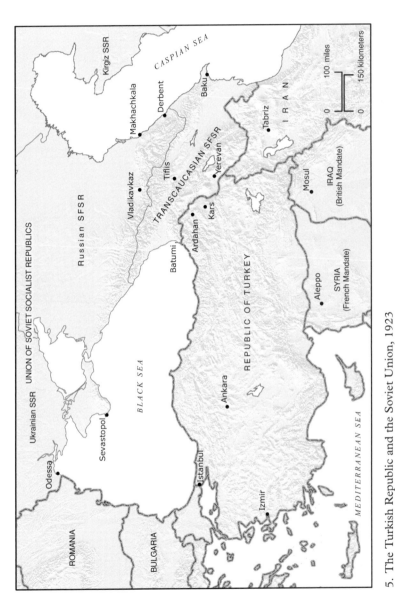

5. The Turkish Republic and the Soviet Union, 1923

Introduction

This is the story of the twilight struggle that the Ottoman and Russian empires waged for the borderlands of the Caucasus and Anatolia. Although the two empires were vastly unequal in their capabilities, the struggle yielded no victor. The instinct for self-preservation brought both empires to the same fate, ruin. Fear of partition led the Ottoman state to destroy its imperial order, whereas the compulsive desire for greater security and fear of an unstable southern border spurred the Russian state to press beyond its capacity and thereby precipitate its own collapse and the dissolution of its empire. The struggle shattered the empires, and the empires in turn shattered the peoples in their borderlands, uprooting them, fracturing their societies, and sending untold numbers to death.

The story begins at a moment of hope and promise, the Young Turk Revolution of 1908. On 23 July, the sultan of the Ottoman empire renounced autocracy and declared the restoration of the constitution he had suspended three decades earlier. The announcement, as contemporary observers and later historians alike have emphasized, sparked outbursts of joy of a kind all but forgotten in the troubled empire. The nineteenth century had been a difficult one for the empire Tsar Nicholas I had derisively dubbed "the Sick Man of Europe." It had been hemorrhaging territory, resources, and people in the face of persistent predation from without and experiencing strife among its constituent peoples within. The restoration of the constitution offered hope that this unhappy history could be reversed. A legal order resting on a constitution would free the empire's servants to modernize the state's institutions, rejuvenate its strength, and enable it to hold its own against outside powers, while its guaranty of liberties promised to dissolve intercommunal tensions and transform the empire into a more harmonious place. As the revolution's "hero of freedom," a dashing young officer named Enver Bey, exclaimed, "Now by working together with all citizens, Muslim and non-Muslim, we will raise our free people, our homeland higher. Long live the people!

Long live the homeland!"[1] The public rejoiced in the streets, celebrants joining arms and dancing together without regard to communal identity. Imams, rabbis, and priests embraced, Greeks stepped with Turks, and Armenians stood with Kurds. It was an auspicious moment, filled with promise, and those who lived it knew it would change their lives.

Enver Bey and his associates acquired from European observers the moniker "Young Turks." They were young – Enver was only twenty-six – energetic, resolute, and capable, and they imparted to that appellation those same qualifiers. They, however, called themselves "Unionists," a derivative of the name of their underground organization, the Committee of Union and Progress (CUP). As their organization's title suggested, they were determined to preserve their empire's unity through the application of progressive reform. They saw themselves as men of destiny and indeed would exert a decisive influence over the fate of their empire.

Yet one decade later their empire would lie in utter ruins. The Unionists, once so bold and full of promise, would flee Istanbul in disgrace, leaving the empire they had vowed to save prostrate and at the mercy of the great powers they had sought to defy. The Balkan provinces had been lost. The Arab lands were either under foreign occupation or in revolt. Anatolia, once a cradle of civilizations, had become a graveyard of peoples. The vision in 1908 of a harmonious community had given way to violence that culminated in the destruction of two of the land's oldest communities, the Armenian and Assyrian Christians. The Turks, Kurds, and others who remained among the living were not much better off. Stalked by death and disease, they were left to subsist at times by eating grass and drinking mud. The Unionists had led their empire not to renewal but to cataclysm.

The contrast between the optimistic vision that beckoned to the Ottoman empire in 1908 and the bitter reality that met it in 1918 was stark, but perhaps not unusual. At roughly the same time, the Ottoman empire's great nemesis, the Russian empire, succumbed to revolution. It drifted into chaos, disintegrated, and fell into a paroxysm of civil wars. Yet a mere four years before his regime collapsed, Tsar Nicholas II had celebrated his dynasty's tercentenary in a grand and opulent style.[2] The tsar was, after all, the sovereign of one-sixth of the world's surface, and the expectation was that this share would increase. Russia possessed enormous natural and human resources, and its economy, though

---

[1] Şevket Süreyya Aydemir, *Makedonya'dan Orta Asya'ya Enver Paşa*, 3 vols. (Istanbul: Remzi Kitabevi, 1971), vol. II, 17.

[2] Orlando Figes, *A People's Tragedy: The Russian Revolution, 1891–1924* (London: Jonathan Cape, 1996), 3–6.

lagging behind those of Western Europe, was industrializing rapidly. To be sure, Russia had its problems. The Russo-Japanese War and the resulting revolution of 1905 demonstrated that the demands of interstate competition were straining the autocracy's ability to rule its empire. The tercentenary celebrations revealed beneath their pomp a widening gulf between an archaic regime and a society becoming increasingly complex and restless.[3] Still, these were growing pains. Overall, Russia's might was waxing and unsettling even Germany and Great Britain.

Despite their contrasting trajectories, the Ottoman and Russian empires met nearly synchronous demises. This fact suggested to many that a common phenomenon, nationalism, best explains the empires' deaths. The contemporaneous collapse of yet another dynastic, polyethnic empire, the Austro-Hungarian, the emergence of a new world order that assumed the principle of national self-determination as a principle for state legitimacy, and the mushrooming of self-proclaimed nation-states throughout the post-imperial spaces of the Middle East and Eurasia testified to the seemingly irresistible power of nationalism. Nationalism, or so it has appeared, was a universal and elemental force capable of bringing down and sweeping away preexisting state institutions and identities.

It is, therefore, little surprise that historians of the Ottoman empire and the Middle East have traditionally approached the late Ottoman period not so much as the final era of an empire but as the prelude to (or resumption of) several distinct national histories. The presentation of late Ottoman history as the story of the awakening of ethnonationalist aspirations and the emergence of nationalist movements among the empire's subjects has the merit of providing a relatively simple framework that can explain both the splitting away of the empire's non-Turkish subjects and the emergence of the Turkish Republic in Anatolia. Thus historians of Turks, Arabs, Armenians, Albanians, Kurds, and others can all share nationalism as the organizing theme for their histories and treat the late empire as a realm of competing nationalisms, despite substantive differences in their approaches, sources, and conclusions.[4] A common

---

[3] Richard S. Wortman, *Scenarios of Power: Myth and Ceremony in Russian Monarchy*, abridged edn. (Princeton: Princeton University Press, 2006), 383–96.
[4] Bernard Lewis, *The Emergence of Modern Turkey*, 2nd edn. (London: Oxford University Press, 1968); Feroz Ahmad, *The Making of Modern Turkey* (London and New York: Routledge, 1993); Stanford Shaw, *From Empire to Republic: The Turkish War of National Liberation*, 5 vols. (Ankara: Türk Tarih Kurumu, 2000); Stanford Shaw and Ezel Kural Shaw, *History of the Ottoman Empire and Modern Turkey*, vol. II, *Reform, Revolution, and Republic: The Rise of Modern Turkey, 1808–1975* (New York: Cambridge University Press, 1977); Taner Akçam, *From Empire to Republic: Turkish Nationalism and the Armenian Genocide* (New York: Zed Books, 2004); George Antonius, *The Arab Awakening: The Story*

perspective underlies their works. The consensus answer to the question posed above of what explains the radical disjuncture between the hopes of 1908 and the outcome of 1918 is straightforward: a clash of irreconcilable nationalisms.

Nationalism as an organizing theme has not dominated Russian historiography as much as it has Ottoman and Middle Eastern historiographies. For most of the twentieth century, the question of the origins and inevitability of the Russian Revolution, pitched generally as a question of contending political visions at the Russian center rather than as a struggle of ethnic or other groups at the imperial periphery, had tended to dominate Russian historiography. The exploration of questions of nationalism was not entirely ignored, but it was left to specialists in the non-Russian areas of the Russian empire and thereby marginalized. Like their counterparts studying the late Ottoman and post-Ottoman Middle East, these scholars strove to distinguish their chosen regions and peoples from the center and searched for the seeds of nationalism in them.[5] One partial but important exception to this tendency to relegate nationalism to the particular was Richard Pipes' *The Formation of the Soviet Union: Communism and Nationalism*.[6] Although arguably it too readily accepted the nationalist framework, it did attempt to integrate the stories of the struggles in the imperial borderlands with that of the center. The fact that Pipes' work, originally published in 1954, was reissued as a largely unrevised second edition in 1997 is a testament both to its inherent value and to the relative lack of debate through four decades on the role of ethnicity in the break-up of the Russian empire and the creation of the Soviet Union.

of the Arab National Movement (Safety Harbor, FL: Simon Publications, [1939] 2001); A. I. Dawisha, Arab Nationalism in the Twentieth Century: From Triumph to Despair (Princeton: Princeton University Press, 2003); James Gelvin, Divided Loyalties: Nationalism and Mass Politics in Syria at the Close of Empire (Berkeley: University of California Press, 1998); Rashid Khalidi, Palestinian Identity: The Construction of Modern National Consciousness (New York: Columbia University Press, 1997); Richard Hovannisian, Armenia on the Road to Independence, 1918 (Berkeley: University of California Press, 1967), Hovannisian, The Republic of Armenia, 4 vols. (Berkeley: University of California Press, 1971); Wadie Jwaideh, The Kurdish National Movement: Its Origins and Development (Syracuse: Syracuse University Press, 2006); David McDowall, A Modern History of the Kurds, 2nd edn. (New York: I. B. Tauris, 2000).
[5] Hélène Carrère d'Encausse, The Great Challenge: Nationalities and the Bolshevik State, tr. Nancy Festinger (New York: Holmes and Meier, 1992); Hakan Kırımlı, National Movements and National Identity Among the Crimean Tatars, 1905–1916 (New York: E. J. Brill, 1996); Ronald Suny, The Making of the Georgian Nation (Bloomington: Indiana University Press, 1994); Tadeusz Swietochowski, Russian Azerbaijan, 1905–1920 (Cambridge: Cambridge University Press, 1985); Serge A. Zenkovsky, Pan-Turkism and Islam in Russia (Cambridge, MA: Harvard University Press, 1960).
[6] Richard Pipes, The Formation of the Soviet Union: Communism and Nationalism, rev. edn. (Cambridge, MA: Harvard University Press, [1954] 1997).

The collapse of the Soviet Union into its constituent national republics, however, refocused the attention of scholars on the polyethnic character of that state and that of its predecessor, the Russian empire. We now possess numerous studies emphasizing the empire's variegated ethnic character, its non-Russian areas, and the evolution of the empire's nationality policies.[7] Calling attention to the way "[s]cholars of the end of the Ottoman, Habsburg, Soviet, and German continental empires have established that the rise of nationalist ideas and practices among the core ethnic groups in each case proved to be among the most important challenges to the viability of the imperial polity," Eric Lohr has argued that "a type of Russian nationalism played a more important role in the last years of the Russian empire than most scholarship has granted."[8] Terry Martin, in what in a sense amounts to a reply to Pipes' juxtaposition of Bolshevik communism against native nationalisms, returned the question of ethnicity to the origins of the Soviet Union by exploring how the Bolsheviks worked with, rather than repressed, nationalism.[9]

Scholars today are comfortable with the idea of nationalism as a global phenomenon. Its seeming ubiquity has moved many to liken it to an irresistible force of nature.[10] Indeed, so embedded is the national idea in our language that scholars, including political scientists who as a disciplinary imperative strive for clarity and precision in nomenclature, speak of "international" relations when what they are really discussing is interaction between states.

There is nothing illegitimate, wrong, or inherently mistaken in undertaking an investigation of the origins of nation-states or national movements. The studies of the aforementioned and cited authors in the fields of Middle Eastern and Russian history have all made lasting contributions to scholarship. But a problem does arise when the focus on nationalism and national identities occludes the impact of other dynamics.

This work takes a different tack. It eschews the national perspective that sees the late Ottoman and Russian empires as mere preludes

---

[7] See, for example, Andreas Kappeler, *The Russian Empire: A Multiethnic History*, tr. Alfred Clayton (New York: Longman, 2001); Theodore Weeks, *Nation and State in Late Imperial Russia: Nationalism and Russification on the Western Frontier, 1863–1914* (DeKalb: Northern Illinois University Press, 1996).

[8] Eric Lohr, *Nationalizing the Russian Empire: The Campaign Against Enemy Aliens During World War I* (Cambridge, MA: Harvard University Press, 2003), 8.

[9] Terry Martin, *The Affirmative Action Empire: Nations and Nationalism in the Soviet Union, 1923–1939* (Ithaca: Cornell University Press, 2001).

[10] See, for example, Martin, *Affirmative Action Empire*, 1; Ernest Gellner, *Encounters with Nationalism* (Cambridge, MA: Blackwell, 1994), 70; Tom Nairn, *The Break-Up of Britain: Crisis and Neo-Nationalism* (London: NLB, 1977), 98.

to the establishment of their successor states in favor of a framework that situates events in the Ottoman and Russian borderlands in their imperial setting and places the two in their global geopolitical contexts. It treats the Ottoman and Russian empires as *state actors* rather than as manifestations of proto-nationalist ideologies or holding tanks of nationalist movements and argues that interstate competition, and not nationalism, provides the key to understanding the course of history in the Ottoman–Russian borderlands in the early twentieth century. At the same time, it devotes significant attention to substate actors, demonstrating how the dynamics of global interstate competition interacted with local and regional agendas to produce new forms of political identity.

States, anarchy, and global society

A few preliminary words should be said in regard to the book's conceptualization of interstate relations. The book takes as its starting point Charles Tilly's influential thesis that the modern state's origins lie in competitive violent interaction between human beings for wealth and resources. The need of sovereigns to generate greater military power than their rivals possessed drove the expansion not merely of armed forces but also of the multiple state institutions and bureaucracies necessary to sustain the armed forces. As Tilly succinctly put it, war made the state, and the state made war.[11]

Several important implications follow from tracing the origin of the state to a process of intense competition among multiple entities. The first is that states do not exist as autonomous units. Rather, they function as parts of a system. The process of state-building in one polity impacts that in others in such a way that the internal development of one state cannot be understood unless seen in the context of its relations with other states and of its place in the system of states. Systems, moreover, produce effects that are greater than the sum of the bilateral relations of any two of their parts. Just as the history of a given state's development cannot be written without reference to its relations with other states, those relations cannot be grasped outside the systemic context in which they are created. Systems generate their own effects that are independent

---

[11] Charles Tilly, "Reflections on the History of European State-Making" in *The Formation of National States in Western Europe*, ed. Charles Tilly (Princeton: Princeton University Press, 1975), 3–84; and Tilly, "War Making and State Making as Organized Crime," in *Bringing the State Back In*, ed. Peter B. Evans, Dietrich Rueschemeyer, and Theda Skocpol (New York: Cambridge University Press, 1985), 169–91. A more refined and nuanced explication of his concepts is provided in Tilly, *Coercion, Capital, and European States AD 990–1992* (Cambridge, MA: Blackwell, 1992).

of the direct actions or desires of their components. Outcomes therefore cannot be interpreted directly as the products of the intentions of system components.[12]

Second, states do not exist solely, or even primarily, as representations or outgrowths of their societies. They originated and exist as members of an interlinked community with "horizontal" ties to each other. These ties are, in fact, often more important for understanding state behavior than the state's "vertical" links to its subjects. The identification of the state with society and the belief that the state's primary function is to provide services to its subjects are comparatively recent developments that stemmed from the state's need to exchange those services for ever-greater resources in order to prevail in warfare. Recent history, alas, provides ample evidence of the illusory nature of modern states' claim to serve the interests of the societies they ostensibly represent.

Third, the anarchic nature of the interstate system impels state elites to be outward-looking. Above the community of states there exists no higher sovereign to enforce law or otherwise regulate behavior and protect its members. Under these conditions states ultimately must rely only on their own capabilities for survival.[13] As theorists of global politics and interstate relations emphasize, anarchy mandates competition between states because any one state's gain in relative power constitutes an implicit threat to others and therefore compels a response from them to offset those gains, such as "self-strengthening" or forming alliances. A necessary preoccupation of state elites is the relative power of their state. In other words, those elites are particularly sensitive to outside challenges and attentive to their state's place in the interstate system. External threats regularly emerge as primary stimuli for internal reform, sometimes to the benefit of a state's inhabitants, oftentimes to the detriment. The state's preoccupation with its relations with other states is reflected in the fact that traditionally the most prestigious posts in a state following that of the executive leader have been those that handle warfare and foreign relations.

Some have contested such structural determinism in interstate relations, arguing that anarchy is "what states make of it." How states respond to anarchy, they contend, is historically and culturally contingent, not uniform and universal, and anarchy does not necessarily lead to competitive behavior.[14] This debate need not concern us, for there is no dispute

[12] Robert Jervis, *System Effects: Complexity in Political and Social Life* (Princeton: Princeton University Press, 1997).

[13] For the most concise and influential statement of this point, see Kenneth Waltz's ambitiously titled *Theory of International Politics* (New York: McGraw-Hill, 1979).

[14] Alexander Wendt, "Anarchy Is What States Make of It: The Social Construction of Power Politics," *International Organization*, 46, 2 (Spring 1992), 391–425.

that in the period we are investigating the interstate system did resemble a Hobbesian "war of all against all" wherein life for the weak was "nasty, brutish, and short." The early twentieth century was a time of intense great power rivalry and high imperialism. Coercion smashed borders. Territories submerged and even disappeared under colonial rule. As Dominic Lieven points out, between 1876 and 1915 fully one-quarter of the world's surface changed hands.[15] It is no coincidence that a historical description of interstate relations in the early twentieth century presaged the starkest explication of the consequences of anarchy, John Mearsheimer's theory of "offensive realism."[16]

To observe that the interstate system is an anarchic one is not to contend that it knows no order. States develop and maintain shared modes of interaction and conventions to manage their quotidian relations, regulate more exceptional issues of war and peace, and arbitrate such questions as who qualifies as a state. The informal rules of a society, while not comparable to a legal codex enforced by a central authority, do shape and channel the interaction of the society's members.[17] These shared understandings or norms thus are not subsidiary to power relations, but are interwoven with them. Understanding interstate relations thus requires that keen attention be paid to the norms of global society as well as to the relative distribution of material power among states.

Global order and the proliferation of the national idea

During the nineteenth century, the doctrine of nationalism became increasingly influential in global society, and by the twentieth century it provided "the hegemonic political discourse of sovereignty" and a fundamental principle of global order.[18] The national idea, the belief that the world should be divided among governments ruling over ethnically homogeneous territories, owed its ascent not to its power of description – even today, the vast majority of states contain ethnically heterogeneous populations – but to its power of prescription. As William H. McNeill and

---

[15] Dominic Lieven, *Empire: The Russian Empire and Its Rivals* (New Haven: Yale University Press, 2000), 46.

[16] John J. Mearsheimer, *The Tragedy of Great Power Politics* (New York: Norton, 2001). Mearsheimer acknowledges the influence of G. Lowes Dickinson's books, *The European Anarchy* (London: George Allen and Unwin Ltd., 1916) and *The International Anarchy, 1904–1914* (New York: The Century Co., 1926).

[17] Hedley Bull, *The Anarchical Society: A Study of Order in World Politics*, 3rd edn. (New York: Columbia University Press, [1977] 2002).

[18] Geoff Eley and Ronald Grigor Suny, "Introduction," in *Becoming National: A Reader*, ed. Geoff Eley and Ronald Grigor Suny (New York: Oxford University Press, 1996), 19.

Elie Kedourie have emphasized, the national idea emerged from Europe and carried an inherent normative preference for the organization of human societies into nation-states.[19] It supplied a blueprint not just for the structure of individual human societies, but also for the proper structure of all humanity. This normative preference for the organization of human societies into nation-states influenced earlier generations of historians no less than statesmen. Thus historians routinely interpreted the break-up of the Ottoman, Russian, and Habsburg empires as a lesson in the irresistible potency and reach of nationalism. Like most memorable "lessons" of history, this one derives power from its normative content. If empire means the domination of one "nation" over other "nations" and the denial of the inherent right of the latter to self-determination, then the destruction of empire becomes a moral necessity, and its occurrence a cause for celebration. The example of an empire's collapse ceases to be a mere historical event and becomes a cautionary tale, thereby acquiring a certain power in the imaginations of both scholars and their audiences. In the twentieth century the very word "empire" became an almost universal word of opprobrium.[20]

Yet a closer inspection of the historical record at the end of World War I reveals the lesson of imperial collapse to be far from clear-cut. Not all empires met their end in World War I. Indeed, several of them expanded, most notably the British, French, and Japanese. The common determining feature of the Ottoman, Russian, and Austro-Hungarian empires was not their imperial structures so much as the fact that they had all been defeated militarily. Had the war's military outcome been different – and it was a very closely run affair – so the list of collapsed empires would have been different. As this study argues, nationalism, understood as the mobilization of groups based on ethnicity for the purpose of asserting a claim to political sovereignty, was at least as much a consequence as a cause of imperial collapse.

In recent decades scholars have written at tremendous length on nationalism. Most case studies of nationalist movements try to locate the origins of their subjects in varying constellations of social, economic, and intellectual factors – e.g., industrialization, print capitalism, proliferation of schools, the formation of intellectual classes – that give rise to

---

[19] William H. McNeill, *Polyethnicity and National Unity in World History* (Toronto: University of Toronto Press, 1986); Elie Kedourie, *Nationalism*, 4th edn. (Oxford: Blackwell, [1966] 1993).

[20] See, for example, Mark R. Beissinger, "The Persisting Ambiguity of Empire," *Post-Soviet Affairs*, 11, 2 (1995), 149–84; and Dominic Lieven, "Empire: A Word and Its Meanings," the first chapter of his comparative examination of empires, *Empire*, esp. 3–7.

such movements. But, as John Breuilly has warned, to search for the apolitical preconditions of nationalism "is to neglect the fundamental point that nationalism is, above and beyond all else, about politics and that politics is about power." Because power in the modern world is principally about control of the state, the "central task is to relate nationalism to the objectives of obtaining and using state power."[21] The story of nationalism in the Middle East and Eurasia, therefore, must be understood as part of the story of the construction of the modern state in those lands, and that story is a geopolitical one. Political scientists have examined the influence of nationalism on interstate politics, and historians and others have explored the ways in which states create and impose ethnonationalist categories and identities. The way global order has fostered nationalist movements, however, deserves more attention.

As noted above, the national idea emerged in Europe, where it provided an important principle, at first implicit and then increasingly explicit, for the conduct of diplomacy and statecraft. The projection of European power around the globe necessarily brought with it the European vision of political order. The correlation between the emergence of "nationalist" movements around the world in the late nineteenth and early twentieth centuries and the assertion by the European great powers of political dominance across the globe is not a coincidence.

The doctrine of nationalism stemmed from an ontology that understood ethnicity as an autonomous category of being deserving of political expression.[22] Not least important, it carried an inherent normative preference for the organization of human societies into nation-states. This is a critical but often overlooked point. Kedourie put it succinctly:

Nationalism is a doctrine invented in Europe at the beginning of the nineteenth century. It pretends to supply a criterion for the determination of the unit of population proper to enjoy a government exclusively its own, for the legitimate exercise of power in the state, and for the right organization of a society of states. Briefly, the doctrine holds that humanity is naturally divided into nations, that nations are known by certain characteristics which can be ascertained, and that the only legitimate type of government is national self-government.[23]

---

[21] John Breuilly, *Nationalism and the State*, 2nd edn. (Chicago: University of Chicago Press, [1982] 1993), xii, 1.
[22] For an overview of how ethnicity acquired such importance, see Josep R. Llobera, *The God of Modernity: The Development of Nationalism in Western Europe* (Providence, RI: Berg Publishers, 1994), 157–76. See also the works of Isaiah Berlin: *The Crooked Timber of Humanity*, ed. Henry Hardy (Princeton: Princeton University Press, 1990), 49–69, 207–37, 238–62; *Against the Current*, ed. Henry Hardy (London: Pimlico, 1997), 333–55; and *The Magus of the North: J. G. Hamann and the Rise of Modern Irrationalism*, ed. Henry Hardy (New York: Farrar, Straus and Giroux, 1994).
[23] Kedourie, *Nationalism*, 1.

The national idea would perhaps have remained a peculiarity of Western Europe were it not for the fact that the societies that embraced it could produce greater amounts of military power by which they compelled other societies to imitate them. This process unfolded in the wake of the French Revolution when the victories of Napoleon spurred neighboring states to follow his example and raise mass armies. The creation of these armies required that soldiers feel a bond with the regime that claimed political authority over them and with the territory that it ruled. Generating this bond became essential to state security. Direct military competition was the first of three processes by which the nation-state as a model of political organization spread throughout first Europe and then the world.[24]

The second route through which nationalism spread was through the dissemination of ideas. Here, too, the perceived need to compete with and match the power of the ascending nation-states played a role. Outsiders in search of the secrets of Western Europe's military, political, and economic success studied European thought and European societies. In this quest they necessarily became acquainted with the concept of nationalism. Nationalism lay at the nexus between mass politics and technological progress, the two phenomena that provided superior power to European societies. Through its function as a provider of a mass identity, nationalism made possible the unification and mobilization of a state's population as a collective entity. At the same time, it also reoriented the public's attention from metaphysical concerns to temporal ones and from traditional sources of authority to technocratic and scientific ones. Western-educated elites came to regard the development of national consciousness as a necessary condition for scientific progress and modernization.

The dynamics of interstate competition and the rules of the global order provided the third way through which the nation-state proliferated. The national idea did not limit its vision to individual societies, but proclaimed that the proper order of all humankind was an order of nations. It provided a template for global order, and marked the long-term polyethnic states such as the Ottoman empire as both empirically impossible and normatively unjust. The awakening of their constituent nations to political consciousness was inevitable and the empire's eventual demise guarantied. In the meantime the empire's existence could not be construed as anything but a violation of the just order. As the statesmen and

---

[24] See Barry Posen, "Nationalism, the Mass Army, and Military Power," *International Security*, 18, 2 (Fall 1993), 80–124. See also Josh Sanborn, *Drafting the Russian Nation: Military Conscription, Total War, and Mass Politics, 1905–1925* (Dekalb: Northern Illinois University Press, 2003).

military leaders of the European great powers extended the dominion of their states around the globe, they imposed this template around the world.

Within the Ottoman empire, the national idea manifested itself first in the Balkans. Given that the Balkans constituted the empire's economically most developed region, this would seem to support the perspective of nationalism as a product of socioeconomic change. Yet even the Balkans possessed a socioeconomic infrastructure unpromising for the cultivation of mass national identities. Its populations were still overwhelmingly illiterate and rural. The economy was heavily agricultural with no significant industry. The institutions of the Ottoman state, although applying and assimilating modern techniques and modes of organization to extend their reach, remained far from capable of shaping positive identities for the mass of Balkan peoples. In short, even here such commonly cited prerequisites of nationalism as mass literacy, industrialization, and pervasive bureaucratic structures were lacking. At the time of Bulgaria's creation its peasants were more commonly literate in Turkish than Bulgarian, and a great many of them, by virtue of religion, labeled themselves "Greek."[25] Similar confusion about "proper" national identities reigned among the inhabitants of the other Balkan states that acquired a national existence.[26]

The Balkans was among the first regions in the world to feel the full impact of Western Europe's rise, its struggles, and its new vision of politics. Contrary to depictions of Oriental lassitude, the Ottomans responded to the European challenge by undertaking progressively more comprehensive programs of internal reform and expansion of state institutions. In their bid to match the might of their European rivals, they replaced their traditional modes and institutions of indirect rule in the Balkans with direct rule. In a pattern repeated the world over, this substitution of direct for indirect rule triggered widespread resentment and resistance that later justified itself with nationalist rhetoric, but in the Balkans processes bound up with interstate competition were decisive for the realization of nation-states.[27]

The disruption wrought by the rise of the European powers was not limited to the projection of material force. The introduction of new concepts of political organization that altered the relationship of states to territory and population was a central part of the disruption. The

---

[25] Mark Mazower, *The Balkans: A Short History* (New York: Random House, 2000), 87–95.
[26] Kemal Karpat, "The Memoirs of N. Batzaria: The Young Turks and Nationalism," *International Journal of Middle East Studies*, 6, 3 (1975), 276–99.
[27] Michael Hechter, *Containing Nationalism* (New York: Oxford University Press, 2000), esp. 71–78.

"emerging Western conception of the globe in its own image," Mark Levene observes, demanded that expertly "demarcated borders between one sovereign state and the next" replace the older and vaguer notion of frontiers.[28] Not least important, the question of who lived within those carefully demarcated borders acquired a new significance. As Eric Weitz has explained, the nineteenth and early twentieth centuries witnessed a "sea change" in the international system. The global order shifted "from traditional diplomacy to population politics, from mere territorial adjustments to the handling of entire population groups categorized by ethnicity, nationality, or race, or some combination thereof."[29] The borders of the state were to be precisely delimited, and they were to correspond to ethnographic ones.

Gazing through the conceptual filter of the national idea, European actors interpreted local rebellions of Balkan Christians as popular national uprisings. When in 1821 rebels in Greece took up arms, the notion that the ancient Greeks' descendants were fighting for freedom enthralled Europeans. Forces from Egypt loyal to the sultan managed to suppress the rebels until the British, French, and Russians intervened in 1827. The subsequent London Protocol of 1830 provided for the establishment of an independent Greek state and thereby "marked the first time that the powers clearly linked a specific population and sovereignty – that is, the Greek state considered as representative of the Greek people."[30] The diplomatic and military support of European powers pursuing their own interests would prove critical to the dissolution of Ottoman rule and the emergence of more nation-states in the Balkans, such as Serbia, Romania, and Bulgaria. This is not to argue that the European powers invented dissatisfaction among the Christian Balkan peoples, though they could stoke and exploit such dissatisfaction when it served them. That dissatisfaction was nonetheless real and stemmed from several sources. Rather, it is to observe that the way these revolts culminated in the establishment of nation-states owes more to exogenous factors such as great power intervention and the available model of sovereign statehood than it does to the endogenous social structures and political agendas of the new "nations" themselves.[31]

---

[28] Mark Levene, *Genocide in the Age of the Nation-State*, vol. II, *The Rise of the West and the Coming of Genocide* (New York: I. B. Tauris, 2005), 221, 313.

[29] Eric D. Weitz, "From the Vienna to the Paris System: International Politics and the Entangled Histories of Human Rights, Forced Deportations, and Civilizing Missions," *American Historical Review* (December 2008): 1314–15.

[30] Weitz, "Vienna to Paris," 1317.   [31] Breuilly, *Nationalism and the State*, 380–81.

The Congress of Berlin

The Congress of Berlin of 1878 revealed concretely the growing influence of the national idea upon global order. The basic goal of the congress was to manage the "Eastern Question," the problem of how to partition the Ottoman empire without triggering a great power war. Russia had handily defeated its Ottoman foe in the Russo-Ottoman War of 1877–78. From the Balkans its armies reached the outskirts of Istanbul and from the Caucasus they penetrated to Erzurum deep inside Anatolia. At peace talks in the village of San Stefano just outside Istanbul, Russia imposed a settlement that provided for the creation of a large autonomous Bulgaria, independence for Serbia, Romania, and Montenegro, and the surrender of Ottoman territories in the Caucasus and the Balkans. Britain and Germany, however, judged the gains Russia awarded itself to be excessive and threatening. Joined by Austria-Hungary, they compelled Russia to enter new peace negotiations in Berlin where the great powers could collectively adjudicate a settlement. The resulting Treaty of Berlin approved the transfer to Russia of the provinces of Kars, Ardahan, and Batumi from the economically strapped Ottomans in substitution for war reparations, but in the Balkans it reduced the size of Bulgaria and limited Russia to annexing southern Bessarabia.[32] Elsewhere it assigned the territory of Kotur to Iran, and its call for rectifying the Ottoman border with Greece led to the Ottomans' loss of Thessaly.

No less important than the congress's impact upon the balance of power was the legacy it left in great power diplomacy and statecraft. By recognizing the independence of Montenegro, Serbia, and Romania, and creating Bulgaria, the congress acknowledged ethnicity as an attribute of human identity carrying distinct political claims. The fulfillment of the national idea was not the goal of the great powers, whose diplomats were woefully ignorant of even basic ethnography.[33] Rather, the national idea emerged as a principle around which the powers organized their competition. Thus, for example, when British diplomats were searching for ways to prevent Russia from claiming the strategic Black Sea port of Batumi, they discovered that a distinct ethnic group, the Muslim Laz, predominated in the area surrounding Batumi. They took it upon themselves to assert the right of the Laz people to independence, before reassessing Britain's overall relations with Russia and dropping the

---

[32] M. S. Anderson, *The Eastern Question, 1774–1923: A Study in International Relations* (London: Macmillan, 1966), 203–19.
[33] Henry F. Munro, *The Berlin Congress* (Washington, DC: Government Printing Office, 1918), 27–33.

ploy.[34] The inconsistent application of the national idea notwithstanding, the congress's affirmation of it reverberated throughout Eastern Europe and the Near East alike. As the Polish historian Jerzy Jedlicki writes, "The Congress of Berlin (1878) opened the epoch of the disintegration of empires and the multiplication of nations. The Bulgarians, Serbs, Montenegrins, Romanians, Ukrainians, Lithuanians, Jews and others all began to claim their rights to a separate existence, justifying such rights by the unique nature of their cultures."[35] Ethnicity had acquired political significance and became a key category in map making and census taking.[36]

The acknowledgment of ethnicity's theoretical claim to sovereignty gave rise to the practical problem of what to do with those ethnicities too small or too scattered to endow with statehood. The inevitable byproduct of the idea that legitimate statehood resides in the popular sovereignty of communities defined by ethnicity in a given territory is the disadvantaging of those who share the same territory but are of different ethnicity. Recognizing this problem, the powers took steps to provide for the protection of those groups that in a reflection of the shift toward the idea of popular sovereignty became known as "minorities."[37] One of those groups was the Armenians, a Christian people indigenous to Eastern Anatolia and the Caucasus. Under Ottoman rule, the Armenians had been subordinated to their more numerous Muslim neighbors and were exposed to various abuses. Thus article 61 of the Treaty of Berlin obliged the Ottoman empire to implement administrative reforms in its eastern provinces to protect Armenians living there against the depredations of their Kurdish and Circassian neighbors. In the event Istanbul failed to provide such security, the treaty reserved to the great powers the prerogative to intervene in Ottoman affairs.

The article's historical impact would stem not so much from its recognition of the dire plight of Armenians in Eastern Anatolia as from the way in which it singled out Armenians based on ethnicity and granted to outside powers the prerogative to intervene on their behalf. The majority of Armenians in Eastern Anatolia were peasants who eked out a precarious existence, bound to Muslim landlords and exposed to raids by

---

[34] B. H. Sumner, *Russia and the Balkans, 1870–1880* (Oxford: Clarendon Press, 1937), 506, n. 1, 541–45.

[35] Jerzy Jedlicki, *A Suburb of Europe: Nineteenth-Century Polish Approaches to Western Civilization* (Budapest: CEU Press [1988] 1999), 260.

[36] On the census, see İpek Yosmaoğlu, "Counting Bodies, Shaping Souls: The 1903 Census and National Identity in Ottoman Macedonia," *International Journal of Middle East Studies*, 38, 1 (2006), 55–77.

[37] Carole Fink, *Defending the Rights of Others* (Cambridge: Cambridge University Press, 2004), 1–38.

nomadic tribesmen. The fact that they were Christians heightened their predicament, as their more numerous and powerful Muslim neighbors and overlords regarded them as social inferiors with limited rights. Yet Armenians were by no means alone in their misery. Kurdish peasants existed in similarly wretched conditions, religion also circumscribed the lives of Anatolia's Christian Assyrians, and the Circassians identified in the treaty as predators were themselves mostly penniless migrants who had been forcibly driven from their native Caucasus by Russia. Article 61, however, established not religion, class, or recent political history but ethnicity as the critical criterion. Since ethnicity now carried an increasingly explicit claim to territorial sovereignty, the introduction of ethnic categories further destabilized a region already undergoing significant socioeconomic transformation and stress.

The great powers' acknowledgment of minority rights no more reflected a commitment to achieving those rights than their assimilation of the national idea reflected a determination to bestow independence upon all putative nations. They lost no time in putting minority rights to the service of their competition. German chancellor Otto von Bismarck, for example, leveraged Romania's Jews.[38] In fact, the motive behind article 61 was not the betterment of conditions for Armenians but the denial of Russia's attempt to arrogate to itself an exclusive prerogative to intervene on their behalf. The "internationalization" of the Armenian Question arguably set the Armenian cause back, as any action on behalf of the Armenians would now require a consensus of powers who were in direct competition. As the duke of Argyll would remark, "What was everybody's business was now nobody's business."[39] The example of Bulgaria fired the imaginations of some young, European-educated Armenians with the dream of replicating the European norm on the edges of the Caucasus and Anatolia. But the Armenians' situation was fundamentally different. Not only were they a distinct minority in much of the land they claimed as their own, they also straddled the contested borderlands of two empires. The aspirations of the Armenians for some form of territorial recognition of their national existence was destined to become a weapon in a broader struggle for regional dominance.

---

[38] Fink, *Defending*, 27–30. Fink describes a "rapid retreat from the façade of humanitarian interventionism back to the ways of traditional *realpolitik*" (30). This is a misleading conceptualization of the problem. Diplomats from the beginning had put these principles at the service of their states' interests, and these principles continued to inform diplomatic practice afterwards.

[39] Richard Hovannisian, "The Armenian Question in the Ottoman Empire," *East European Quarterly*, 6, 1 (March 1972), 9.

The nation-state model presupposes the existence of a sense of shared identity and destiny among its inhabitants. As noted above, however, the bulk of inhabitants of the new Balkan states in 1878 did not subscribe to the concepts of identity on which their states were founded. But if those who should belong did not quite yet know it, those who could not belong were easily identified. The War of 1877–78 resulted in the death and expulsion of roughly 750,000 Muslim Balkaners.[40] These events entered the memory of Muslims as the "'93 sökümü," the "unraveling" or disaster of the Ottoman Rumi calendar year 1293. The trauma would color the perceptions of Ottoman Muslims up through the end of the empire, and worse was still to come.[41]

For the Ottoman empire, the principles embraced in Berlin heralded a death knell, since they stripped the polyethnic empire of its legitimacy as a state and authorized foreign intervention inside the empire on behalf of ethnonational causes.[42] The Congress of Berlin marked the Ottoman empire as anachronistic and illegitimate. The imperial powers' sometimes flagrant violations of the same standards by which they condemned the Ottomans stirred resentment.[43] Resentment, however, could not blunt European power, and some Ottomans began to draw the lesson that maintenance of statehood in the emerging global order required accommodating the national idea.

By virtue of their superior might, the great powers could apply the template of the nation-state selectively and in service of their own interests, but they could ignore the logical implications of the national idea only for a time. The normative contradiction between the national idea and their own colonial empires was too obvious to suppress indefinitely. Critiques of empire being worked out at home were undermining the legitimacy of European empires from within.[44] Doubts about the legitimacy of empire gnawed at imperial administrators and fueled fears, often imaginary, of uprisings by imperial subjects. Because their Muslim

---

[40] Justin McCarthy, *Death and Exile: The Ethnic Cleansing of Ottoman Muslims, 1821–1922* (Princeton: Darwin Press, 1995), 339.

[41] Kemal Karpat, *Studies on Ottoman Social and Political History* (Leiden: Brill, 2002), 63, 367–72, 469, 547.

[42] Karpat, *Studies*, 352–84; Kemal H. Karpat, *The Politicization of Islam: Reconstructing Identity, State, Faith, and Community in the Late Ottoman State* (New York: Oxford University Press, 2001), 183.

[43] One international relations scholar has described great power behavior toward the Ottoman Empire as the apotheosis of "organized hypocrisy." That such behavior was by no means unusual did nothing to change its hypocritical character or camouflage that it rested on might, not right. See Stephen D. Krasner, *Sovereignty: Organized Hypocrisy* (Princeton: Princeton University Press, 1999), 164, 175, 183.

[44] Sankar Muthu, *Enlightenment Against Empire* (Princeton: Princeton University Press, 2003).

subjects' ethnic and religious identities rendered them incontrovertibly distinct from the imperial metropoles, European officials assumed the existence among them of popular currents of potentially explosive anti-imperial sentiments. The fact that Islam exhorts the faithful to pursue and maintain unity reinforced suspicions of subversive activity among Muslims. Notably, whereas officials in the Russian, British, and French empires nurtured fears of pan-Islamic subversion out of all proportion to what the evidence suggested, German strategists for the same reasons fantasized about inciting mass uprisings of Muslims to bring down their rivals' empires. The hopes for and fears of Muslim rage would prove to be vastly exaggerated.

In short, this book argues that nationalism in the borderlands of the Near East and Eurasia is best understood as a form of geopolitics, not as a phenomenon that springs from some non-political base. The rise of the European powers and the Ottoman state's corresponding response upset and overturned existing power relations and patterns of governance in the borderlands of the Near East and Eurasia. The affirmation of the nation-state by the great powers as the normative unit of global politics exerted a tremendous impact upon local politics already in turmoil. It made the language and program of nationalism essential to the central objective of modern politics, obtaining and maintaining control of the state, and thereby facilitated the spread of nationalist ideologies. The structure of the global order and interstate system provided powerful incentives to adopt nationalist ideologies by tying control of the state and its territory to claims made on behalf of the nation. As Breuilly explains, "Nationalist ideology matters, not so much because it directly motivates most supporters of a nationalist movement, but rather because it provides a conceptual map which enables people to relate their particular material and moral interests to a broader terrain of action."[45] Nationalism in these borderlands at this time is better seen as a byproduct of interstate competition than as the stimulus of that competition. Scholars accordingly must be wary of the pitfalls of adopting nationalist teleology retrospectively to classify, analyze, and explain behavior and of ascribing neat, programmatic ideological motives to political actors. A study of politics in the Ottoman and Russian borderlands must put states and substate actors in the foreground, remembering that they were operating under conditions of incomplete knowledge and pursuing multiple and sometimes contradictory goals as they interacted with manifold other actors.

[45] Breuilly, *Nationalism and the State*, 13.

Structure of the book

Chapter 1 traces the course of foreign relations between the Ottoman and Russian empires from the Young Turk Revolution of 1908 up to the July Crisis of 1914. This chapter emphasizes the structural and systemic determinants that shaped Ottoman–Russian relations at the state-to-state or "high politics" level. Using the concept of "competitive anarchy" to describe the nature of international relations at the time, it demonstrates how the search for security shaped Istanbul's and St. Petersburg's relations with each other. Despite the superiority Russia enjoyed over the Ottoman empire, security concerns generated by competition with the other great powers compelled Russia to adopt an aggressive stance toward the floundering Ottoman state. Mutual sympathy and goodwill were not absent from their relations, but were incapable of sustaining warm relations in the context of the age's power politics.

Whereas the first chapter addresses the public, high politics of the Ottoman–Russian rivalry from 1908 to 1914, the next two chapters explore the ways the quest for security entangled the two at the level of "low politics." Unlike nation-states where relatively homogeneous populations mesh with state institutions, empires contain differentiated populations that often possess their own institutions and structures that bypass or compete with those of the state. This creates vulnerabilities unique to empires. Moreover, as contiguous states, the Ottoman and Russian empires shared mixed populations that crossed borders, and this created an unusual dynamic wherein attempts of one to secure its border zones by destabilizing the other's rebounded detrimentally. Chapter 2 examines Russia's policies toward Eastern Anatolia and highlights the way interstate competition shaped local identities and politics through the introduction of the concept of the national idea. Just as the idea of the nation began to transform how tsarist officials conceived of their empire's domestic structure, so, too, did it influence the way they conceived of societies and politics beyond their empire's borders. This had a substantial impact on the organization and conduct of politics in Eastern Anatolia as local Kurdish and other actors adapted to the new framework in pursuit of their own objectives. Chapter 3 explores Russia's use of Muslim spies, Ottoman attempts to exploit Russia's "Muslim" and "Armenian" questions, and the flows of defectors across the borders.

Chapter 4 covers World War I from its outbreak up until the Russian Revolution of 1917. It argues that the Ottoman decision to go to war in 1914 was a calculated gamble undertaken for reasons of security and not an irrational attempt to realize pan-Islamic or pan-Turkist ambitions. Entry into the war was seen as the best way to exploit great power rivalries and obtain an extended, postwar period of stability that would permit the implementation of revitalizing reforms without foreign intervention. The chapter discusses Ottoman collaboration with Ukrainians, Georgians, and Pontic Greeks under Russian occupation as well as Ottoman attempts to mobilize Russia's Muslims for warfare. Chapter 5 examines the interaction of war with the national idea and new concepts of state legitimacy and its impact upon the Ottoman–Russian borderlands. It argues that the wholesale destruction of Ottoman Armenians and incipient Turkification of Anatolia during World War I owed more to calculations of state interest than ethnic passions. It then looks at Russia's attempts to administer occupied Eastern Anatolia, its difficulties in its relations with both Armenians and Kurds, and the way cosmopolitan notions of imperial state interest determined Russian occupation policies.

Chapter 6 analyzes the evolution of Ottoman policy toward Russia and the Caucasus from the breakdown of the Russian army in 1917 through the signing of the Treaty of Brest-Litovsk with the Bolsheviks in March 1918. It demonstrates that Ottoman goals were not fixed by any form of ideology, but changed and adapted to the shifts in the regional balance of power. Believing that Russian weakness was temporary, the Ottomans were determined to exploit it while they could. Initial hopes to restore the 1914 border in the Caucasus expanded to include the annexation of the former Ottoman provinces of Kars, Ardahan, and Batumi and the establishment of one or more buffer states in the Caucasus before Russian power could again assert itself. The seventh chapter looks at the development of Ottoman relations with the Transcaucasian Federation from its emergence in 1917 through the negotiations at Trabzon and Batumi, the Ottoman acquisition of their former provinces of Kars, Ardahan, and Batumi, to the establishment of diplomatic relations with Georgia, Armenian, Azerbaijan, and the North Caucasus. Whereas the emergence of the republics of Georgia, Armenia, and Azerbaijan is commonly assumed to reflect a growth of national consciousness in the Caucasus, the chapter illustrates how in fact interstate competition and the new norms of global order played the decisive role in the creation of these republics.

Chapter 8 follows the Ottoman advance into Azerbaijan and Dagestan. It reveals how geopolitical imperatives, and not notions of ethnoreligious solidarity, continued to determine Ottoman strategic behavior. While the imperative of establishing independent Azerbaijani and North Caucasian states as insurance against the future resurgence of Russian power remained the prime motivation behind the drive on Baku, other exigencies also spurred the Ottoman advance. By the summer of 1918 the Ottomans saw Great Britain and their own nominal ally Germany as additional threats to the survival of their empire. Believing that a negotiated end to the war was imminent, the Ottomans strove to take advantage of their temporary superiority in the region to establish a post-war order that would minimize Russian, German, and British influence by securing the existence of internationally recognized states in Georgia, Armenia, Azerbaijan, and the North Caucasus. The chapter concludes by contrasting the Ottoman reannexation of their former provinces of Kars, Ardahan, and Batumi with their policies toward other parts of the Caucasus.

1 The high politics of anarchy and competition

The event that triggered the Young Turk Revolution had nothing to do with questions of equality or freedom, the principles in the name of which the revolution was made. Rather, it was a meeting in the Baltic port of Reval (today's Tallinn) between the king of England and the tsar of Russia in June 1908 that spurred the Committee of Progress and Union to act (it would later change its name to the "Committee of Union and Progress"). Fearing the meeting was a prelude to the partition of Macedonia, Unionist officers in the Balkans mutinied against Sultan Abdülhamid II and forced him to restore the constitution he had abrogated three decades earlier. A desire to preserve the state, not destroy it, motivated the revolutionaries. They believed the empire was weak for two reasons: its constituent peoples lacked solidarity, and the institutions of its state were undeveloped and decentralized. The Unionists' public formula for generating that solidarity was to restore the constitution and parliament and thereby give the empire's varied elements a stake in the empire's continued existence.

The Unionists' private views, however, were somewhat different. They placed little confidence in the ability of the people to pursue their best interests on their own and distrusted democratic politics. Instead, taking their cue from cutting-edge sociological theories from Europe that emphasized the utility of elitist administration, the leadership of the Committee of Union and Progress (CUP) trusted in the efficacy of marrying the power of scientific reason to the power of the state to guide, control, and transform society. Modern Europe's example also fed skepticism about the possibility of generating between ethnically disparate elements the sort of powerful solidarity that a modern state needed. Since Turks composed a plurality of the empire's population and their fate was bound more tightly to the state than that of any other element, the Unionists identified them as the properly "dominant nation" around which the empire should be organized, not unlike the position of Germans in Austria-Hungary.[1] Only a small minority occupied themselves with Turkism. Saving the empire and state, not asserting Turkism, remained the prime goal of the Unionists, and they embraced the latter in so far as it supported the former.

Whereas the CUP's origins lay in a student secret society founded in 1889, by 1908 military officers, not writers or intellectuals, accounted for the organization's largest constituency. They saw themselves as heirs to a once glorious military tradition, and the defense of their shrinking state had become for them a matter of intense corporate and professional pride. Most of these officers, like the party's membership as a whole, hailed from the empire's Balkan and Aegean borderlands in the west, where the empire's borders were shrinking quickly. They cut their teeth fighting Balkan guerrillas, and they nurtured no illusions that the consequences of the end of the empire for its Muslims could be anything less than dire, and this, too, stiffened their resolve. Service in the borderlands of a declining empire had habituated them to violence, and it convinced them of the need for deep, radical reform of the state they served and of the society that supported it. For them, the application of violence in the name of the state was familiar in practice and permissible, even mandated, in theory. The discipline and cohesion they developed while underground would enable them to operate almost as an institution parallel to the state.

In their endeavor to preserve the empire and reform it from top to bottom, however, the Unionists faced an interlocking dilemma. The first part lay in the nature of the interstate order in the early twentieth century. That order was anarchic, competitive, and dominated by a small, select group of actors. In an environment where no higher sovereign existed to regulate interstate relations, a state's only guaranty of survival was its own power. Gains in power were zero sum. A gain by one meant a loss by another. This state of affairs was, arguably, as old as the state system itself, but now a handful of European states, whose preponderant military, technological, and economic capabilities earned them the sobriquet of "great powers," stood astride the world. Anarchy, competition, and the global reach of the great powers combined to create extraordinary turbulence around the globe in the latter part of the nineteenth century, and the Ottoman lands were among those most buffeted.

The second part of the dilemma stemmed from domestic politics. The Ottoman empire owed its historical expansion and growth to the center's ability to accommodate its multiple varied regions and groups

---

[1] Hüseyin Cahid, "Millet-i Hakime," *Tanin*, 25 Teşrinievvel 1324 [7.11.1908]; M. A. "Osmanlı İttihadı," *Meşveret*, no. 5, vol. 108 (1896), 1–2.

with flexible relations tailored to the specificities of each. This arrangement demanded relatively little of the periphery. By the same token, when measured against the standard of a modern state, this arrangement yielded comparatively little to the center. As the Unionists were aware, the great powers possessed superior abilities both to extract resources from their populations and to mobilize them via a centralized administration. The problem was that replicating such a system in the Ottoman context required not just the erection of new rationalized institutions but also the elimination of the panoply of existing institutions and arrangements that benefited and sustained local elites. Those elites could be expected to resist reform of the status quo in the center's favor. Moreover, the penetration of the great powers into the Ottoman lands offered local elites the option of enlisting outside support to resist and challenge the center. Any attempt by the center to impose its will upon the periphery was fraught with the possibility that the periphery might choose to ally with an outside power, or that an aggressive outside power might exploit such frictions to detach the periphery.[2] A fear and loathing of outside intervention lay at the core of Unionist beliefs. A dispute with other underground opposition groups over the propriety of inviting and manipulating outside intervention to bring down the sultan had precipitated the Unionists' decision to split from the opposition coalition in 1903.

Finance posed a further structural constraint on the state's capacity to carry out revitalizing reforms. Although nominally sovereign in the political sense, the Ottoman empire resembled a "semi-colony" in its economic relations. Its economy was agricultural, and its tax base was tiny. To obtain the capital necessary to fund further development, the Ottomans in the middle of the nineteenth century took loans from the great powers, but then proved unable to service them. To recover the loans, the European powers in 1881 established the Ottoman Public Debt Administration and through it began exacting excise and other taxes as well as control over the Ottoman budget. Adding insult to the injury of foreign control over domestic finances was the ability of European citizens, including predominantly Christian Ottoman subjects who through various avenues obtained European citizenship, to take advantage of a number of extra-territorial legal and economic privileges known as the "capitulations." The arrangement granting European subjects exemption from Ottoman law dated back to the sixteenth century. But due to

---

[2] For an older view that privileges identity and nationalist awakenings over geopolitics, see Hugh Seton-Watson, *Nations and States: An Enquiry into the Origins of Nations and the Politics of Nationalism* (Boulder: Westview, 1977), 110–14. Cf. Mazower, *Balkans*, 87–95.

the vast shift in power in favor of Europe, by the nineteenth century the capitulations had acquired a distinctly exploitative character. Their existence provoked widespread resentment among Ottoman Muslims and sowed social disruption. The Unionists made annulment of the capitulations a prime aspiration.[3]

The mass misery of geopolitics

However neatly the process of Ottoman disintegration may have played out on the maps of diplomats, it inflicted death, pain, and misery on the populations who lived on the landscapes those maps represented. Mass emigration, expulsion, and ethnic cleansing of Muslims accompanied the retreat of Ottoman borders in the Balkans, the Caucasus, and Crimea. The completion of Russia's subjugation of the North Caucasus in 1864 sent hundreds of thousands of Muslim refugees fleeing into Ottoman lands.[4] During the Russo-Ottoman War of 1877–78 an estimated quarter of a million Muslims in Bulgaria lost their lives and up to one million became refugees. Still greater losses in the Balkans were to follow after 1912.[5] A son of refugees living in Edirne (Adrianople) wrote of his childhood at the end of the nineteenth century:

These were not tranquil years. They were pregnant with a bloody, perplexing century . . . Ours was a refugee neighborhood. The flotsam of torrents of refugees, coming every so often from Crimea, Dobruja, and the banks of the Danube because of wars and mass killings, had been pushed back to here step by step with the constantly shrinking borders as armies suffered defeat after defeat for 150, 200 years.[6]

Compounding the despair of such Muslims was the fact that the same advances in knowledge that gave Christian powers and peoples technological superiority were reducing mortality rates and contributing to a Christian demographic boom. Christian populations in Europe and the Balkans were not only growing richer and stronger, but they were also outstripping those of Muslims in sheer numbers.[7] Radical action

---

[3] On the social effects of the capitulations, see Donald Quataert, *Social Disintegration and Popular Resistance in the Ottoman Empire, 1881–1908: Reactions to European Economic Penetration* (New York: New York University Press, 1983).

[4] Kemal Karpat estimates a total of 2.5 million for the period between 1859 and 1914. This is almost certainly excessive. See Kemal Karpat, *Ottoman Population, 1830–1914: Demographic and Social Characteristics* (Madison: University of Wisconsin Press), 65–69.

[5] McCarthy, *Death and Exile*, 90–91, 164; Richard C. Hall, *Balkan Wars, 1912–1913: Prelude to the First World War* (London: Routledge, 2000), 135–37.

[6] Şevket Sürreya Aydemir, *Suyu Arayan Adam* (Istanbul: Remzi Kitabevi, 1995), 9, 18.

[7] Andrew Mango, *Atatürk: The Biography of the Founder of Modern Turkey* (Woodstock, NY: Overlook Press, 2001), 13; Lieven, *Empire*, 155, 208, 216.

and reform would be needed to reverse such a course of events. It was this desperate refugee flotsam from the borderlands that was represented disproportionately in Unionist ranks.[8]

The interstate system at the beginning of the twentieth century was a multipolar one, with no single or two states preeminent. Multipolarity traditionally had afforded the Ottomans the ability to play off one power against the other, which they did at times with consummate skill. Their greatest and most dangerous rival was the Russian empire. Russia bordered directly on the Ottoman empire and had steadily pushed the Ottomans from the Balkans and the Caucasus. And, unlike another neighbor and rival, Austria-Hungary, Russia was growing stronger. Britain and France could project considerable power into the region. They had at times backed the Ottomans against the Russians, and might again in the future. But they, too, had their own economic and geostrategic ambitions in the region and would pursue them to the Ottomans' detriment, as Britain demonstrated in 1878 by absorbing the strategic island of Cyprus in exchange for diplomatic support against Russia. Four years later Britain would occupy Egypt. Italy, too, had its eyes on Ottoman territory in Africa and Albania, and presented a similar, albeit smaller-scale, problem.

That left Germany. Germany was rich and powerful. It shared no direct borders with the Ottoman empire, nor did it have any immediate pretensions to Ottoman territory. Like Istanbul, Berlin had an interest in stymieing the advance of the other powers in the Near East. It alone had opposed the Macedonian reform project without exacting concessions from Istanbul in return. Most important, a deep anxiety about the rise of Russia exercised both capitals. Moreover, a number of influential German foreign policy thinkers by the end of the nineteenth century had become intrigued by the potential of pan-Islam as a revolutionary force to blow up the empires of their Russian, British, and French rivals. Kaiser Wilhelm II was among those fascinated with Islam, going so far as to declare on a trip to Syria that the world's 300 million Muslims had in him an eternal friend.[9] For all these reasons, Germany, so long as it remained outside the Near East, was a logical and desirable ally.

[8] Erik Jan Zürcher, "The Young Turks: Children of the Borderlands?", *International Journal of Turkish Studies*, 9, 1–2 (Summer 2003), 275–85.

[9] On the kaiser's longstanding fascination with Islam, see Donald McKale, *War by Revolution: Germany and Great Britain in the Middle East in the Era of World War I* (Kent, OH: Kent State University Press, 1998), 9–10; Jacob M. Landau, *The Politics of Pan-Islam*, 2nd edn. (New York: Oxford University Press, 1994), 46–47, 98. See also Sean McMeekin, *The Berlin–Baghdad Express: The Ottoman Empire and Germany's Bid for World Power* (Cambridge, MA: Harvard University Press, 2010).

This was the environment in which the Unionists found themselves. Outside their empire, predatory states were engaged in an intense, often bloody, contest of expansion that was often at the Ottomans' expense. Austria-Hungary's brazen annexation of the provinces of Bosnia and Herzegovina in the wake of the 1908 Revolution underscored the unforgiving nature of global society. Inside, the empire's constituents chafed under relative deprivation. Yet efforts to overhaul and streamline the empire's traditionally decentralized administration often provoked only resistance from subjects who opposed ceding greater power to the center and who now had options beyond remaining loyal to Istanbul. The restoration of the constitution had sparked not just joyous celebrations but also a chain of rebellions by tribal leaders in Eastern Anatolia who rightfully feared for the loss of the privileges they had held under the old Hamidian regime. Several of these turned to the Russians across the border for help, and their challenge to the Ottoman state would keep the cauldron of Eastern Anatolia simmering. The reform efforts and diplomatic gambits of the nineteenth century had slowed the empire's partition and disintegration, but they had not stopped it. Something greater had to be done. The Unionists' faith in the efficacy of state power pointed to authoritarian rule as the best bet to resolve the dilemma of pressure to modernize from without and resistance to centralization from within. In the course of the next five years, the Unionists would transform the Ottoman government from a constitutional regime with a parliament to a dictatorship of triumvirs.

Russia's security dynamic: the paradox of power

The position of the Russian empire, it would seem, was fundamentally different from that of the Ottoman. Over the previous two centuries that empire had expanded, not contracted, and had come to dominate the vast Eurasian heartland. It was an emerging industrial power that commanded seemingly inexhaustible natural and human resources. Indeed, the perception of inexorably increasing Russian power was almost universal prior to World War I.[10] The Russian empire, however, inhabited the same anarchic and competitive environment as any other state. Paradoxically, its growth and expansion served to generate rather than alleviate security concerns. St. Petersburg felt an acute vulnerability in the south. The conquest of the Caucasus protected Russia's interior, but it put Russia in control of a troublesome borderland exposed to

---

[10] William C. Wohlforth, "The Perception of Power: Russia in the Pre-1914 Balance," *World Politics*, 39, 3 (April 1987), 380.

competitors. An expanding economy was enriching Russia, but it was also heightening Russia's dependence on the Black Sea Straits for exports. Even Ottoman weakness was a mixed blessing for Russia. Whereas the decline of the Ottomans from the status of true peer competitor was a welcome development, that decline opened the unnerving possibility that another power might manage to exploit it to establish a hostile presence on Russia's southern border and in the Black Sea.

Russia's statesmen, like their Ottoman counterparts, faced the challenge of transforming a polyethnic, multiconfessional, dynastic, imperial state into a modern, efficient, and more centralized state from within, while simultaneously meeting and beating back challenges from without. Russia's territorial expansion and economic growth in the nineteenth century meant the introduction of new constituencies and changing social relations. It subjected the autocracy to severe stress. So long as the tsarist regime proved capable of holding its own against its outside competitors it could keep the internal contradictions in check. But when Japan defeated Russia in 1904–05, the blow to the regime's prestige was so great that a series of revolts, protests, and disturbances erupted across the empire. These events, known as the Revolution of 1905, led Tsar Nicholas II to introduce a constitution and parliament, the Duma. Pressure was alleviated, but only partially, and only for a time.

Southern discomfort

The vectors of Russia's security dilemma came together in January 1908 on the Ottoman–Iranian border. During the previous year Russia had agreed with Great Britain to establish zones of influence in the north and south of Iran respectively in an attempt to regulate both Russia's broader rivalry in Asia with the British empire and to ensure the tranquility of Russian Azerbaijan. But the arrival of the Russians alarmed the Ottomans, in part because they had a border dispute with Iran over Kotur. The Russians' presence also alienated local Kurds, and clashes along the border erupted. Russia's Foreign Minister Aleksandr Izvol'skii sensed an opportunity for a "short, victorious" war to restore the tsarist regime's prestige. With the enthusiastic backing of Army Chief of Staff Fedor Palitsyn, he argued for a war to fulfill "Russia's historical goals in the Turkish East" and floated the possibility of partitioning the Ottoman empire with Britain.[11] Izvol'skii failed to get his way, but that summer the possibility of anarchy in the wake of the Young Turk Revolution spurred

---

[11] I. V. Bestuzhev, *Bor'ba v Rossii po voprosam vneshnei politiki, 1906–1910* (Moscow: Akademiia nauk SSSR, 1961), 150–51; A. A. Polivanov, *Iz dnevnikov i vospominanii po*

him to push again for action. At a special meeting of ministers, diplomats, and military experts he reviewed the options for intervention and resolved to ready a plan to seize the Straits.[12] The unusually powerful minister of the interior, Petr Stolypin, however, was absolute in his conviction that, in the wake of Russia's catastrophic loss to Japan, St. Petersburg must focus its attention and resources on internal reform, and so he quashed the calls for war.[13]

Concerns about Russia's southern strategic position continued to exercise Izvol'skii, but Stolypin received a chance to consolidate control of Russian policy shortly thereafter when the impetuous Izvol'skii blundered. In exchange for a promise to support a new convention permitting the free passage of Russian warships through the Black Sea Straits, he agreed to Austria-Hungary's annexation of Bosnia-Herzegovina. Before Izvol'skii could obtain consent from the powers for the new convention, however, Vienna announced the annexation, leaving Izvol'skii empty-handed and humiliated, and precipitating his departure as foreign minister.[14]

Stolypin's insistence on an inward focus was not a renunciation of expansion. To the contrary, he explained that three or four years of domestic reform would prepare Russia again to assert itself abroad.[15] Until that time, however, Russia needed a rapprochement with the Ottoman empire, and Stolypin saw to the appointment of a likeminded diplomat, Nikolai Charykov, as ambassador to Istanbul. As Charykov explained to Izvol'skii's successor as foreign minister, Sergei Sazonov, rapprochement serves "our fundamental goal: to protect Turkey from disintegrating at a time that would be ill-suited for us." Ottoman collapse was foreordained, but had to be delayed until Russia was strong enough to impose its will on the Ottoman lands. In the meantime, Russia

---

dolzhnosti voennogo ministra i ego pomoshchnika 1907–1916 gg, ed. A. M. Zaionchkovskii (Moscow: Vyshii voennyi redaktsionnyi sovet, 1924), 39.

[12] Protocol of the special meeting called by the minister of foreign affairs, 21.7.1908, [3.8.1908], in A. Popov, "Turetskaia revoliutsiia – 1908–1909," *Krasnyi arkhiv: istoricheskii zhurnal*, 43. (1930), 44–45.

[13] David MacLaren McDonald, *United Government and Foreign Policy in Russia, 1900–1914* (Cambridge, MA: Harvard University Press, 1992), 129, 145–46; Polivanov, *Iz dnevnikov*, 39–48.

[14] Andrew Rossos, *Russia and the Balkans: Inter-Balkan Rivalries and Russian Foreign Policy* (Toronto: University of Toronto Press, 1981), 6. Pavel Miliukov colorfully called Izvol'skii's foul-up a "diplomatic Tsushima": Pavel Miliukov, *Balkanskii krizis i politika A. P. Izvol'skogo* (St. Petersburg: Obshchestvennaia pol'za, 1909), 133. For more on the crisis, see M. S. Anderson, *Eastern Question*, 279–86; Dominic Lieven, *Russia and the Origins of the First World War* (New York: St. Martin's Press, 1983), 33–37; Samuel R. Williamson, Jr., *Austria-Hungary and the Origins of the First World War* (New York: Macmillan, 1991), 69–72.

[15] McDonald, *United Government*, 146–47.

could use the Ottomans to block the Austrians in the Balkans. Even so, aggressively hostile attitudes persisted in Russian military circles.[16]

Despite their suspicions of Russia, both the CUP and its opponents reciprocated Charykov's overtures in 1909. CUP-affiliated newspapers such as *Şura-yı Ümmet* and *Tanin* as well as other leading papers such as *İkdam* ran articles calling for closer ties with Russia. The authors of these pieces included notable figures such as Ali Kemâl Bey, a prominent columnist and CUP opponent, and Dr. Bahaeddin Şakir, a member of the CUP's inner circle. To what extent Charykov personally stimulated this favorable commentary is not known, but his formation of a friendship with the editor of *Tanin* and prominent Unionist deputy Hüseyin Cahid surely facilitated matters.[17]

Their fierce anti-imperialism notwithstanding, the Unionists could hardly afford to spurn overtures for better relations from Russia, since less than a year after coming to power the government was already embattled at home. That April, anti-Unionist elements from the First Army Corps in Istanbul, joined by members of a party called the "Muhammedan Union," marched on the parliament, calling for the government's resignation and the restoration of the *şeriat*, Islamic law. The government fled Istanbul in panic, and across the empire disturbances broke out. In Adana, Muslims lashed out at Armenians, killing thousands. Only the arrival ten days later from Salonica of another faction of the military, an "Action Army" under General Mahmud Şevket Pasha accompanied by Enver Bey, defeated the uprising. The episode failed to shake the Unionists' will to rule. To the contrary, they seized the opportunity to consolidate their control by deposing Abdülhamid II, trying and executing leading mutineers, banning groups bearing ethnic or national names, ordering the formation of special counterinsurgency units in the Balkans, and heightening penalties against bandits and guerrillas. Nonetheless, the so-called counterrevolution taught the Unionists that they could not ignore Muslim sentiment.[18]

When later in 1909 Charykov proposed that Tsar Nicholas II on his way to Rome stop in Istanbul and meet with Sultan Mehmed Reşad V,

[16] Bestuzhev, *Bor'ba v Rossii*, 340; A. M. Zaionchkovskii, *Podgotovka Rossii k mirovoi voine v mezhdunarodnom otnoshenii* (Leningrad: Voennaia tipografiia, 1926), 214; William C. Fuller, "The Russian Empire," in *Knowing One's Enemies: Intelligence Assessment Before the Two World Wars*, ed. Ernest R. May (Princeton: Princeton University Press, 1984), 123.

[17] Akdes Nimet Kurat, *Türkiye ve Rusya: XVIII Yüzyıl Sonundan Kurtuluş Savaşına Kadar Türk–Rus İlişkileri (1798–1919)* (Ankara: Ankara University Press, 1970), 150, 152, 158.

[18] Feroz Ahmad, *Young Turks*, 40–46; Yusuf Hikmet Bayur, *Türk İnkılâbı Tarihi*, 4 vols. (Ankara: Türk Tarih Kurumu, 1940), vol. I, pt. 1, 295–301; Lewis, *Emergence*, 215–18.

the Porte greeted the idea enthusiastically. Within St. Petersburg, however, objections were raised to the idea of the tsar visiting the former Byzantine capital and center of Eastern Orthodoxy – the city the Russians were already calling "Tsargrad," or "Tsar's city" – as a mere tourist. The proposal was dropped and Nicholas II traveled to Rome by train. Charykov attempted to salvage some of the goodwill by mounting an exhibition of Russian industry in Istanbul aboard a ship christened "Nicholas II." Although a commercial success, the exhibition could not rescue the rapprochement. Inside the Russian state bureaucracy too many opposed a closer relationship. Outside, the conservative and liberal press alike criticized the policy, with the former advocating a deal with Austria-Hungary to partition the Ottoman empire. Unsuccessful in their effort to get Serbia, Bulgaria, and the Ottoman empire to resolve their differences in Macedonia, Russia's diplomats ultimately declared the policy barren and dropped it in 1910.[19]

At the same time that he had been restraining his fellow ministers from premature aggression and backing Charykov's efforts to draw Istanbul closer, Stolypin had been pushing for a build-up of Russian military capabilities in the Caucasus and of naval capabilities on the Black Sea. Reports in 1911 that the Ottomans were looking to purchase one or two dreadnoughts raised further alarms. Even if it was true that the Ottomans sought the advanced battleships for use on the Aegean against the Greeks, there would be nothing to prevent them from deploying the vessels on the Black Sea, where Russia's fleet possessed no comparable warships.[20]

A different source of anxiety for St. Petersburg was the possibility that another power might grab control of the Black Sea Straits from the faltering Ottomans. Russian military planners saw the creation of a rapid deployment force as a form of insurance against such a scenario. Indeed, during the disorders of July 1908 and April 1909 the Foreign Ministry had considered landing troops in Istanbul. Reviews conducted in March and June 1911 by the navy and army respectively, however, concluded that Russia's forces remained incapable of executing a surprise assault to seize the Bosphorus. The Council of Ministers concurred with Stolypin that this state of affairs was unacceptable. Overriding objections to the cost, the council backed a Naval Ministry proposal to build eighteen new

---

[19] Kurat, *Türkiye ve Rusya*, 158–59; Bestuzhev, *Bor'ba v Rossii*, 346–48; K. F. Shatsillo, *Russkii imperializm i razvitie flota nakanune pervoi mirovoi voiny (1906–1914)* (Moscow: Nauka, 1968), 94.

[20] Emissary in Sofia to Neratov, 30.6.1911 [13.7.1911], in Kommissia po izdaniiu dokumentov epokhi imperializma, *Mezhdunarodnye otnosheniia v epokhu imperializma* (hereafter *Movei*), series 2, vol. 18, pt. 1 (Moscow: Gosizdat politicheskoi literatury, 1938), 211.

vessels, including three dreadnoughts, on the Black Sea. The tsar and the Duma approved the proposal in May 1911.[21] Over the course of the next two years, Russian anxiety about the straits would intensify as events underscored both Russia's economic dependence upon the waterway and the real possibility of an imminent resolution of the centuries-old Eastern Question by the military destruction of the Ottoman empire.

War with Italy

On 28 September Italy gave the Ottoman empire an ultimatum declaring its intent to occupy Tripoli of Barbary (the provinces of Tripolitania and Cyrenaica). The ostensible motive was to protect Italians living there. The real motive was to prevent Italy from falling further behind its great power peers in the scramble to accumulate colonies. Thus, despite receiving a propitiating response, Rome attacked the next day. Described by one historian as "one of the most unjustified [wars] in European history,"[22] Italy's aggression provided one more example to the Ottomans of the merciless nature of the great powers and the interstate system they dominated, and belied the Europeans' rhetoric of support for stabilizing reforms. To the contrary, the Ottomans concluded, the great powers preferred to keep the Ottoman empire weak and confused, the easier to carve it up. The assessment was not far off the mark. Apprehension that Istanbul's domestic reforms would strengthen its bonds to the African provinces had been among the factors spurring the Italians to attack.[23]

Tripoli represented the last Ottoman possession in Africa. If it went, so would the Ottoman claim to be "an empire on three continents." The Unionists were determined to defend the distant province however they could.[24] A number of Ottoman military officers, including Enver and another promising young officer named Mustafa Kemal, made their way overland to Tripoli, traveling discreetly in small groups to avoid detection as they passed through British-controlled Egypt. With the assistance of such advisors, Tripoli's native tribesmen mounted strong resistance. Unable to impose its will, Italy escalated by bombarding targets on the Ottomans' Aegean and Levantine coastlines.

Italy's expansion of the war into the eastern Mediterranean disturbed St. Petersburg. One-quarter of Russia's total exports passed through the

---

[21] Shatsillo, *Russkii imperializm*, 130–34; Ronald Bobroff, *Roads to Glory: Late Imperial Russia and the Turkish Straits* (New York: I. B. Tauris, 2006), 22–23.

[22] M. S. Anderson, *Eastern Question*, 288.   [23] Bobroff, *Roads*, 22.

[24] M. Şükrü Hanioğlu, *A Brief History of the Ottoman Empire* (Princeton: Princeton University Press, 2008), 168.

Black Sea Straits, and now there was a possibility that Istanbul would block the passage. Since Foreign Minister Sazonov was convalescing, it fell to Vice-Minister of Foreign Affairs Anatolii Neratov to assume the initiative. When the other powers failed to respond to his proposal to act collectively to prevent any disruption to shipping, Neratov had Charykov propose to Grand Vizier Said Pasha that Istanbul accept free passage for Russian warships in exchange for a guaranty to protect the straits and the Balkan status quo, forego a concession to build a railroad along the Black Sea coast, and even revise the hated capitulations. The offer was tempting, but it would make the empire wholly dependent on Russia for its security. Said Pasha and Foreign Minister Âsım Bey decided acceptance would be tantamount to a betrayal of the empire and so declined.[25] All rights and authority over the straits, Said Pasha explained in his response to Charykov that December, belonged to the Ottoman populace and its ruler.[26]

When Sazonov returned to his post in December and learned of Charykov's proposal, he was aghast. With the Tripolitanian War, friction with Britain regarding Iran, and other problems roiling global diplomacy, Sazonov believed it was an inauspicious time to push for change on such a major issue as the straits. He instructed Charykov to inform the Ottomans that his overture had been a wholly private initiative. Then, in April 1912, Russia's fears were realized. When a frustrated Italy, unable to prevail in Tripoli of Barbary, carried out naval attacks on targets near the straits, the Ottomans shut them to traffic for a month. The impact upon Russia was severe: Russian grain exports for the first half of 1912 fell 45 percent from the same period in 1911, an unacceptable situation given that the export of grain from the Black Sea was absolutely essential to Russia's own drive to industrialize and match its rivals.[27] Between 1900 and 1909 the straits accounted for one-third to one-half of Russia's total exports, and shipments of coal, manganese, and oil from the Caucasus and Ukraine were growing in importance.[28]

[25] M. S. Anderson, *Eastern Question*, 289, Kurat, *Türkiye ve Rusya*, 162, 164; Bayur, *Türk İnkılâbı Tarihi*, vol. II, pt. 1, 136–43.

[26] E. A. Adamov, "Vopros o Prolivakh i o Konstantinopole v mezhdunarodnoi politike v 1908–1977 g.g.," in *Konstantinopol' i prolivy po sekretnym dokumentam byvshego ministerstva inostrannykh del*, vol. I, ed. E. A. Adamov (Moscow: Litizdat NKID, 1925), 16.

[27] D. W. Spring, "Russian Foreign Policy, Economic Interests and the Straits Question, 1905–1914," in *New Perspectives in Modern Russian History*, ed. Robert B. McKean (New York: St. Martin's Press, 1992), 212–13; Ia. Zakher, "Konstantinopl' i prolivi", *Krasnyi arkhiv: istoricheskii zhurnal*, 6 (1924), 49.

[28] Alan Bodger, "Russia and the End of the Ottoman Empire," in *The Great Powers and the End of the Ottoman Empire*, ed. Marian Kent, 2nd edn. (London: Frank Cass, 1996), 79.

If the war underscored to Russia the vital importance of the straits, it revealed to the Balkan states the vulnerability of the Ottoman empire. Italy's audacious unilateral grab of Ottoman territory set an instructive precedent. It was permissible, and useful, to act now and attack the hapless Ottoman empire. Bulgaria, Serbia, Greece, and Montenegro all coveted the remaining Balkan territories of the Ottoman empire, and so in 1912 they formed a web of alliances directed against it.[29]

The Balkan Wars and the acceleration of Russian plans

On 8 October 1912, Montenegro got a jump on its Balkan allies and declared war on the Ottoman empire. With yet another war now on their hands, the Ottomans ceded Tripoli and made peace with Italy. They enjoyed no reprieve, however, as the other Balkan states followed Montenegro and attacked Ottoman positions throughout the peninsula. The Balkan armies enjoyed stunning success, inflicting a series of catastrophic defeats on the Ottomans everywhere from Albania to Thrace.

The reasons for the Ottoman army's defeats extended beyond numerical inferiority and the need to fight simultaneously on several fronts. The Ottomans' foreign and domestic challenges had again combined to disastrous effect. The question of the composition of the Ottoman officer corps had become inextricably intertwined with domestic political struggles. As the Young Turk Revolution and the counterrevolution of 1909 had demonstrated, whoever controlled the army could control the course of domestic politics. A group known as the "Savior Officers" (*Halâskar Zabitân*) underscored this lesson again. Upset with the CUP's authoritarian style, the way it had manipulated elections to stack parliament with Unionists earlier that year, and the participation of active-duty Unionist officers in government, the Savior Officers in July 1912 threatened a coup and successfully forced a cabinet change and new elections, thereby driving the CUP from power.

Somewhat ironically, the Savior Officers also required that henceforth all officers swear not to involve themselves in politics. Yet even a seemingly technical question, such as that of military education and promotion, was politically charged. There were two routes into the officer corps. One was through formal training in a military academy, or *mekteb-i harbiye*. The second was promotion through the ranks. These officers, known as *alaylılar* in reference to their emergence through the regiments, or *alaylar*, were as a rule unsuited for command in a modern military force. The Unionists were emphatic proponents of the academy system,

---

[29] Rossos, *Russia and the Balkans*, 35; M. S. Anderson, *Eastern Question*, 291.

both because it meshed with their ideological commitment to modernization and because they counted a disproportionate number of academy graduates, or *mektebliler*, among their supporters. The regimental officers as a group overwhelmingly opposed the CUP.[30] Infighting and a preoccupation with politics took a toll on military preparedness. Disorder and confusion reigned even at the very top. When with war looming in the Balkans the newly appointed war minister Nâzım Pasha, a talented commander and graduate of the French military academy St. Cyr, was asked what the army would do, he was reduced to the reply, "Some plans were apparently made during the time of [the preceding war minister] Mahmud Şevket Pasha; I am going to obtain and examine them."[31]

Crushed on every front, the Ottomans in early November found Bulgarian forces on the outskirts of Istanbul. The Bulgarians' approach alarmed the Russians too. Sazonov, who had earlier encouraged the Balkan alliances, envisioning them as a barrier to Austro-Hungarian expansion, watched in distress as the Bulgarians threatened to take Istanbul and the straits on their own.[32] The Ministry of War on 6 November ordered an amphibious landing force formed in Sevastopol for intervening in Istanbul. Less than forty-eight hours later, the naval minister telegraphed Tsar Nicholas II at 1:30 a.m. to ask that the ambassador to Istanbul, Mikhail Girs, be given discretionary authority to order the intervention. It was an extraordinary request, but the tsar granted his approval. Upon Girs' insistence, the amphibious force was increased to 5,000 men with artillery. A Naval General Staff report advised that Russian forces could deploy to the Bosphorus using the "slightest pretext" and turn their occupation into a permanent one with little difficulty. Although the ostensible mission of the amphibious force would be to protect Istanbul's Christian population from violence expected to result from the influx of defeated and disorderly Ottoman soldiers, Sazonov's intent was to use it to give Russia the "deciding voice" in resolving the fate of Istanbul and the straits.[33]

By mid November the Bulgarian advance had stalled. With the threat defused momentarily, Sazonov returned to his policy of maintaining the status quo until such time as Russia was be strong enough to impose its

[30] M. Naim Turfan, *Rise of the Young Turks: Politics, the Military, and Ottoman Collapse* (New York: St. Martin's Press, 2000), 156–58; Tarık Zafer Tunaya, *Türkiye'de Siyasal Partiler*, vol. I (Istanbul: İletişim Yayınları, 1998), 344–66.

[31] Hüsamettin Ertürk, *İki Devrin Perde Arkası*, ed. Samih Nafiz Tansu (Istanbul: Sebil Yayınevi, 1996), 78; Feroz Ahmad, *Young Turks*, 106–12; Ali Fuad Türkgeldi, *Görüp İşittiklerim*, 3rd edn. (Ankara: Türk Tarih Kurumu, 1984), 60.

[32] M. S. Anderson, *Eastern Question*, 242–44; Rossos, *Russia and the Balkans*, 45–46.

[33] Zakher, "Konstantinopl'," 51–52; Bobroff, *Roads*, 52–54.

will. Explaining to his ambassador to Paris that it was in Russia's interest to maintain room for maneuver, he rejected a French suggestion that France, Britain, and Russia issue a joint declaration against any seizure of the straits. He similarly dismissed a British proposal to make the status quo permanent by internationalizing Istanbul and guaranteeing the neutrality of the straits. Although such an arrangement in principle would satisfy Russia's need for free passage for its commercial and naval ships, legal norms, Sazonov stressed, were effective only in peacetime. In wartime they were, virtually by definition, meaningless.[34] A state's own might, not the promises of others, was the ultimate guarantor of its security.

A renewed Bulgarian threat to Istanbul jolted St. Petersburg again, and again the Black Sea Fleet was put at Girs' disposal. A strong consensus emerged among the Foreign, War, and Naval Ministries that Russia had to take the straits within the next several years since, as a Naval General Staff report put it, "the decisive resolution of the Eastern Question will probably occur in the next few years." The same report argued that because the idea of seizing the straits "had lain in the Russian consciousness for so long and so deeply" it would be dangerous to forego it. Minister of the Navy Admiral Ivan Grigorovich assured Sazonov not only that a powerful fleet could be built on the Black Sea within five years, but also that "the Turkish Straits, the Bosphorus and the Dardanelles, inevitably will become, sooner or later, a Russian possession."[35]

The Naval Ministry drafted a plan to build up the Black Sea Fleet. Calculating that Britain and France would in the event of a *fait accompli* acquiesce to Russian control of the straits, the planners underlined the need for good relations with Greece. Russia between 1915 and 1918 was to concentrate both its Baltic and Black Sea Fleets in the Aegean by making use of Greek ports. Then, at the appropriate time, predicted to be between 1917 and 1919, Russia was to strike and seize the Bosphorus and Dardanelles. Russia's ministers gave the plan their unanimous endorsement.[36]

The message of the Balkan Wars was that the death of Europe's "Sick Man" was at hand. The challenge for Russia was to keep the Ottoman empire around at least until 1917.[37] It is worth noting that Sazonov did

[34] Zakher, "Konstantinopl'," 59, 72.
[35] Zakher, "Konstantinopl'," 64–66; Shatsillo, *Russkii imperializm*, 102–03, 129; M. Petrov, *Podgotovka Rossii k mirovoi voine na more* (Leningrad: Voenizdat, 1926), 158–59; Peter Gatrell, *Government, Industry, and Rearmament in Russia, 1900–1914: The Last Argument of Tsarism* (New York: Cambridge University Press, 1994), 137.
[36] Petrov, *Podgotovka*, 159–61; Zakher, "Konstantinopl'," 66.
[37] I. V. Bestuzhev, "Russian Foreign Policy, February–June 1914," *Journal of Contemporary History*, 1, 3 (July 1966), 107.

not fear that the Ottoman empire was about to disintegrate on its own. To the contrary, he believed that the empire was robust enough to handle its internal problems and that under the right conditions it could continue in existence for some time to come. The existential threat came from the outside, and that was worrisome enough. "[W]e cannot close our eyes to the dangers of the international situation" created by Ottoman weakness, Sazonov cautioned.[38] It was in this context that internal Ottoman conflicts took on heightened significance. As Sazonov remarked, "The Ottoman empire's defects, its inability to rejuvenate itself on legal and cultural bases, have so far been to our advantage, generating that attraction of peoples under the domination of the Crescent to Orthodox Christian Russia which constitutes one of the foundations of our international position in the East and in Europe."[39] The key was to exploit the internal fissures correctly.

External catastrophe and internal consolidation: the final ascent of the Unionists

Thoroughly routed on all fronts, the Ottoman empire signed an armistice on 3 December 1912 and entered peace talks hosted in London. The fact that former subjects, not the great powers, had stripped the empire of its historic heartland and wealthiest lands made the loss all the more bitter. The Unionists seethed. When the Ottoman government, now in the hands of the Liberal Entente (*Hürriyet ve İtilâf Fırkası*), a loose grouping of disparate elements ranging from liberals to tribal chiefs joined together by myriad ideological and material reasons in opposition to the Unionist platform of centralization, decided to enter peace talks, the Unionists fomented popular distress over the surrender of Ottoman territory and channeled it against the government. Suspecting a plot, Grand Vizier Kâmil Pasha ordered the arrests of a large number of Unionists.[40] Those who failed to flee were jailed or exiled to Anatolia.

Kâmil Pasha's preemption was in vain. On 23 January 1912 Enver Bey led an armed group of Unionists in a raid on the Sublime Porte, where they burst in, shot to death War Minister Nâzım Pasha, and forced Kâmil Pasha to resign on the spot. A mistaken fear that the grand vizier had been preparing to surrender Edirne, one of the empire's earlier capitals

---

[38] Report of Sazonov to Nicholas II on November 23, 1913, as cited in Zaionchkovskii, *Podgotovka Rossii k mirovoi voine*, 393; Zakher, "Konstantinopl'," 70.
[39] Zaionchkovskii, *Podgotovka Rossii k mirovoi voine*, 394; Zakher, "Konstantinopl'," 71.
[40] Feroz Ahmad, *Young Turks*, 114–15; Bayur, *Türk İnkılâbı Tarihi*, vol. II, pt. 4, 268–69.

and one of its largest and most important cities, had been the catalyst for the raid. The sultan had no choice but to accept the resignation and permit the Unionists to form a new government. The Unionists remained resolute in opposing peace talks, but in the interests of forming a cabinet and government that would command broad support and rally the empire in self-defense, they opted to appoint only three of their members to the cabinet and amnestied their opponents.[41]

The Unionists' refusal to sue for peace was rewarded in the summer of 1913 when Serbia, Greece, and Romania fell upon Bulgaria on three fronts. The Ottoman army saw its opportunity and opened a fourth front by punching through the Bulgarians' lines at Çatalca to Edirne. The 33-year-old Enver, always with an eye for the theatrical, made sure he was at the head of the Ottoman columns when they entered Edirne on 20 July. The hero of 1908 now claimed the title of the city's "second conqueror," inflating his accomplishment to that of Sultan Murad I's commander, Lala Şahin Pasha, who had captured the city in 1361. The recapture of Edirne boosted the morale of Ottoman Muslims, demonstrating that perhaps defeat was not their only possible fate.[42]

Although Enver's audaciousness had salvaged something from the Second Balkan War, the fact that the empire had experienced a catastrophe remained. In the two-year period between September 1911 and September 1913 the empire had lost over a third of its territory and more than one-fifth of its population. Its already depleted coffers hemorrhaged further.[43] Ethnic cleansing sent hundreds of thousands of Muslim refugees, or *muhacirler*, streaming into the empire, adding yet another economic burden and straining the social fabric. The refugees had their blood shed, homes burned, and families expelled from their birthplaces because as Muslims they were judged to be without legitimate claim to their birthlands in an age of nation-states. When, destitute and embittered, they arrived in what was supposed to be their land, Anatolia, they encountered in Istanbul and along the Aegean coast prosperous communities of Christians, especially Greeks, causing their resentment to burn more intensely. Government offices and private relief organizations ameliorated the refugees' plight somewhat,[44] but the influx of so many desperate and angry people, Russian diplomats

---

[41] Feroz Ahmad, *Young Turks*, 116–23; cf. Turfan, *Rise*, 204–13.
[42] Ertürk, *Perde Arkası*, 98; Şevket Süreyya Aydemir, *Suyu Arayan Adam*, 55; Feroz Ahmad, *Young Turks*, 140.
[43] AVPRI, Asian Turkey and Its Study, 1.5.1913 [14.5.1913], f. 129, o. 592b, d. 7600, l. 1; Feroz Ahmad, *Young Turks*, 152–53.
[44] Shaw, *From Empire to Republic*, vol. I, 49–51.

noted, had injected a dangerous anti-Christian element into the empire's politics.[45]

There is no doubt that the defeats and attendant savagery of the Balkan Wars hardened the attitudes of Ottoman Muslims and of the Unionists and their supporters in particular. As noted earlier, a large proportion of Unionists were from the Balkans, and they felt the loss of their homelands most acutely. In his private letters Enver expressed his anger over the "pitiless" slaughter of Muslims, even "children, young girls, the elderly, women." Calling the Balkan Wars the "latest Crusade," he seethed: "But our hatred strengthens: Revenge, revenge, revenge; there is no other word."[46] Another Unionist, Halil Bey (Menteşe), a future foreign minister, addressed the parliament with an impassioned and militant call not to forget the Balkan lands. That message echoed in speeches, newspapers, and even schoolbooks.[47]

It would be incorrect to explain the savagery of the Balkan Wars as the product of a final reckoning of sorts in the longstanding opposition between Balkan Christians and Muslims. Balkan Christians inflicted upon each other precisely the same savageries that they exchanged with Muslims.[48] More importantly, the emotional impact of the Balkan Wars upon the Unionists' decisionmaking should not be exaggerated. The loss of the Balkans stung, but it did not cause them to lose their heads. Already by September, representatives of the Unionist government met with their Bulgarian counterparts. In an atmosphere of almost joyous amity, they signed a peace treaty. The cause for reconciliation was simple: The shift in the regional balance of power had given Istanbul and Sofia common enemies. Indeed, the two were already considering a formal alliance.[49]

Despite their rhetoric of a Balkan *reconquista*, one lesson the Unionists drew from the Balkan Wars was that the Balkan lands with their predominantly Christian populations were irretrievably lost. Anatolia and the Arab lands were left. The Arab lands were vulnerable. The great powers had extensive interests there. Geography made the Arab lands' naval and military defense difficult, and their ethnic composition made their

---

[45] AVPRI, Dispatch from Ambassador in Constantinople, 12.5.1914 [25.5.1914], f. 151, o. 482, d. 4068, l. 2. On the sociopolitical impact of the war more generally, see Eyal Ginio, "Mobilizing the Ottoman Nation During the Balkan Wars (1912–1913): Awakening from the Ottoman Dream," *War and History*, 12, 2 (2005), 156–77.

[46] M. Şükrü Hanioğlu, *Kendi Mektuplarında Enver Paşa* (Istanbul: Der Yayınları, 1989), 240–42.

[47] Taner Akçam, *Shameful Act: The Armenian Genocide and the Question of Turkish Responsibility* (New York: Metropolitan Books, 2006), 114–16; Mustafa Aksakal, "Not 'by those old books of international law, but only by war': Ottoman Intellectuals on the Eve of the Great War," *Diplomacy and Statecraft*, 15, 3 (2004), 512.

[48] Hall, *Balkan Wars*, 138.   [49] Rossos, *Russia and the Balkans*, 205.

continued inclusion in the Ottoman state difficult to justify under the emerging new global order.[50] Anatolia might well be the last stronghold. But could they hold even it? Recent history had not been encouraging.

The Liman von Sanders crisis

The Ottomans and outsiders alike recognized that the question of the next onslaught against the empire was when, not if. In order to survive even into the near future, the empire had to obtain outside support. Germany was the most logical choice of ally. It was powerful and a rival of Britain, France, and Russia, and held no immediate pretensions to Ottoman territory. Ties between Berlin and Istanbul were already good, and in May 1913 the Ottoman government requested Berlin to provide a military mission to help train and reorganize its army. The Germans agreed that fall to send a detachment of forty officers under the command of General Otto Viktor Karl Liman von Sanders. There was nothing in principle unusual about the agreement; Britain already had a naval mission in the Ottoman empire[51] and the French were training the Ottoman gendarmerie. But the announcement that Liman von Sanders would take command of the army corps responsible for defending the straits provoked a scandal. The idea of a German in control of the straits was intolerable for St. Petersburg, so much so that Sazonov contemplated invading and occupying the Black Sea port of Trabzon or the Eastern Anatolian town of Bayezid in retaliation.[52] After London and Paris, at Sazonov's urging, lodged protests, the Ottomans and Germans cleverly resolved the crisis by promoting Liman von Sanders to full general, a rank that disqualified him from command of a mere army corps.[53]

Yet this did not allay St. Petersburg's fundamental concern, which was rooted in the structure of power in the region more than its fluctuations. In February 1914 Russia's Council of Ministers met to review the options for taking the straits. They concluded that Russia's lack of naval transport and the relative strength of the Ottoman navy rendered such

---

[50] On Unionist attitudes and policies toward the Arab lands, see Hasan Kayalı, *Arabs and Young Turks: Ottomanism, Arabism, and Islamism in the Ottoman Empire, 1908–1918* (Berkeley: University of California Press, 1997).

[51] Chris B. Rooney, "The International Significance of British Naval Missions to the Ottoman Empire, 1908–1914," *Middle Eastern Studies*, 34 (1998), 1–29.

[52] Bobroff, *Roads*, 86; M. S. Anderson, *Eastern Question*, 303; Harry N. Howard, *The Partition of Turkey: A Diplomatic History, 1913–1923* (Norman: University of Oklahoma Press, 1931), 45.

[53] For a detailed treatment of the Liman von Sanders mission and the crisis it created, see R. J. Kerner, "The Mission of Liman von Sanders," *Slavonic Review*, 6, 16 (1927), 12–27; 6, 17 (1927), 344–63; 6, 18 (1928), 543–60; 7, 19 (1928), 90–112.

an operation temporarily unfeasible. In response, they resolved that the army, navy, and ministries of finance, trade, and industry would work together to solve the transport problem, achieve naval supremacy, and increase the number of men and artillery assigned to amphibious operations. They decided also to expand Russia's Caucasian rail network so that it could better support Russia's Caucasus Army in a conflict. The optimal time to seize the straits, they concurred, would be during a general European war. Nicholas II approved the council's plan on 5 April 1914, committing Russia to the creation of the forces it needed to seize Istanbul and the straits.[54] In the meantime, St. Petersburg's task was to avoid a general European war and blunt the Ottomans' efforts to bolster their own fleet. Istanbul had ordered two dreadnoughts from Britain, scheduled for completion in 1914, and was attempting to purchase a third from Chile or Argentina. These two or three warships would give the Ottomans supremacy on the Black Sea until at least 1917 when Russia would launch four planned dreadnoughts. St. Petersburg, in a major departure from its policy of supporting domestic industry, attempted to prevent the Ottomans from acquiring dreadnoughts by preemptively purchasing those ordered by Chile and Argentina and by pressuring London to slow construction of the vessels ordered by the Ottomans.[55] Sazonov succeeded in the latter, and when World War I broke out right before their scheduled delivery, Britain would claim them as its own in a move that produced large and unforeseen ramifications.[56]

The Turkish–Russian Friendship Committee

The main source of contention between the Ottoman and Russian empires throughout 1913 was Russia's insistence that Istanbul implement a reform program in the six provinces of Eastern Anatolia, namely Van, Erzurum, Bitlis, Diyar-ı Bekir, Mamuret ül-Aziz (Harput), and Sivas. The ostensible purpose of the program was to provide better security for the local Armenian population. The rout of the Ottoman army in the Balkan Wars sparked fears in St. Petersburg that the collapse of the Ottoman empire itself was imminent. This spurred Russia to raise the question of the reform of Eastern Anatolia, both as a way to gain leverage over other powers in the event of partition and to prevent instability spilling over into its Caucasian provinces should the Ottoman

[54] Shatsillo, *Russkii imperializm*, 106; Zakher, "Konstantinopl'," 74.
[55] Gattrell, *Government*, 92.
[56] Geoffrey Miller, *Straits: British Policy Towards the Ottoman Empire and the Origins of the Dardanelles Campaign* (Hull: University of Hull Press, 1997), 200–01.

state implode. The reform plan called for placing the administration and policing of the six provinces under foreign control and amounted to the effective surrender of Ottoman sovereignty. To the Ottomans, it eerily resembled the Mürzteg program implemented in Macedonia before that province was lost for good. Istanbul therefore strenuously resisted the Russian proposal, but succeeded only in changing some of the terms before signing a joint agreement on 8 February 1914.

Ironically, the completion of that agreement cleared the way to warmer relations. Sazonov was open to cooperation as a way to preserve the integrity of the Ottoman empire until such time as Russia could violate that integrity on its own terms. The Ottoman government was acutely aware of the dangers of seeking confrontation with a great power and recognized that, given its weakness, it had no chance of abrogating the agreement. Russia, moreover, was bidding to become a member of the Ottoman Public Debt Administration, and there was the possibility that it might back the Ottoman desire to raise customs duties.[57]

In fact, Russians in Istanbul had detected a "Russophilic" tendency among social circles and the press already in the fall of 1913. When a correspondent from the St. Petersburg Telegraph Agency named V. Ianchevetskii proposed taking a group of leading Ottoman professionals to Russia on a tour and sending Ottoman youth there to study so as to improve ties, the leading Unionist and minister of the interior Mehmed Talât Pasha promised his support.[58] The idea of sending students to Russia was not Ianchevetskii's alone. The well-known expatriate from Russian Azerbaijan Ahmed Ağaoğlu (Agaev)[59] was serving in the Ministry of Education and had published articles in the newspapers *Tercüman-ı Hakikat* and *Jeune Turc* calling for Ottoman students to be sent to Europe, including Russia, for education. After meeting with the correspondent, the minister of education assigned Ağaoğlu to draft a plan for sending youth to Russia. Aside from being an expatriate from Russia and an expert in education, Ağaoğlu also taught Russian in Istanbul's university, the Dar ül-Fünun, and was thus an obvious choice to oversee such a program. Ağaoğlu wished to send some of his own students to Russia, lamenting to Ianchevetskii that despite Russia's proximity most Ottomans knew the Russians only as *Moskoflar*, Muscovite barbarian oppressors.[60]

[57] Kurat, *Türkiye ve Rusya*, 213.
[58] AVPRI, Imperial Embassy in Constantinople to Neratov, 31.10.1913 [13.11.1913], Report of Ianchevetskii, 28.10.1913 [10.11.1913], f. 151, o. 482, d. 4347, ll. 2, 3.
[59] For more on Ağaoğlu, see Holly Shissler, *Between Two Empires: Ahmet Ağaoğlu and the New Turkey* (London: I. B. Tauris, 2002).
[60] AVPRI, Report of Ianchevetskii, 28.10.1913 [10.11.1913], f. 151, o. 482, d. 4347, ll. 4–5.

That March, a "Turkish–Russian Committee" was established in Istanbul for the development of closer cultural, economic, and political ties. It planned to accomplish these objectives by influencing the press in the two countries, publishing a monthly newspaper, organizing travel excursions, and holding conferences. It had an executive board of twelve and a total membership of forty, half Ottoman, half Russian. The Ottoman members included Ağaoğlu and were all Unionists.[61]

That Ağaoğlu and the Unionists would have been enthusiastic about such a committee may sound surprising, even suspicious. As a sometime exponent of Turkism and member of the Turkish Hearths (Türk Ocakları), he had penned many articles critical of the Russian government and its treatment of Turks and Muslims. Although it is possible that such Ottomans were merely humoring the Russians with the committee, they supported it financially and were more eager than the Russians to open a branch office in St. Petersburg.[62] The Austro-Hungarian ambassador in Istanbul did not see the committee as mere window dressing, and excoriated its formation.[63]

A pitch for an alliance

The reassignment in the spring of the Russian embassy's chief translator, Andrei Mandel'shtam, known for his hostility to Ottoman Muslims, to the University of St. Petersburg to teach Turkish was interpreted in diplomatic and other circles as a sign of Russia's wish to improve relations.[64] The Porte indicated its desire for closer ties when Grand Vizier Said Halim Pasha proposed to send a delegation to Livadia in Crimea to greet the tsar. The practice of the Ottoman sultan dispatching a delegation to formerly Ottoman Crimea to welcome the vacationing tsar was a ritual established during the reign of Sultan Abdülaziz to symbolize the sultan-caliph's spiritual ties to Crimea's Muslims. Sazonov welcomed the proposal, seeing a visit as an opportunity to push for Russia's inclusion in the Ottoman Public Debt Administration.[65] When Said Halim announced that he would send Minister of the Interior Talât, Hüseyin Cahid Bey in the pages of *Tanin* expressed his support for

---

[61] AVPRI, Charter of the Turco-Russian Committee, 1914, f. 151, o. 482, d. 4347, l. 8. For a list of the leading members, both Ottoman and Russian, see Kurat, *Türkiye ve Rusya*, 216.

[62] AVPRI, Secret Telegram from the Ambassador in Constantinople, 7.7.1914 [20.7.1914], f. 151, o. 482, d. 4347, l. 6; AVPRI, Dispatch from the Ambassador in Constantinople, 7.4.1914 [20.4.1914], f. 151, o. 482, d. 4347, l. 7.

[63] Frank G. Weber, *Eagles on the Crescent: Germany, Austria, and the Diplomacy of the Turkish Alliance, 1914–1918* (Ithaca: Cornell University Press, 1970), 47.

[64] Kurat, *Türkiye ve Rusya*, 217.

[65] Minister of Foreign Affairs to Girs, 15.4.1914 [28.4.1914], *Movei*, ser. 3, vol. 2, 404–05.

the mission while Ağaoğlu similarly boosted the trip in hopes that it would dispel the Russian public's hostile impressions of the Unionist government.[66] Meanwhile, Said Halim warned the Austro-Hungarian ambassador Johann von Pallavicini that the CUP had all but decided to realign with the Entente after Germany lent its support to Greece in a dispute over some Aegean islands. If Said Halim's warning was a bluff, it was a dangerous one, as it led Pallavicini to counsel his German counterpart to undercut the Ottoman effort by offering Istanbul to the Russians. The Habsburg diplomat explained that Russia would soon partition Anatolia and that Germany would be wise to act now and cede the straits on good terms before Russia seized them later.[67]

Talât, accompanied by Minister of War İzzet Pasha, arrived in Livadia on 10 May. The tsar explained that Russia desired a strong and independent Ottoman state so that Istanbul, a vital national interest of Russia, would remain free. He warned that St. Petersburg had not forgotten about the Liman von Sanders crisis and would not tolerate Ottoman dependence on Germany. Talât replied that the Ottomans had little choice but to ask the Germans for technical assistance. When the tsar pointed with pride to the lavish banquet spread and the ornate tableware and boasted that all of it was Russian, Talât coolly remarked, "Because of the capitulations, our situation unfortunately is not the same."[68] An acute sense of their state's disadvantaged position and lack of maneuvering room pervaded the outlook of Ottoman statesmen.

On the day that the Ottoman delegation was to depart, they hosted the Russians with a meal on the sultan's yacht. According to Sazonov's memoirs, after the meal Talât leaned over to Sazonov and proposed an alliance. The suggestion so shocked him, Sazonov later wrote, that he nearly fell over.[69] Talât's account of the meeting, although like Sazonov's given years later, is more convincing. Rather than springing the idea of an alliance in a whisper after lunch, he broached it during a general discussion of the straits. When Talât assured Sazonov that the solution to the straits question was for them to remain in Ottoman hands as they would never be closed to Russian shipping, Sazonov pointed out that, whereas this was true for peacetime, it would not be in the event the Ottoman empire and Greece went to war (a real possibility at the time). Talât then said that an alliance would be a possible solution to the problem. Sazonov just smiled in response.[70]

---

[66] Kurat, *Türkiye ve Rusya*, 218.   [67] Weber, *Eagles*, 54.

[68] As cited in Kurat, *Türkiye ve Rusya*, 221.

[69] S. D. Sazonov, *Vospominaniia* (Moscow: Mezhdunarodnye otnosheniia, [1927] 1991), 160, 164.

[70] Kurat, *Türkiye ve Rusya*, 223.

In the event, nothing emerged from the Livadia overture. The Ottoman press had accorded the run-up much attention, but its silence following Talât's return highlighted the meeting's barren nature.[71] Back in Istanbul, Talât met with Girs. When asked how the meeting had gone, Talât diplomatically explained that he had been anxious about meeting with the "powerful potentate of the mightiest empire" but that the tsar displayed so much goodwill toward the Ottoman empire that he left the Russian sovereign's chambers "touched to the soul and grateful." Talât several times expressed his belief that an alliance with Russia would be beneficial. He also, however, acknowledged that no great power, be it in the Triple Entente or the Triple Alliance, had any use for an alliance with such a weak state. Therefore, he was committed to putting all his efforts toward making the Ottoman empire "a state strong and fully independent of foreign influences." Talât's suggestion of an alliance with Russia surprised but did not stun Girs, who advised Sazonov not to write off the idea since there was a significant faction of Unionists who advocated closer relations with Russia.[72]

Andrei Kalmykov, another Russian diplomat, found Talât to be genuinely concerned about Ottoman dependence on Germany for security and his desire for an alliance with Russia serious. He judged Sazonov's failure to respond seriously at Livadia to be a "great mistake."[73] The course of events in the next several months would show that Talât was right. The great powers put relatively little value on an alliance with the Ottoman empire, preferring instead to look at it as a problem of partition rather than a state with a future. The next several years would prove Kalmykov right, as the Russian empire succumbed to war fatigue and revolution.

[71] Kurat, *Türkiye ve Rusya*, 224.
[72] Girs to Sazonov, 5.5.1914 [18.5.1914], *Movei*, series 3, vol. 1, 212.
[73] Andrew D. Kalmykow, *Memoirs of a Russian Diplomat: Outposts of the Empire, 1893–1917* (New Haven: Yale University Press, 1971), 259.

2 Troubles in Anatolia: imperial insecurities and the transformation of borderland politics

Empires know no necessary or obvious limits to their borders. This boundlessness offers pliability but also breeds insecurity. This held especially true for the Ottoman and Russian empires, whose vast territories were contiguous and whose populations overlapped. Kurds, Armenians, Circassians, Greeks, Tatars, Caucasian Turks, Assyrians, and Cossacks among others inhabited both empires and moved back and forth between them. The imperial states were interpenetrating. They could, and did, project their influence and power beyond formal borders to challenge the authority of the other inside its own territory. The identities, loyalties, and aspirations of their heterogeneous subjects pointed in multiple directions, offering rich opportunities to exploit and creating vulnerabilities to shield. In unstable borderlands, such conditions invite fierce contestation.

It should therefore be no surprise that the Ottoman and Russian empires pursued their competition through channels beyond those of formal diplomacy, channels that included espionage and subversion. No less than formal diplomacy, the hidden pursuit of power was sensitive and responsive to the changing nature of the global order in the early twentieth century. The national idea's effect upon the conduct of interstate competition was profound. It altered not merely the rules of interstate interaction, but also the perceptions of bureaucrats and policymakers, changing the very categories that defined their visions of the political world inside as well as outside the boundaries of their states.

Ottoman and Russian imperial rivalry and insecurities interacted in a particularly complex form in Eastern Anatolia, which constituted a double borderland where the two empires blurred into each other in a zone distinct from the centers of both. The dynamics of global interstate competition spurred the two centers to extend their power into the region. In order to stave off great power – especially Russian – encroachment, the Unionists were determined to assert central control over and extract revenue and resources from the region. Vastly complicating this ambition, however, was the fact that the region's primary communities, nomadic

Kurds and sedentary Armenians, were ambivalent toward Istanbul and locked in conflict with each other over land and the sharply diverging trajectories of their communities. The great powers held the Ottoman government responsible for resolving that conflict, yet Istanbul could barely contain it. External pressure pushed it to support the Armenians, but domestic political calculation dictated that it appease the Kurds.

Ottoman weakness presented a dilemma for Russia. While Russia benefited from its relative superiority and ability to project influence deep into Ottoman Anatolia, Russian policymakers feared that in the event of an Ottoman collapse, a "failed state" might emerge on Russia's southern border and expose its turbulent Caucasus to Kurdish marauders and Armenian subversives freed to operate at will. Still more worrisome was the possibility that another European power might fill the vacuum to Russia's south and use the Kurds and Armenians against Russia. To block such a contingency, the Russians began cultivating allies among Ottoman Kurds resistant to Istanbul's centralizing ambitions, counterproductively sabotaging the establishment of the very stability they desired.

The inhabitants of the Anatolian and Caucasian borderlands were by no means passive bystanders in this imperial contest. They adapted and mobilized in response to the penetration of state power and to the maneuvers of local rivals. In this multifaceted competition, states and non-state actors alike adopted the national idea to legitimize and frame their politics. The ultimate consequences would prove devastating.

Ottoman Eastern Anatolia

The core of the Eastern Anatolian plateau consisted of the Ottomans' so-called Six Provinces (*Vilayât-ı Sitte*) of Van, Erzurum, Bitlis, Diyar-ı Bekir, Mamuret ül-Aziz and Sivas. It extended southward to the province of Musul (Mosul) and eastward beyond Ottoman borders to Lake Urmia in Iran and Yerevan in Russian Armenia in the north. The settlement pattern of the population resembled a mosaic, with the most significant groups – Kurds, Armenians, Turks, Circassians, and Assyrians – intermixed. For reasons ranging from the inherent difficulties of counting nomads through shifting boundaries to deliberate manipulation, population figures for the six Ottoman provinces are inexact and unreliable.[1] The Ottoman state had traditionally surveyed populations for financial

---

[1] For a discussion of some of the difficulties involved, see Fuat Dündar, *Modern Türkiye'nin Şifresi: İttihat ve Terakki'nin Etnisite Mühendisliği, 1913–1918* (Istanbul: İletişim, 2008), 85–106; Hovannisian, *Armenia on the Road*, 34–37; Justin McCarthy, *Muslims and Minorities: The Population of Ottoman Anatolia and the End of Empire* (New York: New York University Press, 1983).

and tax purposes. It did not endeavor to conduct comprehensive counts of whole populations. In line with its traditional understanding of itself as an Islamic state, it categorized its subjects by religion, not ethnicity. The emergence of the Armenian Question in 1878 politicized identity, motivating Ottoman officials and Armenian representatives to manipulate population numbers. Using official Ottoman figures, Kemal Karpat estimates that in 1906–07 the total population of the eastern provinces was 3,147,880. Of these 2,483,135 or 78.89%, were Muslim, and only 664,745 or 21.11% non-Muslim. The Armenian Patriarchate in 1912 counted 1,018,000 Armenians, claiming nearly 40% of the total population in the six provinces.[2] Armenians likely constituted somewhere between one-quarter and one-third of Ottoman Eastern Anatolia's population, i.e., somewhere around one million. In Russia's Caucasus, somewhere between 1,118,094 and 1,500,000 Armenians lived.[3]

Most Armenians in the Ottoman and Russian empires were members of the Apostolic Armenian Church, although small numbers belonged to the Catholic and Protestant churches, and missionaries were active trying to convert more. Another significant Christian group in Anatolia was the Assyrians, who were concentrated in Hakkâri and around Lake Urmia in Iran. The fact that they were divided among multiple churches complicates estimates of their numbers, but 150,000 is probably a fair estimate.[4]

Because the Ottoman census distinguished not on the basis of ethnicity but on religious confession, data on the ethnic composition of Muslims is still less precise. Russian analysts did attempt to distinguish ethnicities. Thus the military ethnographer Petr Aver'ianov in 1912 estimated the number of Kurds in Anatolia at 1,740,000, of whom 1,475,000 were Sunni, 200,000 Alevi, 40,000 Yezidi, and 25,000 Shi'i.[5] The Russian Kurdologist Mikhail Lazarev suggests that before World War I overall there were 5 to 5.5 million Kurds, of whom more than 3.5 million lived in the Ottoman empire, up to 1.5 million in Iran, and approximately

[2] Hovannisian, *Armenia on the Road*, 35–37.
[3] Bakshi Ishkhanian, *Narodnosti Kavkaza: Soslav naseleniia, professional'naia gruppirovka i obshchestvennoe razsloenie Kavkazskikh narodnostei* (Petrograd: M. V. Popov, 1916), 16; Ronald Suny, "Eastern Armenians Under Tsarist Rule," in *The Armenian People from Ancient to Modern Times*, ed. Richard Hovannisian (New York: St. Martin's Press, 1997), 121, 133.
[4] Dündar, *Modern Türkiye'nin Şifresi*, 112–13; cf. David Gaunt, *Massacres, Resistance, Protectors: Muslim–Christian Relations in Eastern Anatolia During World War I* (Piscataway, NJ: Gorgias Press, 2006), 28.
[5] P. I. Aver'ianov, *Etnograficheskii i voenno-politicheskii obzor aziatskikh vladenii Ottomanskoi imperii* (S. Peterburg: Voennaia tipografiia, 1912), 12–13.

150,000 in the Russian empire.[6] Aver'ianov's assessment that the Kurds constituted about one-half of the total population of Eastern Anatolia is reasonable.

From backwater border to frontline frontier

Sultan Selim I incorporated Eastern Anatolia into the Ottoman empire following his victory over Safavid Iran in 1514. Istanbul considered the region as a backwater and remained content to rule indirectly through tribal emirates. The deterioration in the empire's position in the inter-state system, however, compelled Istanbul in the nineteenth century to revise its relationship with its eastern marches. With the empire's territory shrinking and Russia approaching, Eastern Anatolia's value as a resource base and significance as a strategic arena increased accordingly. Thus at mid century Istanbul conducted a "second conquest" of Eastern Anatolia to break up the emirates and impose its writ over the region.[7] Istanbul's attempts to assert state authority over the eastern provinces, however, created a dilemma. Centralization pitted Istanbul against the tribes, but it had few resources to spare for a struggle. The Ottoman economy was small, had virtually no industry, and offered a tiny tax base. Meanwhile, the state was already deep in debt. Along with demands for reforms, external and internal challenges to Istanbul's rule in the Balkans, Africa, and the Arabian peninsula all pressed for attention.

In 1876 a new sultan, Abdülhamid II, ascended to the sultanate and oversaw the introduction of a constitution and the election of a parliament. The ambition was to modernize the state's institutions while simultaneously generating greater popular attachment to them. It was a bold experiment, the first attempt at representative democracy in the Muslim world, but it was short-lived. The outbreak of war with Russia moved the sultan to suspend the constitution and parliament. For the next three decades Abdülhamid II would rule as a pious autocrat, selectively modernizing state institutions and cultivating popular legitimacy among Sunni Muslims through religion while ruthlessly suppressing criticism and any form of opposition.[8]

The Russo-Ottoman War of 1877–78 illustrated the east's new salience. The Russians advanced into Anatolia as far as Erzurum and concluded the war by annexing the three Ottoman provinces of

---

[6] M. S. Lazarev, *Kurdskii vopros (1891–1917)* (Moscow: Nauka, 1972), 26–27.
[7] Martin van Bruinessen, *Agha, Shaikh, and State: The Social and Political Structures of Kurdistan* (London: Zed Books, 1992), 133–82.
[8] François Georgeon, *Abdülhamid II: le sultan calife, 1876–1909* (Paris: Fayard, 2003).

Kars, Ardahan, and Batumi. Demographic upheaval accompanied the war, as tens of thousands of Armenians and Muslims migrated from and to the Ottoman empire respectively. But religion was no guaranty of loyalty. The fact that during the war the Russian army had employed some Kurdish units underscored the mercurial character of loyalty in imperial marches.[9] Istanbul's hold on the region was under challenge.

Abdülhamid II opted to overcome the gap between imperial resources and demands by coopting rather than combating the tribes of Eastern Anatolia. In 1891 he established the eponymous Hamidiye regiments. Composed of Kurdish tribesmen officered by their chiefs, these units were intended to serve as irregular auxiliary forces attached to the Ottoman army in wartime and as an internal security force of sorts in peacetime. In exchange for their allegiance, Abdülhamid II plied the Hamidiye leaders with ranks, titles, money, and land, often expropriated from the Armenians. Although the experiment succeeded in buying the loyalty of a large portion of the tribal leadership, the undisciplined nature of the regiments rendered them unreliable in time of war and downright dangerous in time of peace. The Hamidiye officers, far from being restrained by official ties to the center, felt emboldened to use their new authority and weapons to rob, pillage, and grab still more land, often but not exclusively from Armenians.[10]

For the Unionists, continuing the Hamidian policy of indirect rule was not an option. If the Ottoman state was to survive in the face of the unceasing challenges of the great powers, it would have to marshal and extract more efficiently all potential resources, including those in Eastern Anatolia. They understood their program would encounter resistance from some sectors of society. Their initial hope was that the popular appeal of the Constitutional Revolution's promise of the rule of law and equality for all Ottoman subjects would enable them to overcome the opposition of "reactionary" elements seeking to maintain the privileges they held under the Hamidian regime. Ziya Gökalp, a native of Diyar-ı Bekir and an ethnic Kurd who would later be labeled as the Unionists' chief ideologue of Turkism, as late as 1910 cited the United

---

[9] See P. I. Aver'ianov, *Kurdy v voinakh Rossii s Persiei i Turtsiei v techenie XIX stoletiia. Sovremennoe politicheskoe polozhenie turetskikh, persidskikh i russkikh kurdov. Istoricheskii ocherk* (Tiflis: Izdatel'stvo otdela General'nago shtaba pri Shtabe Kavkazskago voennago okruga, 1900).

[10] On the Hamidiye, see Janet Klein, "Power in the Periphery," Ph.D. dissertation, Princeton University, 2003; and Bayram Kodaman, *Sultan II. Abdülhamid Devri Doğu Anadolu Politikası* (Ankara: Türk Kültürünü Araştırma Enstitüsü, 1987).

States of America and its civic creed of equality and legality as a model for inspiration.[11]

In Eastern Anatolia, however, the seemingly benign promises of the 1908 Revolution acquired a provocative tincture. Global processes were interacting with local social structures to undermine traditional patterns of coexistence and exacerbate conflict especially, but by no means exclusively, between Muslim Kurds and Christian Armenians. Land-holding Kurdish tribal chieftains at the turn of the century continued to occupy a dominant position over most of the Kurdish and Armenian peasantry, who like serfs were bought and sold along with the land on which they lived.[12] Yet whereas the majority of Kurds, nomadic and sedentary alike, remained brutally poor, toward the end of the nineteenth century some Armenians were becoming ascendant in Eastern Anatolia's expanding petty merchant, banking, and quasi-industrial classes.[13] The penetration of the global market had opened economic opportunities that the Armenians were, by virtue of their own openness to education and by the privileged ties they held to Christian European merchants, diplomats, and missionaries, better able to exploit.

The mass of Kurds, by contrast, lacked the basic education and skills that the globalizing economy demanded and so could not compete. Whereas on the eve of World War I most Armenian children in the countryside as well as in towns attended schools (often run by Christian missionaries) and literacy was becoming universal for Armenian boys,[14] not a single Kurd was attending high school as late as 1912.[15] Indeed, as one Russian consul reported, the Kurds' knowledge of medicine and hygiene was so primitive that in Kurdish villages children were few and blindness common. Up to 50 percent of Kurdish newborns perished due to the absence of obstetric help, and by the age of three another 30 percent would fall to smallpox, scarlet fever, typhoid, and snake and insect bites. Trachoma was so widespread that it was rare to meet adult Kurds with healthy eyes.[16] Thus, although Eastern Anatolia overall was growing more prosperous, the social and economic conditions of most

---

[11] Hans-Lukas Kieser, *Vorkämpfer der "Neuen Türkei": revolutionäre Bildungseliten am Genfersee (1870–1939)* (Zurich: Chronos, 2005), 57.

[12] Lazarev, *Kurdskii vopros*, 40; R. Bekguliants, *Po Turetskoi Armenii* (Rostov on Don: Tipografiia Ia. M. Iskidarova, 1914), 74–75.

[13] Lazarev, *Kurdskii vopros*, 41–48; Aver'ianov, *Etnograficheskii*, 18–19.

[14] Richard G. Hovannisian, "Armenian Tsopk/Kharpert," in *Armenian Tsopk/Kharpert*, ed. Hovannisian (Costa Mesa, CA: Mazda Publishers, 2002), 3.

[15] Hans-Lukas Kieser, *Der verpasste Friede: Mission, Etnie und Staat in den Ostprovinzen der Türkei, 1838–1938* (Zurich: Chronos, 2000), 430.

[16] AVPRI, Chirkov to the Chargé d'affaires in Tehran, 14.2.1913 [27.2.1913], f. 180, o. 517/2, d. 3573, l. 25.

Kurds were deteriorating with little prospect of change.[17] The Kurds were acutely aware that these trends were working against them and only accelerating.[18]

The fundamental rifts between the Christian Armenians and the Muslim Kurds stemmed not so much from religion or ethnicity as from clashing ways of life and modes of existence. Most Kurds were nomads, while the Christians generally were peasants. Their relationship was often symbiotic, with both sides benefiting from the specialization of the other, but it was always unequal. The more numerous and powerful Kurds routinely commandeered winter quarters from the Armenians and demanded taxes. Less routinely they plundered Armenian villages.

Islamic norms that prescribed the subordination of non-Muslims to Muslims reinforced the status quo and embedded it in identities, but the religious dimension should not be overemphasized. Sedentary Kurds, too, paid material tribute to tribal overlords. Like non-Kurds they were exploited by the landowning class and subject to depredations of their nomadic co-ethnics and Circassians, too.[19] Christian Assyrians living in the mountains provide an interesting contrast. As observers noted, they resembled the nomadic Kurds in their way of life and martial bearing and demeanor. As a Kurdish proverb put it, "Between us [Kurds and Assyrians], there is but a hair's breadth, but between us and the Armenians a mountain."[20] Finally, Kurdish tribes fought among themselves and with their co-religionists, the Ottoman authorities, as much as they clashed with others.[21]

Shifting patterns of power

At the same time that the global market in the nineteenth century was undermining established socioeconomic relations, the emerging global discourse of the nation was imbuing ethnicity with a heightened significance. It offered to Eastern Anatolia's inhabitants an alternative to the imperial model of politics, one that tied sovereignty and control of

---

[17] Arshak Safrastian, *Kurds and Kurdistan* (London: Harvill Press, 1948), 72; Kamal Madhar Ahmad, *Kurdistan During the First World War*, tr. Ali Masher Ibrahim (London: Saqi Books, 1994), 60.

[18] Dzhalile Dzhalil, *Iz istorii obshchestvenno-politicheskoi zhizni Kurdov v kontse XIX nachale XX vv.* (St. Petersburg: Nauka, 1997), 38.

[19] V. A. Gordlevskii, *Izbrannye sochineniia*, 4 vols. (Moscow: Izdatel'stvo vostochnoi literatury, 1962), vol. III, 119; Lazarev, *Kurdskii vopros*, 11, 39.

[20] F. N. Heazell and Mrs. Margoliouth, eds., *Kurds and Christians* (London: Wells Gardner, Darton and Co., 1913), 121; Gaunt, *Massacres*, 29–30.

[21] AVPRI, Chirkov to the Imperial Chargé D'affaires in Tehran, 14.2.1913 [27.2.1913], f. 180, o. 517/2, d. 3573, l. 25.

land to ethnicity. News of the Treaty of Berlin and its call for internationally supervised reforms to protect Armenians from Kurds and Circassians sparked fears among Kurds that the ascendant Armenians would, with outside help, assume control of Muslim lands, just as Christians in the Balkans had done. Such anxieties provoked the Kurdish Sheikh Ubeydullah to bring together a multitude of Ottoman and Iranian Kurdish tribes in a transborder revolt in 1880. Reflecting the penetration of great power influence and the shift in norms of global order, Ubeydullah appealed to Britain for sympathy and justified his revolt as a bid to form an independent state for the Kurds, who were, he explained, a "nation" unto themselves and ethnically distinct from the Turks and Iranians. Ubeydullah's revolt was significant not, as some have claimed, because it represented an upswelling Kurdish national consciousness – the revolt quickly fell apart as Ubeydullah's followers fell out along tribal lines – but because it demonstrated the dual penetration of European power and of the national idea into Anatolian politics. Ubeydullah did not have a nation, but he understood the utility of speaking as if he did.[22]

The same shifts in global power and politics likewise influenced Armenian imaginations. The Armenians' position was a difficult one. Even as economic opportunities beckoned, the deteriorating political situation was making their existence more, not less, precarious. The example of the Bulgarians, who had with Russian assistance achieved liberation from Ottoman rule in 1878, suggested an alternative was possible and inspired them to dream, while the Treaty of Berlin emboldened them politically.[23] Seven years later Ottoman Armenians in Van formed a political party, but Russia's Armenians soon took the lead in mobilization. Through participation in Russia's underground socialist movement they acquired superior organizational skills and developed more ambitious programs. They founded the two most important Armenian political parties, the Hnchakian Revolutionary Party and the Armenian Revolutionary Federation, often known as the Dashnaktsutiun for short, in 1887 and 1890 respectively. The example of the Bulgarians inspired the Hnchaks and Dashnaks to reject continued the subservience of Ottoman Armenians. Unlike the Bulgarians, however, Armenians were a minority in their own lands. Thus, the Hnchaks and Dashnaks left their ultimate aims – an

---

[22] Hakan Özoğlu, *Kurdish Notables and the Ottoman State: Evolving Identities, Competing Loyalties, and Shifting Boundaries* (Albany: State University of New York Press, 2004), 74–77; Kieser, *Der verpasste Friede*, 127–32; McDowall, *Modern History of the Kurds*, 53–59.

[23] Sarkis Atamian, *The Armenian Community: The Historical Development of a Social and Ideological Conflict* (New York: Philosophical Library, 1955), 66–67.

independent state in a socialist world order or some undefined autonomy respectively – vague and undefined.[24]
Whereas the Hnchaks tended to prefer mass protests, the Dashnaks
formed armed units to conduct guerrilla warfare in the countryside and
terrorism in cities.[25] Vengeance attacks against abusive Kurds and government officials were favorite methods. As gratifying as these tactics
might be, they could never overturn the imperial order. Outside intervention, however, could. Some revolutionaries mounted attacks to provoke
Ottoman reprisals and thereby win European sympathy and, ultimately,
trigger intervention. The cycle of violence peaked in the mid 1890s when,
in massacres abetted if not directed by Sultan Abdülhamid II, Muslims
in Anatolia slew tens of thousands of Armenians.[26] The great powers
reminded the "Bloody Sultan," as European papers now referred to
Abdülhamid II, of the Treaty of Berlin and their prerogative to intervene on behalf of the Armenians. When still worse massacres followed,
however, Russia squelched any plans for intervention for fear that a rival
might exploit the moment to its own benefit, and the great powers stood
aside.

The massacres of 1894–96 revealed the desperate isolation of Ottoman
Armenians, but they failed to crush the revolutionaries. At the turn of
the century the Dashnaktsutiun emerged as the most powerful of the
revolutionary organizations, a force to be reckoned with in Russian and
Ottoman politics alike. In 1907 it joined the Second International of
socialist and labor parties. The Armenian Patriarchate in Istanbul had
served for centuries as the preeminent political institution of the Ottoman
Armenian community, but the Dashnaktsutiun eclipsed it following the
introduction of electoral and party politics in 1908.[27] Despite ample
cooperation between the Dashnaks and the Unionists and other Muslim

[24] Anahide Ter Minassian, *Nationalism and Socialism in the Armenian Revolutionary Move-
ment (1887–1912)*, tr. A. M. Barratt (Cambridge, MA: Zoryan Institute, 1984), 9–20;
Gerard Libaridian, *Modern Armenia: People, Nation, State* (New Brunswick: Transaction
Publishers, 2004), 73–102; Atamian, *Armenian Community*, 97–104.
[25] Razmik Panossian, *The Armenians: From Kings and Priests to Merchants and Commissars*
(London: Hurst and Company, 2006), 216.
[26] Louise Nalbandian, *The Armenian Revolutionary Movement: The Development of Armenian
Political Parties Through the Nineteenth Century* (Berkeley: University of California Press,
1963), 120–28. Christopher Walker puts the number of dead at 100,000: Walker, *Armenia: The Survival of a Nation*, 2nd edn. (London: Routledge, 1990), 165. A commission
of representatives of the six great powers estimated deaths at about 25,000, while the
American consul put the number at 37,085. See Fuat Dündar, *Crime of Numbers: Statistics and the Armenian Question, 1878–1918* (New Brunswick: Transaction Publishers,
2010), 144–45.
[27] M. Şükrü Hanioğlu, *Preparation for a Revolution: The Young Turks, 1902–1908* (New York:
Oxford University Press, 2001), 314–15.

organizations against the Hamidian regime, a fundamental distrust lingered in the Dashnaks' relations with Muslims, Kurds and Turks alike. The clashing priorities of the Dashnaktsutiun and the CUP – one prioritized autonomy and the other the preservation of the empire – could not but generate friction. The fact that the Dashnaktsutiun was not a wholly "Ottoman" organization but a transimperial one that answered to a leadership outside the Ottoman empire irritated the Unionists. The lands the Dashnaks identified as "Armenia" overlapped with lands inhabited heavily by Kurds, or "Kurdistan." Yet they called Kurds "foreigners," portrayed them as backward savages, and targeted them in vengeance attacks.[28] The slogans, methods, and tactics of the Armenian revolutionaries alarmed the Kurds, who by the early 1890s had begun to suspect that the revolutionaries ultimately sought not mere autonomy but the unification of the historically Armenian lands in Anatolia, Iran, and the Caucasus followed by the gradual displacement of non-Armenians. Fears that the Armenians would follow in the Bulgarians' footsteps and establish a state in Eastern Anatolia motivated much of the killing in 1894–96.[29] As one Kurdish poet lamented, "It is heartbreaking to see the land of Jazira and Butan, I mean the fatherland of the Kurds, being turned into a home for the Armenians," and "Should there be an Armenistan, no Kurds would be left."[30] The one-time CUP member and Kurd Abdullah Cevdet posed the problem directly in the title of his famous response to claims advanced by the Armenian newspaper *Jamanak*, "Kurdistan or Armenia?"[31]

Collision course

In 1908, Milli İbrahim Pasha was the most powerful of the Kurdish chieftains. As a favored Hamidiye commander, he ruled the territory between Urfa and Diyar-ı Bekir as his private fief. As soon as he received word of the Constitutional Revolution, he rebelled, understanding that the rise of the CUP meant his demise. The Ottoman army battled his forces and cut him down in the field a month later. Despite his death,

---

[28] J. Michael Hagopian, "Hyphenated Nationalism: The Spirit of the Revolutionary Movement in Asia Minor and the Caucasus, 1896–1910," Ph.D. dissertation, Harvard University, 1942, 343–55; Ali Emirî, *Osmanlı Vilâyât-ı Şarkiyesi* (Istanbul: Evkaf-ı İslâmiye Matbaası, 1334 [1918]), 28, 87, 90.

[29] Selim Deringil, "'The Armenian Question Is Finally Closed': Mass Conversions of Armenians in Anatolia During the Hamidian Massacres of 1895–1897," *Comparative Studies in Society and History*, 51, 2 (2009), 344–71.

[30] Kader Madhar Ahmad, *Kurdistan*, 159.

[31] M. Şükrü Hanioğlu, *Bir Siyasal Düşünür Olarak Doktor Abdullah Cevdet ve Dönemi* (Istanbul: Üçdal Neşriyatı, 1981), 318, 321.

local rebellions of Kurds rippled through Eastern Anatolia that fall. Many more were to follow.[32]

The new government cracked down severely on outlaws and brigands in Eastern Anatolia as part of its program to assert central authority and ensure security, particularly for Armenians. The improvement in security was substantial, as European observers and Armenians attested at the time.[33] Detailing the decrease in banditry and lawlessness, the Russian consul in Bitlis concluded in March 1909, "due to the new government's policy the Kurds have become unrecognizable."[34] For the next two and a half years Eastern Anatolia, including its Armenians, would enjoy markedly improved security.

Resistance to the new regime, however, was building. Alongside the tribal elite who resented the government's effort to displace their authority with its own, many Kurds (and other Muslims) regarded the Unionists' recognition of equal rights for Christians as tantamount to betrayal. Central rule had comparatively little to offer either Kurdish notables or the mass of Kurds other than conscription and taxes. Istanbul's treasury was chronically depleted, and its policies promised in the short term to strip the tribal leadership of its power and in the long term to asphyxiate the rest of the Kurds economically, seemingly to the advantage of the *gâvur*, the unbeliever. Russia's consuls took notice of the dissatisfaction brewing among Ottoman Kurds and began to wonder how they might exploit it in the interests of their empire.

Russia and the Kurds

St. Petersburg's interest in the Kurds dates to at least as far back as 1787, when Catherine the Great commissioned the publication of a Kurdish grammar. The nomadic, armed Kurdish tribes presented a significant security concern on Russia's south Caucasian borders, but also a potential military resource that Russian officials sought to manage. During its series of wars with the Ottoman and Iranian empires throughout the nineteenth century, Russia entered into local and temporary alliances with the

---

[32] Kader Madhar Ahmad, *Kurdistan*, 59; van Bruinessen, *Agha*, 187–89; Gordlevskii, *Izbrannye sochineniia*, vol. III, 116; Hanioğlu, *Preparation*, 106–07; Lazarev, *Kurdskii vopros*, 37, 115–16, 148–49; E. B. Soane, *To Mesopotamia and Kurdistan in Disguise* (London: J. Murray, 1912), 43, 66.

[33] Dikran Mesrob Kaligian, *Armenian Organization and Ideology Under Ottoman Rule, 1908–1914* (New Brunswick: Transaction Publishers, 2009), 96; Manoug Joseph Somakian, *Empires in Conflict: Armenia and the Great Powers, 1895–1920* (London: I. B. Tauris, 1995), 38; Heazell and Margoliouth, eds., *Kurds and Christians*, 204.

[34] Somakian, *Empires in Conflict*, 38.

Kurdish tribes, and even included Kurdish units in its army.[35] Spurred by the demand for knowledge of the Kurds, Russian scholars by the middle of the nineteenth century were conducting multiple studies on them.[36] Similarly, Russian military ethnographers began systematically gathering and analyzing information on the numbers and characteristics of the Kurds of Eastern Anatolia and Iran. Russia's interest in ethnography was not *sui generis*, but was part of a pan-European trend of categorizing and classifying whole population groups according to ethnicity to better predict and manipulate their behavior during wartime. Ethnicity became a prism through which officers and policymakers perceived the political world and categorized actors.[37]

The rebuff encountered at the Congress of Berlin in 1878 coupled with the lure of expansion into Manchuria and the Far East led St. Petersburg to direct its attention away from the Ottoman Near East. Russia's might had long ago eclipsed that of its Ottoman and Iranian rivals, and it had little to fear from them. Indeed, some Russian decisionmakers saw Ottoman weakness as an opportunity to exploit, as the foreign minister and chief of the General Staff had thought in 1908 when they pushed for war with the Ottoman empire as an easy way to restore luster to the tsar's regime.

But if St. Petersburg no longer needed to fret about the Ottoman state as a power, it did worry about the expanding presence of the other European powers along its southern borders. British, German, and French diplomats, spies, businessmen, and missionaries in Anatolia and Iran were opening consulates, laying railroads, building schools, trading, and proselytizing among other activities. An American traveler described the region as "honey combed" with European consulates.[38] In an effort to manage its rivalry with Britain, Russia in 1907 had agreed with Britain to divide Iran into three zones and occupy the northern third. Russian and British officials carefully avoided nomenclature that would suggest partition, but the ease with which the Europeans imposed their will on Iran was not lost on Istanbul. Nor were the facts that Russia had added 400 more kilometers to its 450-km Caucasian border with the Ottoman empire and had even begun settling Slavs in northern Iran. Istanbul's

---

[35] Aver'ianov, *Kurdy*.

[36] For an overview of imperial Russian Kurdology, see A. A. Vigasin, A. N. Khokhlov, and P. M. Shastitko, eds., *Istoriia otechestvennogo vostokovedeniia s serediny XIX veka do 1917 goda* (Moscow: Vostochnaia literatura, 1997), 215–25.

[37] Peter Holquist, "To Count, to Extract, and to Exterminate: Population Statistics and Population Politics in Late Imperial and Soviet Russia," in *A State of Nations: Empire and Nation-Making in the Age of Lenin and Stalin*, ed. Terry Martin and Ronald Suny (New York: Oxford University Press, 2001), 111–44.

[38] Sidney Whitman, *Turkish Memories* (New York: Chas. Scribner's Sons, 1914), 121.

anxiety was not baseless. Russian strategists looking to the longer term concluded that control of the Anatolian plateau would be a vital asset in their competition with the other powers. It would give Russia the ability to dominate Iran, exert influence on the Mediterranean and the Persian Gulf, and threaten Britain's lines of communication to India and its other eastern colonies.[39] As one Russian colonel wrote in an analysis, "Asia Minor, especially in the regions that lie on the Black Sea, and Armeno-Kurdistan, which borders on the Transcaucasus, represents for us a first-class political interest."[40] Russian officials scanned Eastern Anatolia for opportunities to expand their own influence. Given the growing dissatisfaction of the Ottoman Kurds with the Unionist regime, they did not have to look very hard.

Abdürrezzak Bedirhan and the lure of imperial Russia

The new regime's imprisonment of Hamidiye commanders, its appointment of pro-Armenian administrators such as Celâl Bey, the *vali* (governor) of Erzurum, and the sudden change in the status of Armenians from *reaya*, non-Muslim subjects with limited rights, to "citizens with full rights" bewildered the Kurds. As one Russian military analysis observed, "Feeling their strength, they [the Armenians], in alliance with the Young Turks, began to avenge themselves on the Kurds for the former, old offenses. The Kurds, who are not used to this kind of treatment, await further developments in a state of incomprehension."[41] The Kurds, however, did have options. Fed up with the new regime, the chief of the Heyderanli tribe and influential Hamidiye commander Kör Hüseyin Pasha and several others crossed into Iran in early 1910. They took with them several Hamidiye regiments, dealing Unionist plans to restructure the Hamidiye a crippling blow.[42] Inside Iran, increasing numbers of Ottoman Kurds began applying for Russian subject status, embarrassing and distressing Istanbul. Kör Hüseyin went still further

---

[39] M. S. Anderson, *Eastern Question*, 208; "Armeniia – Voenno-geograficheskii ocherk Gen. Liet. Khofmeistera, Geidlberg", *Voennyi sbornik* 11 (November 1914), 143–44; Roderic Davison, "The Armenian Crisis, 1912–1914," *American Historical Review*, 53, 3 (April 1948), 487–88.

[40] AVPRI, Report on Asian Turkey and Its Study, 1.5.1913 [14.5.1913], f. 129, o. 502b, d. 7600, l. 1.

[41] AVPRI, Caucasus Military District to Quartermaster General of the General Staff, 5 January 1910 [18 January 1910], f. 180, o. 517/2, d. 3572, ll. 15–17. See also Noel Buxton and the Rev. Harold Buxton, *Travel and Politics in Armenia* (New York: Macmillan, 1914), 18. For an Armenian taunt of the Kurds' reversed fortunes, see S. V. Bedickian, *The Red Sultan's Soliloquy*, tr. Alice Stone Blackwell (Boston: Sherman, French, and Co., 1912), 114–18.

[42] Lazarev, *Kurdskii vopros*, 150–53; Gordlevskii, *Izbrannye sochineniia*, vol. II, 128.

and made an offer to the Russian viceroy of the Caucasus to hand over all Kurdistan to Russia.[43]

The Russians, however, preferred to concentrate their attention on a Kurd named Abdürrezzak Bedirhan. A grandson of the last independent emir of Botan in the vicinity of Van, Abdürrezzak came from an unusually prestigious clan. He resented the Ottoman state for destroying his grandfather's emirate in 1847 and depriving him of his patrimony. Abdürrezzak had been raised and educated in Istanbul, but he retained an attachment to his native land. When in 1906 he was implicated in the murder of the prefect of Istanbul, he was imprisoned in Tripoli of Barbary along with his extended family. Right after his release under a Unionist-sponsored amnesty in 1910, Abdürrezzak announced to his associates in Istanbul that he was leaving for Kurdistan to "civilise his people."[44]

What made Abdürrezzak particularly attractive to the Russians was his Russophilia. As a young man, he had entered the Ottoman Foreign Ministry and had been posted to St. Petersburg in the early 1890s. What he saw in Russia must have had a powerful effect on him, for Abdürrezzak became a staunch advocate not only of Kurdish political union with Russia, but also of the spread of Russian culture, language, and literature among the Kurds. Through Russia and its culture, Abdürrezzak believed, the Kurds could access the forms of knowledge they required to prosper in the modern world. By cooperating with Russia, the tribal scion hoped, he could solve the predicament of the Kurds and regain his patrimonial lands.

Among the first things Abdürrezzak did was to contact the Russian consul at Van, Sergei Olfer'ev, and ask how an autonomous Kurdistan might be established.[45] By August 1910, he was already distributing pamphlets in the eastern provinces pushing the idea of an ethnically defined Kurdish "beylik," or principality, and praising the "blessedness of Russian rule."[46] In September he applied to the Russian authorities for Russian subject status and requested permission to take up residence in Yerevan. The embassy in Istanbul and the authorities in the Caucasus responded positively, objecting initially only to his desire to settle in Yerevan, which they considered too close to the border. But six months later the Ministry of Internal Affairs approved both Abdürrezzak's requests.[47]

---

[43] Lazarev, *Kurdskii vopros*, 157.
[44] Telford Waugh, *Turkey: Yesterday, Today, and Tomorrow* (London: Chapman and Hall, 1930), 97.
[45] Abdurrezak Bedirhan, *Otobiyografya (1910–1916)*, tr. Hasan Cunî (Ankara: Peri Yayınları, 2000), 26.
[46] Somakian, *Empires in Conflict*, 51.
[47] AVPRI, Letter to K. E. Argirapulo, [no day or month] 1910, Letter of the Minister of Internal Affairs, 3.3.1911 [16.3.1911], f. 180, o. 517/2, d. 3572, ll. 61, 67.

Abdürrezzak and Kör Hüseyin were not the only Kurdish chieftains making overtures to Russia. Ismail Agha Simko, the head of the second-largest tribal confederation in Iran, and another tribal chief named Sheikh Seyid Ali also availed themselves of Russian support. Seeking to take advantage of Italy's declaration of war on the Ottoman empire in 1911, they led rebellions in the regions of Siirt, Van, and Bitlis. They, too, employed ethnicity to legitimize secession, and distributed leaflets declaring "This land is our land" and claiming Bitlis and the neighboring territories as Kurdish.[48]

Although widespread and destabilizing, these revolts were uncoordinated and never posed a fundamental challenge to Ottoman rule. Abdürrezzak recognized the need to unify the rebels and so in May 1912 organized an assembly of prominent Kurdish tribal chiefs in southeast Anatolia. The participants set up a body called "İrşad," meaning "Correct Guidance," to coordinate their actions. İrşad set as its goal the liberation of Kurdistan, and toward that end aspired to establish an armed force of 70,000 men. It formed cells in Van, Diyar-ı Bekir, Urfa, and elsewhere.[49] Russian consular officials had been apprised of the meeting beforehand, and one of the assembly's first acts was to send Abdüsselam Barzani to Tiflis to secure Russian support. Abdüsselam succeeded, and was soon thereafter carrying out attacks along the Ottoman border with Russian weapons and money.[50] In August, another of İrşad's founders, a captain in the Ottoman gendarmerie named Hayreddin Berazi, approached the Russian consulate in Erzurum. Identifying himself on his calling card as "Chef des Kurd," Berazi presented the consulate with a plan to give Kurdistan a status in the Russian empire akin to that of the German principalities in Germany.[51] Berazi's proposal was not unusual. Schemes to join a Kurdish beylik to the Russian empire with a status similar to that of Bukhara or Khiva, where Muslims enjoyed a wide degree of self-rule under the tsar, were also circulating among the Kurds.[52]

Opinion about how vigorously to support the Kurdish rebels varied among Russian officials. The under secretary of war, Aleksei

[48] Lazarev, *Kurdskii vopros*, 201–02.
[49] Dzhalile Dzhalil, "Pervye kurdskie obshchestvennye politicheskie organizatsii," *Tiurkologicheskii sbornik, 1973* (Moscow: Nauka, 1975), 183.
[50] Suat Akgül, "Rusya'nın Yürüttüğü Doğu Anadolu Politikası İçinde İrşad ve Cihandani Cemiyetlerinin Rolü," in *Prof. Abdurrahman Çaycı'ya Armağan*, ed. Abdurrahman Çaycı (Ankara: Hacettepe Üniversitesi Atatürk İlkeleri ve İnkılâp Tarihi Enstitüsü, 1995), 29.
[51] AVPRI, Calling Card of Hayreddin Berazi, Chirkov to Girs, 16.8.1912 [29.8.1912], f. 180, o. 517/2, d. 3572, ll. 96, 99; AVPRI, General Consul in Erzurum to the Ambassador in Constantinople, 19.6.1914 [2.7.1914], f. 129, o. 502b, d. 5350, l. 8.
[52] AVPRI, General Consul in Baghdad to the Embassy in Constantinople, 25.6.1913 [8.7.1913], f. 180, o. 517/2, d. 3573, ll. 186–87.

Polivanov, the future foreign minister, Sazonov, and the Caucasus General Staff advocated an aggressive stance. Charykov and the viceroy of the Caucasus Illarion Vorontsov-Dashkov were wary of lending too much support lest it harm relations or incite disorders that might spread northward, while the finance minister, Vladimir Kokovtsov, objected to the costs involved. Russia's officials found a compromise wherein they agreed to provide Kurdish leaders with money, sanctuary inside Russia and Iran, and support such as advance warning of assassination and arrest attempts, but not to back talk of a Kurdish protectorate or to provide sanctuary inside Ottoman territory. Russia's priority at this point was to prevent Kurdish territory from being used as a platform for attacks on Russian possessions in Iran and the Caucasus. Courtship of the Kurds paid dividends during the Iranian Revolution of 1911 when Kurds followed the direction of Russia's consular officials to attack revolutionaries.[53]

The Kurds' renewed uprisings presented a dual danger to Istanbul. In addition to challenging the state directly, they raised the possibility of provoking a great power to intervene by generating chaos and putting Armenians at risk. The Ottomans recognized that if they could not somehow resolve the tensions between the Kurds and the Armenians they could lose Eastern Anatolia to outside intervention.

A major source of that tension lay in the dispute over land. Land was the essential resource, and one that was becoming more valuable with the growth of population and the advent of commercial agriculture. The majority of Armenian peasants were landless, and Abdülhamid II's policy of facilitating the seizure of Armenian-owned lands, including Church lands, by the aghas had exacerbated the problem.[54] The 1908 Revolution raised hopes among Armenians that they might recover the lands they had recently lost, and the Dashnaktsutiun made the return of those lands a priority.[55] Some Kurdish landowners had in the meantime invested in their new holdings, and the prospect of losing their investments along with the land galled them. Fear that state authorities would confiscate and redistribute the land to the Armenians was a powerful motive behind Kurdish tribal leaders' cooperation with the Russians.[56]

[53] Lazarev, *Kurdskii vopros*, 158–59, 163, 170, 223; Chairman of the Council of Ministers to the Minister of Foreign Affairs, 18.4.1912 [1.5.1912], *Movei*, ser. 2, vol. 19, part 2, 493.
[54] Lazarev, *Kurdskii vopros*, 40–43.
[55] Kaligian, *Armenian Organization*, 53.
[56] AVPRI, Vorontsov-Dashkov to Izvol'skii, 9.3.1910 [22.3.1910], f. 180, o. 517/2, d. 3572, l. 12; General Consul in Erzurum to Girs, 19.6.1914 [2.7.1914], f. 129, o. 502b, d. 5350, l. 5; Lazarev, *Kurdskii vopros*, 153, 202.

The CUP in 1908 in fact had contemplated the distribution of land to peasants throughout the empire, but hesitated to implement it. This failure cannot be explained as the product of a conservative predisposition against land reform. Among the Unionists were exponents of social engineering, and many saw a sociological utility in using land reform to break the power of the landed classes and emancipate the peasantry.[57] Nor is it the case that the Unionists were unwilling in principle to challenge the tribal elite. From the very beginning they had taken on the tribal elites forcefully, disbanding the Hamidiye, imprisoning renegade commanders, appointing unpopular administrators, and extending equal rights and duties, including the bearing of arms and conscription, to Armenians. The granting of permission to Armenians to bear arms and the inclusion of Christians in the ranks of the Ottoman army in 1909 further scandalized the Kurds.[58] In 1910 the state authorities underscored their commitment to the new order by deploying Christian conscripts from the Balkans to Van to acclimate the Kurds to the idea of Christians serving in the Ottoman army.[59] These measures were all provocative, but the Unionists initially did not blench before Kurdish discontent and protest.

The Unionists, however, could not ignore Muslim resentment indefinitely. Muslims were their base constituency, and it was not only in Eastern Anatolia where Muslims suspected the government of favoring Christians. The so-called counterrevolution of 31 March 1909 and the accompanying massacre of thousands of Armenians around Adana had indicated the depth of hostility among Muslims at large toward Christians. In Aleppo, the Unionists' opponents openly derided the CUP as defenders of Christian and Jewish interests.[60] Moreover, many Unionists themselves nursed resentment against Christians, whose interests did not align clearly with the goals of strengthening central rule and preserving the empire. To the contrary, many Christians had benefited from the growing influence of the European powers inside and around the empire,

---

[57] Feroz Ahmad, "The Agrarian Policy of the Young Turks, 1908–1918," in *Économie et sociétés dans l'Empire ottoman (fin du XVIIIe–début du XXe siècle)*, ed. Jean-Louis Bacqué-Grammont and Paul Dumont (Paris: Éditions du Centre national de la recherche scientifique, 1983), 276.

[58] Vice-Consulate in Van to Lowther, 24.3.1913, in Anita L. P. Burdett, ed., *Armenia: Political and Ethnic Boundaries* (Slough, UK: Archive Editions, 1998), 282.

[59] Molyneux-Seel to Lowther, 7.9.1910, as cited in Klein, "Power," 227–28, n. 102.

[60] Keith David Watenpaugh, *Being Modern in the Middle East: Revolution, Nationalism, Colonialism, and the Arab Middle Class* (Princeton: Princeton University Press, 2006), 112.

and few supported the CUP. Balkan Jews, by contrast, feared the collapse of the imperial order and so tended to favor the CUP.[61] Reshaping Eastern Anatolia's administrative and social structures was an enormous, long-term, and inherently unpopular task. The ability of rebels to obtain backing from Russia severely undercut Istanbul's ability to counter them and enact reforms. As one British official wrote in 1910 regarding Russian support for Kurdish rebels, "The mere possibility of this certainly makes it most difficult for the Turkish Government to alienate these Kurdish chiefs by redressing the Armenian grievances about their lands."[62] Moreover, as important as it was, the reform of Eastern Anatolia was just one of multiple urgent issues facing a government with limited resources. The Unionists had to choose their battles, and picking a battle that would demand time, consume significant resources, and put them at odds with a large Muslim constituency made little sense.

The government of Said Pasha did take up the issue of land redistribution. It allocated 100,000 lira to settle Armenian–Kurdish land disputes, and in September 1912 the Council of Ministers resolved to purchase the contested land and return it to its former Armenian owners and distribute the rest to landless Armenians. Despite the plan's provision for compensation, Kurdish landowners saw this plan as yet another state encroachment.[63] In any event, a lack of funds, made still worse by the Balkan Wars, gave the Porte no choice but to abandon the land reform program at the end of the year. Indeed, the Balkan Wars and related economic dislocations constricted further the government's already limited room for maneuver in Anatolia by forcing it to raise taxes and impose new levies on cattle and construction in the region. The result was yet another wave of disturbances led by disgruntled Kurds throughout the region.[64]

The Ottomans' efforts to maintain control over their eastern provinces were undercut by Russia's program to expand its influence. By 1912, the Russians were funneling significant amounts of arms and money to Kurdish tribes.[65] The covert support network extended from local Russian officials in the region all the way up to St. Petersburg, and included army officers, diplomats, academics, and commercial agents.

---

[61] GARF, To the Head of the Special Department of Police Eremin, 23.1.1913 [6.2.1913], f. 529, o. 1, d. 13, l. 4; Mark Mazower, *Salonica, City of Ghosts: Christians, Muslims, and Jews, 1430–1950* (London: Harper Collins, 2004), 282–85.
[62] Cited in Klein, "Power," 322.   [63] Lazarev, *Kurdskii vopros*, 203–04.
[64] Lazarev, *Kurdskii vopros*, 214.
[65] Somakian, *Empires in Conflict*, 52; Lazarev, *Kurdskii vopros*, 223. The sums were large enough that the chairman of Russia's Council of Ministers complained to the foreign minister about them: Kokovtsov to Sazonov, 18.4.1912 [1.5.1912], *Movei*, series 2, vol. 19, part 2, 493.

The Russians used their consulates in Istanbul and the Anatolian and Iranian towns of Bayezid, Bitlis, Erzurum, Khoy, Maku, and Van as safe houses to conduct meetings with Kurdish leaders. They infiltrated saboteurs through Georgia.[66] That October, at least four Russian army officers dressed and disguised as Kurds crossed into Ottoman lands in order to incite the Kurds.[67] Trade missions sent by the Russian governor general of the Caucasus had among their goals establishing contact with Kurdish leaders and the conduct of espionage.[68] The Russian Commerce Bank was used in part to run Russian intelligence operations in Anatolia.[69] A correspondent for the St. Petersburg newspaper *Birzhevyia Vedomosti* traveling through Anatolia in the spring of 1913 was spreading rumors that the Kurds in the vicinity of Diyar-ı Bekir and Bitlis had "declared independence" and were asking for great power protection.[70]

The Ottomans recognized that the Kurdish chiefs' collaboration amounted to "a victory for the Russian government" and a "disaster" and "great danger" for "our state."[71] But Istanbul's inability to undertake structural reform left only a range of tactical measures to keep Eastern Anatolia under control. The most obvious was to suppress the revolts outright, which the Ottoman armed forces did repeatedly. On occasion, the Ottoman forces would, in a reversal of Abdülhamid II's tactic, join with Armenians to fight the Kurds, as in June 1913 when a 500-man force of Dashnaks led by Aram Pasha, i.e., Aram Manukian, fought alongside Ottoman regulars against the Kurds of the Gravi tribe between Van and Başkale.[72] Suppression sometimes achieved notable results, such as when the Ottoman authorities killed Berazi and took several İrşad members prisoner in a firefight in 1913, thereby effectively shutting down that organization.[73] A related tactic was to send undercover agents to capture or assassinate figures such as Abdürrezzak and

[66] BOA, Grand Vizier to the Minister of the Interior, 5 Mayıs 1329 [18.5.1913], DH.MUİ, D. 23, S. 10.
[67] BOA, Vilayet of Van to the Interior Ministry, 5 Teşrinievvel 1329 [18.10.1913], DH.SYS, D. 23, S. 16.
[68] BOA, Directorate of Security to the Vilayet of Van, 14 Cemaziyelevvel 1332 [10.4.1914], DH.ŞFR, D. 40, S. 174.
[69] Kurat, *Türkiye ve Rusya*, 200–01.
[70] BOA, Interior Ministry to the Foreign Minister, 28 Mart 1329 [10.4.1913], DH. SYS, D. 118, S. 13.
[71] BOA, Interior Ministry to Van, 23 Nisan 1330 [6.5.1914], DH. ŞFR, D. 40, S. 151; BOA, Erzurum to Interior Ministry, 10 Kanunuevvel 1327 [23.12.1911], DH. SYS, D. 90, S. 1-6 B. 5.
[72] AVPRI, Telegram from Chirkov, 30.5.1913 [12.4.1913], f. 180, o. 517/2 d. 3573, l. 158.
[73] Dzhalil, *Iz istorii*, 125.

Simko, or to put a bounty on their heads.[74] Yet such measures could secure only momentary victories. Diplomatic pressure on Russia and Iran to keep Abdürrezzak, Simko, Sheikh Taha, and others away from the Ottoman border was similarly, at best, only temporarily effective. Istanbul adopted other tactics besides suppression to pacify the Kurds. One was to exploit the splits and feuds among them. One such rift was the rivalry between the prominent Shemdinan and Bedirhan clans. The head of the Shemdinan clan, Sheikh Abdülkadir, was a CUP member and Ottoman senator who used his influence to try to undercut Abdürrezzak's appeal and reconcile the Kurds to the CUP.[75] Another tactic was to offer amnesty to Abdürrezzak, Sheikh Taha, and other Kurdish rebels working with the Russians.[76] Offers of amnesty, however, ran the risk of diminishing the government's prestige.[77] And there was no certainty that a chief's acceptance of amnesty guarantied he had forsworn anti-government activity. Despite having availed himself of an amnesty, one Sheikh Mahmud Süleyman, resentful at his post-1908 decline, came to the Russians with a proposal to create disturbances and support a Russian invasion, on the understanding that afterwards they would restore his prior privileges and position.[78]

Ottoman officials pursued secret negotiations with Kurds in Iran and managed occasionally to turn Iranian Kurds against the Russians.[79] They also succeeded at times in winning back some Ottoman Kurds. In some instances this backfired, such as when the Ottomans delegated their sometime opponent Sheikh Taha to catch draft dodgers along the border. The unwelcome nature of conscription plus Taha's pillaging and burning of homes in the area caused a score of Ottoman Kurds to flee

---

[74] AVPRI, Telegram of the Vice-Consul in Khoy, 7.11.1913 [20.11.1913], Vice-Consul in Khoy to the First Department, December 1913 [day not specified], f. 180, o. 517/2, d. 3573, l. 232; AVPRI, Vice-Consul in Urmia to Tehran, 31.5.1913 [13.6.1913], f. 180, o. 517/2, d. 3562, l. 160; AVPRI, Telegram from Orlov to Sazonov, 24.6.1914 [7.7.1914], f. 180, o. 517/2, d. 3573, l. 354; Bedirhan, *Otobiyografya*, 40–42.

[75] Özoğlu, *Kurdish Notables*, 392–93; Derk Kinnane, *The Kurds and Kurdistan* (London: Oxford University Press, 1964), 25; V. Nikitin, *Kurdy*, translated from the French (Moscow: Progress, 1964), 290; Naci Kutlay, *İttihat-Terakki ve Kürtler* (Istanbul: Fırat Yayınları, 1991), 34.

[76] AVPRI, Telegram from the Ambassador in Constantinople, 14.12.1912 [27.12.1912], f. 180, o. 517/2, d. 3572, l. 115; AVPRI, Vice-Consul in Khoy to the Imperial Chargé d'affaires in Tehran, 30.10.1913 [12.11.1913], f. 180, o. 517/2, d. 3573, l. 207; Lazarev, *Kurdskii vopros*, 205.

[77] Erdal Aydoğan, *İttihat ve Terakki'nin Doğu Politikası* (Istanbul: Ötüken Neşriyat, 2005), 185–86.

[78] AVPRI, Orlov to Sazonov, 28.2.1913 [13.3.1913], f. 180, o. 517/2, d. 3573, l. 16.

[79] AVPRI, Report of the Court Councilor in Van, 18.3.1913 [31.3.1913], Report of the Vice-Consul in Van, 25.3.1913 [7.4.1913], f. 180, o. 512b, d. 3573, ll. 60–61, 79; Lazarev, *Kurdskii vopros*, 158.

to Iran and plead to the Russian consul in Rumiye for aid, resulting in a deep sense of embarrassment among Ottoman officials.[80] Finally, the Ottoman government at times addressed Kurdish concerns more directly by removing governors that the Kurds resented and appointing Kurds to important positions in Kurdistan. This, however, inevitably alienated the Armenians, to say nothing of when some Unionists, such as Abdülkadir, sought to attract Kurdish support by engaging in rhetorical declamations against Armenians.[81] While the Armenians themselves could be ignored, Istanbul took the threat of great power intervention on their behalf seriously.

This tactic, moreover, led not only to strained relations with the Armenians, but at times also set the Ottoman government against itself. For example, yielding to the lobbying of Abdülkadir, Istanbul appointed a Kurd named İzzet Bey governor to the province of Van for the specific purpose of improving relations with Van's Kurdish notables. But this mission rendered İzzet Bey's relationship with the local army corps commander Cabir Pasha a contentious and embittered one. Cabir Pasha derided the new governor as a "dirty Kurd" who dreamed of a "Kurmanji Beylik."[82] He complained of İzzet Bey's inability to work with the Armenians and at times openly wished that the Dashnaks would kill him. For his part, İzzet, an ardent Muslim and opponent of Russia, accused the army commander of being in league with the Dashnaks and expressed bewilderment as to how such a person could get appointed to a high position. Armenians unsurprisingly favored Cabir and reviled İzzet Bey.[83] Meanwhile, Van's deputy governor despaired that this internal feuding left the province defenseless against Russia's intrigues with Simko and other Kurds.[84]

Inchoate nation

In an analysis of the Kurds' military potential, the Russian army's leading ethnographer of the Kurds, Aver'ianov, wrote in 1912, "the Kurds have neither a clear national self-consciousness nor a sense of patriotism in the Kurdish-national sense, and therefore all of their uprisings against

[80] BOA, Interior Ministry Directorate of Public Communications to Van Province, 25 Kanunuevvel 1326 [7.1.1911], Deputy Governor to the Interior Ministry, 21 Nisan 1327 [4.5.1911], DH.SYS, D. 8-1, S. 1-7.
[81] British Consul in Erzurum to Chargé d'affaires, 9.06.1913, cited in Burdett, *Armenia*, 269.
[82] Kurmanji is one of the three major Kurdish dialects.
[83] AVPRI, Report of Olfer'ev, 18.3.1913 [31.3.1913], Report of Olfer'ev, 25.3.1913 [7.4.1913] f. 180, o. 517/2, d. 3573, ll. 51, 79; British Vice-Consulate in Van to Lowther, 24.03.1914, in Burdett, *Armenia*, 285.
[84] Aydoğan, *Doğu Politikası*, 177.

Turkish domination were put down, were accompanied by fratricidal conflict, never simultaneously took place throughout all of Kurdistan, and never led to the formation of a Kurdish state."[85] This vision of the tribes as an inchoate nation with an inherent but unrealized claim to statehood would have been inconceivable to earlier imperial administrators. But by the end of the nineteenth century the national idea had permeated the Russian bureaucracy, affecting the way Russian officials understood the world inside their empire and outside. No longer did Russians see the tribes as a gaggle of independent entities to be dealt with individually as they existed. Instead they imagined them as a single collective entity defined by what it did not possess – a unifying consciousness and a state of its own.

Aver'ianov's analysis pointed to the military payoff for Russia of such a consciousness. As an aggregate of tribes, the Kurds presented merely an irritant to the Ottomans, but if united they would constitute a formidable military force. This was the argument of the vice-consul in Khoy, Chirkov, for backing Abdürrezzak and his project to bring the Kurds together. Other officials, however, noted two problems with such a policy. The first was the possibility that a union of Kurds could be turned against Russia. The second was that the great masses of Kurds, being illiterate, nomadic, and tied to their tribes, could not be expected to develop a genuinely unifying national consciousness. The idea of a coherent Kurdish entity was illusory, and to pursue it would amount to basing Russian policy on "Turkish emigrants and renegades [*begletsi*]."[86]

Chirkov's viewpoint won out, and Abdürrezzak obtained Russian support at the highest levels in St. Petersburg for his effort to cultivate a Kurdish elite that would transform Kurdish society. Right after the crushing of İrşad, Abdürrezzak together with other former members of that organization founded the Jihandani, or "Upbringing," Society. The Russian consulate in Khoy put the society under its protection, and Chirkov even served as the society's chairman. Among the society's goals were setting up a Kurdish-language press, publishing a weekly newspaper, and opening schools for Kurds.[87]

Exposure to Russian culture formed an integral part of Abdürrezzak's vision of fostering a Kurdish national consciousness. He believed that steeping young Kurds in Russian culture would allow them to raise their people's standards of education, culture, and living.[88] The Kurds,

[85] Aver'ianov, *Etnograficheskii*, 15.   [86] Lazarev, *Kurdskii vopros*, 275–76.

[87] AVPRI, Chirkov to the Chargé d'affaires in Tehran, 14.2.1913 [27.2.1913], f. 180, o. 517/2, d. 3573, l. 23.

[88] AVPRI, Secret Report to the First Department, 1913 [month and day not specified], f. 180, o. 517/2, d. 3573, l. 233; Bedirhan, *Otobiyografya*, 37.

Abdürrezzak explained to Russian officials, were part of the "Indo-European race," but Turkish and Iranian tyranny had blocked them from contact with European civilization. Association with Russia offered an opportunity to remedy this unfortunate legacy. Abdürrezzak wanted a Cyrillic alphabet to replace the Arabic alphabet for Kurdish, and while in St. Petersburg he enlisted Russia's leading orientalists in this project.[89] He envisioned further arrangements to provide for medical assistance and loans and credit for agricultural and educational development.[90] In the meantime, with the Foreign Ministry's blessing, Russia's Khoy consulate began working with Abdürrezzak to create a school for Kurdish children. Simko, too, was brought into the project. Like Abdürrezzak, Simko also looked on Russia's involvement in Kurdish affairs with favor. A visit to Tiflis, the administrative capital of Russia's Caucasus, had made a positive impression upon him regarding imperial Russian culture. Chirkov returned the respect, describing Simko as a man with "a sharp mind and a strong character."[91]

Other Russians who worked with Abdürrezzak and Simko, however, expressed skepticism regarding the characters and true motives of these two figures. Vladimir Minorskii, one of Russia's leading experts on the Kurds, described Abdürrezzak as a "political adventurer."[92] Another assessment belittled him as obsessed with a hatred of Turks, and explained how a proposal of his to divert a hefty portion of the funds earmarked for schools to financing guerrilla bands in the provinces of Erzurum and Van "owed more to a personal desire to get revenge against the Turks than to his worries for his fellow tribesmen." Simko himself objected to Abdürrezzak's proposal. He argued that only a full-scale, united Kurdish uprising to take maximum advantage of the Porte's difficulties in North Africa and the Balkans made sense, and that funds for anything less would be better spent on schools and on protecting Kurdish refugees in Iran.[93] This disagreement cooled relations between the two. Soon thereafter a destructive rivalry developed from which the Bedirhani's prestige and authority never entirely recovered. Some actions of Abdürrezzak cast doubt upon the purity of his passion to exalt his "people." Even as he lambasted the Ottomans, he negotiated with them.

---

[89] AVPRI, Chirkov to the Chargé d'affaires in Tehran, 14.2.1913 [27.2.1913], f. 180, o. 517/2, d. 3573, ll. 23–25; Lazarev, *Kurdskii vopros*, 225; K. N. Iuzbashian, *Akademik Iosif Abgarovich Orbeli (1887–1961)* (Moscow: Nauka, 1986), 34–36.
[90] Klemm to the Office of the Viceroy of the Caucasus, 26.3.1914 [8.4.1914], in *Movei*, seri. 3, vol. 2, 249.
[91] AVPRI, Vice-Consul in Khoy to the Chargé d'affaires in Tehran, 30.10.1913 [12.11.1913], f. 180, o. 517/2, d. 3573, l. 204.
[92] Lazarev, *Kurdskii vopros*, 276.
[93] AVPRI, Khoy to the First Department, 1913, f. 180, o. 517/2, d. 3573, ll. 234–35.

Alongside points such as funding for schools, he also made the provision of special posts and jobs for his relatives a precondition to any agreement. A desire to regain his family's formerly privileged status, and not simply a deep attachment to Kurdishness, motivated his efforts to rally and unify the Kurdish tribes.

Evaluations of Simko were similarly mixed. Simko's tribe, the Shakak, had a reputation for being among the worst robbers and plunderers, and were known for their preference for raiding the settled Christian Assyrians and Shiʿi Azeri Turks of the plains and valleys.[94] Although the governor general of the Caucasus Vorontsov-Dashkov decorated Simko in Tiflis for services to Russia and appointed him governor of Somay, Girs cautioned in internal correspondence that most of Simko's "exploits were little more than poorly disguised banditry" and "boil down to cattle rustling etc."[95] Ottoman officials would have agreed emphatically with this interpretation.[96] They compiled inventoried estimates of the damage that Simko had caused to Ottoman villages and protested Vorontsov-Dashkov's decoration of Simko all the way up to Sazonov. The protests were to no avail since, as the Russian consul in Van bluntly remarked, "[Simko] is someone that we need and we should support him, since his hatred toward the Turks is without limit. And that benefits us."[97]

The first Russian–Kurdish school opened in Khoy in November 1913. Russian military officers and diplomats and Kurdish notables and merchants were among those who attended the opening, and Foreign Minister Sazonov passed on the tsar's gratitude to "the participants in the Kurdish school."[98] The school's mullah commenced the ceremony with a prayer asking God to grant a long life to the tsar and to strengthen the power and greatness of the tsar's state. The Russians' goals for the school aligned with Abdürrezzak's and Simko's. One was to foster a unifying Kurdish identity among the students and to tie this future elite to Russia. Thus, in addition to newly developed courses in Kurdish language and Kurdish literature, the students were also to study the Russian language,

---

[94] Martin van Bruinessen, "Kurdish Tribes and the State of Iran: The Case of Simko's Revolt," in *The Conflict of Tribe and State in Iran and Afghanistan*, ed. Richard Tapper (New York: St. Martin's Press, 1983), 380.

[95] Lazarev, *Kurdskii vopros*, 277–78.

[96] ATASE, Foreign Minister to the General Staff, 4 Şubat 1328 [17.2.1913], BHK, K. 175, D. 72, F. 1-21.

[97] AVPRI, Report of Olfer'ev in Van, 18.3.1913 [31.3.1913], f. 180, o. 517/2, d. 3573, l. 64. One official ascribed Simko's hatred of the Turks to the fact that his father, who had lived in Constantinople and had known Abdürrezzak, died in an Ottoman prison: AVPRI, Telegram of Kokhanovskii, Tiflis, 15.5.1911 [28.5.1911], f. 180, o. 517/2, d. 3572, l. 71.

[98] Dzhalil, *Iz istorii*, 113.

Russian society, Russia's borders, natural resources, governmental structure, legal system, and "wide tolerance for Muslims." Russian literature was to be translated into Kurdish, and Kurdish literature into Russian. The best students were expected to continue their higher education in Russia. Another aim was to bolster Russia's control over northern Iran by winning Kurdish sympathy for the short-term. A longer-term goal was to pacify the Kurds by teaching them the peaceful – and sedentary – pursuits of agriculture, horticulture, metalworking, and carpentry.[99] These three goals would serve the greater objective of facilitating Russian domination of the region by transforming the Kurds from a collection of disparate, often feuding, nomadic tribes inclined to disorder and rebellion into a cohesive, settled society that could become, ideally, a pillar of Russian rule. The Foreign Ministry now sought to improve Russia's capacity to deal with Kurds over the long term by ensuring that St. Petersburg University taught Kurdish language and ethnography on a permanent basis.[100]

A related avenue of enlightenment through which the Russians sought to boost their influence among the Kurds was medical expertise. The Kurds suffered grievously from a lack of basic medical knowledge, the cause of their extraordinarily high rates of child mortality and disease-incurred blindness. Not surprisingly, Russian military doctors proved popular among Kurdish villagers.[101]

The Ottomans and the Germans did not let the opening of the school in Khoy go unnoticed, and responded in kind. The Ottomans managed to scrounge some funds from their depleted coffers to open a school for Kurds outside Van and planned to open more. The Germans decided to bring an annual cohort of Kurds to Germany and to open their schools in Anatolia to Kurds.[102]

The perplexity of imperial security

At the same time that they were winning over the sympathies of Ottoman Kurds, the Russians were destabilizing Eastern Anatolia and eroding their own confidence in the security of the Caucasus. The prospect of Kurdish raiders or especially Armenian revolutionaries from Eastern Anatolia

---

[99] AVPRI, Vice-Consul in Khoy to the Chargé d'affaires in Tehran, 30.10.1913 [12.11.1913], f. 180, o. 517/2, d. 3573, ll. 206–07.
[100] Iuzbashian, *Orbeli*, 34–35.
[101] AVPRI, Chirkov to the Chargé d'affaires in Tehran, 14.2.1913 [27.2.1913], f. 180, o. 517/2, d. 3573, l. 25.
[102] AVPRI, Vice-Consul in Khoy to the Chargé d'affaires in Tehran, 30.10.1913 [12.11.1913], f. 180, o. 517/2, d. 3573, ll. 204–09; Lazarev, *Kurdskii vopros*, 225–26.

spreading disorder in the Caucasus worried Russian officials. The issue of Ottoman Armenians was sensitive because Russia had its own Armenian problem. Exposed through their schooling in Russia and Europe to German Romantic ideals of nation and Russian revolutionary currents, the educated members of Russia's Armenian community had begun to chafe under tsarist rule in the latter half of the nineteenth century.[103] They began to entertain visions of an Armenia that was united, socialist, and autonomous or even independent. Their vision of the future, although vague and undefined, was secular and anti-clerical and did not square with that of the Armenian clergy, heretofore the most influential institution in Armenian life. Consequently, the revolutionaries' popular appeal and support were limited.

In order to head off the development of separatist tendencies, the tsarist regime in 1903 initiated a program to Russify the tsar's Armenian subjects. Among other measures, the regime wrested control of Armenian schools from the Armenian Church, expropriated Church properties, and imposed Russian-style curricula. The effort backfired badly. It drove anti-clerical Armenian socialist groups to rally in defense of the Armenian Church and launch a campaign of violent resistance that with "bullets, bombs, and knives" took the lives of tens, if not hundreds, of Russian state servants. The resistance succeeded. Two years later St. Petersburg backed down.[104]

The liberalization of Russian politics in 1905 allowed Russia's Armenians and others to press their concerns in public. Among the Armenians those concerns included their desire for Russian intervention on behalf of their Ottoman brethren. The tsarist regime could neither wholly ignore the desire for intervention nor indulge it thoughtlessly. Tsarist officials recognized that the occupation or annexation of Eastern Anatolia would bring together the great bulk of Armenians under Russian aegis and thereby enable the Armenian revolutionary movement to concentrate all of its energy on its struggle against Russia.

Indeed, in 1908 the Russian empire, not the Ottoman, came to loom as the greater oppressor for the Armenian revolutionary movement. That year Stolypin ordered a general crackdown on potential subversives, including Armenian activists. In 1909 up to 4,000 Armenians were languishing in tsarist prisons on political charges, and some 3,000 more were in exile.[105] Mass trials of Armenians produced a docket some 20,000

---

[103] Suny, "Eastern Armenians," 118–19.
[104] Hovannisian, *Armenia on the Road*, 18–19; Panossian, *The Armenians*, 220; Suny, "Eastern Armenians," 134.
[105] Bayur, *Türk İnkılâbı Tarihi*, vol. II, pt. 3, 21.

pages in length.[106] Armenian revolutionaries fled Russia and shifted their movement's center of gravity to the Ottoman empire, especially Istanbul and Van, and to Iran.[107] Armenian activists appealing to outside audiences for sympathy and aid hailed the freedom and constitutional order of the Ottomans and contrasted it to the tyranny, torture, and persecution of Russia.[108]

It therefore should be no surprise that the activities of Armenian revolutionaries constituted a major concern for Russian intelligence agents and police personnel posted in the Ottoman empire.[109] Russia's consular officers inside the Ottoman empire were also highly attuned to the activities and often virulently anti-Russian sentiments of the Dashnaks.[110] The view of Armenian revolutionaries as the stalking horse for Russia's imperial ambitions is, therefore, wide of the mark. Although Russia would seek to turn Armenian dissatisfaction with Ottoman rule to its advantage in 1913–14, mutual suspicion and distrust plagued relations between the tsarist state and Armenian revolutionaries.

Balkan shock and Russia's response

The rapidity and extent of the Ottomans' defeats in the Balkan Wars stunned the Russians. They concluded that the empire's demise might well be imminent, and that imminence spurred them to act. St. Petersburg feared that in the event of an Ottoman collapse anarchy in Eastern Anatolia might draw in the populations on Russia's side of the border and that another power might exploit the chance to establish a presence right on Russia's uneasy southern frontier.[111] To forestall these possibilities, the Russians took two courses of action. The first was to expand Russia's support for Kurdish rebels. In a missive dated 28 November 1912, Sazonov instructed Russia's consuls in Anatolia and Iran to seize this moment of Ottoman disarray to strengthen Russia's prestige among the Kurds and draw them away from Istanbul. He ordered his consuls

---

[106] Ter Minassian, *Nationalism*, 52.

[107] Ter Minassian, *Nationalism*, 53; Hratch Dasnabedian, *History of the Armenian Revolutionary Federation Dashnaktsutiun 1890/1924* (Milan: Oemme edizioni, 1990), 93–95.

[108] E. Aknouni, *Political Persecution: Armenian Prisoners of the Caucasus* (New York: n.p., 1911).

[109] See, for example, the files of the police running agents in Istanbul between 1911 and 1914: GARF, Biuro zaveduiushchego zagranichnoi agenturoi Departamenta politsii v Konstantinopole, f. 529, o. 1.

[110] AVPRI, General Consul in Erzurum to Girs, 10.5.1912 [23.5.1912], f. 180, o. 517/2, d. 3708, l. 150; Report of Unnamed General Staff Colonel, 7.1.1913 [20.1.1913], f. 180, o. 517/2, d. 3573, l. 7; Ter Minassian, *Nationalism*, 52–53.

[111] Sazonov, *Vospominaniia*, 168–69.

to study the question of how to unite the Kurds "since only en masse can the Kurds constitute a serious force."[112] Noting Anatolia's strategic importance to Russia and the vulnerabilities stemming from its ethnic heterogeneity, Minorskii advised opening more consulates specifically near non-Turkish populations so as to facilitate subversive work.[113] Overriding Finance Ministry objections to the costs, Sazonov ordered more consulates opened.[114]

Second, Russia suddenly resurrected the dormant Armenian Question in the interstate arena. Whereas during the massacres of 1895–96 Russia had steadfastly blocked the possibility of intervention on behalf of Ottoman Armenians, Sazonov now brandished the issue of the Armenians' security to demand that Istanbul permit Russia to oversee the reform and administration of the six eastern provinces. If conditions for Armenians did not improve, Sazonov threatened, military intervention would follow. Armenians in Russia and in European capitals, urged on by Russian officials, initiated public campaigns for reform.[115]

Opinions of Ottoman Armenians regarding Russia's initiative were mixed. Whereas the patriarch in Istanbul and some members of the Dashnaktsutiun favored the establishment of a Russian protectorate, seeing it as at least a guaranty of desperately needed order, other Dashnaks opposed it. Russia, they believed, was using the Armenians to annex the territory, after which it would impose a regime worse than the Ottoman.[116] The deterioration in security in the east, however, was a real and immediate concern. The Balkan defeats further destabilized matters as refugees bearing tales of atrocities stirred Muslims from Istanbul to Van to threaten vengeance attacks against Christians. Thus throughout 1913 and into 1914, the Dashnaks accelerated preparations for "self-defense" by smuggling weapons and bombs from the Caucasus back into Anatolia and Istanbul and forming "flying battalions" for defense in the event of anti-Christian pogroms.[117]

Russia's demands alarmed an Istanbul already shaken by the disasters unfolding in the Balkans. Following their return to power in January,

[112] AVPRI, Sazonov to Girs, copied to consulates in Van, Urmia, Bayezid, and Savujbulak, 15.11.1912 [28.11.1912], f. 180, o. 517/2, d. 3572, l. 109.
[113] AVPRI, "Asian Turkey and Its Study," f. 129, o. 502/b, d. 7600, ll. 2, 4–5.
[114] Lazarev, *Kurdskii vopros*, 224.
[115] Davison, "Armenian Crisis," 489–90; Hovannisian, "Armenian Question," 22.
[116] GARF, Secret Report to the Head of Agents in Turkey, 23.1.1913 [5.2.1913], To Police Special Department Head Eremin, 1.3.1913 [14.3.1913], To Police Special Department Head Broetskii, September 1913, f. 529, o. 1, d. 11, ll.7, 11, 39.
[117] GARF, To Police Special Department Head Eremin, 7.1.1913 [20.1.1913], f. 529, o. 1, d. 11, l. 3; To Police Special Department Head Eremin, 22.3.1913 [4.4.1913], f. 529, o. 1, d. 12, l. 14; Kaligian, *Armenian Organization*, 181.

the Unionists met several times with Dashnak leaders in 1913 to discuss reforms, despite the latter's public break with them the previous May. At one meeting held in the home of a former Unionist Armenian, Talât offered to fulfill Dashnaks' demands for twenty-two seats in parliament, enforcement of equal rights for Armenians throughout the empire, appointment of Armenians to administrative and judicial posts in the east, and the disarming of the Kurds in exchange for an Armenian refusal to accept European control of the reforms. Aram Vramian answered that the Dashnaks, unlike the Catholicos and Armenian merchants, had never sought European control, since that would involve Russia's participation, and Russian control would destroy their party.[118] Such doubts notwithstanding, some Dashnaks were approaching foreign powers, and the party, albeit divided, ultimately assented to the Armenian National Assembly's preparation of a draft reform project.[119]

Skepticism toward the Russian effort existed among the great powers as well. France, wary that Russian action might precipitate partition and jeopardize its own financial and railway interests in the region, and Germany, suspecting that Russia desired annexation and intended to provoke an intervention, signaled their opposition to any unilateral action by Russia. Russia remained insistent, and so through the summer of 1913 representatives of the great powers met in Istanbul to discuss reform of Ottoman administration of Eastern Anatolia. The Russians put forth a proposal that required, among other things, that the six provinces be combined in a single administrative district over which a Christian, preferably European, governor general appointed by the great powers would preside with extraordinary authority. Istanbul frantically resisted the scheme. It pitched the idea of deploying British officials, whose competence could be expected to achieve results and whose presence would deter Russian encroachment, to oversee reforms and supervise the gendarmerie, the justice system, agriculture, public works, and related government functions.[120]

St. Petersburg, however, made clear to London its determination to control the project, noting that it shared a border with Eastern Anatolia and that it faced pressure from its own Armenian population to impose reforms. London concluded that intimate involvement in the

---

[118] GARF, To Police Special Department Head Broetskii, 27.11.1913 [9.12.1913], f. 529, o. 1, d. 11, l. 69; To Police Special Department Head Broetskii, September 1913, f. 529, o. 1, d.11, l. 39.
[119] Hovannisian, "Armenian Question," 23–24.
[120] Zekeriya Türkmen, *Vilayât-ı Şarkiye (Doğu Anadolu Vilayetleri) Islahat Müfettişliği 1913–1914* (Ankara: Türk Tarih Kurumu, 2006), 33, 35; Cemal Paşa, *Hatıralar ve Vesikalar*, vol. II, *Harp Kabinelerinin İsticvabı* (Istanbul: Vakit, 1933), 292.

project was not worth risking its relationship with Russia and declined the Porte's invitation.[121] The Germans were almost as anxious as the Ottomans to thwart the Russian proposal, and attempted to do so by various stratagems. Not unlike the British with the Laz in 1878, they discovered a utility in invoking the ethnonational rights of indigenous populations. Thus they attempted to counter their Russian interlocutors with the argument that, if it is proper to raise the rights of the Armenians, then it must follow that it is necessary to discuss the interests of the Kurds.[122] In May the Porte put forth its own ten-point reform program, which obtained the approval of the German, British, Austrian, and Italian ambassadors. Girs, however, rejected it, compelling extended negotiations among the powers.[123]

To the Ottomans, the process uncannily resembled those that had preceded the losses of Bosnia and Macedonia. Outside powers were holding Istanbul accountable for its inability to maintain internal order in border provinces while actively fomenting that disorder through the sponsorship of insurgents and rebels. Now Russia was eroding Ottoman sovereignty in Eastern Anatolia from within and simultaneously attacking that sovereignty from without by calling attention to Istanbul's inability to govern the region. The Ottomans were not alone in perceiving a clever link between Russian complaints about the lack of order and threats of "humanitarian" intervention, and their support for Kurdish rebels who were subverting that order. European and American observers noted it as well.[124] Nor were they alone in the belief that the reform project was a last preparatory step before formal Russian annexation of the region and the end of the empire.[125]

German policymakers were among those who suspected Russian cunning, but they had to weigh this against the likelihood that the Ottoman empire was doomed in any event. In a post-Ottoman Anatolia, German ambassador Hans von Wangenheim wrote, "it will be a great asset to have the native Armenian population on our side when we are asserting

---

[121] Davison, "Armenian Crisis," 493–95.

[122] Sverbeev to Sazonov, 29.05.1913 [11.06.1913], in Institut des langues orientales (Russia), *Sbornik diplomaticheskikh dokumentov: reformy v Armenii 26 noiabria 1912 goda – 10 maia 1914 goda* (Petrograd: Gosudarstvennaia tipografiia, 1915), 45; B. A. Bor'ian, *Armeniia, mezhdunarodnaia diplomatiia i SSSR*, 2 vols. (Moscow: Gosudarstvennoe izdatel'stvo, 1928), vol. I, 281–82.

[123] Türkmen, *Vilayât-ı Şarkiye*, 39–41.

[124] Walter Guinness, "Impressions of Armenia and Kurdistan," *National Review* (September 1913–February 1914), vol. 62, 800; W. A. Wigram and Edgar T. A. Wigram, *The Cradle of Mankind: Life in Eastern Kurdistan* (London: Adam and Charles Black, 1914), 36–37; Buxton and Buxton, *Travels*, 153.

[125] Somakian, *Empires in Conflict*, 59; Bayur, *Türk İnkılâbı Tarihi*, vol. II, 114, 117; Davison, "Armenian Crisis," 491.

our rights in Asia Minor."[126] The Armenians' plight was real enough, Russian policies notwithstanding, and by participating in a reform effort Germany would win favor among Armenians. Thus, when the powers proved unable collectively to arrive at a solution, Wangenheim agreed with Girs to resolve the matter through bilateral talks. Wangenheim at the same time hedged his bets and advised his superiors that Germany must redouble efforts to build its influence in Eastern Anatolia by placing in the region more consulates, experts, merchants, missions, and schools.[127]

St. Petersburg throughout the negotiations kept pressure on Istanbul with threats of military action, including invasion. Sazonov warned more than once that, if another massacre of Armenians occurred, Russia would not stand by as it had in 1895.[128]. The Liman von Sanders crisis ratcheted the tension up further, leading Sazonov to consider occupying Bayezid or Erzurum. To underscore that possibility, Russian troops massed on the border. Barring the intervention of a third party, of the sort feared by Russia's naval planners, it seems unlikely the Russians would have mounted a military operation into Ottoman territory. But the deterrent to such a move was the fear of igniting a wider European conflagration, not Ottoman strength nor any notion that such an attack would be illegitimate.[129] As internal Russian correspondence makes abundantly clear, many Russian statesmen regarded the eventual occupation of Eastern Anatolia and Istanbul as all but inevitable.[130] Indeed, some were already suggesting that Russia's sponsorship of the reform plan would win the sympathies of Armenians whose support Russia would find useful against Ottoman Greeks after Russia fulfilled its destiny of occupying "Tsargrad" with its large Greek population.[131]

Germany's success in emerging from the Liman von Sanders crisis without having to make a major concession inclined it to relent and compromise with Russia. Wangenheim urged Grand Vizier Said Halim Pasha to come to an agreement with Russia. Isolated and with its options exhausted, the Porte on 8 February 1914 acceded to Russia's demands.

---

[126] Wangenheim to Bethman-Hollweg, 24.2.1913, in E. T. S. Dugdale, ed., *German Diplomatic Documents, 1871–1914*, vol. IV, *The Descent to the Abyss, 1911–1914* (New York: Harper and Brothers, 1931), 198.

[127] Dugdale, *Descent*, 196–98; Davison, "Armenian Crisis," 492; Somakian, *Empires in Conflict*, 60.

[128] BOA, To the Ambassador in St. Petersburg Turhan Pasha, 2 Kanunsani 1329 [15.1.1914], DH. SYS, D. 23, S. 2; Somakian, *Empires in Conflict*, 50–51.

[129] A. M. Zaionchkovskii, *Podgotovka Rossii k imperialisticheskoi voine: ocherki voennoi podgotovki i pervonachal'nykh planov. Po arkhivnym dokumentam* (Leningrad: Voennaia tipografiia, 1926), 324; Davison, "Armenian Crisis," 502.

[130] Girs to Sazonov, 26.11.1912 [9.12.1912], in Institut des langues orientales, *Reformy v Armenii*, 3; Kalmykov, *Memoirs*, 250; Davison, "Armenian Crisis," 490–91.

[131] Gul'kevich to Sazonov, 27.1.1914 [9.2.1914], *Movei*, ser. 3, vol. 1, 259.

The Ottomans did manage to blunt somewhat the Russian proposal with amendments. The six "Armenian" provinces plus the province of Trabzon were to be reorganized in two parts, not one. The inclusion of Trabzon, which had only a small Armenian population, diluted the Armenian presence overall. The final draft dropped the issue of restitution to Armenians, the exclusion of *muhacirs* from resettlement, and the terms "Armenian" and "Christian." These alterations all aimed at undermining any claims that these territories should or could be regarded as innately "Armenian." Nonetheless, Ottoman sovereignty over Eastern Anatolia had been severely compromised; if recent history was any guide, mortally so.

Although the resolution of the reform question smoothed diplomatic relations between the Ottoman and Russian empires, it did nothing to relieve tensions in the region itself. One reason was that the looming possibility of an end to Ottoman rule maintained all inhabitants in a state of anxiety. Another was that, despite their public protestations of concern for stability in Ottoman Anatolia and their desire to insulate their own border populations from possible unrest in Eastern Anatolia, the Russians continued to cultivate ties with rebellious Ottoman Kurds and thereby were eroding that stability. This contradiction – on the one hand attempting to secure order in Eastern Anatolia by imposing a reform plan while on the other facilitating the disruption of order – was the result primarily of Russia's inability to develop and implement a consistent policy toward the Kurds. This inability in turn stemmed from St. Petersburg's clashing strategic objectives. It preferred to put off the partition of the Ottoman empire until such time as it could ensure it would be able to exert control over that partition. Yet in the meantime it felt compelled to build influence inside the Ottoman lands, and by doing so it was undermining the Ottoman state's ability to administer and control those regions.

The dangers that the Kurdish rebellions might pose to Ottoman Armenians did not escape Russian officials. When Armenians from St. Petersburg expressed such worries to Sazonov, the foreign minister explained that Russia had to pursue relations with the Kurds because they constituted a "potential force" that could further Russian interests in the region.[132] Russian officials introduced Abdürrezzak to Armenian representatives in St. Petersburg in a bid to encourage cooperation between Kurds and Armenians.[133]

---

[132] Somakian, *Empires in Conflict*, 50.
[133] Klemm to the Office of the Viceroy of the Caucasus, 26.3.1914 [8.4.1914], *Movei*, series 3, vol. 2, 249–50.

Kurdish and Armenian leaders at various times attempted to establish conciliatory relations and even a common front against the Ottoman government.[134] But none of these efforts led to substantive results. The fundamental aspirations of the two were too far apart, indeed were fundamentally opposed. The conflict between these two groups was the basic driver of instability in the region. Indeed, Abdürrezzak himself in 1913 had been exhorting his co-ethnics to mobilize and arm themselves lest they find themselves the subjects of the "rich but immoral Armenians."[135] "The Armenian Question," as one Russian consul wrote, "was always the Kurdish–Armenian [Question], since the Armenians suffered and suffer precisely from the Kurds under the weakness and incapacity (intended or not intended – that is also a large question) of the Turkish authorities."[136] In justifying their support for the reform project Russian officials made use of the duality. To European audiences, they pointed to the threat posed to Armenians by Kurds, whereas among themselves they concentrated on the Armenian threat to Russia.[137] But in their execution of policy they could not help but muddle the duality.

The Bitlis uprising

Exactly one month after Ottoman and Russian officials signed the Armenian reform project, a Kurd known as Mullah Selim Efendi al-Hizani declared a general uprising in the area of Bitlis. Mullah Selim called for the imposition of şeriat and the removal of the Ottoman administration, which he accused of disarming the Kurds and selling out the country to foreigners. The demand for Islamic law had become an increasingly popular rallying cry among the Kurds following the restoration of the constitution in 1908 and the rise of the CUP. The governor of Van, Tahsin Bey, described Mullah Selim as an ignorant zealot "famous for pronouncing as blasphemers those who declare the Earth is round" and labeled the uprising "reactionary."[138] The calls for Islamic law,

---

[134] For two interpretations that attempt to argue that such cooperation was possible, see Tessa Hoffman and Gerayer Koutcharian, "The History of Armenian–Kurdish Relations in the Ottoman Empire," *Armenian Review*, 30, 4 (Winter 1986), 1–44; and Garo Sasuni, *Kürt Ulusal Hareketleri ve 15. Yüzyıldan Günümüze Ermeni–Kürt İlişkileri* (Istanbul: Med Yayınevi, 1992).

[135] See the "Manifesto of Abdürrezzak," reprinted in Justin McCarthy, Esat Arslan, Cemalettin Taşkıran, and Ömer Turan, *The Armenian Rebellion at Van* (Salt Lake City: University of Utah Press, 2006), 282–85.

[136] Lazarev, *Kurdskii vopros*, 245; AVPRI, f. 180, d. 3573, ll. 231–32.

[137] Lazarev, *Kurdskii vopros*, 243.

[138] BOA, Cipher from Van Governor Tahsin, 5 Mart 1330 [18.3.1914], DH. KMS, D. 16, 30, S.B. 4.

however, reflected not so much a pious attachment to the legal require-
ments of Islam as distress at the economic ascendance of Christians and
the upending of their traditional legal subordination. As Mullah Selim's
appeal gathered support, panic seized the local Christians. Given past
experience, few of Bitlis's Armenians or Assyrians trusted Selim's assur-
ances that they would not be harmed.[139] Tahsin Bey alerted Istanbul to
the incompetence of Bitlis's governor and the absence of forces in the
province, and warned that, if the government failed to act quickly, "we
will create a Kurdish problem."[140]

Within days some 300 chiefs had pledged their support, and up to
8,000 Kurds had come to Mullah Selim's side. The government meanwhile rushed reinforcements to back up the Bitlis gendarmerie and distributed arms to the Armenians of Bitlis "to defend the city against
reactionaries."[141] The rebels succeeded in seizing half of the town of
Bitlis, but before they could go further government forces counterat-
tacked and put down the uprising on 2 April 1914. Immediately upon the
revolt's collapse, Selim and three other Kurds took refuge in the Russian
consulate in Bitlis. At first, Girs ordered the consulate to get the Kurds
to leave, explaining, "we cannot indulge banditry."[142] When the consulate, now under tight surveillance,[143] replied that expelling the Kurds
would lead to their immediate capture and likely death, the ambassador
relented. He then rejected the grand vizier's repeated appeals, which
included a report on Selim's looting and killing of Armenians,[144] to hand
over the insurgents with the disingenuous argument that the rebellion
had constituted a political, not a criminal, act.[145] The consulate har-
bored Mullah Selim and his compatriots until the formal declaration of
war between the Russian and Ottoman empires in November.

Meanwhile, Ottoman authorities had caught several other leading rebels as they were attempting to cross the border into Russia.
They exiled to the Black Sea towns of Sinop and Trabzon forty-five
Kurds, including a number known for seizing lands from the Armenians, in the hopes that their removal would reduce tensions around

---

[139] AVPRI, Shirkov to Gul'kevich, 12.2.1914 [25.2.1914], Dispatch of S. Tukholki,
20.3.1914 [2.4.1914], f. 180, o. 517/2, d. 3573, ll. 241, 291.
[140] BOA, Cipher from Van, 6 Mart 1330 [19.3.1914], DH. KMS, D. 16, S. 30, B. 3.
[141] Account from the Armenian newspaper *Panper*, as cited in the English-language Istanbul newspaper, *The Orient*, 5, 14 (8 April 1914).
[142] AVPRI, Telegram from the Ambassador in Constantinople, 22.3.1914 [4.4.1914],
f. 151, o. 482, d. 3312, l. 17.
[143] BOA, Talât to Bitlis, 3 Nisan 1330 [3.4.1914], DH. ŞFR, D. 40, S. 24.
[144] BOA, Cipher to Bitlis, 3 Nisan 1330 [3.4.1914], DH. ŞFR D. 40, S.18.
[145] AVPRI, Telegram of Girs, 24.3.1914 [6.4.1914], f. 151, o. 482, d. 3312, l. 19.

Bitlis.[146] The court deported several sheikhs to Medina.[147] The Ottomans also publicly hanged eleven of the rebels. One of those hanged, Mullah Resul, defiantly announced to his executioners, "Thank God that Muslims are hanging me. I have not seen the Russians, but I hope that you will soon and that they will take vengeance on you for me."[148]

The Bitlis uprising failed in large measure because Mullah Selim started it prematurely by several weeks. As a result, major Kurdish figures such as Abdürrezzak and Sheikh Taha were in Russia when it erupted and were unable to do much apart from scrambling to send notes promising support and arms from Russia.[149] Moreover, Mullah Selim was not supposed to have led it. Acting on a tip, the Ottoman gendarmerie arrested him on 8 March for rebellious agitation. Several hours later, however, a raiding party of Kurds attacked the gendarmes transporting Mullah Selim to Bitlis and freed him. He then took it upon himself to declare a rebellion. The intended leader had been a relative of Abdürrezzak's, Bedirhan Paşazade Yusuf Kâmil. Unlike those rebels who fled north to Russia, Yusuf Kâmil fled south, making use of his contacts in the Russian consulates in Aleppo and Beirut. He expressed regret to the Russians for Selim's precipitate behavior and bemoaned the way the Armenians of Bitlis had betrayed the Kurds. Although they had assured the Kurdish plotters of their support prior to the uprising, they failed to act once it began and bore, Yusuf Kâmil alleged, much of the responsibility for the collapse of the uprising. He concluded that it was foolish ever to seek coordination with the Armenians. Yusuf Kâmil received permission to settle in Russia, and from Beirut he set sail via Istanbul to Odessa with guaranties for his safety and security. He was taken to Tiflis, from where the Russians planned to return him to Ottoman Anatolia via Iran. Upon the momentary improvement in Russian–Ottoman relations following Talât Bey's meeting with Sazonov that May in Crimea, however, the Russians instructed Yusuf Kâmil to "sit quietly" in Tiflis for the time being.[150]

Although the Ottoman government forces in the end had suppressed the rebellion, the episode spooked the Unionists. On 4 April they met to

---

[146] AVPRI, Bitlis Consulate to Girs, 12.5.1914 [25.5.1914], f. 180, o. 517/2, d. 3573, l. 327.

[147] BOA, Cipher to the Commandant of Medina, 9 Haziran 1330 [22.6.1914], DH. ŞFR, D. 42, S. 102.

[148] Lazarev, *Kurdskii vopros*, 216.

[149] Abdürrezzak was in St. Petersburg when the revolt erupted: AVPRI, Sazonov to Girs, 4.3.1914 [17.3.1914], f. 151, o. 462, d. 3312, l. 8; Suat Akgül, "Rusya'nın Doğu Anadolu Politikası, "Ph. D. dissertation, Hacettepe University, 1995," 106.

[150] Rossiiskii gosudarstvennyi voenno-istoricheskii arkhiv (RGVIA), Report of Kniaz Shakhovskoi, 31.1.1917 [13.2.1917], f. 2168, o. 1, d. 264, l. 4.

review their regional policy. They resolved to win over the Kurds with a combination of methods, including financial subsidies, making leading Kurds senators, and pressing the Kurds of Istanbul to use their influence over their brethren in Anatolia. The Unionists were relieved that the insurrection had been directed at the government and not at the Armenians, since if the latter had been targets relations with the great powers would have suffered. Thus, in addition to granting the local governors wider latitude to declare martial law and request military reinforcements, Minister of the Interior Talât ordered that special attention be paid to protecting Christians from future attacks.[151] The meeting concluded with a call for less centralization and greater flexibility in the state administration in order to allow for policies to be tailored to regional peculiarities.[152]

Russia's policies, whether by design or not, were eroding Ottoman control of Eastern Anatolia. Repeating the opinion of the local Christians and Muslims, the vice-consul in Bitlis Shirkov wrote, "Turkish rule in Kurdistan is without soldiers and without money, and lacks all prestige and influence, and now with the developing Kurdish movement calls forth disgust and tears." He noted with satisfaction that even the Muslims at the bazaar were openly calling for Russian rule as a way to end the ongoing disorder and chaos, and cited the locals' belief that Russia could take the whole region with just 5,000 soldiers.[153] The Ottoman army would not have contested this judgment. As the inspector general of the Third Army in Erzincan wrote about the military balance in Eastern Anatolia, "Russia will be able to operate as it wants and invade as deep as it wants . . . If there is a war on this front resistance will not be possible."[154]

---

[151] AVPRI, Dispatch of the Ambassador in Constantinople, 31.3.1914 [13.4.1914], Addendum from the Ambassador in Constantinople, 31.3.1914 [13.4.1914], f. Politarkhiv, o. 482, d. 3312, ll. 25, 26.

[152] AVPRI, Dispatch of the Ambassador in Constantinople, 12.4.1914 [25.4.1914], f. Politarkhiv, o. 482, d. 3312, l. 31.

[153] AVPRI, Dispatch to Girs, 29.3.1913 [11.4.1913], f. 180, o. 517/2, d. 3573, l. 86.

[154] ATASE, Telegram from the Inspector General of the Third Army in Erzincan, 14 Kanunusani 1328 [27.1.1913], BHK, K. 131, D. 41, F. 4-1.

3   Visions of vulnerability: the politics of Muslims, revolutionaries, and defectors

Strapped for resources and confronting multiple internal and external challenges, the Ottoman empire could not hope to mount against its Russian rival either a comparable military threat or an effort at subversion. Its armed forces could pose no credible threat, and for subversion it lacked the resources and funds to foment turmoil inside Russia and challenge the Russian state's authority. Nor did it possess the international clout that might have permitted it to exploit Russia's own internal fractures in diplomatic arenas. Nonetheless, the Ottomans were not wholly incapable of projecting influence into the Russian empire. The Russian empire had some fifteen to twenty million Muslim subjects; more, in fact, than lived under the sultan. But the Ottoman empire was the world's greatest independent Muslim state, and as such it could not but perform as a symbol and barometer of the well-being of Islam for Muslims around the world. In addition, the Ottoman sultan had a claim to be the caliph, the successor to the Prophet Muhammad as the head of the community of Sunni Muslims, i.e., the great bulk of Muslims in the world and in Russia outside Azerbaijan. Sultan Selim I first claimed the mantle of caliph for the Ottomans in 1516 when he came upon a descendant of the last Abbasid caliph living among the Mameluks whom he had just defeated. The Ottoman claim to the title was shaky on several grounds, and perhaps for this reason the Ottoman sultans invoked the title sparingly until the last quarter of the nineteenth century, when Abdülhamid II made it a cornerstone of sorts of his legitimacy at home and abroad. With more Muslims falling under the rule of the same European powers that were threatening the Ottoman state, emphasizing the caliph's nominal claim on the loyalties of Muslims around the globe was one way for Abdülhamid II to increase his empire's geopolitical heft.[1]

---

[1] Selim Deringil, *The Well-Protected Domains: Ideology and the Legitimation of Power in the Ottoman Empire, 1876–1909* (London: I. B. Tauris, 1998), 46–50; Georgeon, *Abdülhamid II*, 192–214.

In practice Abdülhamid II's support for pan-Islam was largely rhetorical. The Unionists, however, despised Abdülhamid II's personal piety. They blamed his attachment to Islam for his autocratic conservatism, and some even suspected that St. Petersburg was backing this champion of Islamic values in order to retard the Ottoman empire's modernization and keep it weak. Yet even as the Unionists derided Islam as an obstacle to progress, they bristled at the subjugation of Muslims around the world. They recognized in European imperialism a common foe and accordingly sought to mobilize Muslims as allies.

Iran and the Transcaucasus had been areas of special interest to the CUP when as an underground organization it had to function abroad. They were close to the Ottoman Black Sea coast and Anatolia, contained Ottoman expatriate communities, and offered a relative freedom that was conducive to organizing.[2] While in opposition the Unionists had identified with Iranian revolutionaries and their parallel struggle for constitutional rule and against foreign, particularly British and Russian, domination.[3] In 1907–08, a number of CUP members operating out of Erzurum, including Ömer Naci, Enver's uncle Halil (Kut), and Cevdet Bey, the future governor of Van, traveled to Iran to make contact with Iranian revolutionaries. Later several Unionists fought alongside the Iranians, with at least one losing his life this way in 1911.[4] Erzurum thus became a key location in these borderlands not only for warfare but for subversion, too. During the struggle against Abdülhamid II, a graduate of the Ottoman military academy named Hüseyin Tosun had founded in Erzurum a covert cell for Prince Sabahaddin Bey's League of Private Initiative and Decentralization, an underground Young Turk organization. To evade the police, Tosun posed as a Russian subject. Assisting him were members of the Dashnaktsutiun, who acquired a Russian passport for him and later even secured him a job at the Russian consulate as a mail carrier. Eventually, however, the police uncovered him and compelled him to confess under torture in front of the dragoman from the Russian consulate before sending him to Istanbul for imprisonment.[5] After coming to power the Unionists would use Erzurum as a center to establish contact with individuals and groups in Iran and the Transcaucasus.

The three Caucasian provinces of Kars, Ardahan, and Batumi possessed an unusual status in Ottoman eyes. For centuries they had been Ottoman lands, until 1878, when Russia acquired them. The superior

[2] Hanioğlu, *Preparation*, 161; S. Esin Dayı, *Elviye-i Selâse'de (Kars, Ardahan, Batum) Millî Teşkilâtlanma* (Erzurum: Kültür Eğitim Vakfı Yayınları, 1997), 15.
[3] Bayur, *Türk İnkılâbı Tarihi*, vol. II, pt. 4, 100.   [4] Dayı, *Elviye-i Selâse'de*, 15.
[5] Hanioğlu, *Preparation*, 116–17; Ertürk, *Perde Arkası*, 62–63.

administrative and economic capacities of the Russian empire revealed themselves in the transformation of the infrastructure and economy of the provinces over the following quarter-century.[6] Batumi grew into a major port city whose sight would awe Ottoman visitors accustomed to Trabzon.[7] Russian rule in these lands saw no major disturbances, but not all Muslims reconciled themselves to tsarist rule. Small numbers formed clandestine organizations, and these maintained contact both with other underground groups in the Ottoman empire and with the Ottoman government.[8]

By contrast, no comparable political structures existed among Muslims in Russian Azerbaijan prior to the so-called Armeno-Tatar War of 1905. The superior organization of their revolutionaries had given the Armenians an edge in those clashes, and in response some Azeris formed their own societies, the Defense (Difai) society in Elisavetpol (Gäncä), and the National Defense (Müdafâa-i Millî) society in Baku.[9] The Unionists criticized Abdülhamid II for failing to support the Muslims of Transcaucasia despite his rhetoric, and cautioned those and other Muslim activists outside the Ottoman realm not to expect any assistance from the sultan. The Unionists proffered other noteworthy advice in a series of letters sent by their Paris office to "Our Muslim Brothers in the Caucasus." The letters' message was pan-Islamist in so far as it implored the Muslims of Russia, Sunni and Shi'i alike, to work together and identified the tsarist government and Armenian revolutionaries as the enemies of the Ottomans as well. Yet at the same time the letters' author, the prominent Unionist Bahaeddin Şakir, opined that the tsarist government was working with the Armenians not out of sympathy but rather according to the hoary tactic of using a weaker element to attack a stronger. He reminded the Transcaucasian Muslims that just a few years earlier the Russians had "crushed" the Armenians, and urged them "to come to terms with the Armenians in order to drive out the stronger enemy, the Russians, together." Bahaeddin Şakir went on to identify Russia's Poles and Jews, known for their anti-tsarist sentiment, also as natural

---

[6] İlber Ortaylı, *Osmanlı İmparatorluğunda İktisadî ve Sosyal Değişim* (Ankara: Turhan Kitabevi, 2000), 399–418.
[7] İlhan Selçuk, *Yüzbaşı Selahattin'in Romanı* (Istanbul: Remzi Kitabevi, 1973), 394.
[8] Fahrettin Erdoğan, *Türk Ellerinde Hatıralarım* (Ankara: T. C. Kültür Bakanlığı, 1998), 25–26, 30–32; Dayı, *Elviye-i Selâse'de*, 14–16, 19–20.
[9] Swietochowski, *Russian Azerbaijan*, 42–45; Audrey L. Altstadt, *The Azerbaijani Turks: Power and Identity Under Russian Rule* (Stanford: Hoover Institution Press, 1992), 67; Naki Keykurun, *Azerbaycan İstiklâl Mücadelesinden Hatıralar (1905–1920)* (Ankara: İlke Kitabevi, 1998), 29–45.

allies.[10] The CUP could be quite catholic in its choice of partners in the fight against Russia. Even in opposition they relied upon what they perceived as the interests of the Ottoman state, not identity, to guide them in choosing such partners.

The Unionists' assumption of power after 1908 gave them the opportunity to use government institutions to assist Muslim and other Russian activists and thereby further the goals of the Ottoman state. Six months after the CUP restored the constitution in 1908, the Ottomans resolved to expand the intelligence functions of their network of consulates in Russia.[11] They decided to appoint to each of their consulates, embassies, and missions – in particular those in Batumi, Tiflis, and Kars – one officer from the Ottoman General Staff. The selected officers were to have higher education and were to be selected on the basis of exceptional talent.[12] They were not, however, posted as military attachés. Instead, they operated under the cover of "commercial agents" at the missions where they were stationed. Pursuing intelligence, not trade deals, was to be their real responsibility.[13] As always, however, the paucity of resources restrained Ottoman ambitions. In order to cover the expense involved in maintaining an intelligence officer at the consulates, the government had to reduce the full-time diplomatic staff at each consulate by one official.[14]

The Russian government kept Ottoman diplomats in the Caucasus under close surveillance.[15] It found one Ottoman consul by the name of Cafer Bey to be particularly threatening. In 1910, the Russian authorities in the Caucasus perceived a growing pan-Islamic current and suspected an Ottoman role in it. They assigned agents to trail Cafer Bey, then serving as a consul in Tiflis. They learned that their target had been meeting with local Muslims and urging them to put aside their differences

---

[10] Bayur, *Türk İnkılâbı Tarihi*, vol. II, pt. 4, 84–87. Armenian revolutionaries also put primary blame upon the Russian government: Houri Berberian, *Armenians and the Iranian Constitutional Revolution, 1905–1911* (Boulder: Westview, 2001), 82–84.
[11] In 1910, the Ottomans maintained general consulates in Odessa, Moscow, and Tiflis; regular consulates in Batumi, Kars, Novorossiisk, Rostov on Don, Taganrog, Sevastopol, St. Petersburg, and Warsaw; and vice-consulates in Nikolaev, Kherson, Kerch, Feodosia, and Vladivostok. See AVPRI, Circonscriptions Consulaires des Consulats Impériaux Ottomans en Russie, 1910 [no month specified], f. 129, o. 502b, d. 550, l. 2.
[12] AVPRI, Governor General of the Caucasus to the First Department of the Ministry of Foreign Affairs, 28.12.1908 [9.1.909], f. 151, o. 482, d. 3061, l. 2.
[13] AVPRI, Governor General of the Caucasus to the First Department of the Ministry of Foreign Affairs, 17.2.1909 [2.3.1909], f. 151, o. 482, d. 3061, l. 4.
[14] AVPRI, Charykov to Sazonov, 29.3.1910 [11.4.1910], f. 151, o. 482, d. 3061, l. 7.
[15] V. M. Gilensen, "'Osinye gnezda' pod konsul'skoi kryshei," *Voenno-istoricheskii zhurnal* (September–October 1997), 49–59.

and unite against Russia, whom he labeled the enemy and an oppressor of Muslims. So bold was this consul that he approached the mufti of the Transcaucasus to demand that he include in his public prayers a reference to the Ottoman sultan as the caliph of all Muslims. Cafer Bey even had the temerity to lecture Armenians about how badly they lived in Russia, where the authorities oppressed and persecuted them.[16] Judging Cafer Bey's presence in the Caucasus to be highly inimical to Russia's interests, the Russian viceroy of the Caucasus Vorontsov-Dashkov sought to have him expelled from the region.[17]

Sazonov agreed with Vorontsov-Dashkov's assessment, and instructed the Russian embassy in Istanbul to pressure the Porte to recall Cafer Bey from Tiflis.[18] Although the embassy did not dispute that the Ottoman government engaged in pan-Islamic agitation, it advised St. Petersburg that the Porte routinely denied such charges in public and would strongly denounce any request to recall Cafer Bey unless the request were backed up with evidence. A consular officer recommended instead that the issue be put in terms of Russia's refusal to let Cafer Bey assume a post in Tiflis rather than demand that the Porte recall him.[19] Whatever the tack Russia took, it succeeded. That March the Porte transferred Cafer Bey from Tiflis to Bombay.[20]

The Ottomans also placed intelligence assets in the Transcaucasus under wholly unofficial cover. In 1909, they formed an organization called Canbizâr for the purposes of countering Armenian armed groups in the Transcaucasus. Shortly thereafter, the Ottoman consul in Kars helped put that organization in contact with the local branch of the Azeri Difai society. Then in 1912, Canbizâr, which had its center in the Pasinler district of the province of Erzurum, opened its own branch in Kars with the assistance of Ottoman intelligence operatives.[21] The intelligence section of the staff of the Russian Caucasus Military District reported in November that twelve Ottoman officers dressed as civilians had left Erzurum to organize the Muslims of the Transcaucasus for a possible

---

[16] The mufti rejected Cafer's demand, leading him to declare that he would no longer visit the mufti's mosque: AVPRI, Telegram of Kokhanovskii, 15.12.1910 [28.12.1910], f. 151, o. 482, d. 3068, l. 118.

[17] AVPRI, Telegram of Vorontsov-Dashkov, 15.12.1910 [28.12.1910], f. 151, o. 482, d. 3068, l. 119; AVPRI, Secret Telegram of Vorontsov-Dashkov, 15.12.1910 [28.12.1910], f. 180, o. 517/2, d. 4223, l. 1.

[18] AVPRI, Telegram from Sazonov, 18.12.1910 [31.12.1910], f. 180, o. 517/2, d. 4223, l. 2.

[19] AVPRI, Telegram from Svechin, 19.12.1910 [1.1.1911], f. 180, o. 517/2, d. 4223, l. 4.

[20] AVPRI, Newspaper Clipping from La Turquie, 21.2.1911 [6.3.1911], f. 180, o. 517/2, d. 4223, l. 4.

[21] Dayı, Elviye-i Selâse'de, 20–21.

war with Russia. A similar group was alleged to have left Trabzon for Batumi for the same purpose. In that Russian-held port city the Ottoman consul would conduct propaganda in houses owned by former Ottoman subjects.[22]

In the North Caucasus, small numbers of Ottoman Circassians – a term commonly used to describe descendants of all native North Caucasian peoples, not just the Circassians proper – were active carrying out pro-Ottoman propaganda. When caught, such agitators were expelled.[23] Itinerant preachers crossed into the Caucasus and upset Russian officials with their exhortations to Muslims to forget the differences between Sunni and Shiʻi and work together for their common interests as Muslims. Sometimes such preachers also photographed the cities of the Transcaucasus, an act of possible military utility. The formal attestations of Ottoman consular officers that these alleged preachers were actually merchants in Russia solely for business purposes failed to persuade the Russians and only stoked their suspicions of espionage further.[24]

In a reflection of the disadvantaged position of their state, the Ottomans flipped the conventional use of diplomacy and espionage to exert power abroad and instead used operatives to import power from abroad to remedy weakness at home. Borrowing a page from Sultan Abdülhamid II, who had appealed to all Muslims to contribute money for the construction of a railroad from Istanbul to the Hijaz in Arabia for the transportation of those performing the *Hajj*, the obligatory pilgrimage to Mecca, the Unionists solicited funds from Muslims beyond Ottoman borders for the purchase of battleships. In 1910 they established the "Society of National Assistance to the Ottoman Navy" and dispatched officers and religious figures to raise money among Muslims living in North Africa, Egypt, Sudan, India, and Russia. A delegation of *ulema*, or religious authorities, that visited Crimea in 1910 enjoyed notable success in raising money.[25] Such "fund-raising" trips continued into 1914. At the beginning of that year, the Erzurum branch of the CUP sent two members to the Transcaucasus. Posing as sheep traders, they collected money for the navy and passed it to the consuls in Kars and Tiflis, who in turn sent the

[22] E. K. Sarkisian, *Ekspansionistskaia politika Osmanskoi imperii v Zakavkaz'e nakanune i v gody pervoi mirovoi voiny* (Yerevan: Akademiia nauk Armianskoi respubliki, 1962), 108–09.

[23] AVPRI, Office of the Viceroy of the Caucasus to the First Department of the Foreign Ministry, 9.11.1913 [22.11.1913], f. 129, o. 502b, d. 3575, l. 5.

[24] AVPRI, Vorontsov-Dashkov to Sazonov, 13.11.1912 [26.11.1912], f. 129, o. 502b, d. 5345, l. 1.

[25] AVPRI, Chargé d'affaires in Constantinople to the Governor General of Turkestan, 29.9.1910 [12.10.1910], f. 151, o. 482, d. 3068, ll. 107–08.

money to Erzurum.[26] For their part, the Russians were not averse to trying to glean information from real Ottoman merchants. At the Ottoman border, Russian officials would sometimes stop and interrogate Ottoman Muslim merchants, asking them questions ranging from why they were traveling in Russia, through the location of Ottoman military units near the border, to whether or not the Armenians returning from Russia to Ottoman Anatolia were getting their land back and whether or not they would serve in the Ottoman army.[27]

The Ottomans' interest in the Muslims of Russia extended into Russia's Central Asian colonies. Shortly after the restoration of the constitution, a scholarly organization called the "Scientific Bukharan Society" was founded in Istanbul. The society recruited students from Bukhara and Kashgar, and allegedly placed them in Ottoman military and other government schools. By 1910 the society had roughly 100 students split evenly between those from Bukhara and those from Kashgar. Small numbers of Ottomans traveled to Bukhara via Afghanistan and St. Petersburg to carry out agitation, while religious leaders from Chinese Turkistan came to Istanbul, where they entered into contact with the Unionists and other groups.[28]

When targeting Russian Muslims for agitation the Ottomans did not restrict themselves to appeals to identity. To the contrary, they flogged their constitutional and progressive credentials, too. In a Turkish-language proclamation addressed to the populations of Batumi and Ajaria, the Ottomans called upon them to "awake" and "look at how peoples live in constitutional states and how the government treats all equally." "England, Germany, France, and Turkey . . . these nations, not discriminating by ethnicity or religion and coming together in one body, established their own governments and therefore are progressively moving forward in their tranquil lives." Russia, by contrast, presented a government that was torturing 300,000 in jails, repressing the Iranians, and using the Ajar nobility to persecute the revolutionary committees that were working for the freedom of the Ajars. The appeal concluded with an appeal to the Caucasian sense of manliness, taunting the reader, "Women began a revolution in France before anyone . . . You are men."[29]

[26] Sarkisian, *Ekspansionistskaia politika*, 113.

[27] BOA, Telegram from Bayezid Forwarded by the Governor of Erzurum, 3 Mayıs 1329 [16.5.1913], DH.SYS, D. 64, S. 22, F. 5.

[28] AVPRI, Chargé d'affaires in Constantinople to the Governor General of Turkestan, 29.9.1910 [12.10.1910], f. 151, o. 482, d. 3068, ll. 107–09.

[29] Georgian National Historical Archive, Translation of appeal, f. Kantseliariia namestnika na Kavkaze, op. 27s, d. 3265, ll. 90–91. I thank Peter Holquist for this reference.

In service of state

Fear of pan-Islam was hardly a peculiarity of Russia's imperial administrators. Their British and French counterparts shared it, and in fact it was Europeans who coined the term in the 1870s.[30] The elites of these empires all shared deep anxieties regarding the loyalties of their Muslim subjects. The cultural gap between the dominant populations and their Muslim subjects was too large to make assimilation viable, and in an age increasingly receptive to the idea that sovereignty should be tied to ethnocultural identity, the notion that Muslims might find the benefits of these empires worth association was not persuasive. Logic itself seemed to suggest that at some point the Muslims must seek to separate. The doctrine of pan-Islam, of Muslim unity, intensified imperial anxieties. It conjured up images of brooding Muslim masses resentful of imperial rule and contemptuous of modern practices stirred to vengeful revolt by a fanaticism innate to their faith.

Given pan-Islam's "vitality" in the perception of Russian officials and the presence of so many Muslims in Russia, it is hardly surprising that the tsarist government made efforts to block the spread of the ideology from what many believed to be its source, the Ottoman empire. Among the measures the government adopted were to track the Muslim press in Russia and censor it as necessary; to check the Qurans and Quranic exegeses brought back from Ottoman lands by Muslim pilgrims to confirm they were not propaganda in disguise; to put under surveillance visitors from the Ottoman empire, including those who described themselves as wandering mystics or dervishes; to expel all Ottoman subjects from teaching positions and to ban textbooks printed in Istanbul; to restrict the visits of Ottoman subjects and to interrogate those who did visit.[31]

The activities of émigré Russian Muslims in the Ottoman empire presented a source of special concern to tsarist officials. The Russian embassy in Istanbul identified Ahmed Ağaoğlu and Abdurreshid Ibragimov (also known as Abdürreşid İbrahim) as Pan-Islamic ideologues inimical toward Russia and followed their activities.[32] The embassy's

---

[30] Adeeb Khalid, "Pan-Islamism in Practice: The Rhetoric of Muslim Unity and Its Uses," in *Late Ottoman Society: The Intellectual Legacy*, ed. Elisabeth Özdalga (London: RoutledgeCurzon, 2005), 201.

[31] AVPRI, Report on Muslims [author and date unknown], f. 151, o. 482, d. 3068, l. 132. These and similar policy suggestions raise the question of whom the Russians could employ to read the Muslim press; the number of Christian Russian subjects capable of reading the Muslim press must have been extremely limited and almost certainly the state had to rely on native Muslims to carry out this function.

[32] AVPRI, Chargé d'affaires in Constantinople to the Governor General of Turkestan, 29.9.1910 [12.10.1910], f. 151, o. 482, d. 3068, l. 109.

categorical description, however, reflected a crimped view of Ağaoğlu. Ağaoğlu's sharp shifts in ideological orientation, and in particular his support for building closer ties with the Russian empire and his role in the Turkish–Russian Committee, have already been mentioned. He was hardly an inveterate opponent of Russian civilization.

Ibragimov was more strident, but was amenable to working within the system. A Tatar born in Siberia, in 1857 Ibragimov studied in Medina for four years before returning home to become a mullah and member of the Orenburg Spiritual Assembly.[33] He left Russia and made his way to Istanbul where in 1895 he published what became a notorious attack on Russia's policies toward its Muslims. Its repetition in print of old rumors of an impending tsarist campaign to forcibly convert all the Tatars created a stir in the Volga region. After spending several years traveling to Japan and elsewhere and writing on the theme of Muslim unity, Ibragimov returned to Istanbul. His activism caught up to him in 1904 when Abdülhamid II's police arrested and deported him to Odessa, where authorities held him for two weeks. The opening of Russia's political system the following year offered him the opportunity to enter politics, and he took it. Together with Ağaoğlu and Yusuf Akçura, a Tatar intellectual from Simbirsk who as a child had emigrated to the Ottoman empire where he went on to play a leading role in Turkist thought and to join the CUP, Ibragimov participated in Russia's three "Muslim Congresses" that took place in 1905 and 1906. He helped establish a political party, the Union of Russian Muslims, which joined with the Russian Constitutional Democrat (Kadet) Party in elections for the Duma. During the revolutionary disturbances of 1905–07, Russia's Muslims remained calm, with the exception of some in the Transcaucasus who joined with Russians and Armenians in strikes.[34] Nicholas II's dissolution of the second Duma in June 1907 put an end to the Union of Russian Muslims, and in 1910 Ibragimov returned to Istanbul. There the embassy continued to regard him as an especially effective propagandist and figure behind the "particularly hostile" weekly *Tearüf-i Müslimin* (Muslims' mutual recognition).[35]

Whereas tsarist analyses routinely ascribed pan-Islam to the "aggressive intentions" and "thirst for vengeance" of Turks and Unionists,[36] a sober review of the evidence that the Russians gathered does not support

---

[33] Dzhamaliutdin Validov, *Ocherk istorii obrazovannosti i literatury Tatar* (Kazan: Iman, 1998), 64.

[34] Zenkovsky, *Pan-Turkism*, 35–54; İsmail Türkoğlu, *Sibiryalı Meşhur Seyyah Abdürreşid İbrahim* (Ankara: Diyanet Vakfı, 1997), 20–53.

[35] AVPRI, Report of the Military Agent in Turkey, 23.9.1910 [6.10.1910], f. 151, o. 482, d. 3068, l. 105.

[36] For example, see "Report of the Military Agent in Turkey."

the perception of a menacing pan-Islamic threat. The Russian reports cite individuals or at most small groups as being engaged in subversive activities. They reveal no good evidence of underground networks or arms smuggling, and when discussing events within the Russian empire refer almost exclusively to peaceful activities such as sermonizing, pamphlet distribution, and newspaper printing.

Indeed, one might consider pan-Islamic activity spanning the two empires to have been generated less by a shared *ressentiment* and more by desperation among the Ottomans and frustration among Russia's Muslims. As one embassy report observed, the Unionists were using pan-Islam in order to rally support at home and to raise money abroad to supplement their meager resources.[37] The example of the Chechen rebel Zelimkhan, famed for his attacks on Russian officials in the North Caucasus, is the exception that proves the rule. In 1913, a report alerted the Russian police that Zelimkhan and 300 others had crossed the Russo-Ottoman border with arms. The weapons they carried, however, were Russian-made and they were traveling to Istanbul, not from it, in order to take the Ottomans' side in the Balkan Wars.[38] Contrary to the assumption that pan-Islam was an Ottoman product that inflamed local tensions between the Russian state and its Muslims, such tensions at times produced pan-Islamic sympathies that were exported to the Ottoman empire.

Yet these sympathies, even when strongly felt, very rarely transcended local concerns to inspire physical action as they did in the case of Zelimkhan. Occasionally, the recognition of injustice stifled sympathy. In a series of dispatches on the Ottoman experience in the Balkan Wars that he wrote for Orenburg's Tatar-language newspaper *Vakt*, the Tatar Fatikh Kerimi poured forth his distress at the fate of Ottoman Muslims. The gap between the great powers' high rhetoric of humanitarian values and their cynical indifference to the massacres and barbarities perpetrated against the weaker Muslims disturbed and angered him. Yet the Ottomans' abject weakness also caused Kerimi to draw back and assure his readers that, linguistic and religious links notwithstanding, the Tatars were, in fact, a people separate from the Ottomans.[39] No one likes to

---

[37] AVPRI, Chargé d'affaires in Constantinople to the Governor General of Turkestan, 29.9.1910 [12.10.1910], Dispatch to Sazonov, 19.12.1910 [1.1.1911], f. 151, o. 482, d. 3068, ll. 109–11, 116.

[38] GARF, To the Head of the Special Department of Police Eremin, 7.1.1913 [20.1.1913], f. 529, o. 1, d. 13, l. 1.

[39] Norihiro Naganawa, "Letters from Istanbul: The Ottoman Empire and the First Balkan War Observed by a Tatar Intellectual," paper presented at the American Association for the Advancement of Slavic Studies, 39th annual conference, 15.11.2007.

associate his or her destiny with that of a society floundering on the brink of ruin.

At the same time that some Russian officials nursed inflated fears of pan-Islam and Ottoman subversion, others recognized that the danger was minimal. Junior officials with direct empirical knowledge at times argued against the idea that foreign factors influenced Russia's Muslims and pointed to local conditions as determinative in shaping the attitudes of Muslims. Thus when the minister of foreign affairs asked his subordinates in Istanbul whether the Young Turk movement might have instigated the activities of Ismail Gasprinskii, a prominent Crimean Tatar engaged in the cultural mobilization of Russian Muslims,[40] the response was that Gasprinskii and the Tatar reform movement were products of domestic circumstances and not a foreign-inspired plot.[41] In 1910 Charykov relayed to St. Petersburg an analysis that pan-Islam had little future since Muslims were too concerned with local issues.[42] One Russian Muslim, Ali Shahtahtinskii, who was investigating the activities of Russian Muslim students in Istanbul on behalf of the Russian government, concluded that their number was no more than seventy, and not only were they not engaged in any nefarious activity but they also would have preferred to remain in Russia if the secular educational opportunities for Muslims there had been equivalent.[43] The Russians' own intelligence sources in Istanbul reported that the Ottomans were frustrated by their lack of success in building organizational ties in the Caucasus.[44] Moreover, the circle of writers and intellectuals critical of Russia was quite small. Vastly greater numbers of Russian Muslims – pilgrims, merchants, students, and others – who traveled to and resided in the Ottoman empire preferred to retain their status as Russian subjects, and even many would-be immigrants voluntarily returned to the Russian empire.[45]

---

[40] AVPRI, Minister of Foreign Affairs to V. N. Lamzdorf, 31.12.1900 [13.1.1901], f. 151, o. 482, d. 3068, ll. 2–3.

[41] AVPRI, Zinev'ev to Minister of Foreign Affairs, 9.3.1901 [22.3.1901], f. 151, o. 482, d. 3068, l. 5. The greater irony is that Gasprinskii advocated not separation but the integration of Russia's Muslims into imperial Russian society. For more on Gasprinskii, see Edward Lazzerini, "Ismail Bey Gasprinskii and Muslim Modernism in Russia, 1878–1914," Ph.D. dissertation, University of Washington, 1973; Nadir Devlet, İsmail Bey Gaspıralı, 1851–1914 (Ankara: Kültür ve Turizm Bakanlığı, 1988).

[42] AVPRI, Letter from Charykov, 29.4.1910 [11.5.1910], f. 151, o. 482, d. 3068, l. 98.

[43] James Meyer, "Turkic Worlds: Community Representation and Collective Identity Formation in the Russian and Ottoman Empires, 1870–1914," Ph.D. dissertation, Brown University, 2007, 246, 250; James Meyer, "Immigration, Return, and the Politics of Citizenship: Russian Muslims in the Ottoman Empire, 1860–1914," International Journal of Middle East Studies, 39 (2007), 32 n. 77.

[44] Sarkisian, Ekspansionistskaia politika, 110–11, 116–17.

[45] See Meyer, "Immigration."

Such analyses from their subordinates notwithstanding, senior Russian officialdom exhibited a strong inclination to perceive pan-Islam and pan-Turkism as real internal threats whose origins lay outside the empire.[46] The same year that Charykov submitted his report, a special commission convened by Stolypin concluded that the Tatar reform movement was the result of a carefully organized pan-Islamist and pan-Turkist movement with foreign origins.[47]

Some pan-Islamic activists revealed themselves to be charlatans. One such poseur was a certain Sheikh Said, also known as Mullah Muhammad Said. Sheikh Said came to Istanbul in 1910. He claimed to be the sheikh ul-Islam from Kashgar, and indeed the Russian consul in that Central Asian city had in 1908 identified him as a major pan-Islamic activist. Initially Sheikh Said enjoyed great success in Istanbul, managing to meet with both the grand vizier İbrahim Hakkı Pasha and the sultan. After delivering a speech in fluent Arabic to a meeting of the CUP, he obtained a letter of recommendation from that organization addressed to the people of Kashgar. His act fell apart, however, when some students from Kashgar protested that their native land had never known a sheikh ul-Islam and that Sheikh Said was a deceiver. The Ottomans put the would-be sheikh ul-Islam of Kashgar on trial and discovered that he was in fact an Ottoman subject from Tripoli.[48] This incident of the false Kashgari is notable not simply for what it reveals about Sheikh Said, but perhaps even more for what it reveals about the Unionists and their relative ignorance about Central Asia.

Sheikh Said was not unique in his attempt to claim a tie to the CUP so that he could impress those beyond Ottoman borders with prestigious connections to a seemingly powerful movement. In the spring of 1911, a Doctor Karabekov, identified by Russian officials along with Ağaoğlu and Ibragimov as a leading pan-Islamist, falsely presented himself to the youth of Baku as an official sent by "Young Turkey." Not only was Karabekov, however, not an official CUP or Ottoman representative, but the Ottoman Foreign Ministry was actually working against him by

---

[46] Robert Geraci, *Window on the East: National and Imperial Identities in Late Tsarist Russia* (Ithaca: Cornell University Press, 2001), 277; Elena Campbell, "The Muslim Question in Late Imperial Russia," in *Russian Empire: Space, People, Power, 1700–1930*, ed. Jane Burbank, Mark von Hagen, and Anatolyi Remnev (Bloomington: Indiana University Press, 2007), 334–35.

[47] Robert Geraci, "Russian Orientalism at an Impasse: Tsarist Education Policy and the 1910 Conference on Islam," in *Russia's Orient: Imperial Borderlands and Peoples, 1910–1917*, ed. Daniel R. Brower and Edward J. Lazzerini (Bloomington: Indiana University Press, 1997), 142–43, 151.

[48] AVPRI, Chargé d'affaires in Constantinople to the Governor General of Turkestan, 29.9.1910 [12.10.1910], f. 151, o. 482, d. 3068, l. 107.

tracking his whereabouts and keeping the Russian government informed about the doctor's activities.[49]

Finally, aside from limited knowledge and scarce resources, domestic politics cramped the potential the Ottomans had to mobilize Russia's Muslims. In their zeal to maintain the empire's unity, Unionists closely regulated civil society organizations lest they be used as fronts for separatist activity. Restrictions on the ability of foreign subjects to lead and participate in such organizations impaired the ability of Central Asians and other Russian Muslims to build associations and networks that could, potentially, have been used against the tsarist state.[50]

Forward defense

Given the concern that the activities of Russian Muslim expatriates engendered in St. Petersburg, it is not surprising that the Russian government would instruct its embassies and consulates to keep tabs on them. Muslims could perform such tasks more effectively than non-Muslims, and so the tsarist empire employed them as spies. One such Muslim spy went by the name of Settar. Settar took up residence in the Hotel Caucasus, which was located right across from the Ottoman War Ministry. It was, however, the district's population of expatriate Muslims from Russia and not the War Ministry that interested him. Working with another resident of the hotel named Halid, Settar secretly tracked the movements and conversations of the expatriates and kept the Russian embassy informed of what he was learning. For his services, the embassy paid him a monthly salary of 300 gurushes. By November 1913, however, the Istanbul police were on to his espionage and his ties to the Russian embassy. The chief of the Istanbul police urged that Settar be expelled.[51] The Interior Ministry agreed, and instructed the Foreign Ministry to expel the Russian spy.[52]

Another Muslim Russian agent was the aforementioned Shahtahtinskii. Shahtahtinskii was a native of the Nakhichevan region in the Caucasus and former deputy to the Russian Duma. Before coming to Istanbul he had, together with his fellow Azeri, Ahmed Agaev (Ağaoğlu), published in Tiflis a weekly Turkic-language newspaper called "The Russian

---

[49] BOA, Foreign Minister Mehmed Rifat Pasha to the Interior Ministry, 16 Mart 1327 [29.3.1911], DH.SYS, D. 64, S. 28.

[50] Meyer, "Turkic Worlds," 250–51.

[51] BOA, Chief of the Istanbul Police to the Interior Ministry, 11 Teşrinisani 1329 [24.11.1913], DH.KMS, D. 6, S. 2.

[52] BOA, Interior Ministry to the Foreign Ministry, 13 Teşrinisani 1329 [26.11.1913], DH.KMS, D. 6, S. 2.

East" (*Şark-ı Rus*). In Istanbul Shahtahtinskii took up residence in the neighborhood of the Sublime Porte and commenced spying for the Russian government. Upon receiving a warning about him from the chief consul in Tiflis, the Ottoman foreign minister Mehmed Rifat Pasha urged the Interior Ministry to put the spy under surveillance and then expel him. Rifat Pasha advised that he be kept informed of what was happening in order to avoid any diplomatic missteps.[53] One year later, the Ottoman authorities were ready to act. Although they described Shahtahtinskii as a threat to the empire's "vital interests" and "external and internal security and peace," they were apprehensive lest his arrest spark a row. They decided in February 1912 to arrest him on the street, not in his home, which they feared would be too invasive. After arresting Shahtahtinskii, they were to put him on a ship that preferably would be Romanian, but definitely neither Russian nor French.[54] An irony of the matter was the aforementioned emphatic conclusion of Shahtahtinskii that Russian Muslims reluctantly studied in Istanbul because they could not acquire the equivalent secular education at home.

Not every politically troublesome Russian subject who visited the Ottoman empire was necessarily an agent of the Russian government. One agitator and resident of the Caucasus was Hussein Kami Kerimov, an owner of a publishing house. While in Istanbul, Kerimov took it upon himself publicly to denounce the Ottoman government and its policies. Advertising his lectures as academic in orientation, he invited members of various historical and scholarly societies as well as the Ottoman Naval Society to attend his presentation. But on 22 February 1913, far from a lecture on the state of science or similar topic, he delivered a sharp attack on the Ottoman government and pointed to it as the source of his audience's problems. Although there was no evidence that Kerimov was working directly for the Russian government, the Ottomans established a link between him and another Russian subject they had earlier deported and were convinced that Kerimov had entered their state with the intent to interfere in and disrupt its internal politics.[55] They decided to arrest and expel Kerimov, but were, again, attentive to the need to keep the Russian ambassador informed prior to taking action.[56] The Ottomans

---

[53] BOA, Foreign Minister to the Interior Ministry, 10 Şubat 1326 [23.2.1911], DH.SYS, D. 56, S. 10.
[54] BOA, Foreign Minister on Mehmed Shah Ağa Tahtinsky, 21 Kanunusani 1327 [3.2.1912], DH.SYS, D. 56, S. 10.
[55] BOA, Letter from Istanbul's General Director of Police, 15 Şubat 1328 [28.2.1913], DH.SYS, D. 55 1, S. 96.
[56] BOA, Letter from Istanbul's General Director of Police, 5 Mart 1328 [18.3.1912], DH.SYS, D. 55 1, S. 96.

were more forthright with regard to the case of another Russian subject from the Caucasus named Muhammad Hadi. When Hadi published a provocative essay critical of the practice of veiling among Muslim women, the authorities decided to try and expel him. Not content with the Russian subject's expulsion, this time the Ministry of War instructed the Foreign Ministry to contact the Russian embassy about the collection of the fine that the court had levied against Hadi.[57]

Although the answers to the questions of whether Kerimov and Hadi were working for the Russian empire are unknown, the Ottoman authorities certainly did not regard them as "their own" despite their Muslim faith and had no more compunction expelling them than they did Settar and Shahtahtinskii. They were all foreign subjects, regardless of faith, and therefore they were suspect. This view of non-Ottoman Muslims as subjects of foreign states with dubious loyalties was neither the product of an innovative Unionist attempt to forge an Ottoman identity nor of a Young Turk secularist orientation that downplayed the public significance of religion. Rather, it reflected an ongoing process in the centralization and rationalization of the Ottoman state and dated at least to the reign of Abdülhamid II. In a not so unusual irony of political behavior, the reign of the Ottoman sultan so commonly associated with pan-Islam had also seen the Ottoman state bureaucracy adopt the view that Russian Muslims were foreigners first and Muslims second.[58] The identification of constituents with their states, and the presumption of loyalty of the constituent to the state, affected the identities of those constituents not just at home, but even more so abroad. Regardless of the personal sentiments of individuals, in the modern age their state affiliation marked them abroad as well as at home.

Russian intelligence activities in Istanbul were not limited to passive intelligence gathering. Russia occasionally played a covert but highly disruptive role in the internal politics of the Ottoman capital. While Russian and British views of the Unionists shifted from positive to negative according to circumstance, the Unionists' increasing dominance over Ottoman politics following the 1913 raid on the Sublime Porte and their drift toward Germany concerned St. Petersburg. At the same time, some members of the main opposition party to the CUP, the Liberal Entente, sought to establish ties to the great powers with the hope of securing their outside backing in the struggle against their Unionist

---

[57] BOA, Interior Ministry to the General Directorate of the Istanbul Police, 6 Şubat 1327 [19.2.1912], DH.SYS, D. 57-1, S. 53.

[58] See Selim Deringil, "The Ottoman Empire and Russian Muslims: Brothers or Rivals?", in Deringil, *The Ottomans, the Turks, and World Power Politics: Collected Essays* (Istanbul: Isis Press, 2000), 73–82.

rivals. Although they stood against an increasingly authoritarian CUP, the Liberal Entente was less liberal, and less interested in freedom, than its name claimed. A determination to preserve local privileges and dominance motivated most of the members. Thus when, on 11 June 1913, a team of assassins struck down the CUP government's grand vizier, Mahmud Şevket Pasha, a conspiracy was not out of the question. The son of Georgian parents and raised in Iraq, Mahmud Şevket had been a capable and respected official with a high profile. He had not been a CUP member, but because his presence in the government lent the Unionists prestige he was a prime target for the CUP's opponents. Many observers at the time believed that his murder had been a calculated attempt to sow chaos and bring down the CUP government, and it shook up even the German government.[59]

Suspicion quickly fell on the Russians. One of the suspects in the conspiracy, Prince Sabahaddin, was known to have left Istanbul on a Russian ship shortly before the assassination, and rumors floated about the involvement of the Russian embassy's chief translator and insistent critic of the Unionists, Andrei Mandel'shtam. But the most suggestive evidence was the capture aboard a Russian ship of one of the suspected assassins, Kavaklı Mustafa. It was believed that shortly after the assassination he had fled to Russia. Ottoman authorities received word that Kavaklı Mustafa and another suspect in the assassination, Lt. Şakir Niyazi, were on a Russian vessel sailing between Odessa and Egypt. When on 23 November 1913 the ship docked in Istanbul, the Ottomans made their move. Acting on the orders of the chief of security Cemal Bey and the interior minister Talât Bey, several security officers stormed the ship. They ignored Kavaklı Mustafa's claims to extra-territoriality and seized him.[60] When the Russian ambassador Girs learned that Kavaklı Mustafa had been forcibly taken from a Russian ship, he immediately protested to the Sublime Porte and demanded his return. His appeals were in vain. Allegedly "urgent matters" had required Talât Bey to leave Istanbul for Edirne and in that time Kavaklı Mustafa was strangled to death. After protesting for several days with no result, Girs gave up. As a nominal consolation to the Russian ambassador, the Ottomans reassigned Istanbul's chief of police to Beirut.[61]

Şakir Niyazi, however, had managed to escape capture on the boat by disguising himself and subsequently took refuge in Odessa; he later

---

[59] Bayur, *Türk İnkılâbı Tarihi*, vol. II, pt. 3, 59, 107; Ertürk, *Perde Arkası*, 101.
[60] GARF, To Head of the Special Department of the Police Broetskii, 16.11.1913 [29.11.1913], f. 529, o. 1, d. 13, l. 34; Kurat, *Türkiye ve Rusya*, 200; Ertürk, *Perde Arkası*, 103–04.
[61] Ertürk, *Perde Arkası*, 105.

received an offer of a commission in the Russian army.[62] The CUP considered him enough of a threat that they dispatched two agents, one Turkish and one Armenian, to the Russian port to track his activities.[63] To what degree, if any, the Russians were involved in the assassination of Mahmud Şevket Pasha is not known. But the Unionists had good reasons for suspicion. The Russians had a known preference for the Liberal Entente, they had ties to the suspected assassins of Mahmud Şevket Pasha, and they were assisting other conspirators in Odessa and Batumi plotting to overthrow the Unionists.[64] Indeed, Sazonov personally was facilitating the operations of CUP opponents based in Batumi.[65]

Ottoman–Armenian cooperation against Russia

The Ottomans fully recognized their limited ability to challenge Russia and understood that the regeneration of their empire's power required an extended period of time engaged in internal reform. Thus, if they were to have any prospects for blunting Russian power they needed to maximize Russia's vulnerabilities. The Armenians constituted one such chink, and the Ottomans at times even dared to play the "Armenian card" against the Russians. Ottoman military intelligence in 1911 identified Armenian soldiers as a weak link in the Russian Caucasus Army. Not only did the Armenian soldiers have little loyalty to Russia, analysts wrote, but they were also spreading socialist ideas among the ranks and sapping the morale of the Russian army as a whole. Moreover, the achievements of the Ottoman constitutional regime were winning sympathy among Armenian circles in the Caucasus.[66]

Armenian revolutionaries were at times useful allies against the Russian state. Ottoman collaboration with Armenian revolutionaries against Russia had both passive and active components. The Ottomans, for example, permitted Armenian revolutionaries to shift their base of operations to the Ottoman empire after Stolypin's crackdown in 1908 and to carry out anti-Russian agitation on Ottoman territory. Armenian organizations in Istanbul and in Anatolia openly held fund-raising drives to raise money for bail and lawyers for Armenians imprisoned by the Russians. In 1911,

---

[62] Kurat, *Türkiye ve Rusya*, 200.
[63] GARF, To the Chief of the Gendarmerie of Odessa Zavarzin, 28.11.1913 [10.12.1913], f. 529, o. 1, d. 13, l. 43.
[64] AVPRI, Dispatch of the Ambassador in Constantinople, 31.3.1914 [13.4.1914], f. 151, o. 482, d. 3312, l. 25.
[65] Sazonov to Vorontsov-Dashkov, 3.1.1914 [21.12.1913], in *Movei*, ser. 3, vol. 1, 80.
[66] BOA, Jandarma Captain Nâzım Nazmi Efendi's report on the Caucasus, 14 Ağustos 1327 [27.8.1911], DH.SYS, D. 3, S. 7, F. 2-3.

at least one Ottoman Turkish newspaper, *İkdam*, contributed money for
the hiring of lawyers to defend twenty-one Ottoman Armenians charged
with armed resistance to tsarist authorities.[67] In Istanbul, the Dashnaks
distributed illegal socialist literature to Russian commercial sailors passing through. This disturbed Russian police, but they had no way to stop
it.[68]

Ottoman support for the Dashnaktsutiun also took active forms. In
1910 Russian authorities arrested an Armenian named Boghos Vaganian
for carrying out operations for the Dashnaktsutiun in the region of
Novocherkassk. Vaganian had been a member of the Dashnak Tiflis
committee and represented the federation's eastern bureau at its fourth
congress held in Vienna in 1907. Vaganian was also an Ottoman subject, and on this basis the Ottoman ambassador in St. Petersburg Turhan
Pasha intervened on his behalf. He requested that the Russians release
Vaganian and allow him to return to his homeland. The Russians, however, rejected the ambassador's petition and refused to let Vaganian go.[69]

Inside Iran, however, Ottoman support could be more effective. There,
to the dismay of Russian officials, the Dashnaks had been playing
a "leading role" in armed actions during the Iranian Constitutional
Revolution.[70] Istanbul had an interest in disrupting Russian control of
Iran and frustrating Russian policy. Collaboration with the Dashnaktsutiun was a logical means to that end. Through their consulates in
Khoy, Urmia, and Tabriz, the Ottomans provided Dashnak militants
with weapons, money, and legal protection. Ottoman diplomats issued
Ottoman passports to Armenian revolutionaries and permitted them
to fly Ottoman flags outside their residences, thereby providing them
immunity against Russian arrest.[71] When in March 1912 the Russian
authorities in Khoy detained a Dashnak known alternately as Hovannes
Parumov or Iapon Karabakhskii for assassinating a Russian colonel in
Yerevan, they found they were unable to extradite him. Karabakhskii was

[67] AVPRI, Report of the Translation Office of the Embassy in Constantinople, 22.3.1911
[4.4.1911], f. 180, o. 517/2, d. 3708, l. 108.
[68] GARF, To the Chief of the Gendarmerie Administration of Odessa Krechunesko,
26.6.1913 [9.7.1913], f. 529, o. 1, d. 11, l. 35.
[69] AVPRI, Foreign Minister to Charykov, 10.3.1910 [23.3.1910], f. 180, o. 517/2, d. 3562,
l. 68.
[70] Telegram from Miller (26.08.1911) [8.09.1911], Communiqué of Miller (31.08.1911)
[13.09.1911], in Russia, Ministerstvo inostrannykh del, *Sbornik diplomaticheskikh dokumentov kasaiushchikhsia sobytii v Persii. Vypusk VII (s 1 iiulia po 31 dekabria 1911 g.)*
(S. Peterburg: Gosudarstvennaia tipografiia, 1913), 121, 126. For more on the role of
the Dashnaks and other Armenians, see Berberian, *Armenians*.
[71] AVPRI, Sazonov to Girs, 8.3.1912 [21.3.1912], f. 180, o. 517/2, d. 3562, l. 23.

carrying an Ottoman passport and the Ottoman consul refused to permit extradition.[72]

Among Karabakhskii's accomplices in murder were at least two other Armenians, known as "Avank" and "Ruben." Like Karabakhskii, both were known to be working with the Ottoman consulate in Khoy.[73] Ruben, who earlier had served as a *boevik*, or fighter, in the Yerevan committee of the Dashnaktsutiun in 1905–07, had also taken part in planning an attack on the Russian consulate in Khoy in December 1913.[74] The Ottoman *şehbender*, or consul, in Khoy, Sadullah Bey, oversaw planning for that attack. He offered the mixed group of Armenian and Iranian conspirators the use of his own contingent of soldiers dressed in the style of a *serbaz*, or Iranian militiaman. Although the Armenians liked the idea, the Iranians vetoed it. Only if the Ottomans wore their distinctive fez, they protested, would the "friends of Iranian liberty" be convinced of the depth of Ottoman support against the Russians. Otherwise, the soldiers' participation would have little utility. Sadullah Bey was also alleged to be overseeing in conjunction with the Dashnaks the use of experienced Armenian fighters from the Caucasus for training and leading cells of local subversives. The saboteurs stockpiled explosives in and around the towns of Salmas and Khoy. Indeed, Ruben's own apartment, which served the local subversive network as a sort of headquarters, was located on the grounds of the Ottoman consulate in Khoy. Iranian and Armenian revolutionaries met inside the consulate building where they reportedly agreed to wage a war of terror targeting Russian officials, officers, and groups of soldiers. The hand grenade was their weapon of choice.[75]

In the spring of 1912 an Armenian doctor by the name of Ruben Mığırdıçyan was forced to seek refuge in that same Ottoman consulate in Khoy. He had left Van to sell his pharmacy in Iran and bring back his family. The Russian authorities claimed that he was a Russian subject and demanded that he be turned over to them. They accused him of carrying out anti-Russian agitation among the Armenians and of participating in at least one murder. The Ottoman consul, believing that Mığırdıçyan's life might even be in danger, however, coolly dismissed the Russians' charges. He asserted that the accused was in fact an Ottoman subject and had no ties to any revolutionary political organizations. Also taking refuge in the Ottoman consulate at the same time was a Muslim by

[72] AVPRI, Secret Telegram from Vorontsov-Dashkov, 13.3.1912 [26.3.1912], f. 180, o. 517/2, d. 3562, l. 27.
[73] AVPRI, Dispatch from Sazonov, 9.2.1912 [22.2.1912], f. 180, o. 517/2, d. 3562, l. 8.
[74] AVPRI, Telegram from Chirkov, 20.3.1912 [2.4.1912], f. 180, o. 517/2, d. 3562, l. 34.
[75] AVPRI, Vice-Consul in Khoy to the Imperial Emissary in Tehran, 23.3.1912 [5.4.1912], f. 180, o. 517/2, d. 3562, ll. 72–75.

the name of İbrahim Bakay. The Russians accused him of arming and inciting the Iranian Kurds against them and of participating in the murder of Russian soldiers.[76]

In the northern Iranian city of Tabriz, up to seventy revolutionaries were taking refuge in the Ottoman consulate that same spring. During the day, these revolutionaries moved about the city accompanied by personnel wearing the badge of the consulate.[77] Among the subversives availing themselves of Ottoman support was the Armenian Stepan Gevorkovich Stepaniants, also known as Tserun. After trying and convicting the former resident of Yerevan for a rape in Tiflis, tsarist authorities exiled him to Siberia. From there Stepaniants escaped to Iran. He made contact with the Ottomans and began working with them against the Russians.[78] To ward off the tsarist authorities Stepaniants flew an Ottoman flag over his house in Tabriz.[79]

Not surprisingly, such exploitation of the conventions of diplomatic practice infuriated the Russians. Not only were the Ottomans preventing them from seizing their assailants, but the Ottomans' abuse of diplomatic protocol was also enabling those assailants to flaunt their untouchable status openly. And, what was worse, the range of available responses was limited and the responses less than righteously satisfying. Short of going to war, the Russians could only apply diplomatic pressure to the Porte and set an example of reciprocation by dropping their own support in Iran for subversives working against the Ottoman empire. Thus, the Russian foreign minister ordered his ambassador in Tehran no longer to provide sanctuary to an Ottoman subject named Fettâh Bey lest the Ottomans cite the Russians' own violations of diplomatic norms as a pretext for ignoring their demands.[80]

Russian pressure did yield some results. On orders from Istanbul, Sadullah Bey began to withdraw support from the Armenians and Iranians in April 1912. Soon thereafter he was recalled from Iran following three years of service. Before Sadullah left, however, four Ottoman officers escorted Ruben safely to the town of Ezdihan. Other Armenian

---

[76] BOA, Consular Section of the Foreign Ministry to the Interior Ministry, 26 Teşrinisani 1328 [9.2.1912], Telegram from the Khoy Consul Sedat Bey 10 Mart 1328 [23.3.1912], DH.SYS, D. 13, S. 5, F. 2, 22.
[77] AVPRI, Telegram from Preobrazhenskii in Tabriz, 30.3.1912 [12.4.1912], f. 180, o. 517/2, d. 3562, l. 45.
[78] AVPRI, Sazonov to the Ambassador in Constantinople, 17.4.1912 [30.4.1912], f. 180, o. 517/2, d. 3562, l. 47.
[79] AVPRI, Telegram from Poklevskii in Tehran, 3.3.1912 [16.3.1912], f. 180, o. 517/2, d. 3562, l. 17.
[80] AVPRI, Sazonov to the Emissary in Tehran, 19.3.1912 [2.4.1912], f. 180, o. 517/2, d. 3562, l. 33.

revolutionaries followed afterwards.[81] The removal of Sadullah Bey, however, evidently did not put a complete end to Ottoman cooperation with the Dashnaks. Later that summer, the Russian Foreign Ministry protested to the Porte that a "tide of armed Armenians" had been pouring into Iran from the Ottoman empire. The Ottoman border posts were allowing them to pass freely with their weapons on their way to create havoc in Iran.[82]

Less than a year later the Russian vice-consul in Van argued to his superiors that turnabout was fair play, as Armenians now began bringing arms back into Ottoman Anatolia. At the request of the Iranian government, Russian military authorities on the Iranian border had been searching for and finding weapons smuggled by Armenians crossing into Ottoman territory. The vice-consul noted that the demand for the border inspections and searches had originally come from Istanbul. He advised that the border guards stop conducting such searches because it was the Ottomans themselves who previously had given most of the arms to the Dashnaks for use against Russians. The possibility that the Armenians would now turn those same weapons against the Ottomans only added a poetic justice of sorts.[83]

Improper imperial interaction: defectors, criminals, and converts

Crossborder interaction between the Ottoman and Russian empires was not limited to revolutionaries, terrorists, spies, and political agitators. Merchants, students, bandits, common criminals, smugglers, religious pilgrims, and nomads all crossed the borders in pursuit of their various goals. The human flows across borders sometimes induced cooperation, as when the two states coordinated the provision of armed escorts for merchant caravans.[84] At other times, it triggered competition. The regulation by states of the travel of individuals through the imposition of strict border regimes and implementation of passport control was still an evolving practice in the vast territories of Eurasia and the Middle East, and the two empires squabbled routinely regarding jurisdiction over

---

[81] AVPRI, Vice-Consul in Khoy to the Imperial Emissary in Tehran, 23.3.1912 [5.4.1912], f. 180, o. 517/2, d. 3562, ll. 75–76.
[82] AVPRI, Ministry of Foreign Affairs to the Ambassador in Constantinople and the Emissary in Tehran, 19.7.1912 [2.8.1912], f. 180, o. 517/2, d. 3562, l. 140.
[83] AVPRI, Report of Van Vice-Consul Olfer'ev, 25.3.1913 [7.4.1913], f. 180, o. 517/2, d. 3573, l. 83.
[84] BOA, Cabinet Decision Regarding Merchant Caravan Security, 15 Kanunusani 1327 [28.1.1912], MV, D. 161, S. 15.

itinerant subjects, who often were not above ignoring or exploiting loop-
holes to their personal benefit. For those who lived in the border regions,
especially nomads such as the Kurds, state boundaries were an unfortunate abstraction made concrete hindrance. They impeded but did
not completely sever contact between communities. For others, such
as Armenians, North Caucasian mountaineers, Cossacks, or Crimean
Tatars, the borders' function as a symbol of sovereign statehood was precisely what encouraged them to cross the boundaries, since it promised a
more benevolent order on the other side. Emphasis is, with reason, typically placed on the flow of Christians, generally Armenians, into the Russian empire and of Muslims from the North Caucasus and Crimea into
the Ottoman empire. It is important to note, however, that until World
War I there were important exceptions to this "unmixing of peoples."[85]
Muslims and Christians alike moved back and forth between the two
empires in significant numbers up until World War I.[86]

   But there was another category of migrant whose numbers, although
just a small proportion of the overall flow, were significant enough to
create traffic among government ministries at the highest levels: military
personnel. The movement of deserters went both ways, to the point that
by 1912 the two sides decided that they had to develop a joint protocol to regulate defections. Christian Ottoman soldiers were perhaps the
most obvious constituency for desertion. As part of their program to promote unity and equality, the Unionists in July 1909 had for the first time
in Ottoman history made military service compulsory for all Ottoman
subjects, regardless of religion. The Christian communities were deeply
ambivalent about shouldering the new burden.[87] The potential appeal of
the powerful and seemingly sympathetic Russian empire to disgruntled
Christian Ottoman conscripts is obvious, but Russia managed to attract
Muslim defectors also. Due to its proximity to Russia and the dissatisfaction of much of its population with Ottoman rule, Eastern Anatolia
was a relatively popular site for defections, but they sometimes occurred

---

[85] The phrase is Rogers Brubaker's. See his *Nationalism Reframed: Nationhood and the
National Question in the New Europe* (New York: Cambridge University Press, 1996).
[86] See Meyer, "Immigration." For more examples of North Caucasians seeking to return
to Russia, see AVPRI, Dispatch to the First Department of Internal Communications
of the Ministry of Foreign Affairs, 17.3.1910 [30.3.1910], f. 151, o. 502b, d. 2451,
l. 1. On communities of Cossack immigrants in the Ottoman empire, see "A Russian
Colony in Asia Minor," *The Orient*, 5 31 (5 August 1914), 307; and the notes of the
Ottoman Council of Ministers meetings on 19 Nisan 1327 [2.5.1911] and 8 Mayıs 1327
[21.5.1911], BOA MV 152, F.10/1, 52.
[87] Erik Jan Zürcher, "Ottoman Conscription in Theory and Practice," in *Arming the
State: Military Conscription in the Middle East and Central Asia, 1775–1925*, ed. Zürcher
(London: I. B. Tauris, 1999), 89–90.

elsewhere. Ottoman defeats in the Balkan Wars shook Ottoman authority and raised Russia's prestige among Muslims as well as Christians in Eastern Anatolia. Muslim and Christian military personnel in Istanbul were not immune to this effect, and both were found appealing to the Russian embassy for refuge.[88]

The attitude of Russian consular officials to Ottoman deserters was mixed. On the one hand, the Russians sometimes facilitated desertions by redressing the deserters in civilian clothes and issuing them Russian passports. On the other hand, the Russians were loath to encourage them for fear that the Ottomans might retaliate by inciting desertions among Russian military personnel, particularly Sunni Muslims.[89]

The Russians had cause to worry about desertions, and not only about those of their Muslim soldiers.[90] Christian Russian subjects, too, fled to the Ottoman empire. The defectors' ranks included, in addition to regular conscripts, Cossacks,[91] sailors,[92] officers,[93] and even government officials.[94] Generally, the defectors came over in small groups of one to four, although groups as large as twelve and even thirty also crossed into Ottoman territory to ask for refuge.[95] By land, they generally made their way to Erzurum and Hopa, while by sea they arrived at the Black Sea ports of Giresun and Trabzon.

The motives of the Christian defectors varied. Some were criminals who sought to evade prison sentences by escaping to the Ottoman empire.[96] Others claimed that they were dissatisfied with their

---

[88] BOA, Report from the Mutasarrıf of Beyoğlu, 30 Kanunusani 1328 [12.2.1913], DH.İD, D. 158, S. 9, F. 8.

[89] AVPRI, Telegram from Sablin, 23.8.1912 [5.9.1912], f. 180, o. 517/2, d. 3562, l. 128; BOA, Chief of the Istanbul Police to the Interior Ministry, 30 Kanunusani 1328 [12.2.1913], DH.İD, D. 158, S. 9, F. 5.

[90] ATASE, Telegram from Emin Pasha, 23 Teşrinisani 1328 [6.12.1912], Balkan Harbi Koleksiyonu, D. 72, K. 175, F. 1-3.

[91] BOA, Grand Vizier to the Interior Ministry, 8 Ağustos 1911 [21.8.1911], DH.SYS, D. 4, S. 5, F. 6.

[92] BOA, Chief of the Istanbul Police to the Interior Ministry, 24 Kanunuevvel 1327 [6.1.1912], DH.SYS, D. 4, S. 5, F. 107.

[93] BOA, Dispatch from the Governor of Trabzon, 8 Temmuz 1328 [21.7.1912], DH.SYS, D. 4, S. 5, F. 141; BOA, Ministry of Justice to the Foreign Ministry and the Police, 22 Kanunuevvel 1326 [4.1.1911], DH.İ.UM, D. 19-15, S. 1-12, F. 3.

[94] BOA, Telegram from Vali Mehmed Emin to Erzurum, 1 Kanunusani 1327 [14.1.1912], DH.SYS, D. 4, S. 5, F. 114.

[95] BOA, War Ministry Deputy Undersecretary to the Interior Ministry, 5 Eylül 1327 [18.9.1911], DH.SYS, D. 4, S. 5, F. 30; BOA, Report from the Treasury Ministry Deputy Undersecretary, 29 Kanunusani 1327 [11.2.1912], DH.SYS, D. 4, S. 5, F. 126.

[96] One Russian soldier and an Austrian who sought refuge in the Ottoman empire converted to Islam and explained that they wished to study in Istanbul. An investigation, however, revealed that the two were bandits. The Ottomans decided to expel them: BOA, Chief of the Istanbul Police to the Interior Ministry, 16 Teşrinisani 1327 [29.11.1911], DH.SYS, D. 4, S. 5, F. 95.

government or could no longer bear the harsh treatment and punishment meted out in the Russian army.[97] Ottoman intelligence reports on the Russian Caucasus Army suggest that there was much for the soldiers to be unhappy about. Morale was not high and material conditions were not good. Russian soldiers received salaries even smaller than those of their Ottoman counterparts and were dressed so shoddily that one shocked Ottoman observer compared the dingy condition of their uniforms to a stained chef's apron.[98] Tensions existed not just between Armenians and Russians, but also between Cossacks and Russian soldiers, and at times these tensions could flare into open clashes that demanded the full attention of Russia's generals.[99]

The Russian consul in Erzurum bemoaned the "nearly constant" flow of Russian deserters into the Anatolian town. Some deserters changed their minds about leaving their homeland for the Ottoman empire shortly after crossing over, and applied to the consulate for repatriation to Russia. Most Russian deserters, however, converted to Islam and became Ottoman subjects. The Ottoman authorities openly encouraged these conversions. At times they even invited the chief translator from the Russian consulate to the deserters' conversion ceremonies. Although the issue of converts may have piqued the Russians, it was the presence among the deserters of criminal fugitives who had fled the all too short arm of Russian law that really concerned them. But because Russia did not have a criminal extradition treaty with the Ottoman empire, consular officials had little leverage and had to resign themselves to the matter.[100]

Overall, the Ottoman authorities regarded the arrival of defectors and their expressions of sympathy for the Ottoman government as a cause for joy. But the defectors posed two difficult problems. One was a financial burden. The defectors needed to be fed, transported, resettled, and even sometimes schooled. Local budgets were not sufficient to cope with this added burden, and local officials routinely had to ask Istanbul for additional funds.[101]

Another, more insidious problem was the possibility that the Russian defectors could be criminals, or worse, spies. Interrogating and screening

[97] BOA, Report on Three Russian Soldiers' Defection, 12 Kanunusani 1327 [25.1.1912], DH.SYS, D. 4, S. 5, F. 123.
[98] BOA, Report of Jandarma Captain Nâzım Nazmi Efendi, 14 Ağustos 1327 [27.8.1911], DH.SYS, D. 3, S. 7.
[99] BOA, Report from Erzurum to the Interior Ministry, 28 Teşrinievvel 1328 [10.11.1912], DH.SYS, D. 112-7A, S. 7-49, F. 2.
[100] AVPRI, Consul in Erzurum Shritter to the Ambassador in Constantinople, 25.10.1910 [7.11.1910], f. 129, o. 502b, d. 4431, l. 7.
[101] BOA, Dispatch from the Deputy Undersecretary of the Minister of War, 15 Eylül 1327 [28.9.1911], DH.SYS, D. 4, S. 5, F. 22; BOA, Dispatch from the Interior Minister, 15 Kanunusani 1327 [28.1.1912], DH.SYS, D. 4, S. 5, F. 125.

the defectors constituted the first step to weeding out potential spies.[102] But since semi-competent spies could be expected to pass through a basic examination conducted just after crossing over to the Ottomans by changing their clothing and disguising their identity these measures were not sufficient. Thus, the Ottoman solution to the dilemma of spies posing as deserters was to eliminate the potential utility of any such spies by resettling them in places far from militarily sensitive border regions.[103]

The Ottomans took care also to settle particularly valuable defectors in specially selected areas. In these instances the motive was not to prevent the defectors from doing any harm to the Ottoman empire, but to prevent the Russians from doing any harm to the defectors. The Ottomans took seriously the possibility that the Russians might attempt to snatch and repatriate some of their former subjects forcibly. Russian consulates were the obvious bases and sources of muscle for such operations, so the Ottomans decided to resettle any particularly valuable defectors in areas far from Russian consulates.[104]

---

[102] As part of background checks, the Ottomans sometimes requested information about defectors from the Russian embassy, such as when one Russian who had arrived in Giresun asking to convert to Islam and become an Ottoman subject claimed to be a naval officer. The Ottomans doubted this, and when they asked the Russian embassy for confirmation they discovered that in fact the would-be officer had been an attendant at a military hospital: BOA, Foreign Ministry Deputy Undersecretary to the Interior Ministry, 29 Ağustos 1328 [11.9.1912], DH.SYS, D. 4, S. 5, F. 191.

[103] BOA, Grand Vizier to the Interior Ministry, 21 Ağustos 1328 [3.9.1912], DH.SYS, D. 4, S. 5, F. 189.

[104] BOA, Van Governor Mehmed Emin to Interior Ministry, 1 Kanunusani 1327 [14.1.1912], DH.SYS, D. 4, S. 5, F. 114.

4   Out of the pan and into the fire: empires at war

On 28 June 1914, a young Bosnian Serb terrorist decided to ignore last-minute orders from the Serbian army's General Staff to scrub his mission and fired two shots, killing the Austro-Hungarian heir apparent Archduke Franz Ferdinand and his wife in Sarajevo, the capital of the former Ottoman province of Bosnia. Austria-Hungary, backed by Germany, moved against Serbia on 28 July. The "Third Balkan War" had begun.[1] Russia mobilized in response, spurring Germany to declare war on both Russia and its ally, France, lest it wait and find itself trapped between the Russian steamroller coming from the east and the French in the west. By 3 August war had engulfed the continent of Europe. The Eastern Question that had bedeviled the Ottomans had not disappeared with their retreat, but had remained to plunge Europe and much of the world into the greatest cataclysm humankind had yet witnessed.

The outbreak of war presented a dilemma to the Ottomans. On the one hand, this time the war did not directly involve them, and they were not ready for another. As Enver had advised his fellow cabinet members in the spring, the Ottoman army needed at least five years of peace before it would be ready for a major war.[2] On the other hand, it was not clear that they could have the luxury of sitting it out. General expectations in Europe and elsewhere were that the war would revise the balance of power in Europe and beyond. Since all the great powers had interests and ambitions in the Near East, the war's outcome would necessarily have critical consequences for the future of the Ottoman empire.[3] Most observers expected that it would be short. The prevalent military doctrine held that the opening battles would decide the war in a matter of weeks. Popular economic analysis argued that the combination of modern war's awesome destructive power and economic costs guarantied that the war

[1] The term "Third Balkan War" is from Michael Howard, "The First World War Reconsidered," in *The Great War and the Twentieth Century*, ed. Jay Winter, Geoffrey Parker, and Mary R. Habeck (New Haven: Yale University Press, 2000), 19.
[2] Girs to Sazonov, 10.3.1914 [23.3.1914], *Movei*, ser. 3, vol. 2, 80.
[3] Feroz Ahmad, "The Late Ottoman Empire," in *Great Powers*, ed. Kent, 18.

would be brief.[4] Alongside danger, the eruption of major war in Europe presented Istanbul an opportunity. It transformed the Ottoman empire from the isolated "Sick Man" to a potentially desirable ally. By proffering their allegiance, the Ottomans could at least gain favor from one side or the other, and perhaps even a formal security commitment. And there was the chance that they could avoid entering the war at all.

The search for an ally

The key question was: With which side to join? Germany was a rising power and from a geopolitical perspective it was highly compatible. It shared no borders with the Ottoman empire, yet it did share Russia, Britain, and France as rivals. The German army had been involved in training and advising the Ottoman army for some three decades. The retired German field marshal and strategist Colmar Freiherr von der Goltz had acquired a devoted personal following among Ottoman officers during his nearly two decades of service in the Ottoman empire.[5] Even outside Goltz's circle, many admired the German army's professionalism. The most important of these admirers was Enver, who had served as a military attaché to Germany between 1909 and 1911 before becoming minister of war in 1913.

The Entente powers, however, offered their own advantages. Great Britain was the empire's biggest trading partner, it had been an ally in the past, and its naval advisory mission was nearly as large as Germany's military advisory mission. Russia's status as the greatest threat to the empire suggested counter intuitively that perhaps it might be wiser to accommodate Russian strength and get on the Entente "bandwagon" if this would secure a guaranty of non-aggression from Russia.[6] The logic of Talât's proposition to Sazonov at Livadia in May still held. France wielded great economic influence as the empire's largest lender and investor. The minister of the navy, Cemal Pasha, had long favored closer ties with France, and at his initiative the Ottomans had ordered naval vessels, aircraft, and artillery from France in order to draw that country closer.

---

[4] On military doctrine, see Jack Snyder, *The Ideology of the Offensive: Military Decision Making and the Disasters of 1914* (Ithaca: Cornell University Press, 1984). On economics, see Norman Angell's best-selling *The Great Illusion: A Study of the Relation of Military Power in Nations to Their Economic and Social Advantage* (London: G. P. Putnam's Sons, 1911).

[5] F. A. K. Yasamee, "Colmar Freiherr von der Goltz and the Rebirth of the Ottoman Empire," *Diplomacy and Statecraft*, 9, 2 (July 1998), 91–128.

[6] On "bandwagoning," see Arnold Wolfers, "The Balance of Power in Theory and Practice," in Wolfers, *Discord and Collaboration: Essays on International Politics* (Baltimore: Johns Hopkins University Press, [1962] 1991), 124.

Cemal traveled in July to Paris to sound out the possibilities for an alliance, but returned empty-handed as the French declined to provide any guaranty that might offend their key ally, Russia.[7] Opinion in the Ottoman cabinet was divided, with most members undecided.[8]

Unknown to most cabinet members, Enver had already begun pressing the Germans for an alliance. Senior German officials dismissed the idea initially, scoffing that an Ottoman ally would be a burden, not an asset. Enver countered by warning the German ambassador Hans von Wangenheim that neutrality was not an option for the Ottomans. Whereas he opposed joining the Entente because that would mean becoming Russia's vassal, Istanbul could pursue reforms only if it "were secured against attacks from abroad," and this required "the support of one of the Great Powers."[9] Germany would have to choose between an Ottoman ally and an Ottoman enemy.

The certainty of war with Russia prompted the Germans to recalculate. Kaiser Wilhelm II, roused by visions of angry Muslim hordes rebelling against British and Russian rule, leaned on Wangenheim to pursue talks with the Ottomans.[10] Wangenheim obliged, although some Germans held doubts about the likelihood of the Ottomans committing to enter the war. Enver's suggestion that two German warships being pursued by the British navy in the Mediterranean, the *Breslau* and the *Goeben*, take harbor in Istanbul helped convince Wangenheim that the Ottomans would indeed commit. Harboring the two warships would provoke Britain and also make possible naval and amphibious operations against Russia on the Black Sea.[11] On 2 August 1914 he went ahead and, with the grand vizier Said Halim, who was acting with the knowledge of only Enver and Talât, signed a secret treaty of alliance. The treaty promised German protection of Ottoman territorial integrity for five years and obliged the Ottomans to go to war with Russia if Russia declared war on Germany. Enver, Talât, and Said Halim informed the rest of the cabinet only after the deed. Cemal, though skeptical, assented. The finance

---

[7] Cemal Pasha, *Hatırat*, ed. Metin Martı (Istanbul: Arma Yayınları, [1920] 1996), 105–16; Kurat, *Türkiye ve Rusya*, 228.

[8] Şevket Süreyya Aydemir, *Enver Paşa*, vol. II, 511; F. A. K. Yasamee, "Ottoman Empire," in *Decisions for War*, ed. Keith Wilson (London: UCL Press, 1995), 233–34; M. S. Anderson, *Eastern Question*, 311.

[9] Ulrich Trumpener, *Germany and the Ottoman Empire, 1914–1918* (Princeton: Princeton University Press, 1968), 18–20.

[10] McKale, *Revolution*, 47; Luigi Albertini, *The Origins of the War of 1914*, vol. III (New York: Oxford University Press, 1957), 613; Fritz Fischer, *Germany's War Aims in the First World War* (New York: W. W. Norton and Company, 1967), 121.

[11] Mustafa Aksakal, *The Ottoman Road to War in 1914: The Ottoman Empire and the First World War* (New York: Cambridge University Press, 2008), 103–04.

minister, Cavid Bey, objected vigorously, predicting that mobilization would bankrupt the empire and that a German defeat would lead to the empire's final liquidation.[12] The treaty gave the Ottomans what they had wanted most: a German guaranty of Ottoman security. The cabinet, including Enver and Talât, now sought to delay entry into the war as long as possible, ideally until it was already over. Thus, on 3 August, the government announced both that it was mobilizing the army and that it was maintaining neutrality. Although Germany was already at war with Russia, the Ottomans consistently deflected German pressure to enter the war by arguing that they needed to complete the mobilization of their army first.[13]

Shortly after the signing of the treaty, Enver pitched the idea of an alliance to Girs. He assured Russia's military attaché General M. N. Leont'ev that Istanbul valued friendly relations with Russia for the unimpeachable reason that even a defeated Russia would remain stronger than the Ottoman empire and capable of inflicting damage upon it. Germany, by contrast, shared no border and thus could not avenge itself on the Ottomans so easily. Enver offered to withdraw all forces from the Caucasus and redeploy most of them to Thrace to neutralize the armies of one or more Balkan states or even engage Austria-Hungary. In return the Ottoman empire would recover some of the northern Aegean islands and western Thrace. Enver added that an Ottoman–Russian alliance would render rebellion by Caucasian Muslims and Armenians "inconceivable" and secure tranquility for both empires.[14] Whether or not Enver was at all sincere in his overtures is impossible to know, but Girs, "deeply convinced" that "the historical moment" to "finally subordinate Turkey" had arrived, urged St. Petersburg to consider seriously Enver's proposal. Yet Sazonov brushed off the advice, assuring Girs, "possible action by Turkey against us directly gives us no anxiety."[15]

As the Russians and Ottomans batted back and forth the notion of an alliance, Britain's First Lord of the Admiralty Winston Churchill destroyed what, if any, chance still existed of the Ottomans joining the Entente by commandeering from British shipyards two battleships the Ottomans had ordered and already paid for. The act provoked

---

[12] Türkgeldi, *Görüp İşittiklerim*, 114.
[13] Aksakal, *Ottoman Road to War*, 152, 193; Albertini, *Origins*, 615; Bayur, *Türk İnkılâbı Tarihi*, vol. II, pt. 4, 642–43.
[14] AVPRI, Telegrams from Girs, 23.7.1914 [5.8.1914], 27.7.1914 [9.8.1914], f. 151, o. 482, d. 4068, ll. 10, 28; Kurat, *Türkiye ve Rusya*, 230–35.
[15] Albertini, *Origins*, 619; AVPRI, Telegram from Girs, 23.7.1914 [5.8.1914], Telegram from Girs, 24.7.1914 [6.8.1914], Sazonov to Girs, 27.7.1914 [9.8.1914], Chief of Staff of the Supreme Command to Sazonov, 27.7.1914 [9.8.1914], f. 151, o. 482, d. 4068, ll. 14, 17, 25, 29.

widespread anger among the Ottoman elite and public alike, not least because a popular subscription campaign had helped pay for the ships. The Germans, however, feared that the British might still intimidate the Ottomans to join the Entente. Exploiting such fears, Said Halim extracted from Wangenheim in exchange for definitive permission for the *Breslau* and the *Goeben* to enter Istanbul's harbor a promise to fulfill six conditions: (1) support for abrogation of the capitulations; (2) support for the Ottomans in negotiations with the Bulgarians and Romanians and in the division of any spoils of war with Bulgaria; (3) refusal to conclude any peace until all Ottoman territory had been liberated from enemy occupation resulting from the current war; (4) return of the Aegean islands in the event of Greek intervention and defeat; (5) securing a border change in Eastern Anatolia that would put the Ottomans in contact with "Muslim elements in Russia"; and (6) procurement of the payment of appropriate reparations to the Ottoman empire.[16] The fifth condition shows that the Ottomans had an interest in changing the Russo-Ottoman border. Given their interest in altering their empire's Balkan and Aegean borders, this is perhaps not surprising. Its vague and, given the third condition, even tentative formulation suggests that there was no expectation of overturning the balance of power in the Caucasus, but instead a hope to alter the status quo somewhat in the Ottoman empire's favor.

Upon seeing the German warships slip into Istanbul and out of their grasp, the British demanded that the Porte surrender the vessels or forfeit neutrality. The Ottomans finessed the problem by arranging a sham purchase of the vessels from Germany and redressing the crews in Ottoman naval uniforms. This incident, reports of efforts to arrange an anti-Russian alliance with Bulgaria and Romania, and rumors of Ottoman claims on Batumi raised Sazonov's suspicions that the Ottoman empire had already thrown its lot in with Germany. Some on the Council of Ministers, such as the influential minister of agriculture Aleksandr Krivoshein, hoped this was the case since it would allow Russia to go to war and solve its problems in Asia Minor once and for all.[17] Sazonov learned from a third party, however, that the Ottoman chargé d'affaires in St. Petersburg favored an alliance with Russia. Sazonov saw no point in peremptorily breaking off talks and driving the Ottomans into German

[16] Aksakal, *Ottoman Road to War*, 114–15; Gotthard Jäschke, "Der Turanismus der Jungtürken. Zur osmanischen Aussenpolitik im Weltkriege," *Die Welt des Islams*, 23, 1–2 (1941), 10–11.

[17] B. D. Gal'perina, ed., *Sovet ministrov Rossiiskoi imperii v gody pervoi mirovoi voiny: bumagi A. N. Iakhontova* (St. Petersburg: Dmitrii Bulanin, 1999), 43.

hands.[18] Girs believed that the Ottomans could still be lured from the Germans and found Enver and Said Halim's proposed claims on the Aegean islands and western Thrace reasonable. Sazonov did not rule out such a swap of Balkan territories, and discussed the idea with his ambassadors in Paris and London as well as with Girs.[19] On the Ottoman side, Said Halim and Cavid Bey were seeking ways to work with the Entente so as to undermine Enver's stance and keep the empire neutral, and Cemal, too, suggested possible formulae for Ottoman neutrality.[20] The British, however, grew weary of such temporizing. On 26 September British warships patrolling off the Dardanelles chased an Ottoman torpedo boat back up the straits. In response, the Ottomans shut the straits to all traffic, including commercial shipping.

The closing of the straits effectively ended Ottoman neutrality, and made the empire a power hostile to Russia in all but the formal sense. Writing on 11 October, Girs labeled the straits "undoubtedly the most vital" question for Russia. Russia's security required free passage, and free passage demanded that Russia seize Istanbul for itself. Converting it into a "free city" was not an option, Girs explained, because life does not recognize ownership in common and "a free city can last only until the first caprice of the nearest neighbor." Girs highlighted the "cunning and guile" of the Ottoman officials who utilized their "customary deceit" to cozen the Russians. Yet he was hardly averse to deviousness himself. The catastrophic defeat the Russian army had suffered in early September at the battle of Tannenberg in East Prussia had caused some to argue for war against the Ottomans as a way to acquire easy gains to offset that disaster.[21] Girs disagreed. It would be preferable to convince the Ottomans to remain neutral. This way Russia could crush Germany more expediently. Then, after Germany was defeated, "we will easily find a fully sound pretext for declaring war on Turkey." But in the likely event Istanbul ended its neutrality, Girs counseled, we must obtain "the total abolishment of the straits question."[22]

From September through the first half of October, the Russians had, through intercepted communications and secret agents, been acquiring information about German and Ottoman plans to attack the Black Sea

[18] Bobroff, *Roads*, 98–101; AVPRI, Sazonov to Girs, 30.7.1914 [12.8.1914], f. 151, o. 482, d. 4068, l. 38.
[19] AVPRI, Sazonov to the Ambassador in London, 3.8.1914 [16.8.1914], f. 151, o. 482, d. 4068, l. 58.
[20] Yasamee, "Ottoman Empire," 247.
[21] AVPRI, Telegram from the Envoy in Sofia, 29.9.1914 [12.10.1914], f. 151, o. 482, d. 4068, l. 226.
[22] AVPRI, Girs to Trubetskoi, 28.9.1914 [11.10.1914], f. 151, o. 482, d. 4068, ll. 222–24.

Fleet and conduct an amphibious operation near Odessa.[23] But it was the report of the arrival of German gold that clinched the suspicion that the Ottomans were now irrevocably tied to the Germans.[24] Just as Cavid Bey had warned, the mobilization had nearly bankrupted the government. Enver sidestepped the matter by arguing that, with the German army stymied in France and Austria-Hungary's army suffering setbacks, the war would not end soon. The Ottoman empire's value as an ally, however, was now greater than ever, and it was in any event a propitious moment to ask for a loan. Cavid objected that taking a loan would be tantamount to committing the empire to war, as Germany would demand war in exchange for financing. Cavid's instincts proved right, but Talât, Cemal, and Halil had already moved to Enver's position in favor of closer ties to Germany.[25] The first consignment of gold arrived on 16 October, and the second on 21 October. That same day Enver met with German officers to finalize war plans. As part of those plans, he ordered the Ottoman navy out into the Black Sea to attack without warning any Russian warships and shore targets they encountered.[26]

War formally begins

On 29 October a flotilla of Ottoman warships sailed out on the Black Sea and then divided into two squadrons. One squadron headed for Odessa and the other for Sevastopol and Novorossiisk. The warships shelled targets in and around these port cities, inflicting slight damage but achieving a momentous political effect. The Unionist government in a bald lie publicly described the operation as an act of retaliation. News of the attack sparked a falling-out in the cabinet, where only two or three other ministers beside Enver had foreknowledge of the attack. Whereas some were pleased that the Ottoman fleet had taken the war to the Russians, others were furious. Four ministers, including Cavid, resigned in protest. Enver and Talât managed to retain Said Halim as grand vizier only after much insistent pleading.[27]

---

[23] German Lorei, *Operatsii germano-turestskikh morskikh sil v 1914–1918 gg.* (Moscow: Gosudarstvennoe voennoe izdatel'stvo, 1934), 62; Bayur, *Türk İnkılâbı Tarihi*, vol. III, pt. 1, 203; AVPRI, Dispatch from Girs, 30.9.1914 [13.10.194], f. 151, o. 482, d. 4068, l. 227.

[24] AVPRI, Sazonov to the Commander of Naval Forces in Sevastopol, 7.10.1914 [20.10.1914], f. 151, o. 482, d. 4068, l. 234.

[25] Kurat, *Türkiye ve Rusya*, 243; Trumpener, *Germany*, 48–51.

[26] Mustafa Balcıoğlu, *Teşkilat-ı Mahsusa'dan Cumhuriyete*, 2nd edn. (Ankara: Asil Yayın Dağıtım 2004), 51.

[27] Kurat, *Türkiye ve Rusya*, 245.

The Entente states protested the attacks. In response, the Porte indicated it was prepared to make amends and even pay compensation, but balked at demands to expel the Germans and disarm the German warships in Ottoman service.[28] The Entente states cut relations. On 31 October Tsar Nicholas II declared war on the Ottoman empire and on 2 November Girs quit Istanbul. Britain and France followed with their declarations of war on 4 November, and then the Ottoman empire replied in kind. The struggle for control of Anatolia and the Caucasus was now joined in the open.

There can be little doubt that Enver Pasha had been intent on securing a formal alliance with Germany from the July Crisis onward. But his overtures to Girs had not been meaningless. Although Enver may have been certain that he wanted an alliance with Germany, no such consensus existed in the cabinet of ministers. The disagreements were real. Enver had managed to persuade Talât, Halil, and eventually Cemal, but had still felt compelled to engineer the entrance into the war furtively. What divided the Ottoman leadership was not disagreement over the ultimate ends of policy – the preservation of their state – but rather the tactical question of how best to achieve the external security that would make it possible to carry out the deep and wide-ranging internal reforms the empire required for survival. All recognized the empire's tremendous weakness and that expressions of good intent, conventions, and notions of international law ultimately counted for little and indeed at times served as tools that the strong used to exploit the weak. The empire needed a great power patron that could provide some degree of protection. They differed, however, over how to respond to the outbreak of war in Europe. Enver identified Germany as the best potential patron on account of its geopolitical compatibility and the likelihood of winning the war, and believed it would be better to act sooner while the Ottoman empire's offer of an alliance still held value.[29] Once he obtained that alliance, he delayed the entry into the war in the hope that the war would be over before the Ottomans would have to join in. Enver was no pacifist, but he understood the sorry state of the Ottoman army. The plans and thinking of Russian diplomats and military officials even before the war demonstrate that Enver's assessment of the empire's strategic dilemma – that if it did not act now when it had a chance of joining a victorious coalition it would be snuffed out sooner or later – was sound.

If Russian diplomacy just prior to the war was not as duplicitous as Ottoman diplomacy, it was because St. Petersburg had the luxury of

---

[28] Bayur, *Türk İnkılâbı Tarihi*, vol. III, pt. 1, 248–49, 252.
[29] Aksakal, *Ottoman Road to War*, 193.

adopting a passive stance. St. Petersburg's desire for the Ottoman empire
to stay out of the war was equivocal. Some officials welcomed Ottoman
entrance into the war as an opportunity to destroy it once and for all and
fulfill Russia's ambitions in the straits and Anatolia. Those who preferred
to keep the Ottomans out of the war did so because they believed that it
was more important to concentrate on defeating Germany, not because
they lacked ambitions in the Ottoman lands. This is not to say that such
ambitions were the product of a simple desire for aggrandizement. Hubris
and a thirst for imperial glory did play a role in Russian decisionmaking,
but the structural incentives behind Russian policies were strong. As
World War I would demonstrate, the Black Sea Straits were indeed vital
to Russia. Despite the vastly different places their states occupied in the
global hierarchy, the elites of the Ottoman and Russian empires both had
to make decisions within the same context of a competitive and anarchic
global system in which states rose or fell according to their own efforts
and abilities.

Strategy and rending the fabric of empire

While ambassadors and ministers in Istanbul and St. Petersburg were
busily, if somewhat disingenuously, trading and proffering plans for peace
and good intentions to forestall the onset of war, in the borderlands
hostility had been building steadily. The region remained uneasy in the
wake of the Bitlis rebellion, and the recognition that with the Armenian
Reform Program it was slipping out of Ottoman control kept tensions at
a high level. Kurds in Anatolia and Iran continued to conduct raids, and
the Dashnaktsutiun urged Armenians to arm. In June, a delegation of
Ottoman Assyrians asked the Russian vice-consul in Urmia for 35,000
rifles, promising that they were prepared to rise up at the Russians'
command in the likely event of a war.[30]

As Russian suspicion of Ottoman dealings with Germany grew through
August, so did interest in mobilizing anti-Ottoman elements inside the
empire. In line with Minorskii's advice to split non-Turkish groups from
the center, Sazonov in mid August agreed with Vorontsov-Dashkov that
the Kurds, Armenians, and Assyrians would be of great use in a war. Consular and military intelligence reports predicted that the Ottoman Armenian and Assyrian communities would assist an invading Russian force
and described large numbers of Kurds as sympathetic toward Russia.[31]

[30] A. O. Arutiunian, *Kavkazskii front, 1914–1917 gg.* (Yerevan: Aiastan, 1971), 52.
[31] Arutiunian, *Kavkazskii front*, 53; AVPRI, Telegram from the Head of the Consulate in
Van, 24.7.1914 [6.8.1914], f. 151, o. 482, d. 4104, l. 59.

With a Russian army of some 300,000 mobilized on the Caucasian border, Ottoman authorities found the sympathies and activities of the Armenians worrisome. This gave rise to fearful speculation. Rumors circulated that Armenian revolutionaries were sending their families into Russia – an ambiguous act but one that officials interpreted as a sign of impending rebellion. From the Caucasus came reports of Vorontsov-Dashkov's feting of Armenian leaders and of Armenian gangs threatening Muslims with vengeance for the massacres of 1895.[32] Istanbul instructed its officials in the region to investigate these rumors. The governor of Van reported that not only had no Armenian families left, but the Dashnaks were assisting the government with conscription and that Armenian feeling toward Russia was ambivalent.[33] Authorities in Trabzon, too, related that, contrary to rumors, no Armenian families had left the province for Russia. In his report of 20 August the deputy governor of Erzurum on the one hand questioned the sincerity of Armenian promises to take up arms for the empire but on the other hand noted that the town's Armenians were maintaining cordial relations with their Muslim neighbors.[34] Five days later, however, Erzurum's gendarmerie confirmed that Russian Armenians in the town were sending their families back across the border to Aleksandropol.[35] Three Russian soldiers who defected at the end of August explained that Armenian activists were conducting anti-Turkish propaganda among Russian soldiers and distributing arms to their compatriots along the border.[36] In late September Enver informed the command of the Ottoman Third Army that Hnchak and Dashnak revolutionaries had agreed with the Russians to provoke Ottoman Armenians to rebel.[37]

Enver and other Unionists were not averse to the idea of trying to turn the Armenians against the Russians. Just as the Dashnaktsutiun was wrapping up its eighth congress in Erzurum, a delegation of Unionists led by Dr. Bahaeddin Şakir arrived to propose an alliance. In exchange for inciting a rebellion inside Russia the Dashnaks would receive an

---

[32] ATASE, Telegram from the Ninth Army, 3 Ağustos 1330 [16.8.1914], BDH, K. 2818, D. 59, F. 2.

[33] ATASE, Telegram from the Governor of Van, Tahsin Bey, 12 Ağustos 1330 [25.8.1914], Telegram from the Commander of the 33rd Division, 12 Ağustos 1330 [25.8.1914], BDH, K. 2818, D. 59, F. 2-2, 2-3.

[34] ATASE, Report to the Third Army Command, 7/8 Ağustos 1330 [20/21.8.1914], BDH, K. 2818, D. 59, F. 2-4.

[35] ATASE, Report to the Third Army Command, 12 Ağustos 1330 [25.8.1914], BDH, K. 2818, D. 59, F. 2-4.

[36] ATASE, Report to the Third Army Command, 17/18 Ağustos 1330 [30/31.8.1914], BDH, K. 2818, D. 59, F. 2-5.

[37] ATASE, Enver Paşa to the Third Army Command, 12/13 Eylül 1330 [25/26.9.1914], BDH, K. 2818, D. 59, F. 2-19.

autonomous Armenia consisting of Russian Armenia and several districts around Erzurum, Van, and Bitlis. The Unionists had thin credibility to begin with and, given their commitment to centralized rule, the sudden offer of autonomy probably struck the revolutionaries as fantastic. The Dashnaks declined the offer, diplomatically explaining that Armenians on either side of the border should stay loyal to their respective governments.[38]

On the eastern side of that border, Vorontsov-Dashkov had been urging the arming and mobilization of Ottoman Armenians, Assyrians, and Kurds. Sazonov, not wishing to provoke the Ottomans, initially held off. But on 20 September, convinced that war with the Ottomans was inevitable, he approved Vorontsov-Dashkov's request to arm the Ottoman Armenians and "provoke their uprising at an opportune moment."[39] The Armenian National Council cooperated with the government to establish four volunteer regiments, known as *druzhiny*, to serve in an invasion. Some prominent Ottoman Armenians, such as former member of the Ottoman parliament Karekin Pastermaciyan (Pastermajian), also known by his revolutionary moniker "Armen Garo," joined the regiments. Others declined, predicting that the formation of such regiments would put the safety of Ottoman Armenians at great risk.[40] Nonetheless, hundreds of Ottoman Armenians in the fall began crossing into Russia and Iran to take up arms. Among them was Ruben Mığırdıçyan, the pharmacist who had earlier with Ottoman support carried out attacks on Russians in Iran.[41]

The approach of war saw tensions increase palpably on both sides of the border. Inside Eastern Anatolia and Russian-occupied Iran, where state authority was openly contested and where state agents in places became openly hostile toward state subjects, hostility expressed itself in physical violence. Some Unionists, assisted at times by Germans, were whipping up anti-Armenian and anti-Christian fervor. Public hostility toward Russia hardened. In Erzurum, officials expropriated the property of Russian subjects, including that of Muslims, and confiscated rice and provisions belonging to Armenians.[42] In Diyar-ı Bekir, officials stood

---

[38] Hovannisian, *Armenia on the Road*, 41–42; Somakian, *Empires in Conflict*, 72–73.
[39] Bobroff, *Roads*, 111. Firuz Kazemzadeh writes that the Russians provided 200,000 rubles to the Dashnaks: Firuz Kazemzadeh, *The Struggle for Transcaucasia* (New York: Philosophical Library, 1951), 26. Some cabinet ministers objected strongly to the idea of arming the Dashnaks, seeing them as anti-Russian "criminals": Gal'perina, ed., *Sovet ministrov*, 74.
[40] Hovannisian, *Armenia on the Road*, 44; Somakian, *Empires in Conflict*, 74–75.
[41] ATASE, Report on Developments Around Rumiyye and Selmas, 1 Teşrinievvel 1330 [14.10.1914], BDH, K. 2818, D. 59, F. 2-36.
[42] AVPRI, Telegram from Girs on 4.8.1914 [17.8.1914], f. 151, o. 482, d. 4104, l. 115.

by when an Armenian market went up in flames.[43] Ottoman Assyrians hurried into Iran in search of refuge.[44] Pillaging by Muslim tribesmen increased. According to Girs, by October Ottoman Christians were in incomparably greater danger than they had been in the Balkan Wars.[45]

Inside Russian-occupied Iran, Kurdish bands encouraged by Ottoman propaganda for holy war against infidels began burning churches and wreaking havoc. Christians responded by forming militia units.[46] Russian-backed Kurds, including those led by Simko, and the gangs of the Assyrian Agha Petros struck Ottoman targets. German and Austrian citizens came under harassment, and in Rumiye a Russian army unit ransacked German and Austrian trade houses.[47] As clashes between hostile Kurds and Russian units escalated to regular combat, Vorontsov-Dashkov ordered the army: "Punish the Kurds mercilessly, not neglecting the most extreme measures, especially toward the leaders."[48] By October the border region was already in a virtual state of war.

Although inside Russia no comparable breakdown of order took place, there, too, the mood steadily grew uglier. The press adopted a stridently anti-Ottoman tone. Authorities in Odessa put the Ottoman consul under tight surveillance and took precautions against the possibility of revolt. In Odessa, Sevastopol, and elsewhere along the Black Sea coast the police rounded up some 380 suspected "Turkish spies." In Tiflis the authorities arrested and interrogated leading Muslims on suspicions of espionage.[49]

While there is no dispute that religious antagonism framed much of the violence unfolding in Eastern Anatolia and the Caucasus on the eve of the war, it would be a mistake to conclude that the events represented simply the surfacing of latent currents of hostility. Other factors played important roles. The mobilization imposed intense hardship on all. It sent prices skyrocketing, induced shortages of staples, and fed speculation. Fear of war was roiling other areas, for example spurring Muslims on the Mediterranean coast to flee inland toward Damascus. Ottoman Muslims, not just Armenians, avoided and resisted conscription, at times violently.

---

[43] Somakian, *Empires in Conflict*, 75–76.
[44] L. M. Sargizov, *Assiriitsy stran Blizhnego i Srednego Vostoka* (Yerevan: Aiastan, 1979), 25; Gaunt, *Massacres*, 96.
[45] AVPRI, Dispatch from the Ambassador in Constantinople, 10.10.1914 [23.10.1914], f. 151, o. 482, d. 4068, l. 240.
[46] Sargizov, *Assiriitsy*, 24; Arutiunian, *Kavkazskii front*, 66.
[47] Bayur, *Türk İnkılâbı Tarihi*, vol. III, pt. 1, 223–26.
[48] Vladimir Genis, *Vitse-konsul Vvedenskii: sluzhba v Persii i Bukharskom khanstve (1906–1920 gg.)* (Moscow: Mysl', 2003), 31.
[49] Vahdet Keleşyılmaz, "Kafkas Harekâtının Perde Arkası," *Ankara Üniversitesi Osmanlı Tarihi Araştırma Merkezi Dergisi*, 11 (2001), 283; ATASE, Report from the Foreign Ministry to the War Ministry, 16 Eylül 1330 [1.10.1914], K. 241, D. 2-1001, F. 54.

In an effort to enforce conscription, the Ottoman state began confiscating the property of all draft-dodgers, Muslim as well as Christian. Indeed, resentment of conscription and its enforcement were enough to provoke some Ottoman Muslim Laz to cross into Batumi and consider the possibility of rebelling and attaching their lands to the Russian empire.[50]

Russian and other foreign observers often attributed the increase in pillaging and other forms of depredation by Iranian Kurds to pan-Islamic propaganda conducted by German and Ottoman agents. A closer examination, however, reveals that this explanation is not sufficient. First, the Kurds allied with Russia also conducted raids and looting, the only difference being that their targets were Ottomans and those close to them. Non-Muslim warlords such as the Assyrian Agha Petros had no need for notions of jihad to inspire their acts. Second, to the extent it succeeded, the propaganda of pan-Islam was never far from material incentives. In order to sway the Kurds and other Muslims in Iran to join their jihad, the Ottomans emphasized that all booty and loot acquired in the course of the jihad was *helâl*, or religiously permissible, and belonged in its entirety to its captors.[51] Similarly, in Trabzon the Teşkilât-ı Mahsusa, the so-called Special Organization used to conduct irregular warfare, espionage, and other unconventional missions, experienced difficulties raising recruits and so resorted to amnestying imprisoned Laz bandits in exchange for their participation in operations against Russia.[52] The patterns of behavior of the people residing in the borderlands of Anatolia and the Caucasus suggest that to mobilize groups for violent behavior, spiritual belief or identity is usually insufficient and must be reinforced by material incentives or invested with direct political significance by outside powers.

Ottoman and German strategy

By choosing to enter the war on Germany's side, the Ottomans were tying the fate of their empire to Germany's. It was a calculated risk. Germany stood an excellent chance of winning the war, and it had no immediate designs on Ottoman territory. Its victory would provide the outcome most conducive to affording the breather they needed to implement the

---

[50] AVPRI, Assistant to the Chief of the Kutaissi Gendarmerie, 31.7.1914 [13.8.1914], f. 151, o. 482, d. 4104, l. 173.

[51] Sadık Sarısaman, "Birinci Dünya Savaşı'nda Osmanlı Devleti'nin Bahtiyari Politikası," *Ankara Üniversitesi Osmanlı Tarihi Araştırma ve Uygulama Merkezi Dergisi*, 8 (1997), 305.

[52] AVPRI, Consul in Erzurum, 7.8.1914 [20.8.1914], f. 151, o. 482, d. 4104, l. 130; M. Philips Price, *War and Revolution in Asiatic Russia* (London: G. Allen and Unwin, 1918), 227.

reforms to rejuvenate their empire. From the German perspective, the Ottoman empire could fulfill three functions. It could cut Russia's communications through the Black Sea to the rest of the world, tie down Russian forces in the Caucasus, and "awaken the fanaticism of Islam" to spark rebellions against British and Russian rule in India, Egypt, and the Caucasus.[53]

Around the time of the signing of the secret alliance, Enver and the Germans had discussed a number of speculative war plans, most involving offensives in the Balkans. In the middle of August Enver ordered his German chief of staff to draw up a formal plan for the opening of the war. The plan identified the main axis of effort to be an attack on the Suez to cut British communications to India and left open the option of an amphibious landing in the vicinity of Odessa. Another possibility the plan offered was a joint offensive against Serbia and Russia in the Balkans.[54] Throughout the opening months of the war Ottoman and German planners remained committed to a passive stance in the Caucasus. Indeed, the August mobilization deployed the bulk of the Ottoman army in the west in Thrace, not in the east.[55] The Ottoman force facing the Caucasus, the Third Army, was to brace for an attack and mount a defense around Erzurum. Only in the event of a decisive defeat of the Russians was the Ottoman army to go on the offensive.[56]

When Russian forces began to close in on the Austro-Hungarian city of Lemberg (Lviv), Vienna urged the Ottomans to launch an amphibious invasion near Odessa to relieve the pressure. The initial enthusiasm for the idea of Enver and Austrian and German planners, who entertained ideas of inciting not just Muslims but Georgians, Jews, and even Cossacks to rebel against the Russians, faded once the enormous logistical difficulties involved became clear.[57] They did not give up the idea of an amphibious operation altogether. Major Süleyman Askerî Bey, the

---

[53] Hew Strachan, *The First World War*, vol. I, *Call to Arms* (New York: Oxford University Press, 2001), 695–96; Fischer, *Germany's Aims*, 122, 126.

[54] Cemal Akbay, *Birinci Dünya Harbi'nde Türk Harbi: Osmanlı İmparatorluğu'nun Siyasi ve Askeri Hazırlıkları ve Harbe Girişi* (Ankara: Genelkurmay Basım Evi, 1991), 279–81. See also Ulrich Trumpener, "Liman von Sanders and the German–Ottoman Alliance," *Journal of Contemporary History*, 1, 4 (October 1966), 182.

[55] Edward J. Erickson, *Ordered to Die: A History of the Ottoman Army in the First World War* (Westport, CT: Greenwood Press, 2001), 45.

[56] Genelkurmay Başkanlığı, *Birinci Dünya Harbinde Türk Harbi: Kafkas Cephesi Üçüncü Ordu Harekâtı*, 2 vols. (Ankara: Genelkurmay Basım Evi, 1993), vol. I, 69–71.

[57] Joseph Pomiankowski, *Osmanlı İmparatorluğu'nun Çöküşü*, tr. Kemal Turan, 2nd edn. (Istanbul: Kayıhan Yayınları, [1928] 1997), 74–75; Strachan, *Call to Arms*, 696–99.

chief of the Teşkilât-ı Mahsusa, envisioned smaller clandestine landings
of Ukrainian and other partisans along the Black Sea coast to spark
rebellions.[58]

The Teşkilât-ı Mahsusa and the Program of Revolution

Enver Pasha had founded the Teşkilât-ı Mahsusa in November 1913.[59]
The experience of fighting against insurgents in the Balkans and as an
insurgent against the Italians had impressed upon Enver and other officers the utility of an organization for irregular warfare. Moreover, an
organization that could act in secrecy and lend the Ottoman state "plausible deniability" had obvious utility in the cutthroat yet diplomatically
bounded international environment in which the Ottomans were forced
to maneuver. Enver and his German advisors hoped to use the Teşkilât-ı
Mahsusa to spark uprisings behind the lines of their foes.[60] In August
Teşkilât-ı Mahsusa operatives formed units in Trabzon, Van, and Erzurum to carry out clandestine and guerrilla operations inside Russia and
Iran. Bahaeddin Şakir took command of the unit in Erzurum, the Caucasus Revolutionary Committee.[61] The committee recruited heavily among
Circassians. For purposes of internal security and secrecy, it required
two current members to attest to a candidate's trustworthiness.[62] By mid
September they had formed several bands of Circassians and Iranians
armed with pamphlets as well as small arms and grenades.[63] Addressed
to "our brothers in faith," the appeals of the Caucasus Revolutionary
Committee called upon the Muslims of the Caucasus to rise up against
the "Moskof" oppressor and to drive the "unbeliever" from the Caucasus
entirely.[64] Several operatives left for the North Caucasus and Azerbaijan,

---

[58] Hakan Kırımlı, "The Activities of the Union for the Liberation of Ukraine in the
Ottoman Empire During the First World War," in *Turkey Before and After Atatürk:
Internal and External Affairs*, ed. Sylvia Kedourie (London: Frank Cass, 1999), 183.

[59] Balcıoğlu, *Teşkilat-ı Mahsusa*, 2.

[60] Balcıoğlu, *Teşkilat-ı Mahsusa*, 157; Ali Ihsan Sâbis, *Harp Hatıralarım*, 4 vols. (Istanbul:
Nehir Yayınları, 1990), vol. II, 168.

[61] Keleşyılmaz, "Kafkas," 285.

[62] Balcıoğlu, *Teşkilat-ı Mahsusa*, 157–58; Aydoğan, *Doğu Politikası*, 86; Fuat Dündar, *İttihat
ve Terakki'nin Müslümanları İskân Politikası (1913–1918)* (Istanbul: İletişim Yayınları,
2001), 131, 157.

[63] AVPRI, Telegram from Ianchevetskii in Odessa, 4.9.1914 [17.9.1914], f. 151, o. 482,
d. 4104, l. 274; AVPRI, Telegram from Girs, 19.8.1914 [1.9.1914], f. Politarkhiv,
o. 482, d. 4068, f. 135.

[64] Appeal of the Caucasus Revolutionary Society (Kafkasya İhtilal Cemiyeti), No. 1/714,
personal papers of Bahaeddin Şakir. I thank Şükrü Hanioğlu for this document.

where they made contact with locals, including Mehmed Emin Resulzade of the Musavat Party.[65]

The Kaiser was not the sole German holding high hopes for the revolutionary possibilities of pan-Islam. Extrapolating from the conviction that Islam was a martial religion that could not countenance the rule of unbelievers over Muslims, German policymakers presumed that Muslims under Entente rule were essentially obliged by both belief and psychological constitution to revolt.[66] With much encouragement from them, Ali Haydar Efendi, the Ottoman sheikh ul-Islam – the most senior religious authority in the Ottoman state – proclaimed a jihad on 14 November, three days after the Porte's declaration of war. The proclamation summoned all Muslims, Shiʻi as well as Sunni, to war against Russia, Britain, and France. The call to jihad had little to no effect, except perhaps among the Kurds of Iran, among whom more immediate factors were at work. The idea of waging a holy war in alliance with the infidel powers of Germany and Austria-Hungary was dubious at best. Rumors that Germany had paid for the proclamation circulated inside even the Ottoman empire. Most Muslims did not find that their own circumstances merited war, regardless of what a religious scholar in Istanbul might declare.[67]

The Germans' ardor for pan-Islam loomed greater than their competence or common sense, and they often worked at cross-purposes with their Muslim Ottoman allies, who viewed German efforts in the Middle East with suspicion. The presence in the German effort of unqualified specialists and outright charlatans did not improve matters. The German Foreign Ministry hired a journalist, Max Froloff, to go to the Red Sea region to recruit Muslim holy warriors. Froloff opted to make a shorter trip to Holland where he wrote an account of his imagined experiences. The publication of his book nonetheless had an impact. Its descriptions of Froloff's visits to Mecca and Medina, holy cities strictly barred to non-Muslims, sullied the Ottomans' reputation as guardians of the sacred sites and consequently incensed them.[68] Another German project bordering on the surreal was the dispatching, over the objections of Enver and the Ottoman Interior Ministry, of an Austrian orientalist and Catholic priest,

---

[65] Sadık Sarısaman, "Birinci Dünya Savaşı Sırasında İran Elçiliğimiz ile İrtibatlı Bazı Teşkilât-ı Mahsusa Faaliyetleri," *Ankara Üniversitesi Osmanlı Tarihi Araştırma ve Uygulama Merkezi Dergisi*, 7 (1996), 209–14.

[66] German hopes for revolution abroad were not limited to Muslims, and the notion of revolution itself seemed to exert powerful pull upon the Germans: Strachan, *Call to Arms*, 696.

[67] See, for example, Sâbis, *Harp Hatıralarım*, vol. II, 115–17. Landau's *Politics of Pan-Islam*, 99–103, suggests that a lack of opportunity to participate in jihad rather than a lack of religious fervor explains the failure of the call to jihad. The argument begs the question.

[68] McKale, *Revolution*, 62–63.

Alois Musil, to inspire Muslim Arabs to embark on jihad. Notably, after returning from Arabia, Musil testified to the "complete indifference of the tribes toward holy war and Pan-Islamic ideas."[69] The belief that the Germans were using such missions to prepare the ground for the postwar expansion of German influence haunted the Ottomans, who obstructed German efforts at holy war at several junctures. Frustrated, the Germans moved the center of pan-Islamic operations in 1916 from Istanbul to Berlin.[70]

Perhaps precisely because they themselves were Muslims, many Ottoman officials had been skeptical about the possibilities of pan-Islamic revolution from the beginning. Consular officers in Taganrog, Odessa, Novorossiisk, Batumi, and Tiflis all reported that Russia's mobilization had only caused people, including Muslims, to rally around the tsar. In Tiflis Muslims were praying for Russia's victory. The chargé d'affaires in St. Petersburg Fahreddin Bey predicted that in the event of war the vast majority of Russia's Muslims would not only fail to take active measures on the Ottomans' behalf but would probably fight alongside the Russians as in the War of 1877–78. Most were living in poverty and uneducated, he explained, and those with some education tended to be even more pro-Russian.[71] Indeed, Enver himself advised his subordinates that most of Russia's Muslim Circassians would fight on Russia's side and that the "Türkmen" (by which he probably meant Azeri Turks) and Muslim and Christian Georgians would merely refrain from actively supporting Russia.[72]

The war opens

Before their respective governments had declared war, Russian and British armed forces initiated combat operations against the Ottomans along the Iranian border, in the Persian Gulf, and in the Levant. Russia's initial war plan for the Caucasus provided for an active defense with limited local offensives. Encountering only light resistance, however, Russian forces from Iran pushed further into Ottoman territory to occupy Köprüköy and threaten Erzurum. The Ottoman army then struck, however, and within two weeks had driven their foes back. To the

---

[69] McKale, *Revolution*, 107.
[70] McKale, *Revolution*, 82, 108, 134–35; AVPRI, Telegram from the Envoy in Berne, 12.12.1916 [25.12.1916], f. 151, o. 482, d. 4383, l. 3.
[71] ATASE, Report to the War Ministry on the Situation in Russia, 16 Eylül 1330 [29.9.1914], K. 241, D. 2-1001, F. 54.
[72] ATASE, Enver to the Third Army Command, 12/13 Eylül 1330 [25/26.9.1914], BDH, K. 2818, D. 59, F. 2-19.

north, where the Teşkilât-ı Mahsusa raised a force of some 5,000 Laz and Ajar irregulars, Ottoman forces managed to take the towns of Artvin and Ardanuch. They announced their entrance into the formerly Ottoman town of Ardahan toward the end of December by firing off a telegram to Istanbul boasting simply, "Greetings from Ardahan!"[73] These victories had not been easy, and rifts between the Teşkilât-ı Mahsusa and regular army led Enver to dismiss Bahaeddin Şakir from command, but in the initial confrontations the Ottomans had bested the Russian Caucasus Army.[74]

Sarikamish: gamble and disaster

These early successes emboldened Enver to plan a major offensive to envelop and crush Russian units in the vicinity of Sarikamish (Sarıkamış).[75] In view of the rugged terrain, the winter weather, and the balance of forces, the plan involved tremendous risks, which Enver's subordinates brought to his attention. Enver, however, was not one to fear risk. His meteoric rise had taught him to embrace it. The hero of 1908 had gone from junior officer to minister of war in a mere five years. Moreover, his German chief of staff, Bronsart von Schellendorf, was encouraging him to undertake a major offensive. With Germany's armies bogged down on two fronts and Austria-Hungary on the defensive, the short victorious war the Central Powers had wagered on was growing into a stalemate. If the Ottomans could envelop the Russians on the Caucasian front and inflict a stunning defeat on them as the Germans had done at Tannenberg, the war effort would regain momentum. Enver had no experience commanding large units but, ever self-confident, he arrived in Erzurum to take personal command of the operation.[76]

The offensive commenced on 22 December. Unseasonably warm weather boded well. In the initial days the 95,000-strong Third Army made good progress. By coincidence, the tsar had appeared in Sarikamish

---

[73] Sâbis, Hatıralarım, vol. II, 197; Dayı, Elviye-i Selâse'de, 27; Fevzi Çakmak, Büyük Harpte Şark Cephesi Hareketleri: Şark Vilâyetlerimizde, Kafkasyada ve İranda (Ankara: Genelkurmay Matbaası, 1936), 40–42.

[74] W. E. D. Allen and Paul Muratoff, Caucasian Battlefields: A History of the Wars on the Turco-Caucasian Borders, 1828–1921 (Cambridge: Cambridge University Press, 1953), 245–48; Genelkurmay Başkanlığı, Üçüncü Ordu Harekâtı, vol. I, 347. On the rift, see also Köprülü Şerif İlden, Sarıkamış: Birinci Dünya Savaşı Başlangıcında Üçüncü Ordu Kuşatma Manevrası ve Meydan Savaşı, ed. Sami Önal (Istanbul: Türkiye İş Bankası Kültür Yayınları, 1998), 159; Sâbis, Hatıralarım, vol. II, 175, 197; and Aziz Samih İlter, Büyük Harpte Kafkas Cephesi Hatıraları: Zivinden Peterice (Ankara: Büyük Erkân-ı Harbiye Matbaası, 1934), 28–29, 59.

[75] Bayur, Türk İnkılâbı Tarihi, vol. III, pt. 1, 356–57.

[76] Genelkurmay Başkanlığı, Üçüncü Ordu Harekâtı, vol. I, 349–50.

on a morale-building mission, and some Russians now feared the advancing Ottomans might capture him. The population in Sarikamish and even some Russian generals panicked. But in the meantime the weather shifted dramatically. Temperatures plunged to −36°C and blizzard conditions set in, trapping tens of thousands of poorly clothed Ottoman soldiers in the mountain passes. Most of these were without winter gear and some were without even footwear. Meanwhile, newly arrived reserves enabled the Russians to counterattack. The result was a calamitous rout from which the Ottoman army would never fully recover. Not until 1918 and the disintegration of the Russian army would the Ottomans again be able to go on the strategic offensive on the Caucasian front.[77]

As bad as it was, the disaster of Sarikamish later acquired mythical proportions as part of an effort to discredit the Unionists and Enver in particular. Thus Enver's decision to launch a wintertime offensive with ill-clothed troops in the mountains is often presented as the epitome of stupidity and fanaticism. Total Ottoman losses were crippling, but closer to 60,000 than the 130,000–140,000 of popular legend.[78] One explanation advanced for Enver's otherwise seemingly ineffable heedlessness for entering both the war and the offensive at Sarikamish is a deep-seated pan-Turanism, a grand desire to unite the Turkic and Muslim peoples of the Caucasus, Russia, and Central Asia with those of the Ottoman empire. Such an explanation is not convincing. As noted earlier, Ottoman mobilization plans deployed the army in the west, not on the Caucasian front. Despite the fact that an invasion of the Caucasus was the most obvious and straightforward way to bring the war to Russia, Enver settled on a Caucasian offensive only after discarding for geographic and logistical reasons other options of attack through the Balkans or across the Black Sea.[79] The military stalemate in Europe led Germany and Austria-Hungary to press the Ottomans to launch an offensive against Russia sooner. Enver's concept of encircling Russian units at Sarikamish and cutting them off from their rear was daring but not hare-brained, and in accord with standard military doctrine.[80] Finally, the Ottomans

[77] Erickson, *Ordered*, 59–60; Genelkurmay Başkanlığı, *Üçüncü Ordu Harekâtı*, vol. I, 535–36.
[78] Genelkurmay Başkanlığı, *Üçüncü Ordu Harekâtı*, vol. I, 535. The Turkish estimate of 30,000 for total Russian losses corresponds with other estimates: Allen and Muratoff, *Battlefields*, 284.
[79] Strachan, *Call to Arms*, 717–19.
[80] Arutiunian, *Kavkazskii front*, 141; N. G. Korsun, *Sarykamyshkaia operatsiia* (Moscow: Voenizdat, 1937), 9; Allen and Muratoff, *Battlefields*, 250; Felix Guse, *Die Kaukasusfront im Weltkrieg bis zum Frieden von Brest* (Leipzig: Koehler & Amelang, 1940), 34–35. See also Kurat, *Türkiye ve Rusya*, 68–269; General Otto Viktor Karl Liman von Sanders,

made no effort even to present the operation as pan-Turanist.[81] Liman von Sanders does recollect that Enver commented that he "contemplated marching through Afghanistan to India."[82] A conversational aside is hardly conclusive evidence, and it is notable that Enver stated the objective was India. India was not an objective of pan-Turanism, but *British* India had long been an objective of Britain's rivals, including Germany and Russia.

Given that the advice of Enver's Ottoman and German staff officers alike was split regarding the proposed operation, Enver's personality became critical to the decision to attack. Personal experience had taught the youthful war minister that boldness pays. The Third Army executed the first half of the operation well, but the drastic shift in the weather and the uncommonly swift Russian counterattack sealed its fate; its fate was not sealed from the beginning.[83] The tactical blunder committed by Enver at Sarikamish – emphasized so often to underscore the alleged irrational pull of pan-Turanism upon Enver and the Ottomans in general – is less remarkable when compared with the record of British, French, and German generals fighting on the western front in France, who sacrificed far greater numbers of lives over a longer period of time for no strategic advantage.

Shortly after it had commenced its offensive on Sarikamish, the Ottoman army launched a probe into northern Iran. The idea was that a relatively small force led by the Unionist and Teşkilât-ı Mahsusa commander Ömer Naci Bey, who had fought alongside Iranian constitutionalists in 1907 and knew the region, would rally the Muslims of Iran to rebel against the Russians, stir problems in the Russian rear, and perhaps even facilitate a drive toward Baku, the center of Russia's oil industry. The probe initially made rapid headway when General Aleksandr Myshlaevskii, panicked by the advance at Sarikamish, ordered the abandonment of Urmia and Tabriz. The Russians' sudden withdrawal inspired the Kurds of Iran, including the Russians' erstwhile ally Simko, to swell the ranks of the Ottoman force. The Ottomans and their local allies entered Tabriz on 14 January, looting and wreaking terror upon Assyrian and Armenian villagers along the way. After Russian defenses at Sarikamish had stabilized, however, the chief of staff of the Caucasus Army General Nikolai Yudenich ordered General Fedor Chernozubov immediately to retake Tabriz and secure the northern Iranian plateau.

Five Years in Turkey (Berlin: August Scherl, 1920; reprint, Annapolis, MD: United States Naval Institute, 1927), 38–40.
[81] Erickson, *Ordered*, 53.   [82] Liman von Sanders, *Five Years*, 39.
[83] Erickson, *Ordered*, 60–61.

The return of the Russians in force caused the Ottoman offensive in Iran promptly to collapse.[84]

Attack on the Suez

At the same time that Enver was presiding over the disaster at Sarikamish, Cemal Pasha was readying forces for an offensive on the Suez. The offensive aimed at cutting Britain's lines of communication to India and inciting the Muslims of Egypt and North Africa to rebel against their British and French overlords. Berlin assigned tremendous importance to attacking the British in Egypt and from the beginning of the war had been eager for an attack across the Suez Canal.[85] The Ottomans had not foreseen a multifront war in which Britain was an adversary and so formed a new army, the Fourth, with its headquarters in Damascus. Cemal arrived on 18 November to take command of the offensive. Due to the long distances involved and the poor state of the roads and communications his army was ready only in the middle of January. The Ottoman and German planners hoped to exploit religious sentiment against the British and included in the 4th Army a number of imams for this purpose. A German advisor made the fantastic prediction that 70,000 "Arab nomads" would join their invading Ottoman co-religionists when they reached the canal.[86] The inclusion of a company of Druze, a sect whose beliefs are anathema to mainstream Sunni Islam, however, belies the notion that Sunni fanaticism inspired the offensive.[87]

After skillfully executing a difficult advance across the Sinai to the Suez, the 4th Army launched their attack across the canal on the night of 2 February. Although they achieved tactical surprise, they ran into difficulties at the canal due to improper equipment and a lack of training in water crossings. The British on the opposite bank rushed in reinforcements and repelled those who had made it across. After two days of fighting, Cemal pulled back, having suffered roughly 1,300 casualties.[88]

The offensive had failed in part because Berlin pressured the Ottomans to attack prematurely. Nonetheless, it is doubtful that the offensive would have achieved major results even if the initial assault force had

---

[84] E. V. Maslovskii, *Mirovaia voina na Kavkazskom fronte, 1914–1917* (Paris: Vozrozhdenie, 1933), 153; Gaunt, *Massacres*, 102–05; Genelkurmay Başkanlığı, *Üçüncü Ordu Harekâtı*, vol. I, 570–73; Allen and Muratoff, *Battlefields*, 295–301.

[85] Trumpener, *Germany*, 36–37.

[86] Fischer, *Germany's Aims*, 166; McKale, *Revolution*, 100.

[87] Maurice Larcher, *La Guerre Turque dans la Guerre mondiale* (Paris: E. Chiron, 1926), 251.

[88] Bayur, *Türk İnkılâbı Tarihi*, vol. III, pt. 1, 419; Erickson, *Ordered*, 70–71; Strachan, *Call to Arms*, 737–41.

established a bridgehead on the western bank. Ottoman supply lines were long, Ottoman forces limited, and British military and naval power in and around Egypt was substantial. The outbreak of a rebellion in the British rear perhaps could have assisted the assault, but precisely to preclude such a possibility the British had withdrawn their native Egyptian troops to Sudan and deployed British and Indian troops to the canal. Because the Suez offensive resembled the Sarikamish operation in its timing, ambition, and mismatch between objectives and available resources, historians have tended to locate its origins, too, in an emerging ideology of pan-Islam. They overlook the Central Powers' common interest in cutting British lines of communication and the Ottomans' particular interest in expelling the British from Egypt, a land to which they had strong historical and cultural ties, and which had formally remained part of their empire until the outbreak of the war. The scale of defeat at the Suez was nothing like that at Sarikamish. The Germans, in fact, were satisfied with the operation despite its collapse because it had compelled the British to retain in Egypt troops they could have deployed to Europe.[89]

The crushing defeat of Sarikamish and the failure at Suez deprived the Ottoman army of any offensive capability at the strategic level. The spring 1915 Anglo-French amphibious assault at Gallipoli, British thrusts into Mesopotamia and Palestine, and the steady advance of the Russian army across Anatolia would keep the Ottomans hard-pressed throughout the next two years. They would manage only limited counteroffensives in Anatolia and Mesopotamia, while also contributing substantial forces to joint operations in the Balkans. Deprived of an army and resources, pan-Islam, too, lost whatever strategic significance it may have possessed. In Iran, the Ottomans, backed by the Germans, made appeals to Muslims to join them in the struggle against the infidel Russians and British, but the larger legions and greater resources of the Entente proved to be more persuasive stimuli for the Muslims of Iran.[90] Following their defeats there was little the Ottomans could do beyond backing the activities of a few individuals, such as Enver's younger brother Nuri Pasha, who assisted the Sanussi tribesmen's resistance to the Italians in Tripoli.[91] The fact that pan-Islam exerted little pull on Muslims outside the reach of Ottoman or German material support is not insignificant, as it highlights yet again the ideology's slight power.

[89] McKale, *Revolution*, 101.
[90] See Sarısaman, "Bahtiyari Politikası"; Bayur, *Türk İnkılâbı Tarihi*, vol. III, pt. 3, 123–59; Fahri Belen, *Birinci Cihan Harbinde Türk Harbi*, vol. III, *1916 Yılı Hareketleri* (Ankara: Genelkurmay Basımevi, 1965), 163–200.
[91] McKale, *Revolution*, 88–89.

The Congress of Oppressed Peoples

Up until the end of 1917, the Ottoman empire would remain on the strategic defensive. Although they had no means to exploit it, the Ottomans in this period did not totally cease support for revolutionary work among Muslims abroad. In 1915 Yusuf Akçura along with the Azeri Ali Hüseyinzade, the Crimean Tatar Mehmed Esad Çelebizade, and the native Bukharan Mukimeddin Begcen Bey founded the "Society for the Defense of the Rights of Turko-Tatar Muslims Resident in Russia."[92] Committee members put in appearances in Germany, Austria-Hungary, Bulgaria, and Switzerland on behalf of their cause. Their big success in 1915 amounted to the publication on German printing presses of a pamphlet condemning Russia.[93]

In June 1916 Akçura set out for the Third Congress of Oppressed Peoples. Sponsored by the Union of Nationalities and held in neutral Lausanne, Switzerland, the congress provided a rare international forum for representatives of small nations from the Russian empire and elsewhere to decry the injustices under which they lived. As such, it provided an ideal opportunity for Akçura to speak on behalf of Russia's Tatars. Yet when the congress opened on 27 June, Akçura was nowhere to be found. He had gotten stranded in Sofia, Bulgaria. Desperately shooting off telegrams and racing back and forth from the city center to the train station in vain attempts to get his journey underway, he complained to his supervisor in the Teşkilât-ı Mahsusa that he could not exit Bulgaria because he still had not received a passport. Time was running out and he feared he would have to miss the conference, although he was relieved that at least his train tickets out of Bulgaria were refundable.[94] Akçura did eventually manage to get a passport, and arrived on the third and last day of the congress. Speaking in the name of the Kazan Tatars, he criticized the policies of the current Russian government and in particular its efforts to destroy the Tatar language. He concluded by declaring that, if the Kazan Tatars were to receive the cultural autonomy they desired, their cultural achievements would benefit all of humanity.[95]

Akçura's participation in the Congress of Oppressed Peoples is significant for what it tells us about the scale and nature of pan-Turkist

---

[92] ATASE, Declaration to the Interior Ministry, 6 Mayıs 1332 [19 May 1916], K. 1836, D. 70-38, F. 1.
[93] G. Ieshke, "Poraboshchennye Rossiei narody na Lozanskom kongresse 1916 goda," *Şimalî Kafkasya–Severnyi Kavkaz*, no. 42–43 (October–November 1937), 18.
[94] ATASE, Akçura to Ali Baş Hamba, 6 Haziran 1332 [19.6.1916], K. 1836, D. 70-38, F. 7.
[95] Ieshke, "Poraboshchennye," 21.

or pan-Islamic efforts. Akçura was a prominent figure at the time and close to the leading Unionists. Today he is often regarded as a critical personage in the formation of Turkish nationalism.[96] Yet it is clear that his activities were not a very high priority for the Ottoman government in World War I. Not only could he not obtain a passport in a timely manner, but he also could not count on substantial funding. Given Akçura's pronouncements at the conference one might conclude the government's penury was fortuitous. The émigré averred to speak on behalf only of the Kazan Tatars, not on behalf of all Russia's Muslims and Turks, and appealed merely for cultural autonomy, making no call to rebellion, independence, or political union with other Muslims or Turks. The moderate nature of his demands cannot be explained by limitations imposed by the setting. Speakers at Lausanne were free to employ fiery rhetoric, and several did, including two North Caucasians who called for the revival of the resistance to Russia of Imam Shamil, the legendary Dagestani sheikh who had rallied the North Caucasian mountaineers to fight off imperial Russia for a quarter-century from 1834 to 1859.[97]

Ottoman cooperation with Georgians

In their efforts to subvert Russian control of the borderlands, the Ottomans did not limit their search for allies to Muslims and Turks. They saw Armenians, Georgians, Ukrainians, and Jews at various times as potential allies. The Revolution of 1908 and the restoration of constitutional rule stirred excitement not just in Ottoman lands but in Russia, too. Far from seeing it as an expression of ethnic or religious particularism, many contemporaries saw the revolution as part of a universal march toward representative government and freedom.[98] Attracted to Istanbul's relatively free atmosphere, a heavily socialist community of "illegal" Russian subjects took up residence in the Ottoman capital.[99] Whereas for many Europeans the Ottoman empire functioned as a symbol of an essentially alien Asiatic civilization, to be classed as decrepit and stale or vigorous and young depending upon the prejudice of the observer, for at least some Russian subjects the Ottoman political

---

[96] François Georgeon, *Aux origines du nationalisme turc: Yusuf Akçura (1876–1935)* (Paris: ADPF, 1980).

[97] Ieshke, "Poraboshchennye," 21–22.

[98] Nader Sohrabi, "Historicizing Revolutions: Constitutional Revolutions in the Ottoman Empire, Iran and Russia, 1905–1908," *American Journal of Sociology*, 100, 6 (May 1995), 1383–1447.

[99] The community was sufficiently large and active enough to worry Russian officialdom: AVPRI, B. Serafimov to the Second Political Department of the Ministry of Foreign Affairs, 4.1.1915 [17.1.1915], f. 135, o. 474, d. 18, l. 6

experiment hinted at the beguiling promise of a new civilization that knew no bounds between the old, largely religiously defined boundaries of Europe and Asia. The most famous of the socialists resident in Istanbul was Israel Helphand, better known as "Parvus."[100] Parvus quickly established ties with Unionist and Young Turk circles and between 1911 and 1915 wrote for several publications. Blasting the Ottomans' faith in economic liberalism, he argued strenuously that European investments were not developing the empire, but impoverishing it. Expanded state control of the economy, he contended, was essential for Ottoman liberation. Influenced by Parvus' ideas, Yusuf Akçura noted the unhappy parallel between his empire, where Greeks and Armenians dominated the merchant and business classes, and Poland, where the bourgeoisie was composed entirely of Jews and Germans. The Unionists would make the creation of a new Muslim middle class, and the displacement of the old Christian one, part of their push to liberate their empire from dependency.[101]

The 1908 Revolution inspired other Russian subjects with goals more particularistic than world revolution. These included a group of Georgian separatists who arrived that year in Istanbul. Among them was Archimandrite Nicolas, the former head of Georgia's largest monastery. He began writing appeals to the new government in 1909, describing the Ottoman empire as Georgia's savior from "Russia's oppression and savagery." His appeals failed to generate much of a response. But he spotted the outbreak of war in the summer of 1914 as a chance for Georgia to win independence.[102] In August he and several Georgian colleagues established a nationalist committee in Trabzon. In his requests for Ottoman assistance, Nicolas predicted that the appearance of Ottoman soldiers inside Georgia would spark a popular anti-Russian rebellion led by, of all people, Georgia's 3,000 clergymen. He began working with the Teşkilât-ı Mahsusa to organize a rebellion inside Georgia by conducting anti-Russian propaganda and stockpiling arms. The Germans and Ottomans did contemplate an amphibious invasion fifty kilometers north of Batumi, reasoning that a heavily Georgian area would welcome anti-Russian forces. The outbreak of Ottoman–Russian hostilities cut short the preparations inside Georgia, however, and the

---

[100] On Parvus, see Z. A. B. Zeman and W. B. Scharlau, *The Merchant of Revolution: The Life of Alexander Israel Helphand (Parvus), 1867–1924* (New York: Oxford University Press, 1965).

[101] Georgeon, *Akçura*, 45; Zafer Toprak, *Türkiye'de Millî İktisat 1908–1918* (Ankara: Yurt Yayınları, 1982), 170–71, 390–92, 410–11.

[102] ATASE, Proposal of Archimandrite Nicolas to the Ministry of War, 21 Mayıs 1331 [3.6.1915], ATASE, BDH, K. 1838, D. 45-68, F. 1-1.

Germans and Ottomans ultimately dropped the invasion plan as logistically unfeasible.[103]

One of Nicolas' proposals was to establish on Ottoman soil a Georgian Legion that would fight for an independent Georgian state. Funded by the Germans and deployed alongside the Ottoman army, the legion was a mix of Christians and Muslims and numbered roughly 600 men recruited from prisoners of war and refugees. German observers believed that the Ottomans were hostile toward the legion and sought to undermine it from the start.[104] Ottoman correspondence, however, makes clear that this judgment is overstated. The senior Ottoman leadership did have concerns over the borders envisioned for an independent Georgia – in particular they did not want it to encompass Kars, Ardahan, Elisavetpol, or Aleksandropol (Giumri) – but after the Georgians renounced any claims to these territories the two sides signed agreements to cooperate.[105] The legion's use of Russian military drill and the officers' inability to understand Turkish caused technical problems in the integration of the unit into the Ottoman army, but the Ottoman officers assigned to work with the legion did not regard these incompatibilities as insurmountable.[106] Bahaeddin Şakir at the start of the war was enthusiastic about the Christian Georgians as allies.[107] Others, however, regarded the legion with suspicion. Its use of a Georgian flag rather than the Ottoman standard irritated some. The governor of Trabzon, moreover, dismissed the Georgians as good-for-nothing slackers who dreamed of a long war so that they could continue to draw pay from the Germans. For good measure, he added in his complaints that, leaving aside their loafing and lollygagging, their inability as Christians to offer prayers for the sultan underscored their uselessness.[108] The commanders of the Second and Third Armies, Vehib and Mahmud Pashas respectively, concurred that the Georgians

---

[103] ATASE, Proposal of Archimandrite Nicolas, 4 Mart 1331 [17.3.1915], BDH, K. 1838, D. 45-68, F. 1-52; Proposal of Archimandrite Nicolas, 21 Mayıs 1331 [3.6.1915], BDH, K. 1838, D. 45/68, F 1–2; AVPRI, Intercepted German Dispatch to Constantinople, 1.11.1914 [14.11.1914], f. 151, o. 482, f. 4324, l. 3. See also Strachan, *Call to Arms*, 718; Weber, *Eagles*, 72.
[104] Wolfdieter Bihl, *Die Kaukasus-Politik der Mittelmächte*, 2 vols. (Vienna: Hermann Böhlaus Nachf, 1975), vol. I, 81–82; Mustafa Çolak, *Alman İmperatorluğu'nun Doğu Siyaseti Çerçevesinde Kafkasya Politikası (1914–1918)* (Ankara: Türk Tarih Kurumu, 2006), 154.
[105] Çolak, *Kafkasya Politikası*, 149–50, 157–58; İlter, *Kafkas Cephesi*, 63–66.
[106] ATASE, Cipher to the Third Army Command, 3 Teşrinisani 1331 [16.11.1915], K. 2940, D. 594, F. 9-17.
[107] Cemil Arif, *Birinci Dünya Savaşında Teşkilat-ı Mahsusa* (Istanbul: Arba Yayınları, 1997), 42.
[108] ATASE, Cipher from the Governor of Trabzon Cemal Azmi Bey, 29 Teşrinievvel 1331 [11.11.1915], K. 2940, D. 594, F. 9-8.

presented little utility, an opinion that some Germans came to share.[109] Enver took note of the criticisms. He instructed that the Georgians be permitted to retain their flag, but emphasized that the Georgian Legion should be used to serve Ottoman, and not Georgian, purposes.[110]

Georgian recruits from the legion were occasionally sent on secret missions inside Georgia.[111] In April 1917, however, the Ottomans disbanded the legion. The reason for the decision is not known but most likely stemmed from friction between the Germans and Ottomans over control of the legion. The Ottomans were intensely suspicious of anything the Germans were doing in and around their territory. The Ottomans found the legion of little use and too close to the Germans, who were not only bankrolling it but were also very close to its Georgian head, Prince Giorgi Machabelli. Machabelli had eclipsed Nicolas as the lead Georgian and in 1918 would spar with Ottoman diplomats over the future of Georgia and Eastern Anatolia.

Ottomans and Ukrainians

At the same time that Archimandrite Nicolas established the Georgian Committee, a number of Ukrainians in the city of Lemberg founded the "Union for the Liberation of Ukraine" (ULU). Their goals included getting the Central Powers to proclaim the establishment of an independent Ukraine as a war aim and to form military units from Ukrainian prisoners of war. The ULU promptly dispatched Mariian Basok-Melenev'skii, a leader of the Ukrainian socialist group Spilka, to Istanbul to rally support.[112] The city's socialist expatriate community, however, found the ULU emissary's attempt to square the project of a constitutionalist monarchy headed by a German prince with socialist principles unconvincing.[113] Basok-Melenev'skii had better luck when he renewed his contacts with Parvus, who helped put the ULU in contact with the Teşkilât-ı Mahsusa.[114] The ULU was assigned key roles in the Central Powers' plans to foment rebellion in Ukraine, conduct amphibious

[109] Balcıoğlu, *Teşkilat-ı Mahsusa* 160; Çolak, *Kafkasya Politikası*, 160–61.
[110] ATASE, Enver Pasha to the Deputy Chief Commander, 2 Teşrinisani 1331 [15.11.1915], K. 2940, D. 594, F. 9-11.
[111] RGVIA, Report of the Chief of the Kutaisi Gendarmerie Colonel Treskin, 9.12.1916 [22.12.1916], f. 2168, o. 1, d. 553, ll. 249–50; David Marshall Lang, *A Modern History of Soviet Georgia* (Westport, CT: Greenwood Press, 1962), 183.
[112] Roman Smal-Stocki, "Actions of 'Union for the Liberation of Ukraine' During World War I," *Ukrainian Quarterly*, 15, no. 2 (June 1959), 170–71.
[113] AVPRI, Serafimov to the Second Political Department of the Ministry of Foreign Affairs, 4.1.1915 [17.1.1915], f. 135, o. 474, d. 18, l. 6.
[114] Kırımlı, "Union," 183.

operations at Odessa and the Kuban, and incite mutiny in the Russian Black Sea Fleet. ULU members took part in discussions of these plans along with the head of the Teşkilât-ı Mahsusa Major Süleyman Askerî Bey, Enver, and German and Austro-Hungarian military officials. Because these plans all demanded capabilities beyond what the Central Powers possessed, nothing came of them beyond the infiltration of ULU members from Istanbul into Russia.[115] In the meantime, ULU officials recruited among Russian prisoners of war in Izmir, separating the prisoners not according to self-identification but according to whether or not the prisoner was born within the borders of the imagined Ukrainian state. They then lectured these prisoners on Ukrainian history and revolutionary politics to inculcate in them their "proper" ethnopolitical identity.[116] These prisoners were supposed to be enrolled in a Ukrainian Legion that would fight alongside the armies of the Central Powers.

ULU activities and contacts were not restricted to military and intelligence channels. They succeeded in getting the Istanbul press to run articles on their cause, and in December two Ukrainians secured meetings with Said Halim and other cabinet ministers. Battlefield losses to the Russians and the specter of Ukrainian separatism in Galicia dampened Vienna's enthusiasm for the ULU and the Ukrainian cause, and so the ULU headquarters moved to Berlin in the spring of 1915. The ULU Istanbul delegation continued its efforts to build support among the Ottomans, publishing books and pamphlets and lobbying officials. In early 1915 Basok-Melenev'skii obtained from Talât the first public endorsement of an independent Ukraine by a Central Power.[117] For the next three years that endorsement would mean nothing, but the fall of the tsar and the collapse of the Russian empire would endow the ULU–Ottoman relationship with geopolitical significance.

Russia drives into Anatolia, 1915–1916

The disaster at Sarikamish left just some 52,000 Ottoman soldiers spread over a 600-km front facing the much better equipped Russia's Caucasus Army with roughly 78,000 effective combatants.[118] With the initiative on their side, the Russians began to push steadily forward. In the north, they threw back the Ottoman and Laz–Ajar formations and recaptured Artvin before the end of March. To the south, in Iran, where the Russians had hastily abandoned Tabriz to invading Ottoman regulars and anti-Russian Iranian Kurds, General Chernozubov rallied Russian forces

---

[115] Kırımlı, "Union," 184–92.
[116] AVPRI, Report of Serafimov, 14.12.1914 [27.12.1914], f. 135, o. 474, d. 18, l. 4.
[117] Smal-Stocki, "Actions," 171.   [118] Erickson, *Ordered*, 106.

and retook Tabriz in January. The Ottomans managed to stem a determined offensive toward Erzurum in May, push the Russians back at Malazgirt in July, and recapture Van in August after losing the city to Armenian rebels and Russian forces in May. By early fall, however, they had again to surrender these positions and were in full retreat.

The Ottoman reversal at Sarikamish encouraged Britain and France to contemplate a large-scale operation against the Ottoman empire to knock it out of the war. They began planning an amphibious operation to seize the Dardanelles and then Istanbul and thereby reopen a critical supply route to Russia.[119] Nervous Russian officials, fearing Russia might lose in this, urged Sazonov to move to seize Istanbul and the straits unilaterally. Sazonov was no less ardent to gain control of Istanbul and the straits and indeed made it a prime objective of the war. However, he recognized that the war presented a rare opportunity to obtain Britain's and France's acquiescence to Russian control of the straits. Sazonov's patience was rewarded on 10 April 1915 when Britain and France, fearing that Russia might otherwise opt out of the war, concluded a secret agreement that conceded to Russia the right to take possession of Istanbul and the straits.[120]

Britain had wasted no time in taking the war to the Ottomans, seizing the Persian Gulf port of Basra in November 1914 and marching on Baghdad. The Ottoman empire was in a fight for its life. With the Russian army advancing from the east, the British coming up from the south, and the British and French landing at Gallipoli in April, the Ottoman government panicked and began preparations to abandon Istanbul and relocate to Konya in the Anatolian interior. The nightmare scenario of a last stand in Anatolia was unfolding.

At Gallipoli a titanic struggle took place that lasted from the spring into the fall. During the battle a young commander named Mustafa Kemal demonstrated his exceptional talents and won fame throughout the Ottoman officer corps. The defenders of Gallipoli eventually prevailed, albeit at a heavy cost. Beaten, the British and French withdrew to sea. In Mesopotamia, the Ottomans managed to keep the British out of Baghdad. These defensive successes, however, came at a tremendous cost in lives and supplies. By November 1915, the Ottomans had managed to put close to 800,000 men under arms, but this marked the peak of their manpower for the next two years.[121] In 1915 alone they had sustained total losses of nearly half a million men.[122]

[119] Allen and Muratoff, *Battlefields*, 287.
[120] Bobroff, *Roads*,118–24, 131–38; M. S. Anderson, *Eastern Question*, 324–25.
[121] Allen and Muratoff, *Battlefields*, 289.   [122] Erickson, *Ordered*, 75.

Before the Ottomans could consolidate their forces and regain their balance in Anatolia, the Russian Caucasus Army struck without warning in January 1916 and in February claimed the strategic prize of Erzurum. The loss of Erzurum, the key to the control of the Anatolian plateau, demoralized the Ottomans and thrilled a sullen Russian public, which had been receiving from the western front report after report of defeats. Accordingly, the Russian press gave the triumph widespread coverage and throughout the empire Russian clergy said celebratory masses.[123] More Russian victories followed. One month later, the town of Rize on the Black Sea fell and then Trabzon in April. The port of Trabzon had served as a critical logistics center for the Third Army, enabling it to bypass Anatolia's underdeveloped road and rail network. The port was of no less advantage to the Russians, who could now exploit the more direct and far shorter lines across the Black Sea to provision their soldiers deep in Anatolia. With Erzurum and Trabzon in hostile hands, the Ottomans were in a desperate position. The Russians inflicted more punishing defeats in July, taking Bayburt and Erzincan. Meanwhile, the British were again on the move in Mesopotamia.[124]

The Ottomans, though despondent, refused to break. They dealt the British a humiliating blow and stymied their advance on Baghdad in spring 1916 when Enver's uncle Halil Pasha cut off and compelled the British vanguard to surrender at Kut ül-Amara. The Russians had failed to relieve the British as planned because in June they had withdrawn before an Ottoman force invading Iran. In a summer counteroffensive in Anatolia, units under Mustafa Kemal Pasha managed to recapture Muş and Bitlis from the Russians, albeit briefly.

None of these successes, however, changed the overall strategic situation. The counteroffensive in Anatolia petered out, accomplishing little beyond chewing up the last of the Ottomans' strategic reserve, the highly capable divisions that had fought at Gallipoli. The Ottomans had lost 100,000 men with little to show for it.[125] The Russians returned to Iran and again rolled back the Ottomans. The British accumulated strength for a new drive on Baghdad. The Ottoman army, barely able to feed and equip its personnel, was hemorrhaging thousands more in the form of deserters, whose practice of forming gangs and roaming Eastern Anatolia's desolate landscape in search of food only exacerbated difficulties. With its army bled white and its morale low, the empire in late 1916 was in a precarious condition.

[123] Kurat, *Türkiye ve Rusya*, 291.
[124] Allen and Muratoff, *Battlefields*, 299; Maslovskii, *Mirovaia voina*, 159, 164–65.
[125] Erickson, *Ordered*, 135.

The strategic situation of the Russian empire, however, was also troubled. As early as October 1915 the Russian army's chief of the General Staff General Mikhail Alekseev had begun warning that Russia simply was not capable of fighting simultaneously on multiple fronts and that it had better make peace with the Ottoman empire so as to concentrate on the western front against Germany.[126] Russia had lost Poland and the Baltic territory of Kurland (Kurliandiia) to the Germans. The failure of the Gallipoli campaign dashed all hopes of breaking Russia's isolation, and the economic and military strain of war was subjecting the tsarist regime to severe stress at home. The capture of Erzurum, however, had created "an important psychological moment" that "should not be missed." Here, Alekseev implored, was an opportune moment to make peace with the Ottomans and redeploy the Caucasus Army against the Germans. The recovery of Kurland was more important for Russia even than the straits. Above all, victory over Germany in the shortest time possible had to take precedence.[127]

The possibility of a separate peace had been broached as early as January 1915 when some Unionists contacted a former Russian embassy translator posted to the Italian embassy who had the official job of looking after Russian property and the unofficial duty of spying. Sazonov, however, shot down the idea of peace talks for fear that they would block the definitive resolution of the straits question in Russia's favor.[128] Members of the Ottoman opposition throughout 1915 and 1916 pitched peace proposals to Entente officials, but none generated any real interest for the obvious reason that their promoters would first have to achieve power before they could deliver. A proposal made in the name of Cemal Pasha by an Armenian intermediary in December 1915 bestirred greater interest in Petrograd, the recently renamed capital of imperial Russia. Allegedly, Cemal Pasha was willing to cede Istanbul and the straits in exchange for recognition of him as the new sultan of a revised Ottoman empire based in Damascus. It is by no means clear that Cemal Pasha in fact ever actually made such a proposal.[129] But it is a moot point in any event. The Entente powers in the meantime agreed on a plan for the final partition of the Ottoman empire with the Sykes–Picot–Sazonov agreement, and so each became wary of revisiting that sticky question for fear that it might not receive its "fair share" and would be put at

[126] Kundashev to Sazonov, 8.10.1915 [21.10.1915], in M. N. Pokrovskii, "Stavka i Ministerstvo inostrannykh del," *Krasnyi arkhiv: istoricheskii zhurnal*, 28 (1928), 10.

[127] Kundashev to Sazonov, 5.2.1916 [18.2.1916], in Pokrovskii, "Stavka," 30.

[128] Minister of Foreign Affairs Sazonov to the Ambassadors in Paris and London, 7.1.1915 [20.1.1915], *Konstantinopol' i prolivy*, ed. Adamov, 237–38.

[129] Bayur, *Türk İnkılâbı Tarihi*, vol. III, pt. 3, 224–35.

a disadvantage in the postwar struggle. Rivalry infected even relations among allies engaged in a existential struggle.

The Central Powers and the Entente made several peace offers to each other during the course of the war, but none went anywhere. Members on each side suspected the others of deception, and neither side was willing to offer the other significant concessions.[130] Yet had the Entente offered Istanbul a separate peace on lenient terms, they may have spurred the Ottoman empire to quit the war. The war among the Ottomans had been controversial from the very beginning, hence Enver's resort to deceit. Conditions in the empire had declined precipitately from the beginning of the war. By 1917 the Unionist government had become so unpopular it was forced to rely on German soldiers to guard its buildings in the capital. Indeed, Enver feared the possibility of a "peace coup" enough that he created a secret armed force to suppress any such attempt.[131] Germany's financial support to the CUP, Russia's downward spiral into revolutionary chaos in 1917, and the opportunity to realign the regional balance of power that Russia's collapse offered kept the Ottomans in the war. It is, of course, impossible to know whether Istanbul would have obliged had Russia and its allies made a credible peace offer in 1916 or earlier, but, just as the Unionists entered the war for the sake of preserving their empire, they would have withdrawn for the sake of the same. The Entente's avowal to hold the Unionists responsible for the massacres of Armenians would perhaps have complicated negotiations, but it is not inconceivable that the allies would have been willing to overlook this in exchange for an Ottoman withdrawal from the war.

Conclusion

The Ottoman decision to ally with Germany, even at the cost of war, was a rational response to the empire's predicament of being too weak not only to defend itself from outside attack but even to pursue internal reform in the face of subversion. Powerful, wealthy, and distant, Germany could provide the best counterbalance to Russia, their greatest existential threat, as well as Britain and France, which had already seized Ottoman territories and aspired to grab more. The outbreak of war in continental Europe boosted the geopolitical weight of the Ottoman empire, allowing Enver to exploit this leverage and obtain an alliance. The Central Powers

---

[130] Bernadotte E. Schmitt and Harold C. Vedeler, *The World in a Crucible, 1914–1919* (New York: Harper and Row, 1984), 466–67.

[131] Enver hid the force even from Talât and, when the latter learned what Enver had done, he decided to organize his own personal armed guard: Bayur, *Türk İnkılâbı Tarihi*, vol. III, pt. 4, 158–63.

stood an excellent chance of vanquishing the Entente, and Russia in particular, and thereby provide the Ottomans the breather required for the successful implementation of reforms. The alternatives to alliance with Germany would, at best, only delay predation on the Ottoman empire.

Ottoman war plans were fluid and hardly predetermined by ideological commitments. The primary concern was Russia. When Bulgaria's deferral of entrance into the war blocked the possibility of an offensive through the Balkans against Russia, Ottoman and German planners considered various amphibious operations along Russia's Black Sea coast before concluding that logistical and other difficulties rendered these unfeasible. That left the Caucasus and Iran as the only possible theater for operations against Russia. With the war stalled in the west, Germany and Austria-Hungary pressured the Ottomans to take the war to Russia. Enver embraced the idea of a decisive battle but, instead of winning the desired Caucasian Tannenberg, he led the Ottoman Third Army to catastrophe at Sarikamish. Cemal Pasha's Suez offensive also aimed at delivering a crippling blow, this time against Britain, but fell short. As part of their war plan, the Ottomans combined the techniques of partisan warfare they had learned in the Balkans and North Africa with the German strategy of revolutionary warfare. The Teşkilât-ı Mahsusa carried out these missions, and targeted Georgia and Ukraine as well as the Muslim Caucasus, Iran, Afghanistan, Egypt, and North Africa. Outside its successes with Circassian–Laz–Ajar partisan units in the invasion of the southwest Caucasus in 1914 and with some Kurdish tribes in northern Iran, the Teşkilât-ı Mahsusa was not remarkably effective, due in large part to a lack of trained personnel, organizational infrastructure, and resources.

For Russia, the Caucasian front was secondary. All the same, it managed to inflict a series of sizeable defeats upon the Ottomans and advance deep into Anatolia and along the Black Sea coast. In the diplomatic arena it secured British and French acquiescence to possession of Istanbul and the straits as well as a significant part of Eastern Anatolia. Yet, as General Alekseev warned, this success came with the risk of a high, even fatal cost.

5 Remastering Anatolia, rending nations, rending empires

Even as the outcome of the world war hung in doubt, tsarist officials were thinking about the postwar challenges that Eastern Anatolia would pose to their empire's security. They had entered the war without firm plans for the region, and the advance of the Russian army only complicated matters. Some voices advocated taking formal possession of the fruits of war. The Naval Ministry coveted Trabzon and the Black Sea coast. Others, especially the energetic minister of agriculture Krivoshein, advocated colonizing Eastern Anatolia with Cossacks and Russians. Despite the appeal of annexation, up until 1916 Russia's official position on Eastern Anatolia remained that after the war the land would revert to nominal Ottoman control, albeit with enhanced Russian supervision of the region's administration. Senior tsarist officials were cool to the idea of annexing Eastern Anatolia because they regarded the Armenians as "the most difficult" of the heterogeneous populations they had to rule.[1] The tsar's ministers believed an Armenia would only "become a burden" and a "future source of various complications," and regretted that some circles abroad believed that the creation of an Armenia was a Russian war aim. Indeed, they feared that Russia might inadvertently bring an Armenian state into existence.[2]

When British and French officials presented to Petrograd their proposal for partitioning the Ottoman empire, the so-called Sykes–Picot plan, the Russians initially found it unacceptable because it assigned to France territory from the Levant as far north as Diyar-ı Bekir and Lake Urmia, i.e., abutting the Russian empire. "The appearance on a large stretch of our Asian frontier, in regions of a mixed and turbulent population, of a great European power, albeit even one currently allied to

[1] Ambassador Paléologue to Briand, 11.3.1916, in Arthur Beylerian, ed., *Les Grandes puissances, l'empire ottoman et les Arméniens dans les archives françaises (1914–1918)* (Paris: Université de Paris I, Panthéon, Sorbonne, 1983), 177.
[2] A. N. Iakhontov, *Prologue to Revolution: Notes of A. N. Iakhontov on the Secret Meetings of the Council of Ministers 1915*, ed. Michael Cherniavsky (Englewood Cliffs, NJ: Prentice Hall, 1967), 36–37.

us," Sazonov advised the tsar, was "undesirable."[3] The British author of the plan, Sir Mark Sykes, however, managed to clear the way for a compromise by suggesting to Sazonov in March 1916 that the division of the Armenian population between France and Russia would dissipate Armenian antagonism toward Russia. A French-controlled "southern" or Cilician Armenia would, due to Cilicia's special significance for Armenians, become the focus of Armenian national sentiment. In turn, the more conservative Cilician Armenians would moderate the "anarcho-socialist" tendencies of their Caucasian brethren. No less important, Sykes pointed out, was the brute fact that deportations, massacres, and disease had effectively eliminated the Armenian population in the northern provinces. Muslims handily outnumbered Armenians, and this further diminished any challenge the Armenians might pose. Sazonov found Sykes persuasive and over the objections of officials in Russia's Naval and War Ministries, who pushed for the acquisition of Sinop as well as Trabzon and who warned that if the French were permitted into Anatolia they would later incite the Kurds and Armenians against Russia, reached an agreement with Britain and France on how to partition the Ottoman empire. Russia would take the provinces of Van, Erzurum, Bitlis, and Trabzon, "to a point to be defined on the shore of the Black Sea west of Trabzon," as well as the region of "Kurdistan" to the south of Van and Bitlis, and the district of Mergever. France would take possession of "Lesser Armenia," including Sivas, Harput, Diyar-ı Bekir, and Cilicia.[4] Thus, despite its initial reluctance, the Russian empire found itself the successor to the Ottoman empire as the sovereign of Eastern Anatolia. Yet again, the dynamics of global interstate competition had spurred another empire's expansion into Ottoman lands.

Harnessing intercommunal warfare: the exploitation and administration of fear and hatred

Russia could be as adept as any other power at advancing its interests in the Near East within the discursive frameworks of progress and national liberation. At home and abroad Russia presented its war with

[3] Memorandum of Sazonov, 29.2.1916 [13.3.1916], *Razdel Aziatskoi Turtsii po sekretnym dokumentam byvshego Ministerstva inostrannykh del*, ed. E. A. Adamove (Moscow: Litizdat NKID, 1924), 160–61.

[4] C. Jay Smith, *The Russian Struggle for Power, 1914–1917: A Study of Russian Foreign Policy During the First World War* (New York: Philosophical Library, 1956), 368–82. The Entente's recognition in 1917 of Italy's claims to Izmir and Konya in the agreement of St. Jean de Maurienne rounded out Anatolia's planned partition although due to revolution Russia never ratified the agreement.

the Ottoman empire not as a clash of states but as a struggle to liberate oppressed nations from an obscurantist tyranny. Tsarist authorities "operationalized" this concept by arming Armenians, Assyrians, and Kurds on the eve of the war. Such a policy served Russian ends at the war's outset. These elements would augment Russian forces at the front and create fractures in the Ottoman rear, but, as experienced imperial administrators, the Russians understood that the loyalties of borderland populations were often ambivalent. Thus, even as they generated propaganda blasting the "Turk" for barbarism and hailing their invasion of Anatolia as a liberation of the Christians of Anatolia, they regarded those same populations with unease. They knew that the agendas of some in these groups could differ fundamentally from that of the Russian state. Although Russian authorities never repudiated the notion of a war of liberation, they consistently subordinated it to the imperatives of imperial power. Nonetheless, despite their experience in running one of history's largest and most complex empires, Russian officials found the challenge of ruling Eastern Anatolia severe. Exploiting intercommunal hostilities for the sake of waging war could be easy, but taming them for the sake of establishing order was not.

The dilemmas that confronted Russian rule in occupied Anatolia were not unlike those that had bedeviled the Ottomans prior to the war. Resource-strapped and distracted administrators had to maintain order among disparate communities that were in fundamental conflict with each other, hostile to the state, and with access to outside sources of support. The traditional formula for rule over a heterogeneous region, an imperial order, had in the age of the national idea lost much legitimacy. It was no longer a compelling vision, even for many imperial administrators. Moreover, the possibility that today's imperial administrators might be gone tomorrow tempered the willingness of locals to trust or accommodate newly arrived imperial institutions and officials. The best that tsarist administrators in Eastern Anatolia could achieve was an equilibrium that was in perpetual flux and in need of constant maintenance. They could not ignore the conflicts swirling beneath them, yet involvement brought the danger that those conflicts would seep into the administrators' ranks, divide those ranks, and tear them apart.

As Russian authorities on the eve of the war were moving ahead with plans to mobilize and arm Armenians, Assyrians, and Kurds, Sazonov cautioned that the enrollment of these populations in Russia's war effort would expose them to the "justified retribution" of the Ottomans. Sazonov's concern was not so much the suffering these populations might undergo but rather the damage to Russia's prestige that would ensue from their exposure to retribution. Concerns for their objects of liberation were not foremost in the minds of Russian officials. When in December 1914 Catholicos Kevork V submitted a plea to Nicholas II to establish an autonomous Armenia under Russian rule, the tsar blithely assured him, "Tell your flock, Holy Father, that a most brilliant future awaits the Armenians."[5] In fact, an incomprehensibly devastating future awaited them.

Cutting the Gordian Knot

Prior to the war, the Unionists had seen Eastern Anatolia slide inexorably from under their control. The six years following the Constitutional Revolution had been marked by a chain of crises, one after another, foreign and domestic, that afforded neither Unionist nor other Ottoman governments the opportunity to formulate, let alone implement, solutions for governing the *Vilayât-ı Sitte*. Due in no small measure to Russia's patronage of Kurdish rebels, the Unionists had failed in their effort to pacify the Kurds and bring them under state control. Consequently, they could not satisfy Armenian demands for basic security, let alone for land reform, and the situation remained volatile. The imposition of the Russian-backed reform plan in 1914 heralded the end of real Ottoman sovereignty in that region, and inside and outside the empire alike observers expected the end of nominal sovereignty to follow soon after. Only the outbreak of the war had blocked the plan's implementation, and in December 1914 the Ottoman government formally abrogated the plan as part of its policy of total independence.[6] The act marked a return to the status quo ante, but the lesson the Unionists drew from their experience was that if they were to remain sovereign in Eastern Anatolia the status quo was unsustainable. In the coming year they would cut the Gordian Knot through the most aggressive form of social engineering.

The widening gyre

As discussed earlier, the trauma and political uncertainty that ensued following the Balkan Wars caused intercommunal tensions in Eastern Anatolia to simmer up through the summer of 1914. The outbreak of war in August and the looming likelihood of war between the Ottoman and Russian empires stoked tensions in the borderlands of Anatolia and the Caucasus until they exploded in a crescendo when the empires openly joined in warfare. First, localized violence became regional, and then central state institutions targeted whole populations. General Vladimir

---

[5] Hovannisian, *Armenia on the Road*, 45.   [6] Türkmen, *Vilayât-ı Şarkiye*, 83.

Liakhov took a significant step in escalation. When in January 1915 he retook Ajaria and neighboring areas in Georgia from the invading Ottomans and their Laz and Ajar irregulars, he ordered his Cossacks to kill Muslim natives on sight and burn every mosque and village, and reduced Artvin and the Chorokhi valley to a cinder.[7] Armenian militias participated in exacting revenge. Ottoman officials estimated that up to 30,000 Muslim males had been killed and thousands more women and children left without shelter in the winter. Istanbul urgently informed the embassy of Italy, then still a neutral power, of alleged inhumane treatment of Ottoman prisoners by Armenians in the Russian army.[8] David Lang estimates that the punitive expeditions in the Chorokhi valley took the lives of 45,000 Muslims, leaving just 7,000 alive.[9]

By January's end the Russians had beaten back the Ottomans and restored order behind their lines. Nonetheless, Vorontsov-Dashkov ordered the deportation of some 10,000 Muslims living along the border into the interior of Russia. Fears of bringing infectious disease and pan-Turkism inside Russia, however, led officials subsequently to dump roughly half of the deportees on uninhabited Nargen Island in the Caspian Sea. Measures more extreme were proposed. A majority of Russia's cabinet ministers backed the radical idea of deporting all Muslims from the provinces of Kars and Batumi and then stripping them of citizenship. Following the war, these Muslims would be expelled from the empire altogether and Russian peasants resettled on their land. Russia's Foreign and Justice Ministries, however, advised that international law made no allowance for mass expulsions and warned that such an act would invite a reciprocal torrent of refugees from the Ottoman lands into Russia. Protests by Georgian Duma members that the deportees were not ethnic Turks but in fact Ajars prompted an investigation that concluded that the deportees had not been guilty of hostile acts but, to the contrary, had been victims of Cossack and Armenian pogroms.[10] Once the threat of invasion had been squelched, Russia's Caucasus remained tranquil until late 1917 when the empire as a whole began to unravel. Russia's institutions and legal culture had managed to uphold order, but just barely. Even a shallow offensive mounted by a weak opponent had nearly brought the edifice of empire in the Caucasus down upon itself.

---

[7] Price, *War*, 224; Maslovskii, *Mirovaia voina*, 150.
[8] İsmet Binark, ed., *Osmanlı Belgelerinde Ermeniler*, 2nd edn. (Ankara: T. C. Başbakanlık Devlet Arşivleri Genel Müdürlüğü, 1994), 20–22.
[9] Lang, *Soviet Georgia*, 185.   [10] Lohr, *Nationalizing*, 151–52.

Square pegs into round holes: ending an imperial order

Whereas Russia's Caucasus remained secure, the picture on the Ottoman side in early 1915 was different. To the front, the powerful Russian army loomed. To the rear, Armenian partisans were cutting telegraph wires, attacking military and police posts, and assassinating military and civilian officials. Through spies and agents in St. Petersburg and Iran, the Ottomans knew of Russian plans to provoke Armenians to a general uprising.[11] The partisan activity was especially unnerving because the main Armenian population centers lay astride the only two railways in the Third Army's area of operations. Also carrying out attacks were Kurds loyal to Abdürrezzak and others. Ottoman officers eyed developments to the front and rear nervously.[12]

The Russian army's establishment of four Armenian volunteer regiments (*druzhiny*), calls by prominent Armenians abroad to their co-ethnics to support the Allied war effort, and knowledge of Russian communications with Ottoman Armenians fed Ottoman suspicions of imminent revolt around the city of Van. In November, Ottoman gendarmes learned from two captured Armenian couriers that a large uprising was in the offing.[13] In response Ottoman security forces stepped up sweeps of villages to uncover arms, redeployed a gendarmerie unit from Bitlis to Van, and placed Armenian conscripts into labor battalions where, without arms and to the rear, they could neither pose a threat nor defend themselves. Ottoman fears were realized in April 1915 when the Armenians of Van rose and seized control of the city. The lightly equipped militias and gendarmes deployed near the city were unequal to the task of suppressing the revolt, forcing the Ottoman army to divert regular units from an offensive in Iran to invest the city. The fighting in and around Van was merciless. While Ottoman regulars and Kurdish militiamen besieged the town, tribesmen roamed the outlying areas. Armenian males twelve years or older were targeted for death, and Armenian women liable to kidnapping and rape. Inside the town the well-armed rebels held the advantage, and they, too, gave no quarter, exacting retribution on Muslim women and other non-combatants.[14]

---

[11] McCarthy, *et al.*, *Rebellion*, 185.
[12] Erickson, *Ordered*, 98–99; Edward Erickson, "Bayonets on Musa Dagh: Ottoman Counterinsurgency Operations – 1915," *Journal of Strategic Studies*, 28, 3 (June 2005), 533–34.
[13] Nâzım Bey to the 3rd Army Command [29.11.1914], Document no. 1812, *Askerî Tarih Belgeleri Dergisi* 31, 81 (1982), 50.
[14] Rafael de Nogales, *Four Years Beneath the Crescent*, tr. Muna Lee (New York: Charles Scribner's Sons, 1926), 57–100; Çakmak, *Büyük Harpte*, 94–95. See also "Oborona Vana," in M. D. Amirkhanian, ed., *Genotsid Armian i russkaia publitsistika* (Yerevan: Muzei-Institut genotsida armian, 1998), 143–89; Anahide Ter Minassian, "Van 1915,"

General Yudenich was aware of the uprising and was determined to exploit the opportunity it provided. He ordered the Russian Caucasus Army to drive on Van from Iran. Along the way he took care to deploy his cavalry across the countryside so as to produce a spectacle of mass force and awe Iran's Kurds into submission. The Ottomans around Van, still unable to prevail over the rebels, had little chance of stopping the Russian column. Accordingly, they withdrew on 15 May. Tens of thousands of fearful Muslims accompanied them. Two days later Yudenich's vanguard, composed of Armenian volunteers and Cossacks, relieved the city.[15]

The question of whether the Armenian revolt in Van is best understood as an act of self-defense or of treacherous collaboration remains hotly debated. As a sizeable city lying astride supply routes, Van was strategically critical. The Ottomans' prophylactic measures were unremarkable and, in themselves, hardly evidence of a plan to massacre the Armenian population. Moreover, the armaments, organization, and numbers of rebels at Van reveal that the uprising had been far from spontaneous. Ottoman fears of a threat were neither groundless nor overblown. The rebels did, after all, accomplish a military feat historically quite rare for guerrilla forces, namely taking and holding a city behind enemy lines.

Yet at the same time, the Armenians had ample reasons other than treachery to arm themselves. They had not forgotten the Hamidian massacres some two decades previously. The 1908 Revolution had brought a modest improvement in security, but this proved temporary. In recent years the Ottoman government had, at best, failed to provide security to Armenians. At worst, its own officials had fanned and manipulated anti-Armenian sentiment. Amidst the region's chronic political instability, tensions between Muslims and Armenians continued to build through 1914. The natural response of any population living under such conditions of malevolent anarchy would be to arm and organize itself, and such behavior is not in itself an indication of bad faith or betrayal. Still less can the revolt be described as an obtusely opportunist bid to exploit the war by assisting Russia. Many of Van's revolutionaries had been avowedly hostile toward tsarist Russia. The decline in order and the outbreak of war, however, had put Van's Armenians in an impossible situation. Pogroms against Armenians in areas surrounding Van in the months preceding the revolt reinforced Armenian fears of impending massacre.[16] Conditions

in *Armenian Van/Vaspurakan*, ed. Richard G. Hovannisian (Costa Mesa, CA: Mazda, 2000), 209–44; and McCarthy, *et al.*, *Rebellion*.

[15] Erickson, *Ordered*, 105; Maslovskii, *Mirovaia voina*, 161; Allen and Muratoff, *Battlefields*, 299–301. On the difficulties in the advance, see Arutiunian, *Kavkazskii front*, 176–77.

[16] Gaunt, *Massacres*, 57.

deprived the option of remaining neutral of any rationality. Collaboration with Russia offered the best hope for survival.

The debate about whether the revolt at Van was an act of self-defense or collaboration is thus pointless because it assumes that a meaningful distinction can be made between the two. Self-defense amounted to collaboration, whether intentionally or not. The relationship between Ottoman and Armenian fears was not static, but dynamic, and is better understood through the concept of the "security dilemma."[17] Operating under conditions of anarchy wherein trust was impossible, both the Ottoman authorities and the Armenians found themselves compelled to assume the worst intentions lay behind the capabilities of the other. Hence, Ottoman authorities regarded the stockpiling of arms and the organization of armed bands as an indicator of Armenian intentions to orchestrate a general uprising, while the Armenians interpreted the deployment of Ottoman forces near Van as an indicator of an intention to eliminate them.[18]

At the same time as the Van rebellion was unfolding, the Russians were entering from the east, the British pushing on Baghdad from the south, and, most ominously, the British and French were storming ashore at Gallipoli. The simultaneous attacks stretched the wobbling Ottoman army to breaking point. As the Unionists debated how to handle the Van uprising, an Ottoman colonel pointed to Russia's expulsion of Muslims into Ottoman territory and urged a reciprocal expulsion of the rebels and their families either into Russian territory or into the interior of Anatolia. He suggested also that, barring objections from others, Muslim refugees be resettled in and around Van.[19]

Small-scale deportations of Armenians had begun in February, but it was the combination of the Van uprising and the landings at Gallipoli that triggered the decision to deport the Armenians en masse. The Ottomans shut down all Armenian political parties and associations and arrested

---

[17] The "security dilemma" refers to the paradoxical phenomenon that when under conditions of anarchy what one does to enhance one's own security provokes reactions from others that, in the end, make one less secure. For example, the decision to arm oneself, even if for the sole purpose of self-preservation, may well be interpreted by one's neighbor as preparation for a future act of aggression. It may thus provoke the neighbor to acquire arms, thereby establishing a vicious circle. The classic exposition of the security dilemma is Robert Jervis, "Cooperation Under the Security Dilemma," *World Politics*, 30, 2 (January 1978), 167–214. Barry R. Posen applies this concept to ethnic conflict in his article, "The Security Dilemma and Ethnic Conflict," *Survival*, 35, 1 (Spring 1993), 27–47. As Posen observes, "the drive for security in one group can be so great that it produces near-genocidal behavior towards neighboring groups" (30).

[18] Anahide Ter Minassian alludes to this dynamic in her discussion of the role of fear: Ter Minassian, "Van 1915," 224; see also "Oborona Vana."

[19] Dündar, *Türkiye'nin Şifresi*, 280–81.

their leadership. In Istanbul during the first two days they arrested 2,345 Armenian leaders and thereby decapitated the Armenians politically. On 9 May Talât ordered deportations from Van, Erzurum, Bitlis, and Zeytun. After the loss of Van, Talât expanded the areas to be "cleansed" of Armenians to include the provinces of Adana, Antep, and the western half of Halep (Aleppo). He instructed that deportees were to be resettled in parts of Musul, Deyr ül-Zor, Halep, and Syria in such a way that individual settlements did not exceed fifty households and their numbers did not exceed 10 percent of the surrounding Muslim population.[20] Reports of widescale massacres and atrocities accompanying the dislocations spurred the Allies on 24 May 1915 to issue a note condemning the Ottoman government for what, in terminology coined by Russian legal scholars, they labeled "crimes against humanity and civilization" and for which they promised to hold responsible members of the Ottoman government and their agents.[21]

The decision to define whole populations as suspect and to uproot, expel, and relocate them was not particular to the Ottomans or Unionists. The manipulation of borderland populations was hoary imperial practice.[22] In the nineteenth century, however, two things changed. The first was that, beginning in Europe, state institutions began to employ sciences such as statistics, sociology, and ethnography to vastly increase their capacity to identify, classify, and control population groups. The second was that these institutions, including armies, came to imagine ethnicity to be a key predictor of political behavior. Armies anxiously trained ethnographers to advise on how to manage and exploit the ethnic identities of friendly and hostile populations alike.[23] By the beginning of the twentieth century, forced population exchange was emerging as an almost routine practice, one that many regarded as logical and even salutary. In November 1913 the Ottoman empire and Bulgaria had engaged in reciprocal expulsions of Slavic Muslims and Christians. When in the spring of 1914 war with Greece appeared likely, the Ottomans expelled Ottoman Greeks from strategically vulnerable stretches of the Aegean coast. Girs approved, opining to Sazonov that the "cleansing" of the Greeks would promote reconciliation, not bloodshed, between the Ottoman empire and Greece.[24] During World War I, Russia forcibly relocated not just

---

[20] Dündar, *Türkiye'nin Şifresi*, 274–86.

[21] Peter Holquist, "Armenian Occupation," in *A Question of Genocide*, ed. Ronald Grigor Suny (Oxford: Oxford University Press, forthcoming).

[22] Mark Pinson, "Demographic Warfare: An Aspect of Ottoman and Russian Policy, 1854–1866," Ph.D. Dissertation, Harvard University, 1970.

[23] See Holquist, "To Count, to Extract, and to Exterminate."

[24] The term "cleansing" (*ochishchenie*) is Girs': Girs to Sazonov, 13.6.1914 [26.06.1914], *Movei*, ser. 3, vol. 3, 439.

Muslims from the border region in the Caucasus but also Germans and Jews by the hundreds of thousands on its western front.[25] As noted earlier, Ottoman military officers referenced the Russian precedent in the Caucasus during the debate on how to respond to the uprising at Van.

The deportations of Armenians thus were not unique in their origin, but they acquired several dimensions that distinguished them from conventional wartime deportations and indicate a motivation more radical and ambitious than immediate security concerns. The first is that deportation orders were applied not just to Armenians in militarily sensitive areas but to virtually all Armenians outside Istanbul, Edirne, Izmir, and the Arab provinces. In June and July 1915 Talât expanded the deportation orders to include virtually all Armenians in Eastern Anatolia and then in the west outside the three aforementioned cities. The second is that the acts of deportation were often preceded and accompanied by massacres, many of which were organized and facilitated by state officials. In some locations, such as Diyar-ı Bekir, the butchery reached demonic levels.[26] Disease, hunger, and thirst exacted the greatest toll on those who remained.

The third is that the destruction of the Armenians was not a self-contained operation against one troublesome population. Instead, it must be understood as part of a nascent program of ethnic homogenization that involved the resettlement of a multitude of other population groups, including Muslim Kurds, Albanians, Circassians, and others in small, dispersed numbers so as to break up clan and tribal ties and facilitate assimilation, and the substitution of Muslim place names for non-Muslim ones. These measures were aimed at the long-term Turkification of Anatolia. This larger program, in turn, was a direct response to the global order's adoption of the national idea. If the legitimacy, and thus security, of state borders was dependent on the degree of correspondence to ethnographic lines, the Unionists would ensure that the latter conformed to the former. They would reshape the square peg of Anatolia to fit the round hole the global order favored.

As mentioned earlier, it is no coincidence that nearly half of the Unionist leadership came from the Balkan and Aegean borderlands, i.e., those

---

[25] Mark Von Hagen, "The Great War and the Mobilization of Ethnicity in the Russian Empire," in *Post-Soviet Political Order: Conflict and State Building*, ed. Jack Snyder and Barnett Rubin (New York: Routledge, 1998), 42, 46. For an overview, see Peter Gatrell, "War, Population Displacement, and State Formation in the Russian Borderlands, 1914–1924," in *Homelands: War, Population, and Statehood in Eastern Europe and Russia*, ed. Nick Baron and Gatrell (London: Anthem Press, 2004), 10–34.

[26] Uğur Ü. Üngör, "'A Reign of Terror': CUP Rule in Diyarbekir Province, 1913–1918," M.A. Thesis, University of Amsterdam, 2005.

territories that had witnessed repeated violent expulsions and massacres of Muslims and the establishment of nation-states.[27] Significantly, these men fostered no fantasies of irredentism in the Balkans. They nurtured no illusions about the relative power of the Ottoman state. Difficult though it must have been for them, they recognized that their homelands had been lost for good. They were not dreamers but cunning, resolute, and desperate men for whom the idea of a last stand was no romantic abstraction. They and their families had tasted the sting of imperial decline. Despite their efforts and those of earlier generations of Ottoman statesmen to stabilize their empire, they saw what remained crashing down around them. Unlike the Russians who were ambivalent toward Eastern Anatolia, the Unionists were grimly determined to preserve Ottoman sovereignty over the region. Experience had taught them that the global community of states accorded no legitimacy to pluralistic but weak empires. As long as Anatolia remained ethnically pluralistic it would be vulnerable to subversion and partition. The homogenization of Anatolia was the surest solution to the dilemma they faced. If the Gordian Knot that was Eastern Anatolia had to be cut, they were willing to do it.

The state-guided demographic transformation of Eastern Anatolia had begun under Abdülhamid II, who boosted the numbers of Muslims in the region by resettling Muslim refugees there. However, the losses of North Africa, Egypt, and then Muslim Albania and Macedonia, as well as the creeping emergence of the Kurdish question into the interstate sphere, all underscored the reality that the Ottoman state no longer had a privileged claim on territories populated predominantly by Muslims. Ethnicity was the critical criterion. Unionists such as Ziya Gökalp prior to the war had begun to think about the need to transform Anatolia into a more ethnically homogeneous Turkish territory, but these ideas remained in the realm of conjecture. Istanbul's acceptance of the 1914 reform plan signaled that they would stay there.

The war, however, presented an opportunity to remaster Anatolia's demographics and thereby block future partition.[28] The beginning of the war found hundreds of thousands of refugees from the Balkans still on the move and in need of permanent settlement. The advance of Russia's Caucasus Army sent Muslim villagers and nomads alike fleeing from the east, further swelling the numbers of itinerant Muslims, and by the summer of 1915 the deportations of Christians were in full swing. In response to the influx from the Balkans the Ottomans in 1913 had established a department for the resettlement of refugees under the Interior Ministry. Then in 1916 under the same ministry they set up a Directorate for the

---

[27] See Zürcher, "Young Turks."   [28] Dündar, *Türkiye'nin Şifresi*, 282.

Settlement of Tribes and Immigrants. Talât instructed the directorate to distribute non-Turkish refugees among Turkish populations in such a way as to promote the refugees' long-term linguistic and cultural assimilation. The measures taken included restricting in some places resettled Muslim refugees to no more than 5–10% of the local Turkish population and separating the tribal elites, the sheikhs and aghas, from ordinary tribesmen in order to break down the tribe's internal structures and thereby facilitate sedentarization, assimilation, and state control.[29]

Whereas the assimilation of Muslims was conceivable, the assimilation of Christians was not. Accordingly, in January 1916 Enver ordered that inside the "Ottoman lands" place names in "Armenian, Greek, Bulgarian, and non-Muslim languages" be changed to Muslim ones.[30] The presence of Armenians in the eastern provinces was especially problematic in the Unionists' view. Because it provided a readymade pretext for intervention, it constituted a weapon that the great powers wielded against the Ottoman empire. As Talât put it in his address to the Unionists' 1916 Congress, Russia had been using the Armenian Question as "an instrument of war." It was not the only great power to do so. Britain, too, he reminded his audience, covetously eyed the Armenian provinces, had used its Anatolian consulates to incite Armenians, and desired an independent Armenian state in Anatolia as a buffer against Russia.[31] That same year the Ottoman Foreign Ministry commissioned a historical review of the Armenian Question from 1877 to 1914. The review concluded that Britain, France, and Russia had "always worked against us on the Armenian Question and caused us a great many troubles," while Germany, Austria-Hungary, and Italy more often than not had accommodated those "malicious policies."[32] As long as a substantial Armenian presence remained inside Ottoman Anatolia, the land would be vulnerable to outsiders' meddling. Deporting the Armenians would neutralize not just the immediate threat of partisans and saboteurs, but also the long-term threat of foreign intervention and partition.

Talât followed the progress of the deportations and resettlement closely, regularly soliciting confidential statistical reports on the numbers of Armenian deportees and Muslim refugees. These reports were not for publication but were strictly confidential and kept for internal purposes.

---

[29] Dündar, İskân Politikası, 137–55; Dündar, Türkiye'nin Şifresi, 399–418.
[30] BOA, Instruction of Enver, 23 Kanunuevvel 1331 [5.1.1916], DH.İ.UM, D. 48, S. 17, F. 18.
[31] Zafer Toprak, "İttihat ve Terakki Fırkası 1332 Senesi Kongre Raporu," Tarih ve Toplum, no. 22 (June 1986), 136.
[32] Münir Süreyya Bey, Ermeni Meselesinin Siyasî Tarihçesi (1877–1914), ed. Uğurhan Demirbaş, et al. (Ankara: Başbakanlık Basımevi, 2001), 103.

According to the statistics kept by Talât, a total of 924,158 Armenians were forcibly relocated.[33] Roughly 800,000 were deported from the eastern provinces. Some 250,000 Armenians managed to escape deportation by fleeing into Russian territory. Of the 800,000, only 500,000 made it to their designated resettlement areas.

"The scenes that I have witnessed are beyond any possible conception of horror," wrote Auguste Bernau, a German based in Aleppo, before describing what he saw while traveling along the Euphrates in 1916: piles of 200 to 300 bodies of victims of "hunger, deprivation, dysentery, and typhus," and desperate groups of women and children – the men having earlier been slain – roaming "along the riverbank in search of a few stalks of grass in order to still their hunger." Survivors told of mass rapes and children drowned in rivers.[34] As an Armenian poet wrote, "So great is the anguish and suffering of the Armenians, so hideous and unprecedented, that the infinity and fathomlessness of the universe must be considerate in gauging it; there are no words in the dictionaries to qualify the hideousness of the terrors. Not a single poet can find words."[35]

That the deportation of so many people in such a short amount of time would exact such a high death toll could not have been a surprise, particularly as Talât personally tracked the deportations.[36] This, combined with copious accounts from multiple sources of massacres and the choice of Deyr ül-Zor, a desert province known to Talât as inhospitable, as a terminal point for most of the deportees suggests that the goal of the deportations was if not the extermination of the Armenian community, then the devastation of it such that it could no longer have a credible claim to Eastern Anatolia. Indeed, by 1916, virtually no Armenians remained in the Ottoman-held eastern provinces. The much smaller community of Assyrian Christians was also swept up in the deportations and suffered similarly. The deportations, Talât explained, had accomplished "the definitive solution to the Armenian Question."[37] When the

[33] Murat Bardakçı, ed., *Talât Paşa'nın Evrak-ı Metrûkesi* (Istanbul: Everest Yayınları, 2008), 77.
[34] Walker, *Armenia*, 228–29
[35] As cited in Martin Gilbert, *The First World War: A Complete History* (New York: Henry Holt and Company, 1994), 167.
[36] Taner Akçam, "*Ermeni Meselesi Hallolunmuştur*": *Osmanlı Belgelerine Göre Savaş Yıllarında Ermendilere Yönelik Politikalar* (Istanbul: İletişim, 2008), 271–329; Dündar, *Modern Türkiye'nin Şifresi*, 248–348. Some charge that Dündar overstates Talât's knowledge and control of events. See Ayhan Aktar and Abdülhamit Kırmızı, "'Bon Pour l'Orient': Fuat Dündar'ın Kitabını Deşifre Ederken…," *Tarih ve Toplum Yeni Yaklaşımlar*, 8 (Spring 2009), 175–79.
[37] Fuat Dündar, "Pouring a People into the Desert: The 'Definitive Solution' to the Armenian Question," in *A Question of Genocide* ed. Suny.

Turkish author Halide Edib queried him about the fate of the Armenians, he answered in an angry and defensive tone. He decried the world's
"criminal silence" about the massacre of Muslims in the Balkan Wars
and then concluded, "I have the conviction that as long as a nation
does the best for its own interests, and succeeds, the world admires it
and thinks it is moral. I am ready to die for what I have done and I
know that I shall die for it."[38] His words leave little doubt he understood the radically transgressive nature of his resolution of the Armenian
Question.

Talât's vision of remaking Anatolia was radical in its ambition, but not
in its conception. The idea of using state power to make ethnic settlement
patterns congruent with state borders represented the logical converse
of the national idea of drawing state borders according to ethnic criteria.
If borders could be altered to match ethnic settlement patterns, so too
could ethnic settlement patterns be reshaped to fit borders.[39] It would be
wrong, however, to infer from this that the destruction of the Armenians
or Assyrians was planned before the war. Rather, as Donald Bloxham and
Fuat Dündar have argued, the deportation and massacre of Armenians
emerged from a series of limited but linked measures in a process of
cumulative radicalization.[40] Immediate security concerns related to the
protection of supply lines and the rear aligned with anxieties about the
long-term viability of the empire. With refugees already on the move and
deportations underway in the context of total war, it was a relatively short
step to expand the use of the techniques of resettlement and mass death
for the creation of a more homogeneous population, a population that
would secure the state and its claim to the land. In short, in order to save
the state, the Unionists had to destroy the empire.

A doctrinal commitment to Turkism was not the prime driver behind
the Unionists' demographic policies. Throughout their tenure in power
the Unionists had one constant guiding them: their determination to
preserve their state.[41] To the extent that senior Unionists had Turkist
proclivities, it was because they identified ethnic Turks as the bulwark of

[38] Halidé Edib Adıvar, *Memoirs of Halidé Edib* (London: Century Co., 1926), 387.
[39] Norman Naimark, *Fires of Hatred: Ethnic Cleansing in Twentieth-Century Europe* (Cambridge, MA: Harvard University Press, 2001), 18; Donald Bloxham, *The Great Game of
Genocide: Imperialism, Nationalism, and the Destruction of the Ottoman Armenians* (Oxford:
Oxford University Press, 2005), 120.
[40] Bloxham, *Great Game*, 96; See also Donald Bloxham, "The Armenian Genocide of
1915–1916: Cumulative Radicalization and the Development of a Destruction Policy,"
Past and Present, 181 (November 2003), 141–92; Dündar, *Türkiye'nin Şifresi*, 276–323.
See also Michael Mann, *The Dark Side of Democracy: Explaining Ethnic Cleansing* (New
York: Cambridge University Press, 2005), 111–79.
[41] Hanioğlu, *Preparation*, 316–17.

their state's power. They responded to the multiple crises that chronically beset them while in and out of power in the years from 1908 through 1918 by adopting *ad hoc* a wide variety of policies. As Taner Akçam has written, their drift toward Turkism was the result of necessity much more than of doctrinaire preference.[42]

This is not to absolve the Unionists of responsibility for their policies. Instead it is to underscore the contingency of the process by which they arrived at the decision to remaster Anatolia with such brutal speed and force. Rather than representing the implementation of a carefully considered and comprehensive plan to remake Anatolia, the Unionists' deportation policies emerged during the war out of responses to immediate concerns, be they security concerns or the need to resettle refugees. Once presented with the opportunities opened up by the war to reshape Anatolia's demographics, however, the Unionists seized them, inflicting death upon hundreds of thousands of non-combatants.

Although it is impossible to obtain precise numbers of deaths in Eastern Anatolia during World War I, there is no question that mortality rates were staggering. Estimates are that 40 percent of the Muslim population in the provinces of Van, Erzurum, and Bitlis perished in the years 1914–21. It is reasonable to assume that at least half, if not more, died between 1914 and 1918.[43] This is an astoundingly high death rate, yet when one remembers how tentative life in Anatolia was before the war for the Kurds and other nomads, who suffered from appallingly high rates of infant mortality and disease, it is not unfathomable. Wartime conditions and hundreds of thousands of soldiers, refugees, and deportees crisscrossing Anatolia disrupted seasonal migration and agricultural patterns, wrecked local economies, and condemned countless more to death by starvation and sickness. The deportations of Armenians, who formed essential components of Anatolia's economy, contributed to the economic collapse and the emergence of famine and paradoxically undermined the Ottoman army's ability to feed itself. When Grigoris Balakian, an Armenian priest who traveled Anatolia *incognito* and witnessed the destruction of his own people, came upon tens of thousands of Turks and Kurds, "the survivors of the hundreds of thousands of Muslims who had fled the Russian armies and the Armenian volunteer regiments", he remarked:

Decimated by starvation and epidemic, these Muslims would die in the severities of the coming winter. I passed through the Turkish neighborhoods along the river and came upon thousands of Turkish and Kurdish refugees – women, girls,

[42] Akçam, *From Empire to Republic*, 136.   [43] McCarthy, *Death and Exile*, 230.

and children – on the flagstone pavements in front of the mosques. They were living ghosts, reduced by starvation to skeletons; for clothing they had only rags hanging from their shoulders, and the dirt that covered them rendered them unrecognizable. There was no visible difference at all between these refugees and Armenian exiles in the deserts of Der Zor.[44]

Although Anatolia's Muslims sustained greater losses in absolute terms, Armenians and Assyrians bore the greater losses proportionately, a function of their being targeted for deportation and massacre. The most thorough study of the statistical data puts the number of Armenian dead at 664,000, or about 45 percent of prewar Anatolia's 1.5 million Armenians.[45] Other scholars estimate that 800,000, perhaps as many as one million, Armenians ultimately perished from massacre, starvation, and disease.[46] Losses for the Assyrians were at least comparable in proportionate terms.[47] The exact figures will never be known, but the result was a radical one in the truest sense of the word, the effective eradication of the presence in Anatolia of two peoples who had been rooted there for millennia.

Imposing empire, rending empire

Russian policies toward the peoples of Anatolia varied according to the needs of the imperial state. When the mission was conquest, tsarist authorities did not refrain from inflaming and exploiting intercommunal tensions. When the mission shifted to the administration of conquered territories, they strove to establish an order that did not discriminate according to religion or ethnicity. The challenge of ruling an ethnically and religiously heterogeneous population was a familiar one to Russians, but governing war-riven Anatolia would prove extraordinarily difficult even for imperial administrators as practiced as the tsar's. By the time the Russians established their authority, intercommunal rifts had turned into chasms. The calamitous living conditions of wartime Anatolia added to tensions. Disease and starvation ravaged the population. Refugees, bands of deserters, and nomads wandered the land in desperate search of shelter and sustenance. The future was uncertain and competition for scarce

---

[44] Grigoris Balakian, *Armenian Golgotha*, tr. and ed. Peter Balakian and Aris Sevag (New York: Alfred Knopf, 2009), 356–57.

[45] Fuat Dündar, *Crime of Numbers: The Role of Statistics in the Armenian Question (1878–1918)* (New Brunswick: Transaction Publishers, 2010), 151.

[46] Akçam, *Shameful Act*, 183; Bayur, *Türk İnkılabı Tarihi*, vol. III, pt. 4, 787; Bloxham, "Genocide," 141. Documents from Talât's personal collection, although problematic, suggest a figure around one million: Bardakçı, ed., *Talât Paşa'nın Evrak-ı Metrûkesi*, 108–09.

[47] Gaunt, *Massacres*, 301.

resources harsh. Survival dictated the strengthening of intracommunal bonds.

The Russians initially sought to exploit intercommunal strife in the service of their goals but also to contain it. Thus, even as the Russians were arming Armenians, Assyrians, and Kurds, Vorontsov-Dashkov at the outset of the war instructed the Caucasus Army that it was to treat all peoples in occupied territories equally. Muslims were to enjoy precisely the same privileges as Christians, and violence was to be directed only against armed formations.[48] But the problems inherent in employing ethnic militias revealed themselves from the very beginning. Already in December 1914 a tsarist official was complaining that the Armenian regiments "abandon themselves above all to the looting and destruction of the homes of the peaceful Muslim population, thereby settling their centuries-old scores."[49] In response, an advocate of the regiments argued for their utility but assented that, indeed, tighter supervision to curb "excesses" was warranted.[50] Yet the impulse for vengeance was strong. Armenian women in communities victimized by Kurds exhorted Armenian militiamen entering Anatolia to "Give them what they have given to us."[51] In areas of Anatolia where local Armenians vouched for the righteous behavior of their Kurdish neighbors who sheltered them, Caucasian Armenians nonetheless identified and dealt with them as enemies.[52]

Throughout 1915 a debate was waged over the utility of the Armenian volunteer regiments. While Armenian spokesmen and some tsarist officers hailed their bravery and zealotry, other Russian officials pointed to their predilection for looting and massacring Muslims. The alienation of Muslims had negative military consequences, the latter contended, and preventing this had to take precedence. In the summer of 1915, the Russian army High Command vetoed the formation of new Armenian regiments and began discouraging Armenians from abroad from volunteering.[53] Then in December it abolished the regiments altogether, absorbing willing Armenian personnel into the regular army, executing

[48] AVPRI, Order to the Caucasus Army No. 106, 31.10.1914 [13.11.1914], f. 151, o. 482, d. 3490, l. 48.

[49] AVPRI, Telegram from "Stolitsa," 19.11.1914 [1.12.1914], f. Politarkhiv, o. 482, d. 3490, l. 150.

[50] AVPRI, Gul'kevich to the Diplomatic Official under the Viceroy of the Caucasus, 21.11.1914 [3.12.1914], f. 151, o. 482, d. 3490, l. 51.

[51] Price, War, 136.   [52] Bedirhan, Otobiyografya, 46.

[53] AVPRI, Prince Kudashev, Chief of the Diplomatic Office Under the Staff of the Supreme Commander, June 1915; Chief of Staff of the Section on Organization and Service of Forces to A. A. Neratov, 1.7.1915 [14.7.1915], f. 151, o. 482, d. 3490, ll. 55, 63.

an undetermined number of Armenian volunteers, and disbanding the rest.[54]

Military effectiveness and the preservation of the neutrality of the Muslims, however, were not the only concerns that influenced the Russian decision to dissolve the volunteer regiments. By the middle of 1915 fear of Armenian separatism was again informing Russian policy. Tsarist officials began to see the volunteer Armenian formations as two-edged swords that could be turned against their own empire as easily as against the Ottoman empire. Thus the Russian consulate in Salonica in the summer of 1915, at the height of Armenian massacres and deportations rejected the requests of roughly 100 Ottoman Armenians to enter Russia and join the army. Despite Petrograd's official condemnation of the Unionist government in the note of 24 May, the consul dismissed the applicants' complaints of mistreatment by the Ottoman government as economic, not political, in origin. He further justified his decision to his superiors by suggesting that among the applicants were revolutionaries and even "Turkish spies."[55] Similarly, General Yudenich blocked the admittance of a group of Armenians from Bulgaria as "undesirable" because, he believed, they were almost certainly Dashnaks.[56] Others suspected that Armenian units were arming themselves at Russia's expense yet refraining from combat against the Ottomans in order to preserve their strength for a postwar struggle against Russia.[57]

One tsarist official, Prince Vasilii Gadzhemukov, bluntly laid out the case against the Armenians in a report to Yudenich. Armenian participation in military operations had yielded "only negative results." Armenian merchants were gumming up army logistics by abusing their access to railroads to ship commercial goods. Worse, the unchecked marauding of Armenian gangs antagonized the Kurds and other Muslims. With their indiscriminate slaughter of Muslims at Van, he explained, "the Armenians themselves" had given the "signal for the barbaric destruction of the Armenian nation in Turkey." And, although that destruction left "the positive result that Turkey has left us Armenia without Armenians," the legacy of Van had been to stiffen Muslim resistance to Russian arms

---

[54] Somakian, *Empires in Conflict*, 109; RGVIA, Gadzhemukov to Iudenich, 14.3.1917 [27.3.1917], f. 2168, o. 1, d. 274, ll. 1–3.
[55] AVPRI, General Consul in Salonica to the Second Political Department of the Ministry of Foreign Affairs, 11.7.1915 [24.7.1915], f. 151, o. 482, d. 3490, l. 64.
[56] AVPRI, Chief of the Department of Organization and Service of Forces of the General Staff to A. A. Neratov, 9.10.1915 [22.10.1915], f. 151, o. 482, d. 3490, l. 123.
[57] V. S. Diakin, *Natsional'nyi vopros vo vnutrennei politike tsarizma (XIX–nachalo XX vv.)* (St. Peterburg: LISS, 1998), 540.

"for fear of falling into Armenian hands."[58] Gadzhemukov was not alone in his opinions. Boris Shakhovskoi, a former consul in Damascus who oversaw ties with the Kurdish tribes for the Russian General Staff, complained bitterly about "brutal Armenian lawlessness [toward the Kurds]." Armenian nationalists wanted "to exterminate all Muslim residents of the areas we occupied" and their savagery provoked "desperate Kurdish resistance" that "terribly complicated our [military] operations."[59] As the Assyrian Agha Petros testified, refugees who had been victimized in atrocities were filling up the ranks of Kurds hostile to Russia.[60] While less quick to blame the Armenians for the Kurds' estrangement, the consular officers and orientalists Vladimir Minorskii and Vladimir Gordlevskii also lobbied the army to pay greater attention to the Kurds' security and other concerns.[61]

The Armenians were not the only group persecuting Kurds. The Cossacks had a special reputation for dealing harshly with them. When General Nikolai Baratov's Cossacks recaptured the Iranian town of Rawanduz, reportedly only 20 percent of the Kurdish population managed to survive.[62] Yet many regular Russian officers also reviled them as a "thoroughly uncultured people" who "recognize only force and who always will obey only the stronger."[63] The formula "the Kurd is the enemy," wrote Viktor Shklovskii, "deprived the peaceful Kurds, including the children, of the protection of the laws of war." One Russian general even boasted of being an "exterminator of Kurds."[64] The Russians' local allies often abetted this line of thinking. One Assyrian officer urged his superiors to drop the "Russian rule" of conciliating one's enemy peacefully in favor of all-out warfare on Muslims.[65] The British Major E. W. C. Noel described the "extermination of the town of Rowanduz and the wholesale massacre of its [Muslim] inhabitants" by what he dubbed the "Christian Army of Revenge" of Agha Petros as one example of a long record of outrages

---

[58] RGVIA, Gadzhemukov to Iudenich, 14.3.1917 [27.3.1917], f. 2168, o. 1, d. 274, ll. 1–2.

[59] Kamal Madhar Ahmad, *Kurdistan*, 93–94.

[60] RGVIA, Report of the Urmia Unit, 31.12.1916–8.1.1917 [13.1.1917–21.1.1917], f. 2168, o. 1, d. 264, l. 17.

[61] Gordlevskii, *Izbrannye sochineniia*, vol. III, 456–57.

[62] John Joseph, *The Modern Assyrians of the Middle East: Encounters with Western Christian Missions, Archeologists, and Colonial Powers* (Leiden: Brill, 2000), 143–44.

[63] RGVIA, Generals Devitt and Gerasimov to the General-Commissar of Turkish Armenia and the Other Regions Occupied by the Right of War, 26.8.1917 [8.9.1917], f. 2168, o. 1, d. 277, l. 39.

[64] Viktor Shklovskii, *Sentimental'noe puteshestvie* (Moscow: Novosti, 1990), 101.

[65] RGVIA, Report of the Chief of the 4th Assyrian Reconnaissance Company and Translator of the Vice-Consulate of Urmia, 16.12.1916 [29.12.1916], f. 2168, o. 1, d. 264, l. 27.

perpetrated by Russia and its allies that, he asserted, could easily match that of the Turks.[66] Another British officer went further, describing the "conduct of our Russia allies" as "worse by far than that of the Turks."[67] An American described the Kurdish victims of mass Russian reprisals as among "the most pitiful examples we have encountered in our travels . . . so near the starvation point that it was not uncommon to see them eating the undigested grains out of manure."[68]

Not surprisingly, this hostility and distrust hampered Russian efforts to mobilize Kurds. Abdürrezzak adopted the title Sultan ul-aşair (Sultan of the Tribes)[69] and joined the Russian forces with his own Kurdish units in the fall of 1914. Abdürrezzak called upon Ottoman Kurds to join with him to drive out the *Rum*, or "Romans," i.e., the oppressive government in Istanbul. He enjoyed initial success, winning over even Kurds who otherwise rejected the idea of following those who "carry Crosses." Yet despite their service to Russia, Abdürrezzak and his men were detained and disarmed by their Russian comrades in arms. Still more problematic, however, was the conduct toward Kurds of the Armenian regiments, which ranged from stealing livestock to rape and indiscriminate murder. Although Abdürrezzak personally emphasized the need for Armenian–Kurdish cooperation, he found himself forced to promise fearful Kurds that he would retaliate should Armenians attack them.[70]

From the Armenian perspective, matters looked different. The Russians' declared policy of treating all inhabitants of Anatolia equally appeared to them to be less a principled stance of universalism than a cynical ploy to deny Armenians their due. After occupying Van, the Russians appointed the leader of the rebellion, the Dashnak Aram Manukian, as governor. Manukian promptly decried the Russians' decision in June 1915 to permit the return of Kurdish tribesmen to Van. He pointedly reminded Yudenich that, just a month earlier, Russia, together with Britain and France, "had declared all the participants in the massacre and plundering of Armenians personally responsible for their crimes before the whole civilized world." Yet now Russia was welcoming these criminals back. This, Manukian argued, was morally repugnant. It was also dangerous, he warned, because it would weaken the resolve of

---

[66] As cited in Shaw, *From Empire to Republic*, vol. II, 922.
[67] Arnold T. Wilson, *Loyalties: Mesopotamia 1914–1917* (London: Oxford University Press, 1930), 266.
[68] Charles E. Beury, *Russia After the Revolution* (Philadelphia: George W. Jacobs & Company, 1918), 36.
[69] BOA, General Security Directorate to Van, 25 Eylül 1330 [8 October 1914], DH ŞK, D. 45, B. 215.
[70] Bedirhan, *Otobiyografya*, 46, 51–52, 59, 64, 66, 68, 71.

the Armenians to fight, strengthen the Kurds' belief they could kill and steal with impunity, and permit the Ottomans to obtain intelligence from spies among the Kurds.[71] In his response General Andrei Nikolaev acknowledged Manukian's "irreconcilable feelings toward the Kurds" for their "barbarous, savage, and traitorous reprisals against the Armenian population." However, he explained, military and administrative expediency were paramount, and even Kurds who temporarily submit to Russian authority are preferable to those who resist. For these reasons, he refused also to rescind the order enjoining Armenians "not to attack or steal from the Kurdish population."[72]

At times the Russians had not been above exploiting anti-Armenian sentiment for tactical advantage, such as when in August 1915 they charged an innocent Armenian soldier with stealing from a Kurdish prisoner of war. After a cursory trial they hanged him in front of an audience of Kurdish and Turkish prisoners of war. The following day an officer gave the prisoners a short lecture on Russian justice: "That is how we deal with those who harm imprisoned Turks. He who does harm to one of you will be sentenced to death and shot. We Russians always act this way and will always act this way." The prisoners were then released with clean clothes, boots, sugar, and tea to tell their comrades about the attraction of life in Russian prison camps.[73]

Worse still for the Armenians was the fact that not only was the tsarist regime unwilling to accommodate a sovereign Armenia, but parts of it were hostile even to the presence of Armenians inside Armenia. Already in March 1915 Minister of Agriculture Krivoshein had begun advising Sazonov that Van, Erzurum, and parts of Bitlis, now being emptied of their Armenian natives, were suitable for Russian colonists.[74] Indeed, tsarist officialdom was not eager to see the return of Armenians to their lands in Anatolia. In April 1915 General Yudenich urged Vorontsov-Dashkov not to permit the Armenians to resettle their refugees on lands cleansed of Muslims and advocated instead that Cossacks be brought in to create a Cossack buffer to separate Anatolia from the Caucasus and thereby simplify Russian control and annexation.[75] Although Russian authorities could be callous, their callousness was more often a function

---

[71] AVPRI, Governor of Van to the Commander of the Caucasus Army, 26.6.1915 [9.7.1915], f. 151, o. 482, d. 3490, ll. 49–51.
[72] AVPRI, Major General Nikolaev to the Governor of Van, 4.7.1915 [17.7.1915], f. 151, o. 482, d. 3490, l. 52.
[73] AVPRI, Unsigned Telegram, 26.8.1915 [8.9.1915], f. 151, o. 482, d. 3490, l. 102.
[74] Krivoshein to Sazonov, 28.2.1915 [13.3.1915], *Razdel Aziatskoi Turtsii*, ed. Adamov, 360–62.
[75] Bor'ian, *Armeniia*, vol. I, 356; Hovannisian, *Armenia on the Road*, 57–58.

of indifference to Anatolia's inhabitants than one of active hostility. Thus, for example, tsarist authorities barred the return to Anatolia of all but 10,000 of the 250,000 Armenian refugees, but they did so less out of animosity toward Armenians than out of concern that the influx of large numbers of refugees would precipitate a supply and food crisis for the army.[76] And while some Russian officials, like Yudenich and Krivoshein, did advocate the settlement of more reliable Slavs and Cossacks in the lands abandoned by Armenian refugees, none suggested forcibly removing more Armenians. Similarly, although the army during its campaigns in Anatolia did uproot and expel Kurdish villagers from tactically significant positions, it did so for reasons of military expediency, not because it aimed to reshape settlement patterns in Anatolia.

Tearing the fabric of administration

Despite its espousal of the principle of strict impartiality toward all inhabitants of the occupied lands, the tsarist administration could not avoid getting drawn into the bitter rivalry between Kurds and Armenians. As those officials who worked with one or the other grouping gradually became partisans of their contacts, they bickered and conspired against each other. By the time imperial Russian rule collapsed, pro-Kurdish and pro-Armenian officials were resorting to false accusations and frame-ups, each charging the other with betrayal of the empire's interests for the sake of their clients.

In March 1917 the counterintelligence section of the First Caucasus Army Corps uncovered an anti-Russian movement in the town of Erzincan. The ringleader of the movement was not a Muslim Turk, Kurd, or Circassian, but an Armenian junior officer named Devoiants. The discovery of an Armenian plot within the Russian army itself was perhaps sensational but not a total surprise. Many officers and officials complained of what they regarded as the clannishness of the Armenians, their rumor mongering, and their irritating and suspicious habit of banding together. According to Prince Gadzhemukov, the Armenians were subverting Russian control by, of all things, using money intended to ransom Armenian refugees instead to bribe the Kurds to oppose the Russians and support an "Armenian revolution." Gadzhemukov named Devoiants as a player in this seemingly fantastic conspiracy.[77] Several months earlier Boris Shakhovskoi had warned that according to his sources the

---

[76] Holquist, "Armenian Occupation."
[77] RGVIA, Gadzhemukov to Iudenich, 14.3.1917 [27.3.1917], f. 2168, o. 1, d. 274, ll. 1–3.

Armenians, under orders from their leadership in Moscow, were conferring with Kurds and Yezidis about forming an anti-Russian front. The Russians were weak, they advised the Kurds. Expecting that peace would soon come, Manukian and others allegedly were reaching out to the former governor of Van, Cevdet Bey, in the hope that they might retrieve something from the war.[78]

Devoiants claimed he was the target of intrigues and pointed to a certain Colonel Mustafa Vefa Bey who maintained contact with Kurds as the source of the accusations. An investigation vindicated the Armenian in May.[79] He did not have to wait long for satisfaction. The previous month Shakhovskoi had been arrested and transported to Tiflis on charges of promoting ethnic discord and arming the Kurds.[80] Shakhovskoi had been a consistent critic of the excessive influence of the Armenian elite in Tiflis over policy, and now he had fallen to that elite.[81] Only the intervention of a senior Russian general and the promise that he would not leave Tiflis saved Shakhovskoi from imprisonment or worse.[82] Several days later the dismissal of another leading pro-Kurdish voice, Gadzhemukov, was announced.[83]

The removals of Shakhovskoi and Gadzhemukov coincided with a marked pro-Armenian shift in policy by Russia's Provisional Government, which came to power following Nicholas II's abdication in March 1917. The liberals in the new government were sympathetic to the Armenians, and in May 1917 the government recognized the provinces of Van, Erzurum, and Bitlis as "age-old Armenian" lands, encouraged the settlement of Armenians in those regions, and forbade the return of Muslims who had fled with the Ottoman army.[84] This shift in policy, coupled with the disintegration of Russian authority in Anatolia, led to what Shakhovskoi and Gadzhemukov had warned of: the resumption of open hostilities between Armenians and Kurds and a swing of the tribes to the Ottomans.

---

[78] AVPRI, Shakhovskoi to the Caucasus Army Chief of Staff, 8.10.1916 [21.10.1916], f. 151, o. 482, d. 4120, ll. 2–3.
[79] RGVIA, Major General Gerasimov to the Commander of the First Caucasus Army Corps, 29.4.1917 [11.5.1917], f. 2168, o. 1, d. 533, l. 4.
[80] AVPRI, Bulletin of the Petrograd Telegraph Agency, 4.4.1917 [17.4.1917], f. 151, o. 482, d. 4466, l. 2.
[81] Lazarev, *Kurdskii vopros*, 444–45.
[82] AVPRI, Telegram from the Civil Servant for Border Affairs in the Caucasus, 16.5.1917 [29.5.1917], f. 151, o. 482, d. 4466, l. 8.
[83] RGVIA, Telegram from the General Quartermaster, 21.5.1917 [3.6.1917], f. 2168, o. 1, d. 533, l. 15.
[84] Lazarev, *Kurdskii vopros*, 345.

Russian paranoia about Armenian collaboration with the Ottomans was perhaps not as preposterous as it sounds in retrospect. The resentment of prominent Armenians toward Russia was well known, and for many Armenians living conditions in Russian-occupied Anatolia were no better than those under Ottoman rule before the war and often were worse.[85] Moreover, negotiated peace and return of conquered territories to the Ottomans was not inconceivable. In such an event it would have behooved the Armenians to keep their lines open to Istanbul, if for no other reason than to salvage what they could from a calamitous position.

Greeks and Russians

A similar dynamic of ambivalent loyalties and political uncertainty lay beneath relations between the Pontic Greeks and Russians. As skilled imperial administrators, the Russians never took the loyalties of borderland populations for granted. They remained wary of the possibility of betrayal by the Ottoman Greeks and were seemingly rewarded for their skepticism when in the spring of 1917 they uncovered a "very well-organized" espionage network along the Black Sea coast involving Greek businessmen, bankers, and clergy among others as well as Muslims.[86] The Ottomans were pursuing other forms of subterfuge. Working through agents in Odessa and Athens, they were paying money to editors at the Greek-language newspapers *Argonautis* in Batumi and *Faros-Anatolis* in Trabzon to publish articles with upbeat pro-Ottoman themes. Thus appeared articles reporting that the former governor of Trabzon, Cemal Azmi, continued to maintain a positive attitude toward Greeks and praising the Greek Orthodox metropolitan of Trabzon, Chrysanthos, for his humane attitude toward Turks.[87]

Even without such questionable endorsements Chrysanthos was already attracting Russian suspicion for espionage. The visit of the commander in chief of the Caucasus Army and viceroy of the Caucasus Grand Duke Nikolai Nikolaevich to Trabzon in the summer of 1916 revealed tension between the Russian commanders and Chrysanthos.[88] The Russian military knew him to have had personal ties to Enver Pasha

---

[85] Somakian, *Empires in Conflict*, 111.
[86] RGVIA, Beliankin to the Senior Adjutant of the Intelligence Section of the Caucasus Army, 21.4.1917 [4.5.1917], f. 2168, o. 1, d. 535, l. 43.
[87] RGVIA, Dispatch to Quartermaster General of the Caucasus Army, 8.10.1916 [21.10.1916], f. 2168, o. 1, d. 553, ll. 1–2; RGVIA, Translation of Article Planted in *Faros-Anatolis*, 1.2.1917 [14.2.1917], f. 2168, o. 1, d. 553, l. 55.
[88] Diary of the wife of General Shvarts, Aleksandr Vladimirovich Shvarts papers, Box 1, Bakhmateff archive, Columbia University. My thanks to Halit Akarca for this citation.

and by the spring of 1917 believed he was passing on information to Istanbul through trusted couriers.[89] Although a certain degree of paranoia may have influenced the Russians' suspicions of the metropolitan, they had reasons to fear his duplicity. In an assessment of attitudes among the population of the province of Trabzon toward the Russians, a civil official highlighted the fact that the Russian occupation had deprived Chrysanthos of much of his authority and significance. Whereas under the Ottoman regime he had functioned effectively as the leader of the roughly 42,000 Greek Orthodox Christians of Trabzon, under Russian rule he had become a mere spiritual figure. As an ambitious man, it was difficult for Chrysanthos to accept his fall in status, and this, analysts concluded, stoked his resentment toward the Russian occupation authorities. Chrysanthos represented more than just his own person. He also represented Trabzon's Greek clergy, who remained loyal to him, and this further worried the Russian authorities.[90]

Whether or not the metropolitan of Trabzon in fact was in secret contact with the Ottomans is not known, but events would bear out the wisdom of maintaining such ties. In the wake of the February Revolution of 1917, Chrysanthos and others under Russian occupation grew increasingly nervous about the possibility of a Russian withdrawal and the future legal status of Eastern Anatolia. In the event that Trabzon did revert to Ottoman control, Chrysanthos would find it necessary to rebuild ties. As it happened, the Ottomans took the initiative. During the approach of the Ottoman Third Army toward Trabzon in February 1918, Vehib Pasha named Chrysanthos interim administrative head of the city. When receiving visitors, Chrysanthos emphasized not only his appointment by Vehib but his personal friendship with the general as well.[91]

Even combatants preserved imperial ties and could call on them when they found it expedient. Investigating anti-Ottoman guerrilla activity around Samsun in the summer of 1917, the commander of the Caucasus Armies Group General Ahmed İzzet Pasha reported that it did not stem from Pontic Greek nationalism but from bandit activity, and included many Georgians and local Muslims as well. A Pontic Greek gang leader explained that "We Rum [Anatolian Greeks] know the Russians as the greatest enemies of our nation and church" and that Russian occupation

---

[89] RGVIA, Report from the Chief of the Counter-Intelligence Department of the Caucasus Army, 22.3.1917 [4.4.1917], f. 2168, o. 1, d. 553, l. 199.

[90] AVPRI, Report of the Collegiate Councilor on the Attitude of Trabzon's Populace Toward the Russians, 1916 [no month], f. 151, o. 482, d. 4128, l. 26.

[91] Hüsamettin Tuğaç, Bir Neslin Dramı: Kafkas Cephesinden, Çarlık Rusyasında Tutsaklıktan Anılar (Istanbul: Çağdaş Yayınları, 1975), 202–03.

"will mean the destruction of Pontic Greekness" ("Rumluğun mahvı demek olur"). They had no ties to the Russians, and could be won over to the Ottoman side. Moreover, as Vehib noted, the gang leader had earlier served the Ottomans under Hüseyin Hilmi Pasha in the Balkans fighting Bulgarian and Serbian bands.[92]

Conclusion

Surveying the damage and suffering inflicted upon the populations of the Ottoman–Russian borderlands during World War I, the British correspondent M. Philips Price concluded, "I now see clearly that the guilt of war-atrocities upon civil populations cannot be put down to any one combatant... The more one dispassionately looks at the facts, and collects the stories told by sufferers of all races and creeds on the spot, as I have done in the course of eighteen months, the more it becomes clear that it is impossible to charge any one government with the crime."[93] Price was correct to note the ubiquity of atrocities and mass death caused by massacre, starvation, and disease, as well as the parallels in the treatments both empires meted out to the borderland populations. Nonetheless, there were substantial differences that stemmed from the dissimilar objectives of the two empires. Although powerful voices inside the tsarist bureaucracy advocated remaking Anatolia's demographic structure in order to strengthen Russia's grip upon the region for the long term, overall the tsarist empire was ambivalent regarding the annexation of Anatolia. Thus, aside from the beginning of the war when tsarist authorities expelled Muslims from Ajaria en masse, Russia refrained from large-scale manipulation of populations. Cossack and Armenian units fighting under Russian colors did acquire a reputation for brutality toward Muslims, Kurds especially, yet Russian authorities in general attempted to treat all populations equally. This policy sat poorly with the Armenians, who rightly saw it as aimed in part at the suppression of Armenian nationalist ambitions. The rift between Armenians and Kurds became so wide that the feud between the two groups began to consume the tsarist bureaucracy itself.

Whereas the Russians judged the consolidation in Anatolia of a comparatively cosmopolitan order to be in the Russian state's best interests, the Ottomans undertook to transform Anatolia's demographics toward the goal of Turkification. This switch from an imperial policy to a nationalist one was rooted in an instrumental logic. The Unionists

---

[92] Türk Tarih Kurumu, Vehib to Enver, 2.7.1333 [15.7.1917], Enver Paşa Arşivi, 1426.
[93] Price, *War*, 234.

had identified Anatolia as the place they would make their last stand in an existential struggle and understood that the homogenization of the land would bolster their ability to hold on to it. Polyethnicity had become a burden that a weak state could not carry. Most infamously, the Ottomans uprooted and destroyed the Armenian and Assyrian communities in Eastern Anatolia and at the same time sought to resettle Muslim refugees and nomads in such a way as to facilitate their assimilation to Turkishness. The impact of this effort at social engineering was tremendous in terms of lives taken and disrupted. Yet the sophistication of this effort at social engineering should not be overestimated, nor should the consistency or scope with which it was applied. The number of personnel overseeing and tracking the movements of people was limited, and throughout the war the Ottomans remained sensitive to the possibilities of harnessing non-Muslims to their war effort. Ensuring the survival of the state remained the primary motivation of its servants throughout the war and, indeed, thereafter.

Plate 1   Ottoman minister of war İsmail Enver Pasha (Louis Fischer, *The Soviets in World Affairs*, 2nd edn.)

Plate 2   Russian foreign minister Sergei Sazonov (TsGAKS)

Plate 3   Muslim refugees from Salonica en route to Istanbul (Hoover Institution, Emile Holman Papers)

Plate 4   Grand Duke Nikolai Nikolaevich with Tsar Nicholas II (Hoover Institution, Russian pictorial collection)

Plate 5   Laz fighters in Samsun (Hoover Institution, Tarsaidze papers)

Plate 6 Ottomans rally for war (Hoover Institution, World War I
pictorial collection)

Plate 7   Cossacks on the Caucasian front (TsGAKS)

Plate 8   Russian soldiers on the Caucasian front (TsGAKS)

Plate 9 Ottoman soldiers with captured Russian machine gun (*Harb Mecmuası*, February 1915)

Plate 10 Chief of Staff and later commander in chief of the Caucasus Army General Nikolai Yudenich (TsGAKS)

Plate 11   Chief of the Teşkilât-ı Mahsusa Major Süleyman Askerî Bey
(*Harb Mecmuası*, May 1916)

Plate 12   From the right, seated: Rauf Bey, Vehib Pasha, General Otto
Viktor Karl Liman von Sanders (*Harb Mecmuası*, August 1916)

Plate 13   Russian prisoners of war held in Sivas (*Harb Mecmuası*,
February 1915)

Plate 14   Officers of imperial Russia's famed Muslim "Savage Division"
(Hoover Institution, Tarsaidze collection)

Plate 15   Ottoman and Russian delegates at the Erzincan Armistice,
December 1917 (*Harb Mecmuası*, December 1917)

Plate 16 Leon Trotsky with Adolf Ioffe arriving at Brest-Litovsk in December 1917 (Imperial War Museum, Q23903)

Plate 17 German general Max Hoffmann, Austro-Hungarian foreign minister Ottokar von Czernin, Ottoman grand vizier Talât Pasha, and German foreign minister Richard von Kühlmann at Brest-Litovsk (Hoover Institution, Arthur M. Free photograph collection)

Plate 18 Germans on the march in Georgia (Hoover Institution, Tarsaidze collection)

Plate 19 German officers confer with peasants in Georgia (Hoover Institution, Tarsaidze collection)

Plate 20 Enver Pasha to Vehib Pasha on the danger of an Armenian
state (27 May 1918) (ATASE)

Plate 21 Armenian soldier and British officer from Dunsterforce defend Baku (Imperial War Museum, Q24891)

Plate 22 Armenians drill in Baku (Imperial War Museum, Q24926)

Plate 23   Indigent woman and child in postwar Trabzon (Hoover Institution, Roy E. Wayne photographs)

Plate 24   Refugees, most likely Armenians, in the Caucasus (Library of Congress, Prints and Photographs Division)

Plate 25   Kurd carries child who died of starvation to burial (Imperial
War Museum, Q24728)

6   Brest-Litovsk and the opening
of the Caucasus

The condition of the Ottoman empire at the beginning of 1917 was desperate. The afterglow of the victories at Gallipoli and Kut ül-Amara had long dissipated. In the previous year the Russians had taken Erzurum, Rize, Trabzon, and Erzincan and in the process had mauled the Ottoman forces opposing them. On the Caucasian front alone the Ottomans had lost over 100,000 men to combat, desertion, and hunger. They had committed their last standing reserves, seven divisions, to the European front in support of the Austro-Hungarian army and had none left. In the Anatolian countryside tribesmen roamed without clothing and were reduced to eating grass, mud, and coal.[1] Starvation stalked even Istanbul, where prices for essentials were soaring uncontrollably and the possibility of bread riots loomed. The empire as a whole was exhausted, worn down, and bankrupt. Only the onset of an unusually severe winter, which brought combat operations to a halt on the Caucasian front, preserved what remained of the army and prevented military collapse.[2]

Russia's generals, by contrast, were "full of fight" at the outset of 1917. The Entente had achieved material superiority on virtually every front, American entrance into the war looked more likely with every passing day, and the Russian economy was now capable of supporting a modern industrial war. Russia's increase in productive capacity, however, had come at a prohibitive cost. It imposed extreme dislocation and disruption upon Russian society, and ultimately society snapped.[3] In early March 1917, or late February according to Russia's old calendar, a series of protests in Petrograd against rising bread prices snowballed into mass demonstrations. Unable to maintain order in his own capital, tsar Nicholas II abdicated on 15 March. The event, dubbed the February

---

[1] Shklovskii, *Sentimental'noe*, 102; RGVIA, Kiamil Bey to Shakhovskoi, 22.12.1916 [4.1.1917], f. 2168, o. 1, d. 264, l. 14.
[2] Erickson, *Ordered*, 120–37; Maslovskii, *Mirovaia voina*, 296–98, 403–11. Cf. Belen, *1916 Yılı Hareketleri*, vol. III, 3–107.
[3] Norman Stone, *The Eastern Front, 1914–1917* (London: Hodder and Stoughton, 1975), 282.

Revolution, stripped the Russian empire of its axle. The empire's geographic expansion, the growth in its bureaucracy, the development of its economy, and the stratification of society had all subjected the imperial apparatus to increasing strain. The tsar, as the symbol of the empire and its central institution, had held it all together. The fall of the tsar meant that the whole imperial project was open to question, from the future form of government through property rights to the empire's borders. Everything was up for grabs.

The announcement of the tsar's abdication shook the army hard. Discipline slackened instantly. Responding to the revolution's promise of democracy, soldiers began forming independent committees, vetoing orders, and selecting their own commanders. While Petrograd reconsidered Russian war aims, the question of whether the war should be prosecuted at all became a topic of acrid debate dividing soldiers from officers, junior officers from senior, and even the infantry from the artillery.[4] In a surreal twist, tsarist officers found themselves with little choice but to cooperate with the revolutionary movements churning in the ranks. Thus, for example, General Yudenich took part in an army congress sponsored by the socialist Mensheviks in May 1917.[5]

The Ottomans took note of the dissension spreading through the Russian ranks. They grasped the broader political meaning of the February Revolution and attempted to turn it to their own ends. In propaganda leaflets distributed by aircraft and ground patrols they hailed the "felicitous revolution" (*ihtilâl-i mesut*), drew parallels between revolutionary Russia and their own constitutional regime, and underscored their common commitment to "civilizational progress" (*terakkiyat-ı medeniye*).[6] They dispatched small delegations of soldiers to meet face to face with their Russian counterparts. The Russians explained that they held no animosity toward the Ottomans who, unlike the Germans, did not occupy their lands.[7] Denunciations of the "imperialists' war" in Anatolia and declarations such as "We don't want the Dardanelles" circulated in the Russian ranks, suggesting the unpopular nature of the war against the Ottomans. By the summer, Russia's war-weary peasant soldiers were quitting the front in large numbers and streaming home, where, rumors claimed, a mass redistribution of land was imminent.

[4] ATASE, A. 5/5649, K. 3913, D. 55, F. 6-14, cited in Selami Kılıç, *Türk–Sovyet İlişkilerinin Doğuşu* (Istanbul: Dergâh Yayınları, 1998), 25–26.

[5] Allan K. Wildman, *The End of the Russian Imperial Army*, vol. I (Princeton: Princeton University Press, 1980), 325.

[6] Sadık Sarısaman, *Birinci Dünya Savaşı'nda Türk Cephelerinde Beyannamelerle Psikolojik Harp* (Ankara: Genelkurmay Basım Evi, 1999), 91.

[7] ATASE, A. 1/2, K. 384, D. 1526-359, F. 6-14, cited in Kılıç, *Türk–Sovyet*, 88–89.

Yet, even as the Russian Caucasus Army disintegrated literally before their eyes, the Ottomans in Anatolia remained passive. Enver planned to exploit Russia's deterioration not with an offensive toward the Caucasus, but instead with one to retake Baghdad, which had fallen to the British in March. The concept was to use the divisions returning from Romania and Galicia to form a new army, the "Thunderbolt Army" (*Yıldırım Ordusu*), in upper Mesopotamia. The Thunderbolt Army would march on Baghdad southward along the Euphrates, and the Sixth Army of Halil Pasha would attack east along the Tigris. These two armies would trap and destroy the British in a pincer movement. Although the scale and boldness of the plan excited Enver, the logistics involved in transporting the units from Europe to Mesopotamia in a timely manner proved too difficult.[8] Reluctantly, Enver dropped the plan in September and shifted the newly formed army to his second priority, Palestine.[9]

The mood in the Ottoman rear was no more belligerent than at the front. The February Revolution inspired Istanbul's newspapers to call not for new campaigns, but for peace. *Tasvir-i Efkâr* announced, "We long for peace," while *Tanin* admonished, "The continuation of the war will be a crime against humanity."[10] In a newspaper interview in the middle of May 1917, Talât painted a positive picture of the empire's position, stating that things were going well on all fronts, with the British on the defensive in Syria, matters beginning to shift in the Ottomans' favor in Iraq and Arabia, and the Caucasian front quiet. Although the meaning of Russia's revolution, he explained, was not yet clear, the collapse of tsarism augured well, since a "free Russia" would not be systemically compelled to destroy the Ottoman empire. Peace was what the Ottomans desired. Further, he emphasized, only negotiations could end the war.[11]

Talât's upbeat spin notwithstanding, the Ottomans were still in a precarious position in the fall of 1917. The collapse of morale in the Russian army did not trigger a corresponding rise in the Ottoman army, nor did it improve material conditions.[12] Writing from near the front, the Assyrian

---

[8] One of the factors disrupting the logistics was an explosion at the Haydar Pasha train station in Istanbul so massive that it blew out windows across the Bosphorus. The authorities fingered some Greeks as responsible and executed several of them: RGVIA, Intelligence Report on the Enemy, Staff of the Commander in Chief of the Caucasus Front, 15–25.10.1917 [28.10–6.11.1917], f. 2320, o. 1, d. 16, l. 339.

[9] Erickson, *Ordered*, 166–71; Şevket Süreyya Aydemir, *Enver Paşa*, vol. III, 296–97.

[10] RGVIA, Reports on the Enemy, Staff of the Commander in Chief of the Caucasus Front, 5–15.11.1917 [18–28.11.1917], f. 2320, o. 1, d. 16, l. 303.

[11] Türk Tarih Kurumu, Report to Enver, 6 Mayıs 1333 [19.5.1917], Enver Paşa Arşivi, 1419.

[12] RGVIA, Telegram to the Staff of the Caucasus Army, 26.10.1917 [8.11.1917], f. 2168, o. 1, d. 227, l. 211.

patriarch Mar Shimun XXI Benyamin described the Ottoman army as a pathetic, pitiful rabble filled with starving teenagers who beg for bread and soup.[13] Indeed in October Mustafa Kemal warned Enver, "The war has brought all of the Ottoman peoples, without exception, to the brink." Enver did not disagree, but he added that the condition of their enemies was not much better.[14] On this Enver was right. In fact, Russia's situation was about to grow even worse.

The promise of the Bolsheviks, ceasefires, and peace talks

On 7 November 1917 the Bolshevik Party led by Vladimir Lenin over-threw the Provisional Government in Petrograd in a violent coup and plunged Russia into a full-fledged civil war or, rather, a concatenation of civil wars. Russia's deepening disorder comforted the Ottomans.[15] As the newspaper *Vakit* observed in an editorial entitled "The Russia of Tomorrow," Russia represented an eternal danger, but "the Russian revolution . . . has saved us from an immediate threat . . . and . . . we can now take a deep breath."[16] Yet the rise of the Bolsheviks held out the possibility of more than just greater turmoil inside Russia. While in oppo-sition the Bolsheviks had consistently denounced the war as an imperialist project, and the day after they came to power they published a "Decree on Peace" in which they called for an immediate end to the war and a peace "without annexations and indemnities."[17] Lenin's explicit condemna-tion of the Entente's secret agreements to partition the Ottoman empire and Leon Trotsky's publication of those agreements in the newspaper *Izvestiia* further thrilled the Ottoman press. The Bolsheviks, it seemed, really were sincere about peace. And if peace could be made with Russia, the rest of the Entente would almost certainly have to follow.[18]

When in late November the Bolsheviks radioed to the Germans a cease-fire request, Enver immediately instructed the commander of the Third Army Vehib Pasha to propose a ceasefire to Russia's Caucasus Army. Vehib complied, but cautioned Enver against withdrawing forces from the Caucasian front prematurely.[19] Due to the fractured and confused nature of political relations in Russia – neither Russia's Caucasus Army nor

---

[13] RGVIA, Translation of Letter from the Assyrian Patriarch, 28.10.1917 [10.11.1917], f. 2168, o. 1, d. 258, l. 8.

[14] Şevket Süreyya Aydemir, *Enver Paşa*, vol. III, 311–16.

[15] Kurat, *Türkiye ve Rusya*, 328.

[16] "Yarınki Rusya," *Vakit*, 27 Kasım 1333 [27.11.1917].

[17] The English text of this decree can be found in John Wheeler-Bennett, *Brest-Litovsk, the Forgotten Peace, March, 1918* (London: Macmillan, 1938), 375–78.

[18] Kurat, *Türkiye ve Rusya*, 327–28.

[19] Genelkurmay Başkanlığı, *Üçüncü Ordu Harekâtı*, vol. II, 425.

Caucasian civil authorities recognized the embattled Bolshevik government in Petrograd – there could be no assurance that an armistice would
be accepted or obeyed as Enver hoped. Vehib's concern was not that
Enver would overcommit to the Caucasus, but the opposite, that he
might be lulled into redeploying forces elsewhere. Finally, on 18 December in the town of Erzincan the Ottoman government and the Russian
Caucasus Army signed an armistice.

On 3 December the Ottoman foreign minister Ahmed Nesimî Bey
informed the Chamber of Deputies that the government was opening
peace talks with Bolshevik Russia. There was no reason, he declared
to stormy applause, why excellent relations should not exist between
Russia and the Ottoman empire, especially since Russia "like us needs
to work in peace on reforms for many years." More thunderous applause
greeted his expression of hope for a comprehensive peace. One deputy,
however, did dissent from Nesimî's vision of peace without preconditions.
He reminded his giddy colleagues that parts of the empire were under
occupation. Baghdad and the Hijaz were lands as vital to the Ottoman
empire as Alsace-Lorraine was to Germany, and their recovery should be
no less a priority for the Central Powers. Yet although determination to
recover the lands the empire had lost was a powerful sentiment, relief at
the prospect of peace remained the dominant theme.[20]

Brest-Litovsk

That same day delegations from the four Central Powers met with the
Bolsheviks' representatives at the German army headquarters in the town
of Brest-Litovsk. The Bolshevik formula of peace without annexations
and indemnities framed the Ottomans' expectations. At a minimum, it
seemed to guaranty the return of the 1914 border. And if the formula
were applied retroactively – something not inconceivable given the Bolsheviks' professed radical idealism – then the Ottomans could recover
the 1877 border and Kars, Ardahan, and Batumi (known as "Elviye-i
Selâse," the "three provinces"), which they had ceded to Russia in lieu
of an indemnity in 1878. Enver in December informed the Germans
that the Ottomans would like to see the 1877 border returned, pointing
out that the Ottomans alone among the Quadruple Alliance had lost
territory.[21] In remarks passed on to the German ambassador Johann
Heinrich von Bernstorff, Enver explained also that given the tremendous
suffering the Ottomans had endured in the war so far, some territorial

[20] Bayur, *Türk İnkılâbı Tarihi*, vol. III, pt. 4, 104–08.
[21] PA-AA, A41666, Bernstorff to the Foreign Ministry, Rußland 11041, 12.12.1917.

adjustment would help shore up his legitimacy and that of the sultan. The territories lost in 1878 were former Ottoman territories and inhabited by Muslims, and thus their return to Istanbul, after all, made sense. Moreover, Germany in 1914 had promised to support a border change in the Caucasus.[22]

Return of the 1877 border, however, was an outside hope. The empire's diplomats were painfully conscious of their empire's weak bargaining position. Their state was a junior partner to Germany, and their wish to compel Russia's withdrawal from Anatolia by asserting the principle of no annexations clashed with Germany's desire to preserve control over the East European lands it occupied and with Bulgaria's claims on Dobruja and parts of Serbia. Austria-Hungary was desperate for peace and had no patience for Ottoman demands that might place that peace in jeopardy. Indeed, whereas Germany, Austria-Hungary, and Bulgaria all endorsed Enver's call for the withdrawal of all Ottoman and Russian forces from Iran they were pointedly ambivalent regarding Russia's evacuation of Anatolia. Fear that the Germans would abandon them to pursue bilateral talks dogged the Ottomans throughout the peace talks, and so they refrained from voicing loud demands for territory beyond the 1914 border.[23]

From Bolshevik anti-imperialist rhetoric and slogans the Ottomans drew hope that a kinder and gentler new world order might be dawning. The world order of the great powers had resembled that described by the Athenians to the Melians – the strong did what they would and the weak suffered what they must. Under that order a notion of international law and certain conventions existed, but these were invoked inconsistently and often disingenuously. That order had disillusioned the Ottomans long ago. Now the self-declared enemies of imperialism had come to power in Russia with a starkly different vision of order.

Yet at the same time the Ottomans retained some suspicion and were careful not to mistake Russia's current chaos as permanent. As the ambassador to Berlin, İbrahim Hakkı Pasha, cautioned, "Although Russia may be in a weakened state today, it is always an awesome enemy and it is probable that in a short time it will recover its former might and power."[24] Permanent or not, Russia's weakness was real, and Enver's inclination was still to use the moment to turn from Russia. When as a condition of an armistice the Bolsheviks insisted that the signatories keep their

---

[22] PA-AA, A5018, Note from Hertling, Rußland 11041, 14.12.1917.
[23] Bayur, *Türk İnkılâbı Tarihi*, vol. III, pt. 4, 108–13; Kılıç, *Türk–Sovyet*, 64, 123; Kurat, *Türkiye ve Rusya*, 358–59.
[24] Kurat, *Türkiye ve Rusya*, 357–58.

armies in place, Enver immediately ordered one division from both the Second and Third Armies withdrawn to the west lest they be committed to the Caucasian front for the duration of the war. Similarly, when the Bolsheviks, with the concurrence of the Germans, Austro-Hungarians, and Bulgarians, pointed out that the precipitate removal of Russian and Ottoman forces from Iran might invite the expansion of British influence, Enver acknowledged the merit of the concern but emphasized that there could be no compromise on Iran's independence.[25] Enver prioritized securing Russia's disengagement over the possibility of extending Ottoman influence.

On 15 December the Central Powers and Bolsheviks signed an armistice and agreed to begin final peace negotiations one week later.[26] At the first bilateral meeting between the Ottomans and the Bolsheviks the following day, the temporary head of the Ottoman delegation Zeki Pasha requested of Lev Kamenev that the Bolsheviks put an end to atrocities being committed on Russian-occupied territory by Armenian partisans against the Muslim populace. Kamenev assured Zeki that the Soviet government would take appropriate measures and then explained that the Bolsheviks believed that an international commission should be established to oversee the return of refugees and deportees to Eastern Anatolia. After the resettlement of the displaced persons the form and structure of the region's administration would be decided in accord with the population's wishes.[27] It was the opening salvo in the battle of ideals, rhetoric, and material to determine the post-Great War fate of Eastern Anatolia.

The opening of the talks on the peace agreement

Aware that their bargaining leverage was limited, the Ottomans were keen to maintain flexibility prior to the opening of the peace negotiations. The former minister of foreign affairs and current minister of justice Halil Bey wired his successor Nesimî Bey the following instructions. The foreign minister was to continue to resist German pressure for separate negotiations. If Germany and Austria-Hungary saw fit to make annexations, then the Ottomans should, too. Obtaining reductions in the debt, however, would be an appropriate substitute if German support for annexations

---

[25] ATASE, A. 1/1, K. 151, D. 678-200, F. 108-2, cited in Kılıç, *Türk–Sovyet*, 72.
[26] Wheeler-Bennett, *Forgotten Peace*, 379–84.
[27] ATASE, Zeki Pasha to Enver Pasha, 15 Kanunuevvel 1333 [15.12.1917], K. 530, D. 2070-928, F. 1-36; Kılıç, *Türk–Sovyet*, 163; Stefanos Yerasimos, *Türk–Sovyet İlişkileri: Ekim Devriminden "Milli Mücadele"ye* (İstanbul: Gözlem Yayınları, 1979), 14; Kurat, *Türkiye ve Rusya*, 364.

was not forthcoming. Russia should be required to evacuate the lands it occupied before Germany withdrew from the territories it had taken, and because large swaths of Ottoman territory had fallen into enemy hands the question of private reparations should not be neglected.[28]

The Bolshevik Adolf Ioffe opened the substantive negotiations on 22 December by reciting the tenets of the Bolshevik peace program.[29] These tenets were by now familiar to all gathered, and boiled down to the principles of no indemnities, no annexations, and the right of every nationality to self-determination. After taking a two-day break to consider the Bolshevik proposal, the two sides reassembled. In the name of the Central Powers, the Austro-Hungarian foreign minister Count Ottokar von Czernin announced that the main lines of the Russian proposal would be acceptable if the Entente powers also agreed.[30] The announcement pleasantly surprised the Bolsheviks.

Czernin made his statement with the expectation that Britain and France would not assent, but it caused discord among the Central Powers all the same. The mere suggestion that Germany forego annexations spurred German newspapers to assail their foreign minister Richard von Kühlmann for surrendering at the negotiating table what "had been bought with the blood and lives of hundreds of thousands."[31] The Bulgarians, whose poor command of French and German permitted them only a vague idea of what their allies were proposing, obstinately refused to surrender their claims to Dobruja and parts of Serbia when they caught on. In response, German general Max Hoffmann had to solicit a telegram from Bulgarian tsar Ferdinand overruling his own justice minister and head of the Bulgarian delegation.[32] Nesimî Bey made two objections. The first was that the Bolsheviks be required to withdraw all Russian troops from the occupied territories in Anatolia and the Caucasus upon the conclusion of the peace agreement. The second was that the Bolsheviks must pledge more explicitly to refrain from interfering in the internal affairs of other states. The Germans stifled the first objection since it would

[28] Bayur, *Türk İnkılâbı Tarihi*, vol. III, pt. 4, 112.
[29] See Wheeler-Bennett, *Forgotten Peace*, 117–18; United States, Department of State, *Proceedings of the Brest-Litovsk Peace Conference: The Peace Negotiations Between Russia and the Central Powers, 21 November 1917–3 March 1918* (Washington, DC: Government Printing Office, 1918), 38–39; Judah L. Magnes, *Russia and Germany at Brest-Litovsk* (New York: Rand School of Social Science, 1919), 31–32.
[30] Magnes, *Brest Litovsk*, 32; Wheeler-Bennett, *Forgotten Peace*, 118–19.
[31] Wheeler-Bennett, *Forgotten Peace*, 118–19.
[32] Ottokar Czernin, *In the World War* (New York: Harper and Brothers Publishers, 1920), 248–49; Wheeler-Bennett, *Forgotten Peace*, 120; Max Hoffmann, *War Diaries and Other Papers*, vol. II, tr. Eric Sutton (London: Martin Secker Ltd., 1929), 200–01; Kılıç, *Türk–Sovyet*, 116.

require in turn that they withdraw from Poland, Kurland, and Lithuania, while Czernin persuaded Nesimî to drop the latter by assuring him that whereas Austria-Hungary had more to fear from Bolshevik intrigues he did not feel any need to insist on such a pledge.[33]

Ironically, General Otto von Lossow was at this time urging Enver to carry out propaganda to incite Russia's Muslims to separate from Russia.[34] Lossow, joined by Bernstorff writing from Istanbul, also advised Kühlmann to support the Ottoman claim to Kars, Ardahan, and Batumi. The Ottomans sought the recovery of *Elviye-i Selâse* not because they desired territorial expansion but because it would give their government something to show for the war. The foreign minister softened his position. Whereas a few days earlier he had dismissed the idea of the return of the lands,[35] on 25 December he informed Enver that he did not believe the Bolsheviks would resist the reincorporation of the three provinces. Proclamations from locals in the three provinces expressing their wish to rejoin the Ottoman empire made an impression on Kühlmann, and he suggested the possibility of arranging reunification through a plebiscite.[36]

Global order's local reflection or mirage: the Caucasus Committee

The proclamations to which Kühlmann referred had been telegraphed to the Ottoman grand vizier Talât Pasha, the Bolsheviks, and the German and Austro-Hungarian foreign ministries. They purported to speak in the name of the people of Ardahan, Batumi, Acara, Çürüksu, Livane, Kars, and Şavşat. Enver had been a step ahead of Kühlmann and had ordered the formation of a "Caucasus Committee" to lobby for the inclusion of Kars, Ardahan, and Batumi. On 22 December Enver informed the Ottoman embassies in Berlin, Vienna, and Sofia that a delegation from the committee had left Istanbul by train and instructed them to assist the delegates in their lobbying. The delegates had little success. Reporting from Berlin in the middle of January, they complained that not only did the Germans and Austro-Hungarians not support the reincorporation of the three provinces, but that the Bulgarians' insistence on the annexation

---

[33] Czernin, *In the World War*, 247; Wheeler-Bennett, *Forgotten Peace*, 119–20; Hoffmann, *War Diaries*, 201.

[34] Kılıç, *Türk–Sovyet*, 119.

[35] Yerasimos, *Türk–Sovyet*, 14–15; Tülay Duran, "I. Dünya Savaşı Sonunda Türk Diplomasisinin İlk Başarısı: Brest-Litovsk Hazırlıkları," *Belgelerle Türk Tarihi Dergisi*, 12, no. 67–68 (April–May 1973), 45.

[36] Kılıç, *Türk–Sovyet*, 120–22.

of Dobruja and the Germans' unwillingness to withdraw from Eastern Europe were undermining their case.[37]

Given the committee's disappointing reception in Berlin, Talât considered sending it on to Petrograd in the hope that perhaps it might gain some support directly from the Bolsheviks. But when he wired Galip Kemalî Bey, who had recently arrived in Petrograd as the head of the Ottoman delegation to an economic and cultural commission and who was the closest official the Ottomans had to an ambassador, to ask if the committee might have some success, Galip's answer was negative. The Bolsheviks, he emphasized, were generally fulfilling their rhetoric of self-determination by permitting autonomy to those who desired it on condition that they remain tied to the Russian Republic. Moreover, he observed, the notion that the Caucasus Committee, six of whose ten members were Ottoman subjects and among whom were prominent Ottoman officials, could pretend to represent the aspirations of a population that for the last forty years had been under Russian rule did not seem plausible. It was a fair point. The committee in fact knew little about the three provinces it purported to represent. Indeed, after the committee members had departed Istanbul, Enver had to wire to them a basic statistical profile of the population of Kars and Batumi taken from a Russian source. Bernstorff's doubts about the committee's legitimacy led him to check on its members' backgrounds and note that many were Ottoman, not Russian, subjects.[38]

Galip then came to the heart of the matter with the Caucasus Committee. "The really important question for us," Galip warned Talât, "is whether or not we will have to listen to assertions along these lines [of self-determination] from some nations inside our country."[39] Indeed, the chief of the Georgian Committee, Prince Machabelli, was applying precisely that tactic in Berlin, threatening that, if the Ottomans persisted in claiming Kars, Ardahan, and Batumi, they might hear calls for self-determination from Lazistan and Kurdistan.[40]

The issue of self-determination sparked the first major row at Brest-Litovsk when the severe advocate of *Machtpolitik*, General Hoffmann, resolved to disabuse the Bolsheviks of their illusions and clarified that German forces would not withdraw to the 1914 Russo-German border because as far as the German government was concerned Poland,

---

[37] ATASE, A. 1/64, K. 1867, D. 167-20, F. 2-10, F. 2–12, cited in Kılıç, *Türk–Sovyet* 127–28.

[38] Kılıç, *Türk–Sovyet*, 126.

[39] Galip Kemalî Söylemezoğlu, *Hariciye Hizmetinde Otuz Sene*, 4 vols. (Istanbul: Şaka Matbaası, 1950), vol. I, 438–39.

[40] Kılıç, *Türk–Sovyet*, 129, 270 n. 239.

Kurland, and Lithuania had already exercised their right to self-determination and seceded from Russia. The announcement sent the Bolshevik delegation into convulsions. Displaying an unseemly state-centric attitude for a revolutionary, the future court historian of the Soviet Union Mikhail Pokrovskii broke down, sobbing and sputtering, "How can you talk of peace without annexation when nearly eighteen provinces are torn from Russia?"[41] The resulting tumult and Bolshevik threats to break off the talks rattled the Austro-Hungarians, who were desperate for peace and resented the Germans' intransigence.[42] The flare-up did not upset the Ottomans, who in private talks that afternoon obtained from the Bolsheviks a promise to evacuate the occupied territories.[43]

The Germans mollified the Bolsheviks somewhat the following day by agreeing to withdraw their troops and hold referenda in the German-occupied territories. They refused, however, to specify whether the withdrawals would precede or follow the referenda. When the Bolsheviks requested that a referendum be held in Armenia, the Germans spotted the logical parallel to Eastern Europe that the Bolsheviks might draw and retorted that this was an internal Ottoman affair. On other matters of importance to the Ottomans, the Bolsheviks assented to the abolition of the capitulations and to granting commercial shipping free passage through the Black Sea Straits for two years until a new regulatory regime could be drafted.[44]

The second round of talks

In going to Brest-Litovsk, the Bolsheviks were interested not in conclud-ing a peace but in the opposite. They desired to drag out the talks in order to increase war fatigue and stoke revolutionary ferment in Germany and elsewhere until a workers' revolution erupted in industrialized Western Europe. Toward that end, Lenin dispatched Trotsky to lead the Bolshevik team at the second round of talks that began on 9 January 1918. Trotsky's arrival helped create one of the most curious and fascinating spectacles in all diplomatic history. The Bolshevik and Central Power delegations espoused diametrically opposed conceptions of politics. Where the Cen-tral Powers operated in a framework of territorial states and sought to delineate geographic borders and secure economic concessions, the Bol-sheviks worked from a Marxist template of revolution wherein the very

---

[41] Wheeler-Bennett, *Forgotten Peace*, 125.
[42] Czernin, *In the World War*, 253–54; Max Hoffmann, *War Diaries*, 202–03; Wheeler-Bennett, *Forgotten Peace*, 125–27.
[43] Kılıç, *Türk–Sovyet*, 173.   [44] Bayur, *Türk İnkılâbı Tarihi*, vol. III, pt. 4, 117.

concept of state was to disappear and a whole new social order was to arise.

Complementing the conceptual contrasts were those of personality, with the brash, brilliant, and self-obsessed revolutionary Trotsky squaring off against the quintessential representative of the old order, the cool, cosmopolitan, polished aristocrat Foreign Minister Kühlmann, who lacked neither experience nor intelligence yet retained an ability to laugh at himself. For the next four weeks Trotsky would keep his opponents off balance, hammering constantly at their positions in charged, even emotional, debates. His rudeness, grandstanding, and refusal to acknowledge that they, not he, represented the victorious side, however, would infuriate the Germans, and hand the Ottomans an unexpected diplomatic triumph.[45]

The principle on which both sides sparred so passionately was one both claimed to value, the right of nations to self-determination. One might be tempted to dismiss the German and Bolshevik stances on national self-determination as cynical exercises in power politics. The Germans, after all, openly advocated *Machtpolitik*, and the Bolsheviks would build their empire by subverting and conquering nations and local movements all along Russia's periphery. Nonetheless, this interpretation would be simplistic and misleading. Although both sides did exploit the national idea in the service of extending their power and influence, they also expended considerable energy not merely accommodating national identities but actually fostering them. During their occupation of Eastern Europe the Germans consciously implemented programs to transform Belorussians, Jews, Latvians, Lithuanians, Poles, and others from mere "peoples" into proper "nations" with all the markers of such.[46] In creating and ruling their empire, the Bolsheviks would reveal a profound "ethnophilia" by requiring every Soviet subject to adopt a national identity and endowing all Soviet nationalities with the requisite markers of nationhood.[47]

Talât's arrival and the decree "On Armenia"

Talât Pasha, now holding the post of grand vizier, also arrived for the second round of talks. After introducing him, Kühlmann whispered within earshot of the Turk that he considered him to be "Europe's best

---

[45] Max Hoffmann, *War Diaries*, 211–12; Wheeler-Bennett, *Forgotten Peace*, 156–57; Lev Trotskii, *Moia zhizn'* (Moscow: Vagrius, 2001), 355–59, 367–68.

[46] Vejas G. Liulevicius, *War Land on the Eastern Front: Culture, National Identity, and German Occupation in World War I* (New York: Cambridge University Press, 2000), 113–50.

[47] On Soviet "ethnophilia," see Yuri Slezkine, "The USSR as a Communal Apartment, or How a Socialist State Promoted Ethnic Particularism," *Slavic Review*, 53, 2 (Summer 1994), 414–52.

diplomat." The ploy further stirred Trotsky's contempt for the German and his old-school diplomatic tricks of flattery.[48] Talât, however, had not come to satisfy his vanity. There had been talk in German and Austrian newspapers of holding a plebiscite in Eastern Anatolia, and this raised the possibility that Ottoman sovereignty over the region might again be compromised or denied outright. Recovery of those lands was critical for his government's reputation and success. Talât fretted that Nesimî and Hakkı would not be assertive enough and so decided to attend the talks in person.[49]

Ottoman estimations of the Bolsheviks' commitment to establishing a new world order changed fundamentally when on 13 January the Bolshevik mouthpiece *Pravda* published decree no. 13, "On Armenia." Galip Kemalî Bey immediately wired the news from Petrograd to his colleagues at Brest-Litovsk. Signed by Lenin and Commissar for Nationalities Joseph Stalin, the decree recognized the Armenians' right to self-determination, called for the creation of an Armenian militia to facilitate the withdrawal of Russian troops from Anatolia, and proclaimed the right of all Armenian refugees to return to their lands. Until a referendum could be held to determine Armenia's future, a Soviet of People's Deputies assisted by the Bolshevik extraordinary commissar for the Caucasus and ethnic Armenian, Stepan Shaumian, would act as Armenia's provisional government.[50] The information confirmed the growing suspicions of the Ottoman diplomats that the Bolsheviks had no real intention of returning the occupied territories. After discussion, they identified two ways to recover what they termed "our land." The first was to obtain a guaranty from Germany to withdraw from Russian territories and thereby achieve a precedent to compel the evacuation of Eastern Anatolia and the Caucasus. The delegates anticipated that Petrograd would respond by declaring it had no authority over Russian army units remaining in the South Caucasus, and so they recommended to Enver that he prepare to execute an amphibious landing at Batumi with German naval support. But if Germany was an unwilling or undesirable partner, a suggested option was to conclude a peace treaty with Ukraine and then mount the same amphibious operation but with the remnants of the Russian Black Sea Fleet under Ukrainian command in support.[51]

---

[48] Trotskii, *Moia zhizn'*, 362.   [49] Kurat, *Türkiye ve Rusya*, 366–67.

[50] USSR, Ministerstvo inostrannykh del, *Dokumenty vneshnei politiki SSSR*, vol. I (Moscow: Politizdat, 1959), 74–75; Hovannisian, *Armenia on the Road*, 100; Bayur, *Türk İnkılâbı Tarihi*, vol. III, pt. 4, 120–21.

[51] Kılıç, *Türk–Sovyet*, 241–42. The Ottomans soon learned that the second option was unfeasible as the Black Sea sailors would obey no one: ATASE A. 1/1, K. 153, D. 682-380, F. 4-9, 4-10, cited in Kılıç, *Türk–Sovyet*, 241, n. 146.

The next day Nesimî met with Trotsky. He argued that arming the population of a territory that did not belong to Russia and encouraging it to declare independence was contrary to the Bolsheviks' own principles. The attempt to instruct Trotsky in Bolshevik doctrine was unsuccessful. Searching desperately for some form of leverage, Nesimî then suggested that in exchange for Russia's unconditional return of Ottoman territory in Asia, Germany would return Russian land in Europe. Trotsky could not have been impressed by an offer from the Ottoman foreign minister to arrange the withdrawal of German forces from Eastern Europe.[52]

The Ottomans' suspicion that an ulterior agenda lay behind the decree "On Armenia" had foundation. The Bolsheviks at the time were encouraging the repatriation of Armenians serving in the Russian army outside the Caucasus to Armenia and were also releasing political prisoners and common criminals to take up arms in the Caucasus.[53] Trotsky dismissed Nesimî's concerns about the arming of the Armenians. Once the Armenians had weapons, he explained, the Kurds would not be able to do anything to them and the two groups would have no choice but to compromise and get along.[54] The reality was that the Bolsheviks were trying to make the best of a bad situation. Despite Trotsky's occasional boasts, the fact was that they had no influence over the Caucasus Army, let alone control. The Caucasus Army itself had effectively dissolved, and in November 1917 its command desperately authorized the formation of Armenian and Georgian units, as only soldiers from these regions had a stake in resisting an Ottoman advance. The reinforcement of those Armenian units offered a way to keep the Ottoman army at bay until such time as the Bolsheviks could consolidate their power in the Caucasus.

Talât speculated that Trotsky might be partial to the establishment of an independent Armenian state in part because one of the principal Bolshevik delegates, Lev Karakhan, was an Armenian, or at least resembled one.[55] One night before dinner the Ottoman delegation decided to test this suspicion by having Hrand Bey, their legal advisor from the foreign ministry and an ethnic Armenian, call Karakhan on the telephone and address him in Armenian. Hrand Bey rang the Bolshevik, but could not understand a word until he and Karakhan spoke in French. The question of Karakhan's ethnicity continued to intrigue the Ottomans. Later, while

[52] Kurat, *Türkiye ve Rusya*, 370–71; Kılıç, *Türk–Sovyet*, 242–43; Bayur, *Türk İnkılâbı Tarihi*, vol. III, pt. 4, 122–23; Yusuf Hikmet Bayur, "Birinci Genel Savaştan Sonra Yapılan Barış ve Anlaşmalarımız," *Belleten*, 29, 115 (1965), 510–11.

[53] Jacques Kayaloff, *The Battle of Sardarabad* (The Hague: Mouton, 1973), 73–74.

[54] Kurat, *Türkiye ve Rusya*, 371–72; Bayur, *Türk İnkılâbı Tarihi*, vol. III, pt. 4, 122–23.

[55] Kılıç, *Türk–Sovyet*, 304; Wheeler-Bennett, *Forgotten Peace*, 85.

serving in Moscow, Galip Kemalî would "discover" that Karakhan was a Georgian.[56] In reality, he was an Armenian.

Talât had more on his mind than telephone tricks. Two could play at the Bolsheviks' game. In a telegram to Galip Kemalî in Petrograd, Talât explained that Lenin's government was assisting the establishment of an independent state "on our occupied territory" and permitting Armenians to massacre Muslims. The surest way to apply countervailing pressure on the Bolsheviks was to incite Russia's Muslims. In particular, he asked if Yusuf Akçura could be sent to attend a rumored upcoming congress of Muslims in Kazan and if Akçura could also contact Muslim newspapers and mobilize opposition to the spilling of Muslim blood in Anatolia. Galip Kemalî answered that Akçura was in Moscow meeting with the Red Crescent Society, but if necessary could be sent to visit prisoners of war. He cautioned Talât, however, that little could be expected from Russia's Muslims or from the congress to be held in Ufa, not Kazan. They were not organized and were too divided politically, and the poor state of communications in Russia blocked the dissemination of information.[57]

Ukraine: the key to remaking the regional balance of power

The third round of talks began on 30 January under Talât's chairman-ship. Although he was impatient to return to Istanbul to attend to pressing domestic matters, he decided to await Trotsky's return from Petrograd and the resolution of the major outstanding problems.[58] Trotsky's obfus-cation and grandstanding at the second session had strained the Central Powers' cohesion, but the Bolsheviks' unity was also unraveling. Lenin's dispersal by bayonet of the popularly elected Constituent Assembly in January had caused the Bolsheviks' domestic enemies to coalesce. Many of the Bolsheviks now judged a continuation of hostilities with Ger-many to be too risky.[59] Still worse for Trotsky, his diplomatic oppo-nents would teach him a trick or two of their own. The question of Ukraine would dominate the third sitting, and the Central Powers' solu-tion to it would precipitate the breakdown of the talks.

One day after the signing of the armistice, a three-person delegation from Ukraine arrived at Brest-Litovsk. Barely beyond their student years, the Ukrainians were representatives of the Rada, the Ukrainian Central Council. The youths as yet had no concrete agenda but hoped to get a

[56] Söylemezoğlu, Hariciye Hizmetinde, vol. I, 429.
[57] Söylemezoğlu, Hariciye Hizmetinde, vol. I, 442–43.
[58] Kurat, Türkiye ve Rusya, 374–75.   [59] Wheeler-Bennett, Forgotten Peace, 183–93.

sense of the situation and then plot a course. The Germans were happy to have the Ukrainians around, since they could use their presence as a reminder of the issue of self-determination and thereby pressure the Bolsheviks and keep the Austro-Hungarian delegation in step.[60] The Austro-Hungarians feared both Ukrainian territorial claims and the possible repercussions of Ukrainian statehood for their empire's stability. Vienna's desperation for peace and grain, however, gave Czernin little choice but to go along with the Germans.[61]

The Ottomans could not hope to manipulate the Ukrainians like the Germans could, but they were pleased to have the Rada delegates' company. As Ottoman planners recognized at the beginning of the war, the emergence of an independent Ukraine would cripple Russia by stripping it of rich lands, a large population, and much of its Black Sea coast. As Russia's political crisis deepened throughout 1917, the Ottoman embassy in Stockholm – the Ottomans' overseas center for the collection and analysis of intelligence relating to the Russian empire – emphasized the singular importance of the emergence of an independent Ukraine. Whereas Russia's Muslims lacked strength and were at an elementary level of organization, the more sophisticated and educated Ukrainians possessed the capability to redraw the geopolitical map of the Black Sea and surrounding regions to the benefit of the Ottoman empire.[62] Ottoman intelligence analysts cautioned that the odds for a total break between Ukraine and Russia were less than even, but concluded that the impact of such a break would be decisive.[63] The Ottoman attaché in Stockholm accordingly moved to support the Ukrainian independence movement.[64] In January 1918 the Teşkilât-ı Mahsusa issued passports to ULU members and dispatched six of them to Ukraine via Batumi.[65]

Trotsky and Kühlmann had skirmished on the Ukrainian issue at the opening session, but on 1 February Czernin let the Rada representatives take the floor in a bid to ratchet up the pressure on the Bolsheviks. The youthful Ukrainian socialists seized the opportunity and spoke with

[60] Max Hoffmann, *War Diaries*, 209; Wheeler-Bennett, *Forgotten Peace*, 155; Hakan Kırımlı, "Diplomatic Relations Between the Ottoman Empire and the Ukrainian Democratic Republic, 1918–1921," in *Turkey Before and After Atatürk*, ed. Kedourie, 201.

[61] Czernin, *In the World War*, 258, 262, 267–69, 279.

[62] ATASE, Report from Stockholm, 12 Temmuz 1333 [12.7.1917], K. 302, D. 937-1231, F. 87.

[63] ATASE, Report on Conditions in Russia, 28 Haziran–28 Temmuz 1333 [28.6–28.7.1917], K. 1843, D. 129-67, F. 1-24, 1-37.

[64] ATASE, Attache in Stockholm to the General Staff, 10 Temmuz 1333 [10.7.1917], K. 302, D. 937-1231, F. 85.

[65] ATASE, Passports and Copy of List of Ukrainians, [n.d.], K. 332, D. 817-1332, F. 2, 2-8, 3-5; Kırımlı, "Union," 195.

vengeful abandon. They loosed one rhetorical broadside after another, contemptuously denouncing the Bolsheviks for their cowardly and two-faced use of force against the Constitutional Assembly, Ukrainians, Caucasians, and others. The humiliating impact of the verbal assault was, to the amusement of the Quadruple Alliance delegates, visible in Trotsky's pained and sweating visage.[66] Trotsky recovered enough wit to crack that the Rada delegates represented no territory greater than the rooms they occupied at Brest-Litovsk; Hoffmann judged the comment "unfortunately not to be without foundation."[67]

In a telegram to Enver that day Talât wrote that the new Bolshevik Russia had revealed itself to be the same expansionist Russia of old and was assaulting Finland and Ukraine with the objective of creating a "United Russian Republic." With approval he related how the Germans and Austro-Hungarians had decided to recognize Ukraine, sign a peace treaty with it, and then march on Petrograd to force the Bolsheviks to come to terms.[68] On 8 February the Central Powers did in fact sign a peace treaty with Ukraine and, in exchange for Ukrainian grain, eggs, sugar, manganese, linen, and other products, they pledged to support the Rada against the Bolsheviks. Austria-Hungary was to cede the province of Cholm to Ukraine, create a Ukrainian province out of Bukovina and the Ruthenian districts of Galicia, and grant linguistic rights to the Ruthenians of Western Galicia.[69] The high diplomacy, however, bore no relation to the facts on the ground, and everyone knew it. As Czernin mused in his diary that evening, "I wonder if the Rada is still really sitting at Kieff?"[70] In fact, earlier that very day the Rada government had fled Ukraine's capital as Bolshevik soldiers entered the city.[71] Still, Trotsky's furious protests against the peace treaty had come to nothing. Impotent, he declared the war over in a feeble gambit to duck the issue of a formal peace treaty and left for Petrograd.[72] The talks had collapsed.

Although Trotsky's departure disappointed the Ottomans, overall they had cause for satisfaction. As Talât put it to a German reporter, the formal failure of the talks was not as important as the practical result. The peace with Russia was not official, but it was a peace of sorts that provided security to the Ottomans.[73] And the treaty with Kiev was a

---

[66] Czernin, *In the World War*, 274; Wheeler-Bennett, *Forgotten Peace*, 209–10. Cf. Trotskii, *Moia zhizn'*, 369–70.

[67] United States, Department of State, *Proceedings*, 145; Max Hoffmann, *War Diaries*, 216.

[68] Talât to Enver, 1.2.1918, as cited in Emin Ali Türkgeldi, "Brest–Litowsk [sic] Konferansı Hatıraları," *Belgelerle Türk Tarihi Dergisi*, 3, 13 (March 1986), 48–49.

[69] Kılıç, *Türk–Sovyet*, 290; Wheeler-Bennett, *Forgotten Peace*, 220.

[70] Czernin, *In the World War*, 278.   [71] Pipes, *Formation*, 126, 130–31.

[72] United States, Department of State, *Proceedings*, 169–72.   [73] Kılıç, *Türk–Sovyet*, 313.

considerable achievement in itself. As the semi-official CUP mouthpiece *Tanin* exulted Russia had lost much of its malign relevance.[74]

The Ottoman advance begins

Kühlmann warned Trotsky before he left that failure to conclude a formal peace agreement would leave the Central Powers no choice but to continue the war. He made good on his word. As the Bolsheviks debated what to do next, he issued an ultimatum, and on 18 February the Germans resumed their advance. In just four days they covered 240 kilometers. "Trotzsky's [sic] theories could not resist facts," Hoffmann later wrote.[75] With the Germans approaching an all but defenseless Petrograd, Lenin ruled that a peace treaty had to be signed, whatever the terms, lest the Germans snuff out the revolution. Because Trotsky had no desire to sully himself with so ignominious an act, Bolshevik Central Committee member Grigorii Sokol'nikov led the delegation back to Brest-Litovsk.

Shortly after arriving, Sokol'nikov discovered more unpleasantness. Whereas Kühlmann's ultimatum had demanded that the Russians withdraw from the ambiguously titled "Eastern Anatolian provinces," the draft peace treaty handed to Sokol'nikov required the Russians to evacuate specifically the provinces of Kars, Ardahan, and Batumi.[76] The amendment represented a triumph of Ottoman diplomacy. As İbrahim Hakkı Pasha, the former grand vizier and expert in international law,[77] had advised the foreign ministry, diplomatic convention forbade the augmentation of ultimata subsequent to their presentation. Convention notwithstanding, Hakkı quietly took up the matter of *Elviye-i Selâse* with the chief German representative at Brest-Litovsk, Baron Frederic von Rosenberg, and managed to persuade him that Kars, Ardahan, and Batumi rightfully belonged to the Ottomans and that the phrase "Eastern Anatolian provinces" properly referred to them as well as to the territories to the west of the 1914 border.[78] Kühlmann opposed allowing the Ottomans to gain a foothold in the Caucasus and was not inclined to agree. The German Foreign Ministry had its own plans for the future exploitation of the Caucasus, and these did not include

[74] Kırımlı, "Relations," 204.   [75] Max Hoffmann, *War Diaries*, 220.
[76] The text of the ultimatum can be found in Wheeler-Bennett, *Forgotten Peace*, 255–57, and United States, Department of State, *Proceedings*, 176–77.
[77] For a portrait, see Carter Findley, *Ottoman Civil Officialdom* (Princeton: Princeton University Press, 1989), 195–209.
[78] Hakkı Pasha to the Foreign Ministry, 2.3.1918, as cited in Türkgeldi, "Brest-Litowsk," 52–53.

partnership with the Ottoman empire.[79] Germany's quartermaster general and chief strategist, General Erich von Ludendorff, however, was disposed to punish the Bolsheviks for their insolent intransigence and so approved amending the clause to read:

> The Russian State will do all within its power to ensure the immediate evacuation of the provinces of Eastern Anatolia and their lawful return to the Ottoman state. The districts of Ardahan, Kars, and Batumi will likewise and without delay be cleared of Russian troops. The Russian State will not interfere in the reorganization of the national and international relations of these districts, but leave it to the population of these districts to carry out this reorganization in agreement with the neighboring states, especially with the Ottoman State.[80]

Notably, the terms did not assign Kars, Ardahan, and Batumi to the Ottoman empire but paid obeisance to the principle of self-determination. Hakkı and Rosenberg next persuaded the Austrians and Bulgarians to accept the new wording. The matter, however, was not guarantied. The Austro-Hungarians made their support for the amendment dependent on the condition that it not cause any delay in the signing of the treaty.[81]

That delay threatened on 3 March, the morning scheduled for the signing, when Sokol'nikov opened his remarks with a sustained and blistering attack on the injustice of including the three provinces in the treaty.[82] Hakkı Pasha's anxiety soared. If the Bolsheviks hesitated to sign, the Ottomans' allies would almost certainly scrap the amendment for the sake of concluding the treaty once and for all. He seized the chance to speak and rebutted Sokol'nikov with an impassioned defense of Ottoman claims, delivering a masterful lecture on the history of the region, its relationship to the Ottoman empire, and its loss to Russia in 1878.[83] Then, feigning surprise at the Bolsheviks' objections, he contended that the return of the three provinces was perfectly consonant with their revolutionary principle of peace without annexations and reparations. He closed with an acidic jab at the Bolsheviks' ideological pretensions: "And why are we talking at all about victors and vanquished? Are we not really all victors, and is not the one whom we have all vanquished our common enemy, Russian tsarism?"[84] Sokol'nikov seethed. He had identified the

---

[79] Fischer, *Germany's Aims*, 551.

[80] Kılıç, *Türk–Sovyet*, 343–44, 378; Wheeler-Bennett, *Forgotten Peace*, 405–06.

[81] Türkgeldi, "Brest-Litowsk," 52–53.

[82] Jane Degras, ed., *Soviet Documents on Foreign Policy*, vol. I (New York: Oxford University Press, 1951), 48–50; USSR, Ministerstvo inostrannykh del, *Dokumenty vneshnei politiki*, 117–19.

[83] Türkgeldi, "Brest-Litowsk," 52; United States, Department of State, *Proceedings*, 183.

[84] G. Ia. Sokol'nikov, *Brestskii mir* (Moscow: Gosudarstvennoe izdatel'stvo, 1920), 20–22.

amended clause as especially objectionable in a cable to Lenin, but Lenin stuck to his strict instructions to sign. Sokol'nikov obeyed, and the Bolshevik delegates put their signatures on the treaty. Only then did Hakkı relax.[85]

The Ottoman reaction to the Brest-Litovsk peace

The next day Minister of Justice and Minister of Foreign Affairs Halil Bey announced to the Chamber of Deputies the achievement of peace with Russia and the return of "our three provinces" (*üç sancağımız*). He cheered the deputies further with his prediction of the imminent signing of a third peace treaty, with Romania (the first having been signed with Ukraine), and his hope that the Brest-Litovsk treaty would convince the Entente to cease hostilities and bring a rapid end to the war.[86] The deputies praised God for the empire's good fortune, rejoiced at the destruction of the throne of Ivan the Terrible and "Crazy Petros," as the Ottomans called Peter the Great, and expressed their wishes for subsequent victory on the Palestinian and Syrian fronts. They greeted the defeat of Russia with joy because it seemingly heralded the end of the war as well as the disappearance of the Russian threat. Not one suggested that the treaty provided an opportunity for expansion of Ottoman territory into Central Asia or the Caucasus beyond *Elviye-i Selâse*.[87]

The criticism of one deputy is telling in this regard. After congratulating the government for its success in negotiating a peace treaty, the Azeri émigré and now deputy from Karahisar-ı Sahip, Ahmed Ağaoğlu, explained that he could not refrain from bringing to the government's attention certain facts that had been overlooked. Whereas other allied governments had not forgotten nations related to their ethnicity or type and had secured certain guaranties from the Bolshevik government on those nations' behalf, such as the Germans did for Estonia, Kurland, and Lithuania, the Ottoman government had done nothing for the Muslim governments established in Ufa, Crimea, and similar places. He concluded by remarking that Halil Bey had not said anything about these matters and accused the government of failing to perform its duty.[88]

Enver Pasha took up Ağaoğlu's charge. Responding to him by name, Enver averred that the government had not seen any need to resolve this problem twice. Governments in "Ufa, Kazan, and Orenburg" now

---

[85] Türkgeldi, "Brest-Litowsk," 53.
[86] Türkiye Büyük Millet Meclisi, *Meclis-i Mebusan Zabıt Ceridesi* (hereafter *MMZC*) (Ankara: TBMM Basımevi, 1991), vol. III, pt. 2, 656–57.
[87] *MMZC*, II/3, 658.   [88] *MMZC*, II/3, 658.

existed and the Bolsheviks had "already accepted the right of all nations to determine their own fate." In the Caucasus a government composed of various nations was emerging, Enver explained, and "we will not refrain from assisting in every way and recognizing other governments that will emerge and wish to maintain good neighborly relations with us due to their proximity in addition to [the governments of those] nations that share our ethnicity and religion." "Hence in my opinion," Enver concluded, "the things that Ahmed Bey Efendi has described have been dismissed."[89] The next day Halil Bey wanted to add "two words" to Enver's reply to Ağaoğlu, "The government did not neglect its duty in this matter, it remembered [its duty] very well. Tomorrow, while examining the Foreign Ministry's files he [Ağaoğlu] will see and understand very well that the government did not neglect its duty; but only those things that are possible can be done. What could be done was done."[90] Sympathy for Muslims outside the empire was one thing; placing the interests of Ottoman Muslims in jeopardy for their sake was another.

Given the evolution that took place in the Ottoman leadership's opinion about the nature and intentions of Bolshevik Russia, these responses, and Enver's in particular, were less than wholly forthcoming, and amounted to dissembling. By mid January 1918, Talât and Enver had become convinced of the Bolsheviks' commitment to centralized rule at the expense of the independence of the non-Russian borderlands. If assisting Russia's Muslims to attain independence, let alone seeking to unite with them, had been one of the Ottoman government's goals at Brest-Litovsk, then the Ottoman performance would have to be judged a spectacular failure. Lenin's rationale for signing the treaty had been to enable the Bolsheviks to focus their energy and forces against their internal enemies, and among those they crushed during or soon after the signing of the Brest-Litovsk Treaty were Muslim governments and movements in Kazan, Ufa, and Kokand.[91]

The first part of Halil Bey's defense that "Only what is possible can be done," would be a more compelling rebuttal of Ağaoğlu's charge were it not for the second part, "What could be done was done." Clearly, unlike the Germans the Ottomans did not possess the military wherewithal to threaten the Bolsheviks in such a way as to decisively influence the course of events in Kazan or elsewhere in the interior. The second part of Halil's defense, however, was misleading, since it suggested that the Ottomans

[89] *MMZC*, II/3, 658–59.   [90] *MMZC*, II/3, 709–10.
[91] Pipes, *Formation*, 108, 158–59; Azade-Ayşe Rorlich, *The Volga Tatars: A Profile in National Resilience* (Stanford: Hoover Institution Press, 1986), 132–33; Zenkovsky, *Pan-Turkism*, 170–78.

188   Shattering Empires

at Brest-Litovsk held the assistance of Muslim independence movements in Russia as one of their goals and that the Ottomans accomplished or at least attempted to accomplish something to benefit those movements. But evidence that the Ottoman government at Brest-Litovsk sought to assist the Muslim independence movements is weak. At Enver's direction, Hakkı Pasha did ask the Germans on 27 February 1918 to demand recognition of rights for the Muslims of Kazan, Orenburg, Turkistan, and Bukhara.[92] The request went nowhere and was dropped. Neither the Ottomans nor anyone else put the fate of Russia's Muslims on the agenda at Brest-Litovsk.

More importantly, when the Ottomans did consider assisting the various Muslim movements, such as when Enver oversaw the establishment of the Caucasus Committee or when Talât inquired about whether Yusuf Akçura could be used to stir up Russia's Muslims, the criterion for Ottoman interest was whether or not such movements could further the Ottomans' goal of recovering their lost territory, and not whether the Ottoman government could assist these Muslims in gaining independence. Although they may have liked to see the establishment of a Muslim state in Crimea, they prioritized relations with Ukraine because of its geopolitical importance and therefore did little to assist the Crimean Tatars.[93]

Indeed, Ottoman military intelligence evaluated Brest-Litovsk as a success precisely because it meant that the Bolsheviks would be preoccupied with internal rebellions and would not pose a threat across the Caucasus. Writing in the middle of June 1918 to the Directorate of Eastern Affairs, the Ottoman military attaché from Moscow made it clear that Ottoman state interests, and not those of Russia's Muslims, were his primary concern. After noting that peace had been made between the Germans and Ukrainians on the one side and the Bolsheviks on the other, he advised, "the Russians will be able to use their forces against the rebels. The continued existence of Bolshevik rule in Russia is to the advantage of the Ottoman government because [Russia] will not be able to unite itself on account of internal conflicts and will not be capable of creating problems for Turkey from the Caucasus."[94]

While ministers, bureaucrats, parliamentary deputies, and military officers in Istanbul, Damascus, and elsewhere exchanged notes of congratulations and celebrated, those outside government hailed the news

---

[92] Jäschke, "Der Turanismus," 23–24.
[93] Kırımlı, "Diplomatic Relations," 207; Balcıoğlu, *Teşkilat-ı Mahsusa*, 146.
[94] ATASE, "Information Regarding Conditions in Russia," 17.06.1334 [17.06.1918], D. 142-121, F. 1-20.

as well. In an article entitled "Brest-Litovsk in History" in the newspaper *Tasvir-i Efkâr*, Yunus Nadi Bey praised Brest-Litovsk as signifying the elimination from the world map of the threat of "nightmarish Muscovite tsarism" and rejoiced at the return "of one of our most important defensive points."[95] Ahmed Emin Bey, writing in the pages of the newspaper *Vakit* under the headline "Ardahan, Kars, and Batumi" approvingly quoted Foreign Minister Halil Bey's words, "we have been saved from the Muscovite danger and oppression for at least a century." Describing the Ottoman achievement at Brest-Litovsk not as a "conquest" but as "the repair of an old injustice," he noted, "We have such burdensome duties in the matter of reforming and adapting our country to a way of life appropriate for this century that we cannot leave things unfinished as they are and we cannot waste time even thinking of conquests."[96]

Conclusion

The toppling of the tsar in March 1917 was a stroke of immense good fortune for the struggling Ottoman empire. Russia's descent into chaos inspired the war-weary Ottomans to hope that a general peace was near and that the empire might manage to survive the war intact. The dissolution of Russia's Caucasus Army relieved the military threat from the east. Enver hoped to exploit this opportunity not by pushing to the Caucasus but instead by regrouping Ottoman reserves to retake Baghdad and Palestine from the British. The Bolshevik seizure of power in November buoyed Ottoman spirits as it promised further turbulence for Russia. The Bolsheviks' anti-imperialist formula of peace with no annexations and no indemnities also excited the Ottomans, who set off for the peace negotiations at Brest-Litovsk with the expectation that they would attain at a minimum the restoration of the 1914 border and at a maximum perhaps the return of the 1877 border and the three provinces of Kars, Ardahan, and Batumi.

At Brest-Litovsk the national idea emerged as the center of gravity in the diplomatic struggle between the Central Powers and the Bolsheviks. In order to preserve or extend their own influence over space, both sides invoked the principle of national self-determination in their debates over the future of Russian-occupied Anatolia and German-occupied Eastern Europe. The Bolsheviks' caginess on withdrawal from Eastern Anatolia and their decree "On Armenia" disillusioned the Ottomans, who concluded that the new Bolshevik Russia would not fundamentally differ

[95] "Tarihde Brest-Litovsk," *Tasvir-i Efkâr*, 3 Mart 1334 [3.3.1918].
[96] "Ardahan, Kars ve Batum," *Vakit*, 6 Mart 1334 [6.3.1918].

from the old. They weighed the option of inciting Russia's Muslims in retaliation but judged their co-religionists to be too disorganized and dispersed to be of use. Yet, if the essence of the new world order was the same as the old, the form was decidedly different. Thus, the Ottomans mobilized the Caucasus Committee to make claims on behalf of the Muslims of *Elviye-i Selâse*, and the Germans anointed Ukrainian youth from the Rada as the representatives of an independent Ukraine. Due to a fortuitous combination of quiet but persistent lobbying, German exasperation with Bolshevik temporizing, and Lenin's decision to conclude a peace treaty at any cost, the Ottomans succeeded in achieving a Russian commitment to withdraw from Kars, Ardahan, and Batumi. In line with the new conventions of state legitimacy, the Treaty of Brest-Litovsk did not transfer those territories to the Ottoman empire, but instead assigned the Ottomans the leading role in organizing the plebiscite by which the provinces' inhabitants would determine their own fate.

The Treaty of Brest-Litovsk represented an enormous success for the Ottomans. The creation of an independent Ukraine promised to cripple Russia, and the recovery of *Elviye-i Selâse* gave the government a tangible prize for the war. Nonetheless, it was incomplete. The Ottomans nurtured no illusions about Russia's ability to recover from the crisis into which it had fallen. They knew they had little time to accomplish their next objective, expelling Russia from the Caucasus and putting space between their empire and Russia. Thus far, however, the Caucasus had declined Ottoman entreaties to break from Russia and embrace independence. The idea of a greater and democratic Russia exerted an attraction. Forcing the Caucasus to be free would be the Ottomans' challenge.

7 Forced to be free: the geopolitics of independence in the Transcaucasus

Following Brest-Litovsk a rapidly evolving diplomatic environment continued to demand that Ottoman statecraft remain flexible and creative. The goals of building a bulwark against the resurgence of Russian power and recovering *Elviye-i Selâse* would guide Ottoman policy toward the Caucasus, but unlike at Brest-Litovsk, where the Ottomans were junior partners without leverage over either their enemy or their allies, in the Caucasus the Ottoman state enjoyed comparative advantages in strength and stability. For the moment, the Ottoman state was the most powerful entity in the region. The Ottomans' interlocutors in the Transcaucasus, by contrast, were isolated, confused about what they represented, and uncertain about who they were. Transcaucasia's political elites came from the same currents of democratic socialism as those who lost Russia to the Bolsheviks, and they would display many of the same flaws of naiveté, arrogance, and irresolution. Fate dealt them a weak hand of cards, and they would play that hand badly. The Transcaucasians aspired to remain part of a democratic Russia, but geopolitical pressure would force them to be free, splitting them into three separate and independent republics – Georgia, Armenia, and Azerbaijan. Each of these republics was born in the shape of a nation-state, and each would fit that shape poorly.

The Transcaucasus alone

Right after Tsar Nicholas II abdicated, his viceroy in the Caucasus, Grand Duke Nikolai Nikolaevich, also stepped down. The architecture of tsarist rule had broken apart. Abandoned by the center, the peoples of Transcaucasia had no choice but to take matters into their own hands. Transcaucasian members of the Duma formed a Special Transcaucasian Committee (Ozakom) in Tiflis that took nominal control of civil affairs in the name of the Provisional Government in Petrograd, while General Yudenich assumed command of the Caucasus Army. Socialists dominated Transcaucasian politics and, as elsewhere in the empire, they established multiple local councils, or "soviets." The two most important

191

were in Tiflis and Baku. Working through a regional center located in Tiflis, the soviets exercised what real institutional power existed in the region. In an approximation of the Menshevik ideal wherein "proletarian" organs of self-rule directed the "bourgeois" government, the Ozakom duly echoed the resolutions of the soviets.[1] The Transcaucasians believed that the future of their region was inside a united and democratic Russia. The disintegration of Russia's Caucasus Army, however, had left the region exposed to Ottoman or German invasion. It was also sending tens of thousands of unorganized but armed young men in packs streaming across the Transcaucasus toward their homes beyond. Despite the breakdown in order, the Transcaucasus in 1917 remained relatively calm and undisturbed by mass violence.

When news from Petrograd of the Bolshevik seizure of power reached Tiflis, the Regional Center of Soviets and the Army Committee of the Caucasus Army alike roundly condemned it as an attack on the revolution. They reiterated their allegiance to Russia's Provisional Government and emphasized that only the future All-Russian Constituent Assembly could legitimately decide the fate of "our dear mother land."[2] A week later the Bolsheviks issued their famous "Declaration of the Rights of Peoples," recognizing the prerogative of the empire's peoples to exercise self-determination and even to form sovereign states. In an act that has confounded later historians, the Transcaucasians ignored this offer of independence.[3] Although by no means without nationalist sentiment, most of Transcaucasia's socialists believed that nationalism in the sense of the aspiration of each nation to be sovereign was impractical and already an obsolescing principle. Democratic union, not ethnic separatism, would best serve the peoples of the empire, including their own.[4]

The Bolsheviks, too, for their part, did not regard national separatism as a lasting force. Their expectation was that the empire would be reconstituted as a "voluntary and honest union" bearing no resemblance to Lenin's famous description of Russia as a "prison house of peoples."[5] Indeed, the Bolsheviks anticipated that socialist revolution would spread to Western Europe and across the globe, alter the world irrevocably, and render national differences ultimately irrelevant.

---

[1] Pipes, *Formation*, 98.
[2] Resolutions of the Army Committee and of the Regional Center of Soviets, 26.10.1917 [8.11.1917], Republic of Georgia, *Dokumenty i materialy po vneshnei politike Zakavkaz'ia i Gruzii* (Tiflis: Tipografiia pravitel'stva Gruzinskoi respubliki, 1919), 1–2.
[3] See, for example, Kazemzadeh, *Struggle*, 57.
[4] Stephen F. Jones, *Socialism in Georgian Colors: The European Road to Social Democracy, 1883–1917* (Cambridge, MA: Harvard University Press, 2005), 259–60, 265–66.
[5] I. Minets and E. Gorodetskii, eds., *Dokumenty po istorii grazhdanskoi voiny v SSSR*, vol. I (Moscow: Politizdat, 1941), 18–20.

When in the wake of the Bolshevik Revolution Transcaucasia's political elites met to decide the region's future, their mood was dour. The
decision not to recognize the Bolshevik government was an unpleasant
one. As the Menshevik leader Noi Zhordaniia put it to those assembled,
"A misfortune has now befallen us. The connection with Russia has been
broken and Transcaucasia has been left alone."[6] When four days later
they proclaimed the "Transcaucasian Commissariat," they did so in an
exculpatory manner, not a celebratory one. Extraordinary circumstances
compelled them to assert a degree of independence, and even so they had
formed not a sovereign entity but a provisional body intended to exist
only until the convocation of the All-Russian Constituent Assembly.[7]
Their house was falling apart, and the Transcaucasians had unwittingly
taken their first steps toward independence.

First contacts

The Ottomans made their first contacts with the Transcaucasus on 25
November, when Vehib Pasha sent a ceasefire proposal to the Caucasus
Army. Delegations from the two armies met in the town of Erzincan.
When General Mikhail Przheval'skii, who succeeded Yudenich as commander in chief of the Caucasus Army, made a pretense of representing
an independent Transcaucasian state, he spooked the Ottomans, who
feared Przheval'skii wanted to use a ceasefire agreement as a ruse to
obtain Ottoman recognition of a sovereign state. Recognition of such a
state, Enver warned, would likely mean "we will encounter problems in
the evacuation of the occupied lands."[8] Others imagined a diabolical trap
wherein the Russians would annex Iranian Azerbaijan and "part of Anatolia" to this nominally independent Caucasian state.[9] Thus the Ottomans
were careful to ensure that the text of the armistice, signed on 18
December, skirted the issue of the commissariat's sovereign status. The
armistice also forbade all strategic regroupings, a condition the Transcaucasians had wanted so as to prevent the Ottomans from redeploying
forces away from the Caucasus against the British in Mesopotamia.[10]

---

[6] Noi Zhordaniia, *Za dva goda: doklady i rechi* (Tiflis: Istoricheskaia kommissia Ispolnitel'nogo Komiteta Soveta rabochikh deputatov, 1919), 51–52.
[7] First declaration of the Transcaucasian Commissariat, 18.11.1917 [1.12.1917], Georgia, *Dokumenty i materialy*, 8–9.
[8] ATASE, A. 4/3671, K. 2897, D. 310-398, F. 3-61, cited in Kılıç, *Türk–Sovyet*, 98.
[9] ATASE, A. 4/10481, K. 3627, D. 117, F. 30-1, cited in Kılıç, *Türk–Sovyet*, 102.
[10] Kazemzadeh, *Struggle*, 81–82; Excerpt from the Log of Meeting of the Transcaucasian
Commissariat, 21.11.1917 [4.12.1917], Telegram to the Commander in Chief of the
British Mesopotamian Army, 22.11.1917 [5.12.1917], Georgia, *Dokumenty i materialy*,
11–12, 14.

The armistice put a formal end to the long dormant hostilities between armies on the Caucasian front, but it acknowledged another ongoing conflict, that between Armenians and Kurds. The unraveling of the Caucasus Army had spurred Armenians in the spring of 1917 to begin forming units on their own initiative. At the end of November Przheval'skii, now desperate for manpower, authorized the incorporation of Armenian and Georgian national units into what remained of his Caucasus Army.[11] The Armenian units had free rein and again began to prey upon Muslims, especially Kurds, engaging in episodic massacres and lesser outrages such as extorting "taxes," expelling them from their homes, and settling others in their place. From the area of Hınıs in June 1917 the Russian army received reports that gangs of Armenians were pillaging Kurdish villages daily,[12] and in Kars Armenian units perpetrated massacres of elderly Kurdish men, women, and children.[13]

Even Kurds sympathetic to the Russians were pleading for protection from the Armenian militias, threatening otherwise to defect to the Ottomans.[14] Kurdish activity in the regions of Dersim and Mt. Ağrı (Ararat) in Anatolia and Kotur in Iran became especially worrisome. The Kurds of Dersim were predominantly Alevis, and as such had a long history of persecution by the Sunni Ottomans. Russian military intelligence before the war had identified them as likely allies, and they assisted the Russians by attacking the Ottomans.[15] Yet by the middle of 1917, robbery, stealing of cattle, and "ceaseless assaults upon Kurdish women" perpetrated by Russian and Armenian forces alienated them and turned them against the Russians.[16] The picture around Urmia in Iran was similar.[17] Earlier in the war Urmia had been the site of widespread slaughter of Christians. Now, the breakdown of Russian authority led to vengeance attacks by Christians against Muslims. Muslims fearing for

---

[11] Gabriel Gorganian, "Armenian Participation in World War I on the Caucasian Front," *Armenian Review*, 20, 4 (Winter 1967), 78.

[12] RGVIA, Telegram from the Erzurum Chief of Staff, 27.5.1917 [9.6.1917], f. 2168, o. 1, d. 48, l. 33.

[13] RGVIA, Captain Kablitskii to the General of the Caucasus Army, [undated], f. 2168, o. 1, d. 48, l. 4. See also the draft order on l. 50.

[14] RGVIA, Petition from the Population of Zilandere to Kiamil Bey, 31.1.1917 [13.2.1917], Appeal to Shakhovskoi from Kiamil Bey, 22.12.1916 [4.1.1917], f. 2168, o. 1, d. 264, ll. 10–11, 35; Telegram from the Commissar of the Bayezid Region, 21.5.1917 [3.6.1917], f. 2168, o. 1, d. 277, l. 3.

[15] Allen and Muratoff, *Battlefields*, 438, 461.

[16] RGVIA, Lt. Devoiants to the Caucasus Army Staff's Senior Reconnaissance Section Adjutant, 22.6.1917 [5.7.1917], f. 2168, o. 1, d. 277, ll. 16–17; Çakmak, *Büyük Harpte*, 263–65; Kâzım Karabekir, *Doğunun Kurtuluşu: Erzincan ve Erzurum'un Kurtuluşu. Sarıkamış, Kars, ve Ötesi* (Erzurum: Erzurum Ticaret ve Sanayi Odası, 1990), 79.

[17] Kamal Madhar Ahmad, *Kurdistan*, 124.

their lives crowded onto the Russian consulate's grounds in June 1917, causing Urmia's vice-consul to lament that the "Russian flag can no longer serve as a symbol of security and justice for the Iranians." The Russian Refugee Council implored the imperial army to adopt "extreme measures for the cessation of the violence perpetrated by Christians against the Muslim population."[18]

The Russian army representatives at Erzincan worried that the vacuum created by the collapse of Russian power would precipitate a major clash as Armenians and Kurds rushed back to reclaim their lands. Russia's liberal Provisional Government was sympathetic to the Armenian cause and that spring passed legislation allowing Armenian refugees to return home. Before the end of the year 150,000 had done so.[19] Przheval'skii feared that the conclusion of an armistice would encourage Kurdish refugees also to return to the eastern provinces and thereby stoke further violence. The Russians knew that the Ottomans were already exploiting intercommunal tensions to their rear by inciting Kurds to mount attacks.[20] Thus article eleven of the armistice called upon the Ottoman command to restrain the Kurds and recognized the Russians' right to deal with the Kurds as "bandits" if necessary.

Invitation to independence

In January 1918, Enver reversed his stance on Caucasian independence. He came to favor the idea for two reasons. One was that an independent Caucasian state would serve as a barrier to Russia. The second was that it could potentially neutralize the Armenians if it was based on a dominant coalition of Caucasian Muslims and Georgians. But "whatever form and shape it takes," Enver advised Vehib, "we will immediately recognize and acknowledge such a Caucasian government formally."[21]

---

[18] RGVIA, Dispatch of the Executive Committee of the Council for the Settlement of Refugees, June 1917, f. 2168, o. 1, d. 288, ll. 53–54.

[19] Hovanissian, *Republic of Armenia*, vol. I, *The First Year 1918–1919*, 16.

[20] Enver in January 1918 recommended that irregular units be formed from Kurds to follow the withdrawing Russians and protect Muslims from reprisals: ATASE, Enver to Vehib, 6 Ocak 1334 [6.1.1918], K. 2928, D. 545, F. 1. Some Christian Russian subjects allegedly were collaborating with Ottoman infiltrators: RGVIA, 14th Infantry Regiment Commander to the Chief of the 4th Caucasus Rifle Division, 19.4.1917 [2.5.1917] and Chief of the Counterintelligence Section to the Senior Adjutant of the Intelligence Section of the Caucasus Army, 21.4.1917 [4.5.1917], f. 2168, o. 1, d. 535, ll. 16, 36. Some Armenians continued to serve in the Ottoman army. One such Armenian officer was covertly feeding the Russians information: RGVIA, Telegram to Colonel Batashev, 23.5.1917 [5.6.1917], f. 2168, o. 1, d. 258, l. 1. See also Sâbis, *Hatıralarım*, vol. IV, 168.

[21] ATASE, Enver to Vehib, 9 Ocak 1334 [9.1.1918], K. 2921, D. 511, F. 1-24.

In a letter to the Transcaucasian General Ilia Odishelidze on 14 January, Vehib Pasha recalled General Evgenii Vyshinskii's earlier claim to represent an independent state and explained that Enver was now interested in establishing relations with such a state. Vehib's letter forced the Transcaucasian Commissariat to grapple head on with the questions of what it was and whom it represented. The commissariat, however, was schizophrenic precisely on these basic questions. It called itself a regional government subordinated to the greater Russian one, yet refused to recognize Russia's Bolshevik government. By authorizing the signing of the Erzincan Armistice, the commissariat had already asserted itself as a sovereign state in the interstate arena, even if it preferred to pretend that it had not. As the Ottomans noted, even General Vyshinskii had not abided the fiction that the Russian Caucasus Army signed the armistice.[22]

The commissariat's provisional answer to the question of its status had been to defer to the authority of the future All-Russian Constituent Assembly. The Bolsheviks' disbandment of the assembly in January, however, stripped Tiflis of this illusory option. No longer could Tiflis defer to another body. Nonetheless, it tried. After spending nine days in debate, the commissariat managed only to thank the Ottomans for the proposal to become independent and to ask for three more weeks in order to consult the "opinions and views of the other autonomous governments" in Russia.[23] But before this reply could even reach him, Vehib extended an invitation for Tiflis to come to Brest-Litovsk and achieve recognition as an independent state.[24] The idea won the support of only a small group of Georgian National Democrats.[25] Partly out of a fear of standing on their own, but also out of belief in the fundamental unity of Russian revolutionary democracy and a lingering "imperial loyalty," the other parties rejected the idea of independence.[26] It was a fateful decision.

Forward into the Caucasus

On 12 February, in coordination with the Germans' resumption of their advance on Russia following the breakdown of the talks at Brest-Litovsk, the Ottoman army undertook offensive operations toward the Caucasus. Throughout 1917 Vehib Pasha had been sensitive to the unsettled

---

[22] Letter of Vehib Pasha, 1.1.1918 [14.1.1918], Georgia, *Dokumenty i materialy*, 24–25.
[23] Answer to Vehib Pasha, 15.1.1918 [28.1.1918], Georgia, *Dokumenty i materialy*, 35–36.
[24] Invitation to the Brest-Litovsk Conference, 1.2.1918 [14.2.1918], Georgia, *Dokumenty i materialy*, 52.
[25] Hovannisian, *Armenia on the Road*, 120–21.
[26] Zurab Avalov, *Nezavisimost' Gruzii v mezhdunarodnoi politike, 1918–1921 gg.* (New York: Chalidze Publications, [1924] 1982), 31.

nature of the Caucasian front and so had husbanded the Third Army's manpower. He lost one division to Enver's Thunderbolt Army but managed to fend off requests for forces for the Mesopotamian, Iranian, and Palestinian fronts. On 23 January he received the order from Enver to begin preparations for an offensive. Taking into account the dissolution of the Russian army and the emergence of the Armenian and Georgian militias, Vehib appointed as commander of the First Caucasus Army Musa Kâzım Karabekir Pasha, a commander known for his experience in fighting partisans in Macedonia.[27] Karabekir's First Caucasus Army was to advance inland toward Erzincan and Erzurum, and Vehib's Third Caucasus Army was to march along the Black Sea coast toward Trabzon. The armies were to avoid combat with remaining Russian forces, firing only if fired upon, and to focus on retaking the occupied territory. Waiting for them, however, were also some 10,000 Georgians and 21,000 Armenians in armed formations.[28] For such a large front these were small forces, but they had the advantages of a skilled officer corps, defensible terrain, and ample stockpiles of weaponry, equipment, and food left by the Russians.[29] What the formations of Russian Armenians lacked, however, was the will to fight for the lands of their Anatolian co-ethnics. Instead of attempting to mount any form of defense, they preferred to withdrew and perpetrate "extraordinary acts" against the Muslim villages they passed through.[30]

The Ottoman advance followed repeated protests against the treatment of Muslims in occupied Anatolia and the Caucasus. As Vehib explained to Odishelidze, the Armenians' apparent determination to annihilate the Ottoman Muslim population in the occupied territories "as part of an organized plan" required Ottoman forces to advance for the sake of "humanity and civilization."[31] Caucasian Muslim representatives

---

[27] Karabekir, *Doğunun Kurtuluşu*, 61.   [28] Allen and Muratoff, *Battlefields*, 459.
[29] Antranik Çelebyan, *Antranik Paşa*, tr. Mariam Arpi and Nairi Arek (Istanbul: Peri Yayaınları, 2003), 221–23.
[30] Antranig Chalabian, *Revolutionary Figures: Mihran Damadian, Hambardzum Boyadjian, Serob Aghibur, Hrair-Dzhoghk, Gevorg Chavush, Sebastatsi Murad, Nikol Duman*, trans. Arra S. Avakian (USA: A. Chalabian, 1994), 298–99.
[31] "Ermenilerin müretteb bir plan dahilinde birbirini vely ve takib edib ve edeceğinden de zerrece şübhe olmayan ihrak-ı buyut, katl-i nüfus, nehb-i emval ve hetk-i ırz gibi cinayetlerle Osmanlı ehl-i İslamının mahv ve ifnasını tasmim eyledikleri." ("The Armenians are determined to destroy and annihilate the Ottoman Muslims by way of crimes such as burning homes, massacres, looting of property, and the 'rending of honor' [rape], about which there is no doubt that the Armenians are committing and will be committing as part of an organized plan.") ATASE, To the Commander of the Caucasus Armies, General Przheval'skii, [n.d.], K. 2930, D. 5530, F. 8. This phrase does not appear in the similar but not identical and abbreviated Russian text, "Telegramma Vekhiba-Pashi o perekhode turetskikh voisk v nastuplenie," 30.12.1917 [12.1.1918],

complained consistently about the cruel treatment they were suffering. Internal correspondence makes clear that this concern for the safety of Ottoman Muslims was not a mere pretext.[32] Enver wired his own head-quarters that retreating enemy forces were acting contrary to "the laws of states and civilization," carrying out cruelties such as gouging eyes, attacking hospitals, dismembering the sick and wounded, and looting the property of Muslim Ottoman subjects.[33] Later he wanted to make "end-ing atrocities against the Muslims living in our occupied provinces" a priority at Brest-Litovsk.[34] Vehib urged his officers to advance rapidly in order to deliver Muslims from the massacres.[35] Not wishing to lend even rhetorical legitimacy to the Armenian formations, Karabekir and Vehib agreed not to employ the phrase "Armenian army" but only "bands" (*çete*) in their correspondence.[36] Although the available evidence does suggest serial massacres, the small Armenian forces were incapable of carrying out a program of annihilation.

The Ottomans rolled forward meeting light resistance, taking Erzincan, Mamahatun, and Bayburt in the first week. Against Enver's wishes, Vehib Pasha halted his forces outside Trabzon for three days to give the Russian, Georgian, and Armenian forces an opportunity to withdraw from the city. The defenders availed themselves of Vehib's offer. On 24 February, as their opponents left by sea, Ottoman forces reentered Trabzon without bloodshed and to the accompaniment of a Russian brass band.[37]

Peace talks in Trabzon

At the end of February the Transcaucasian Seim, or parliament, declared itself authorized to make peace, yet still refrained from proclaiming inde-pendence. The Seim envisioned a peace based on the 1914 borders and the granting of self-determination to the peoples of Eastern Anatolia and autonomy to Ottoman Armenia, and readied a delegation for peace talks

---

Georgia, *Dokumenty i materialy*, 47–49. Unlike the Ottoman version, the Russian one includes a warning from Vehib Pasha that he "was no longer in a state to keep his forces in the role of silent witnesses, who hear and understand that their parents and children, wives and relatives are doomed to extermination."

[32] Kılıç, *Türk–Sovyet*, 261–62. Cf. Hovannisian, *Armenia on the Road*, 123; Sarkisian, *Ekspansionistskaia politika*, 336; Trumpener, *Germany*, 171.

[33] ATASE, Telegram to the General Headquarters, 28 Kanunuevvel 1333 [28.12.1917], K. 511, D. 27-1995, F. 1-1.

[34] ATASE, Cipher from Zeki Pasha to Enver Pasha, 15 Kanunuevvel 1333 [15.12.1917], K. 530, D. 2070-928, F. 1-36.

[35] ATASE, A. 1/1, K.153, D. 682-380, F.15, cited in Kılıç, *Türk–Sovyet* 261.

[36] Karabekir, *Doğunun Kurtuluşu*, 74, 81.

[37] Genel Kurmay Başkanlığı, *Üçüncü Ordu Harekâtı*, vol. II, 452–53.

with the Ottomans in Trabzon.[38] Before the delegation had departed
Tiflis, news of Brest-Litovsk and the surrender of Kars, Ardahan, and
Batumi arrived, stunning the Transcaucasians. The Seim dashed off fervent denunciations of the treaty to capitals throughout the world. The
delegation set out for Trabzon by ship, deluding itself that it could defy
the terms of Brest-Litovsk.

The amateurish 61-man delegation made a poor initial impression. As
one onlooker cracked when seeing it disembark, "If this is the entire population of Transcaucasia it is indeed very small; if, however, it is only a
delegation, it is much too large."[39] The Transcaucasians' diplomacy was
no better. The Ottomans repeatedly pressed them to clarify the commissariat's legal status. With hopelessly convoluted logic the Transcaucasians
insisted that they were still part of Russia but were not bound by the treaty
of Brest-Litovsk because they did not recognize Russia's Bolshevik government. The Ottomans outlined the illogic and inconsistencies in this
position and berated them for Tiflis' failure to follow Ukraine's example
and Istanbul's earlier solicitation to participate at Brest-Litovsk.[40]

As the two sides talked in Trabzon, the Ottoman army continued to
advance toward the 1914 border. When Vehib chastised Karabekir for
moving too quickly and exposing his flanks, the latter countered that the
rapid movement was keeping Armenian units on the run and preventing
further massacres. Another, more prosaic force spurring the Ottomans
forward was hunger. Karabekir could keep his forces fed only by leaping
ahead to capture abandoned Russian supply depots. Often he did not
know if he was really searching for the enemy or simply more depots.
Low supplies compelled him to storm Erzurum on 11 March in defiance of Vehib's orders to wait for reinforcements.[41] Karabekir's gamble
paid off when the defending Armenians under the famous commander
Andranik Pasha (Ozanian) fled the city without a fight.[42] Erzurum's vast
stockpiles of food and arms inspired wonderment among the badly provi-
sioned Ottomans who could not understand how it was that the wealthy
and powerful tsarist empire collapsed.[43] The discovery of such bounti-
ful supplies inspired Enver to entertain plans to push deeper into the
Caucasus.[44]

[38] Resolutions Taken by the Transcaucasian Seim on the Question of Peace, Georgia,
    Dokumenty i materialy, 83–84; Hovannisian, *Armenia on the Road*, 125–30; Kazemzadeh,
    Struggle, 87–90.
[39] Avalov, *Nezavisimost'*, 34.
[40] Kazemzadeh, *Struggle*, 94–95; see also Georgia, *Dokumenty i materialy*, 113–19.
[41] Karabekir, *Doğunun Kurtuluşu*, 97–99, 108–09, 124–48.
[42] Hovannisian, *Armenia on the Road*, 134–36; Kazemzadeh, *Struggle*, 86.
[43] Karabekir, *Doğunun Kurtuluşu*, 130.
[44] PA-AA, A7013, Bernstorff to the Foreign Ministry, Rußland 11042, 15.2.1918.

From Erzurum the Ottomans pushed on, retaking one town after another and reaching the 1914 border on 24 March. All the while, the Transcaucasians at Trabzon remained stubbornly oblivious both to the dubious merits of their legal case and to the increasingly unfavorable correlation of forces between themselves and the Ottomans. They persisted in their attempts to persuade the Ottomans that their state could be simultaneously part of Russia and exempt from the terms of Brest-Litovsk.

In private meetings with the Ottoman negotiators, however, separate parties of Transcaucasians sought to establish closer relations. Some Muslim Transcaucasians urged the Ottomans to push deep into Trans-caucasia as far as Baku.[45] At the end of March, Baku's Bolsheviks had joined with the city's Dashnaks to violently suppress the Musavat Party, which as the leading party of Baku's Muslim majority represented the Bolsheviks' most formidable opponent and the Dashnaks' greatest enemy. The relatively well-armed and disciplined Bolsheviks and Dash-naks succeeded in crushing the Musavat and establishing a coalition government known as the "Baku Commune." In the process they turned the Caspian port into a "redoubt of terror and pogrom" not just against the Musavat, but against Muslims as a whole. Up to 12,000 Muslims perished in this episode, and one-half of the city's Muslims fled to the countryside. Known as the "March Events," it added urgency to the Caucasian Muslims' calls for help.[46]

Armenian and Georgian politicians also approached the Ottomans confidentially. The mayor of Tiflis, founder of the Armenian National Council, and Dashnak Aleksandr Khatisian proposed to the head of the Ottoman delegation Naval Minister Hüseyin Rauf Bey (Orbay), that in exchange for permitting some 400,000 Armenian refugees to return to their homes in Eastern Anatolia, the Armenian delegates at Trabzon would come out in favor of restoring Kars, Ardahan, and Batumi to the Ottoman empire.[47] The Transcaucasian foreign minister and Georgian

---

[45] Enis Şahin, *Trabzon ve Batum Konferansları ve Anlaşmaları (1917–1918)* (Ankara: Türk Tarih Kurumu, 2002), 335.

[46] Jörg Baberowski, *Der Feind ist überall: Stalinismus im Kaukasus* (Munich: Deutsche Verlags-Anstalt, 2003), 138; Kazemzadeh, *Struggle*, 69–76; Michael G. Smith, "The Russian Revolution as a National Revolution: Tragic Deaths and Rituals of Remembrance in Muslim Azerbaijan (1907–1920)," *Jahrbücher für Geschichte Osteuropas*, 49, 3 (2001), 375–78; Şahin, *Trabzon*, 391–95; Ronald Grigor Suny, *The Baku Commune, 1917–1918: Class and Nationality in the Russian Revolution* (Princeton: Princeton University Press, 1972), 214–33; Hovannisian, *Armenia on the Road*, 147–49. For a detailed analysis, see Solmaz Rustamova-Togidi, ed., *Mart 1918 g. Baku: azerbaidzhan-skie pogromy v dokumentakh* (Baku: n.p., 2009).

[47] Kurat, *Rusya ve Türkiye*, 471–72.

socialist Akaki Chkhenkeli confided to Rauf that he regarded the Armenians as a "harmful element." He explained that he had supported the call for an autonomous Ottoman Armenia only to prevent the Armenians from sowing anarchy inside Transcaucasia. Already they were collaborating with the British, and could be controlled only if the Georgians and Caucasian Turks cooperated. Rauf listened dutifully to these conversations and noted these internal fractures.[48]

The arrival at the beginning of April of a delegation from the Union of Allied Mountaineers of the North Caucasus added another source of complexity to the talks. The UAM was a pan-mountaineer movement composed of the predominantly Muslim indigenous peoples of the North Caucasus who comprised a dizzying array of ethnicities and languages. Like the commissariat, the UAM had sprung up in the wake of the tsar's abdication and advocated the inclusion of the Caucasus within a democratic and federal Russia. A Bolshevik invasion of the North Caucasus that winter, however, spurred the UAM to look to break from Russia. The North Caucasus was too small to stand alone, they reasoned, and so they sent to Tiflis a delegation led by their president, the Chechen oil baron Abdulmejid Chermoev, and foreign minister, the Dagestani Kumuk lawyer Haidar Bammatov (Bammate). The mountaineers narrowly missed the Transcaucasian leadership and so proceeded to Trabzon. There they asked to join the Transcaucasian Commissariat, contending that only a united Caucasus stood a chance against the Bolsheviks. The Transcaucasians, however, still could not sort out their state's sovereign status, and so they demurred, neither rejecting nor accepting the mountaineers' proposal.[49] Nesimî, by contrast, found the argument for a single, unified Caucasian state compelling,[50] as did Enver, who wrote that it would be desirable if Chkhenkeli could be persuaded to form a government with the North Caucasus.[51]

If the primary goal of the Ottomans was to block the reemergence of Russian power in the region, a secondary objective was to minimize, if not eliminate altogether, Armenian influence. The prospect of an Armenian stalking horse discomposed Enver and Talât. The Bolsheviks' decree on Armenia had demonstrated continued Russian interest in the Armenian Question, and France's and Britain's pro-Armenian sympathies were known. Facilitating the establishment of a united Caucasian state offered

---

[48] Şahin, *Trabzon*, 336–39.   [49] Kurat, *Türkiye ve Rusya*, 483; Şahin, *Trabzon*, 388.

[50] ATASE, K. 1847, D. 61, F. 5-11, cited in Mesut Erşan, "Birinci Dünya Harbinde Osmanlı Devletinin Kuzey Kafkasya Siyaseti," Ph.D. Dissertation, Atatürk University, Erzurum, 1995, 47.

[51] ATASE, Dispatch to the Third Army Command, 14 Nisan 1334 [14.4.1918], K. 526, D. 2054-369, F. 3-2.

the dual advantage of serving both Ottoman objectives. A Caucasian state joining Muslims and Georgians would prove a stronger buffer against Russia. Its population would not only be greater but it would also be of higher quality: Ottoman analysts believed the Georgians' comparatively high educational levels would make for a stronger state.[52] At the same time, it would also contain Armenian influence by submerging the Armenians as a minority in a larger formation dominated by the Christian Georgians and Caucasian Muslims. Enver speculated hopefully that the Georgians and Dagestanis might form a state that included the Armenians but would divide the Armenians' lands between them and thereby keep them in check.[53]

Throughout the spring of 1918 the Ottomans at Trabzon worked to isolate the Armenians from their neighbors. With the Russians withdrawn beyond the horizon and conflict with Muslims deepening, the Georgians were the Armenians' only potential ally. During the war the Georgians had resented Vorontsov-Dashkov's Armenophile policies and watched the Armenians with unease.[54] The Ottomans were aware of friction between the Georgians and Armenians,[55] and Enver made preventing an alliance between them one of his objectives.[56] The Georgians presented themselves as eager to accommodate the Ottomans against the Armenians, as Chkhenkeli had suggested to Rauf when he cursed the Armenians. The Georgian Transcaucasian minister of war Evgenii Gegechkori would similarly disparage the Armenians by complaining, "the massive Russian and Ottoman empires could not cope with these fellows. How can my tiny Georgia deal with these troublemakers?"[57]

Although in private correspondence Ottoman military officers approvingly quoted their Georgian counterparts' comments that no serious basis for Ottoman–Georgian hostility existed, ownership of Batumi loomed as a major obstacle to an alliance between them. The Georgians insisted adamantly on retaining the port. The Azeris and the North Caucasians backed the Georgians, and urged the Ottomans to leave Batumi to the Georgians as a sign of goodwill. This would keep the Georgians from aligning with the Armenians, and a cooperative Georgia would facilitate the delivery to the north of the arms the mountaineers needed to repel the

---

[52] ATASE, Col. Tevfik to Vehib, 17–18 Nisan 1334 [17–18.4.1918], K. 2918, D. 496, F. 1-35.
[53] ATASE, Enver to Vehib, 9 Ocak 1334 [9.1.1918], K. 2921, D. 511, F. 1-24.
[54] Diakin, *Natsional'nyi vopros*, 541; Price, *War*, 264–65.
[55] ATASE, A. 1/2, K. 227, D. 941-574, F. 61, cited in Kılıç, *Türk–Sovyet*, 231.
[56] Kılıç, *Türk–Sovyet*, 250.
[57] Halil Menteşe, *Osmanlı Mebusan Meclisi Reisi Halil Menteşe'nin Anıları* (Istanbul: Hürriyet Vakfı Yayınları, 1986), 229.

Bolsheviks.[58] Rauf and Vehib similarly advised foregoing Batumi. Good relations with the Georgians were necessary, Vehib argued to Enver, because the Muslims of the Caucasus were unreliable, and sooner or later the Caucasus would again fall into Russia's grasp. Annexing Batumi, he warned, would drive the Georgians to the Armenians and drag "the [Ottoman] state into a tragic quagmire." "Today it is in your hands whether to sink or save the state," he concluded.[59] Enver, however, was adamant that the Ottoman state reclaim Batumi. It was a key port for the whole of the Caucasus, and its recovery would boost his government's floundering legitimacy.[60]

As reports about the Ottoman army's steady progress toward Batumi continued to come in, the dithering Seim belatedly began to grasp the depth of its problems. In early April the Transcaucasians offered to surrender parts of Kars and Ardahan and to soften their demands regarding Eastern Anatolia, explaining that their interest in reform of that region was to relieve themselves of the burden of Armenian refugees, not to interfere in internal Ottoman affairs.[61] For Rauf these concessions were too little and too late. As far as he was concerned, the only negotiable questions were technical ones involving the transfer of Kars, Ardahan, and Batumi. Frustrated with the Transcaucasians' temporizing, on 6 April he issued an ultimatum demanding that Tiflis declare independence and accept the terms of Brest-Litovsk as the basis for negotiations within forty-eight hours.[62]

From Trabzon Chkhenkeli frantically urged the Seim to propose to surrender significant portions of Kars, Ardahan, and Batumi. Rauf rejected the offer out of hand when it came. Chkhenkeli by telegram implored the Seim immediately to comply in full with the ultimatum. Then, bewailing his legislature's dilatory manner, he acted without authorization and told Rauf that Tiflis now recognized the Treaty of Brest-Litovsk. Desperate to find some kind of support for the isolated commissariat, Chkhenkeli requested that Rauf agree to permit the other Brest-Litovsk signatories to participate in the drafting of a peace agreement between the Ottoman empire and Transcaucasia. Rauf coolly responded that this would be possible only after Transcaucasia first declared independence.[63]

[58] Şahin, Trabzon, 388, 415–16.
[59] Genelkurmay Başkanlığı, Üçüncü Ordu Harekâtı, 479.   [60] Şahin, Trabzon, 414, 458.
[61] Declaration of the Transcaucasian Delegation with the Proposal of Territorial Concessions, 23.3.1918 [5.4.1918], Georgia, Dokumenty i materialy, 152–55.
[62] Ultimatum of the Turkish Delegation, 24.3.1918 [6.4.1918], Georgia, Dokumenty i materialy, 155–56.
[63] Ottoman Declaration on the Conditions of Including the Central Powers in the Talks, 31.3.1918 [13.4.1918], Georgia, Dokumenty i materialy, 162; Hovannisian, Armenia on the Road, 152.

Tiflis defends Russian democracy

On 12 April Vehib reached the outskirts of Batumi. He gave the city's garrison commander until four o'clock the following afternoon to withdraw. That night the Seim met. Rather than deliberate, member after member indulged in fiery oratory to proclaim his unshakeable will and that of the people of Transcaucasia to defend democracy and the revolution.[64] The Seim brashly declared war and issued appeals to the people of the Transcaucasus to take up arms for the sake of "Russian democracy."[65] It was wonderful revolutionary theater. Crowds surged through the streets of Batumi, stoked with bravado and "unworried and full of joy" on the eve of war.[66] The lone dissonant voice was that of a member of the Musavat Party, Shafi Bek Rustambekov, who averred that religious ties barred the Caucasus Muslims from actively fighting against the Ottomans but assured his fellow Transcaucasians of their support. Rustambekov's citation of religious ties was something of a subterfuge, for the predominantly Shi'i Azeri Turks had for centuries clashed with the Sunni Ottoman Turks. Rather, the Musavat's concern was to expel the Bolsheviks from Baku, and the Ottoman army presented the only force capable of doing that.[67]

The passionate intensity expressed in Tiflis came to naught. The capacities of Transcaucasia's defenders failed to match the rhetoric of its parliamentarians, and in a matter of hours the Ottoman army captured Batumi.[68] As one Georgian wryly observed, "On the same day that Noi Zhordaniia declared, 'We are officially entering the military arena,' the Turks perfectly officially entered Batumi."[69]

On 19 April Enver entered the newly captured city and addressed the Batumi city duma. After thanking the duma and the city's population for expressing their loyalty, he emphasized that he and his men could not be conquerors because Batumi had for centuries been part of the Ottoman empire. He announced that the Ottoman authorities had no

---

[64] Log of the Joint Meeting of the Presidium of the Transcaucasian Seim, Transcaucasian Government, and Representatives of Seim Factions, 31.3.1918 [13.4.1918], Georgia, *Dokumenty i materialy*, 166–84; Kazemzadeh, *Struggle*, 99–100.

[65] Appeal of the Seim to All Peoples of the Transcaucasus, 31.3.1914 [13.4.1914], Appeal of Transcaucasian Social Democracy to the Democracy of Russia, 1.4.1918 [14.4.1918], Georgia, *Dokumenty i materialy*, 185–87.

[66] Avalov, *Nezavisimost'*, 28.

[67] Kazemzadeh, *Struggle*, 100; Hovannisian, *Armenia on the Road*, 154. Hovannisian writes that Rustambekov cited "racial-religious" bonds. This is incorrect. Rustambekov made reference only to religious bonds: Georgia, *Dokumenty i materialy*, 178.

[68] Allen and Muratoff, *Battlefields*, 465; Genelkurmay Başkanlığı, *Üçüncü Ordu Harekâtı*, 488–89.

[69] Avalov, *Nezavisimost'*, 33.

interest in disrupting the work of the council or of other city institutions. He concluded with the promise that the "population without regard to faith or nationality is under the defense and protection of his majesty the sultan, who wishes to see the prosperity and well-being of the provinces rejoined to his empire."[70]

The loss of Batumi compelled the Transcaucasians at last to confront the reality of their position. Isolated and powerless, they had only one real choice to make: declare independence and make peace with the Ottomans on the Ottomans' terms, or cling to the ideal of a unified Russia and be overrun. The Seim finally declared the Transcaucasus an "independent Democratic Federative Republic" on 22 April. Even in these desperate circumstances the declaration proved controversial. The Musavat backed it, the Armenians opposed it, and the Georgians were split, leaving the Seim evenly divided. But the Dashnak Hovhannes Kachaznuni, just returned from Trabzon with no illusions about Tiflis' predicament, glumly endorsed the declaration and provided the edge for the resolution to pass. Discomfited and confused, the Transcaucasians had created an independent state.[71]

The Seim chose Chkhenkeli as prime minister, and the next day he ordered General Foma Nazarbekov to cease hostilities and surrender the fortress of Kars. Karabekir, having again defied Vehib's instructions to move at a more deliberate pace, was already at Kars and negotiating with the garrison commander, a Russian colonel of French extraction named Morel. Nazarbekov asked the Ottomans to permit a full month for the evacuation of Kars. Karabekir read the request as a play for time wherein more massacres would be organized and demanded that Morel quit the city in one day.

Karabekir's concern was not feigned. Aside from providing fodder to Istanbul for complaints to domestic and international audiences about Armenian inhumanity, the steady flow of atrocity reports and Muslim requests for protection affected Ottoman field commanders, spurring them to move still faster.[72] In response to the outrages he discovered on his advance, Karabekir promised local Muslims he would take vengeance,

[70] Extract from Minutes of the Batumi City Duma, 6.4.1918 [19.4.1918], Georgian Archive, Houghton Library, Harvard University, box 19, reel 63.
[71] Declaration of Independence of the Transcaucasus and Renewal of Talks with Turkey, 9.4.1918 [22.4.1918], Directive of the Transcaucasian government, 10.4.1918 [23.4.1918], Georgia, *Dokumenty i materialy*, 200–23; Kazamzadeh, *Struggle*, 103–05; Hovannisian, *Armenia on the Road*, 160.
[72] For Russian documentation of these acts, see for example RGVIA, Telegram from the 5th Corps Commander, 31.12.1917 [13.1.1918], f. 2168, o. 1, d. 506, l. 7; RGVIA, Telegram from the Commander of the Second Turkestan Corps, 30.1.1918 [12.2.1918], f. 2168, o. 1, d. 506, l. 46; RGVIA, Shakhovskoi to the Caucasus Army Chief of Staff,

and ordered that Armenian "bandits" and "outlaws" be put to death "wherever they are found."[73] At other times, however, he and other commanders such as Vehib issued emphatic instructions that Russian and Ottoman subjects alike were to be treated strictly according to the law, stating that "all women and children without regard to ethnic and sectarian identity" were to be treated with "a nobility and compassion appropriate to Ottomanness."[74] To what extent, if any, the latter tendency prevailed is uncertain.

Since the decision to surrender Kars had already been made, Morel had little choice but to comply with Karabekir's demand to quit the city straight away. The sudden order to pull out confounded Kars' Armenian defenders, who had expected to make a stand in the fortress. The result was a replay of the abandonment of Erzurum: the city's Christians fled pell-mell, joined by a confused Armenian militia. The sight of fires in the city, combined with fresh reports of massacres of local Muslims by Yezidis and Armenians, provoked the Ottomans to violate the agreement to wait a day and instead enter the city that evening on 25 April. Yet despite the chaos, no blood was spilled inside or around the city. The fire consumed some buildings, but to the Ottomans' great fortune it spared Kars' tremendous stores of ammunition and supplies.[75] The abandonment of Kars reverberated throughout the Caucasus as Armenians angrily accused Chkhenkeli of treachery and nearly brought down his government.[76]

Batumi peace talks

The Ottoman empire duly recognized the Democratic Federative Republic of the Transcaucasus, and the two sides resumed peace talks in Batumi on 11 May. The chief negotiator for the Ottomans, Halil Bey, opened the talks by proposing to admit the foreign minister Bammate to the talks. Although that same day in Istanbul Chermoev declared the North Caucasus an independent state, the UAM continued to aspire to join the Transcaucasus to form a unified state, and to that end had sent Bammate

31.1.1917 [13.2.1917], f. 2168, o. 1, d. 264, ll. 1-3; RGVIA, Dispatch of General Major Vyshinskii, 13/14.11.1917 [26/27.11.1917], f. 2168, o. 1, d. 493, l. 30.

[73] Muhammet Erat, "Kâzım Karabekir'in Nahçıvan ve Çevresindeki Faaliyetleri," *Kafkas Araştırmaları, IV* (Istanbul: Acar Yayınları, 1998), 52; Karabekir, *Doğunun Kurtuluşu*, 342–43.

[74] ATASE, Karabekir to the Command of the 36th Caucasus Division, [undated], K. 3920, D. 86, F. 2-3a; ATASE, Declaration to Townspeople and Villagers, [undated], K. 2908, D. 444, F. 6-4.

[75] Karabekir, *Doğunun Kurtuluşu*, 311–22.

[76] Hovannisian, *Armenia on the Road*, 162–69.

to Batumi. All present consented to admit Bammate to the conference. Halil's next proposal, however, proved distinctly less popular. Tiflis' decision to resist the terms of Brest-Litovsk by arms, Halil explained, entitled Istanbul to make additional territorial demands. Specifically, Halil wanted the cession of the Kars–Aleksandropol–Julfa railroad, the Akhaltsikh and Akhalkalaki districts of Tiflis province, the city of Aleksandropol and most of the district of that name, and part of the Echmiadzin district. The heart of Halil's demands concerned the Kars–Julfa railroad, which the Ottomans needed for the rapid deployment of forces to Azerbaijan and northern Iran, where they feared growing British activity. The additional territories that Halil demanded were necessary for the railroad's control and defense. To the Transcaucasians these terms were harsh indeed, as they deprived their state of its major transportation artery and reduced Armenia to a rump territory.[77]

Even as geostrategic concerns guided general Ottoman territorial objectives, the national idea was shaping their precise formulation. During the course of the talks in Batumi, Halil Bey received deputations from Muslims throughout the Caucasus, including Baku, Elisavetpol, Nagornyi Karabakh, and Tiflis, asking for assistance.[78] A petition in the name of the Muslim population of the latter two areas pleaded for the territorial incorporation of all of Akhaltsikh and part of Akhalkalaki within the Ottoman empire for the sake of "rescuing the Muslims of the aforementioned districts from total extinction." Notably, the petition invoked the right to self-determination granted by the Russian Revolution. It observed that the two districts had been forcibly taken from the Ottoman empire in 1828 and claimed that their Muslim populations had never cut their spiritual ties to the Ottoman empire and that ethnic tensions in the region had escalated to a level that threatened the very existence of the Muslims. The petition further asserted that the Transcaucasian government neither trusted the Muslim population nor fulfilled their just requests, and concluded with the statement that the Muslims resident in Akhaltsikh and Akhalkalaki had hereby informed the Transcaucasian government of their inclusion into the Ottoman empire.[79]

[77] Avalov, *Nezavisimost'*, 41–42; Kazemzadeh, *Struggle*, 109–10; Hovannisian, *Armenia on the Road*, 173–74; Şahin, *Trabzon*, 612; Karabekir, *Doğunun Kurtuluşu*, 360–61. According to statistics the Ottomans obtained from Russian sources, the populations of Akhalkalaki, Aleksandropol, and Echmiadzin were reportedly 76.6, 88.8, and 62.4 percent Armenian respectively. Only Akhaltsikh had a predominantly (71.9 percent) Muslim population: ATASE, Population Statistics for the Provinces of Baku, Elisavetpol, Yerevan, and Tiflis, Kutu 60, Gömlek 59.

[78] Ahmed Refik, *Kafkas Yollarında* (Istanbul: Kütübhane-i Askerî ve İslâm, 1919), 76.

[79] Decree of the Delegates from the Muslim Population of Akhaltsikh and Akhalkalaki, Georgia, *Dokumenty i materialy*, 26.5.1918 [8.6.1918], 310–12.

Yet even so Vehib Pasha was already considering the possibility that the Ottomans might do better to cede the two provinces. Since Akhalkalaki was populated predominantly by Armenians, he wrote, giving it to Georgia would ensure tension between the two neighboring republics, and this would be good for the Ottomans. As for Akhaltsikh, he suggested it could be left as an autonomous and neutral province, since this would serve Ottoman goals as effectively as annexation would.[80]

Hoping that they could stymie the Ottomans with outside support, the Transcaucasians decided to try to stall in Batumi and win time for Gegechkori to make it to Berlin and secure German backing.[81] The Ottomans, however, had lost all patience with the Transcaucasians' chronic "diplomatic evasion and double talk." [82] Enver ordered Halil Bey to advance on Tiflis. That midnight Halil sent his secretary to rouse the Georgian negotiators and inform them that he was crossing the Arpachay River and would take Tiflis if they did not hand over the railroad and the adjoining territories. After a perfunctory protest the Georgians agreed to comply. This left the Armenians, whose forces held Aleksandropol and the rail line junctures, to face the advancing Ottoman army alone.[83] Halil and Vehib pleaded with the Armenians to cede the rail lines and make peace, promising to see personally to the return of the railroad following the war while warning that Talât and Enver would not offer such generous conditions. The confused Armenians were unable to respond.[84]

Halil thereupon ordered Vehib to cross the Arpachay River on 15 May. Once again the Armenian defenders crumpled and Aleksandropol fell.[85] Enver was keen to exploit this moment of Ottoman superiority and now sought control of the next strategic crossroads at Karakilise. Şevki and Karabekir drove Nazarbekov's and Andranik's Armenian formations from their positions at Amamli and Güllü-Bulak outside Karakilise.[86] Vehib, still seeking to end the conflict with the Armenians, agreed to parley with Nazarbekov in Aleksandropol. Nazarbekov, however, failed to show. In a note to the Armenian commander, Vehib explained that the breakdown of the talks in Batumi and rejection of Ottoman proposals had created a new situation. He warned that, just as the Ottomans would react

[80] ATASE, Intelligence Summary Regarding the Caucasus, 27 Mayıs 1334 [27.5.1918], K. 526, D. 2059-369, F. 50.
[81] Kazemzadeh, *Struggle*, 111; Trumpener, *Germany*, 182.
[82] Kazemzadeh, *Struggle*, 111.   [83] Menteşe, *Anılar* 229–30.
[84] Hovannisian, *Armenia on the Road*, 175.
[85] Menteşe, *Anıları*, 229–230; Hovannisian, *Armenia on the Road*, 175; "Nota Ottomanskoi delegatsii o propuske turetskoi armii cherez Zakavkaz'e," 14.5.1918 [27.5.1918], Georgia, *Dokumenty i materialy*, 269–70.
[86] Genelkurmay Başkanlığı, *Üçüncü Ordu Harekâtı*, vol. II, 514; Allen and Muratoff, *Battlefields*, 472.

with mercy and solicitude to sincere and favorable behavior, so too they would react "severely and swiftly" to "underhanded and ill-intentioned behavior."[87]

The Ottoman advance was already disquieting the Germans, who eyed Baku's oil and the rail network that transported that oil to Batumi from where it could be exported to Europe. Baku was in Bolshevik hands, but the Bolsheviks' grip on it was tenuous. Bolshevik control rested on an uneasy alliance with the Dashnaks against the majority Muslims. Baku was isolated from Russia. Located in Moscow, to where in early 1918 he had moved his government, Lenin recognized that he had no way to reinforce the Bolsheviks of Baku.

Berlin and Moscow both wanted to stop the Ottoman advance, but each realized that alone it was powerless to do so. If they cooperated, however, together they might manage to stymie the Ottomans. Germany made the first overture and offered to mediate between Russia and Tiflis. Although Tiflis had rejected the Bolsheviks' request to participate in the Batumi talks without recognizing the independence of the Transcaucasian Federation, the commissar for foreign affairs, Georgii Chicherin, had little choice but to accept Germany's offer. Moscow at the same time underscored its continued rejection of Transcaucasian independence with rhetorical attacks on the Transcaucasian Federation that questioned the federation's popular legitimacy, undercut Tiflis' claims to non-Georgian regions such as Abkhazia and Southern Ossetia, and fanned the dissatisfaction of Armenians with Tiflis.[88] National self-determination, the Bolsheviks showed, could be a two-edged sword indeed.

Despite Moscow's inability to intervene in the Caucasus, the specter of a resurgent Russia continued to exercise the Ottomans, who believed it was imperative to wring as much as they could from their moment of superiority before Russia regained its strength, even at the risk of conflict with Germany.[89] Indeed, Germany's own ambition to fill the vacuum left by Russia only underscored the need to move quickly and exploit the moment fully. Thus when Germany's observer in Batumi, Colonel Lossow, offered to mediate the peace negotiations between Tiflis and Istanbul, Halil rejected the proposal out of hand. Lossow was "an uncompromising advocate of German supremacy in the Caucasus,"[90] and Halil

[87] Genelkurmay Başkanlığı, *Üçüncü Ordu Harekâtı*, vol. II, 517–18.
[88] Note to Lossow, 19.5.1918, Note from Lossow, 21.5.1918, Georgia, *Dokumenty i materi-aly*, 290–92, 302–03; Note of the Temporary Deputy Minister of the People's Commissar of Foreign Affairs, 15.5.1918, in *Dokumenty vneshnei politiki*, USSR, Ministerstvo inos-trannykh del, vol. I, 302–03; Kurat, *Türkiye ve Rusya*, 475–76; Hovannisian, *Armenia on the Road*, 171.
[89] Kurat, *Türkiye ve Rusya*, 476.   [90] Fischer, *Germany's Aims*, 555.

saw his offer for what it was – a wedge through which Germany could insert its influence at the Ottoman empire's expense.

Upon Halil's refusal, Lossow quit Batumi. As he left he predicted that the federation would come apart.[91] The colonel was in a privileged position to foresee the impending collapse of the Transcaucasian state because he was complicit in its demolition.[92] In secret meetings with the Georgian National Council, Lossow had been urging them to break from the Transcaucasian Federation. Germany could use Georgia as a toehold from which to extend its hegemony over the region as a whole following the victorious conclusion of the war.[93] For the Georgians the advantages of close ties to Germany were clear. An alliance with a state that was wealthy, militarily powerful, technologically advanced, and too distant to suffocate Tiflis would be attractive even in less desperate times. But the cost of German protection would be steep.

Armenian nightmares

Enver had in December 1917 stated his view that the Armenians could exist autonomously within a union with the Georgians and Caucasian Muslims as long as they made no claims on Ottoman Anatolia. The possibility of an independent Armenia, however, filled the Ottoman leadership with dread. What worried the senior leadership remained the fear that the British, or others, would use Caucasian Armenia as a base from which to drive the Ottomans out of Eastern Anatolia. The experience of the Balkan wars and the defeat suffered at the hands of the Bulgarians shaped estimations of the Armenians for the worse. Writing to Halil on 24 May, Talât expressed his opposition to the idea of an Armenian government in any form:

I am absolutely not in favor of the Armenians establishing a government.

A small Armenian autonomous [government] will five years later become a five-million-strong Armenian state, it will dominate the Caucasus, and it will become the "Bulgaria of the East." All the Armenians in Iran and America will gather there and, as you describe, they will get every form of aid from the English and French, and in the future they will move against us with the Christian Georgians and also with great ease with the Iranians *Âcem'lerle*. Therefore, were it possible, the best thing would be to lance the boil [*çıbanı kökünden temizlemek*]. Since it is not possible, it is necessary that Armenia be formed in an extremely weak and unviable form.[94]

[91] Refusal of Lossow to Participate, 25.5.1918 [7.6.1918], Georgia, *Dokumenty i materialy*, 307.
[92] Fischer, *Germany's Aims*, 555.   [93] Fischer, *Germany's Aims*, 552–54, 558.
[94] Kurat, *Türkiye ve Rusya*, 661–62.

Enver came to agree. Writing three days later to Vehib Pasha to warn him that an Armenian proposal to be compensated for territorial losses to the Ottomans with land taken from the Caucasian Muslims was dangerous, he echoed Talât's fears but found the notion of an independent Armenia even less acceptable:

In my opinion this is a very big mistake. If today in the Caucasus a small Armenia possessing a population of 500 to 600 thousand and sufficient territory is formed, in the future this government, together with the Armenians who will come mainly from America and from elsewhere, will have a population of millions. And in the east we will have another Bulgaria and it will be a worse enemy than Russia because all the Armenians' interests and ambitions are in our country. Consequently, in order to remove this danger, the formation of even the smallest Armenian government must be prevented. Land from the Muslims must not be given to the Armenians; rather, to the contrary, I prefer that the Muslims occupy provinces such as Yerevan.[95]

Vehib at the time was driving toward Yerevan. It was precisely at this juncture that Armenian forces now stood their ground. With their backs to the wall, they fought desperately at Karakilise and Sardarabad, declaring, "if we must be destroyed, let us be destroyed with our honor."[96] They threw back the attacking force and compelled the Ottomans to scale back their ambitions. Vehib warned headquarters,

We do not have the strength to defeat the Armenians. The three-day battle in Karakilise shows that as long as their existence is in danger they will prefer to die fighting. We must not bring on a battle with the force that 1,200,000 Armenians can raise. If the Georgians join in the hostilities, it will be impossible to advance . . . In short, we must come to terms with the Armenians and Georgians.[97]

The Ottomans lacked the men and resources for a protracted confrontation with Armenia and Georgia and, as even Talât and Enver understood despite their vivid fears of a second Bulgaria, there were more pressing strategic concerns.

The victory at Sardarabad stirred some Armenian commanders to dream of going on the offensive. Nazarbekov, however, entertained no such fantasies and ordered that hostilities cease. Nazarbekov's call was a prudent one but, in the wake of the debacles at Erzurum and Kars,

---

[95] ATASE, Enver to Vehib, 27 Mayıs 1334 [27.05.1918], K. 2919, D. 499, F. 3-31.
[96] Cited in Mustafa Çolak, *Enver Paşa: Osmanlı–Alman İttifakı* (Istanbul: Yeditepe Yayınevi, 2008), 148.
[97] ATASE, Intelligence Summary Regarding the Caucasus, 28 Mayıs 1334 [28.05.1918], K. 526, D. 2059-369, F. 50. W. E. D. Allen's assessment (Allen and Muratoff, *Battlefields*, 476) that the Armenians' battlefield performance at the end of May had less impact on Ottoman plans than did the Georgian tactic of temporizing is incorrect.

Andranik saw it as the final betrayal of the idea of a "greater Armenia."[98] Embittered and angry, he and his men set off to take vengeance. They wound up entering Nakhichevan (Naxçivan) where they "crushed one Tartar village after another" and sent thousands of Caucasian Muslims into flight.[99]

Independence: lamentation and regret

Vehib's concern about a Georgian–Armenian alliance was misplaced. As the Armenians were making their last stand, the Georgians abandoned them. In Tiflis, Noi Zhordaniia rebuked Khatisian, telling him that the Armenians had brought misery upon themselves through their own actions and admonishing him that their insistence on opposing the Ottomans was endangering the Georgians. "We cannot drown with you," he told Khatisian.[100] Georgia would go its own way, separate from the federation, and save itself by accepting German protection. On the following day the Seim dissolved itself. The Armenian and Azeri members exited the hall while the Georgians remained behind. The red flags of revolution were brought down, the Georgian flag was put up, and independence was declared. Notably, the Georgians' act of independence disavowed any active role in achieving independence. Its language was mournful, not celebratory. The new government did not take credit for Georgian independence but rather laid the blame for it on Russia's inability to fulfill its obligation to protect Georgia.[101] The Transcaucasian Federation was no more.

When the Armenian National Council received news of Georgia's break, it instantly accused the Georgian Mensheviks of treachery but, beyond that, the council remained paralyzed, unable to chart a course. It fell to the Dashnaktsutiun to insist that the council proclaim Armenia independent and rule as a dictatorial government. On May 30 the council belatedly issued a saturnine statement that shunned bold words such as "independence" or even "republic," but instead spoke of the "grave circumstances" that compelled the Armenian National Council to "temporarily . . . pilot the political and administrative helm of the Armenian provinces."[102] Independent Armenia was poor, small, and isolated, and

[98] Çelebyan, *Antranik*, 274–78.   [99] Hovannisian, *Armenia on the Road*, 192–94.
[100] Hovannisian, *Armenia on the Road*, 184–85.
[101] For the text, see the Georgian Act of Independence, 26.5.1918, Georgia, *Dokumenty i materialy*, 336–38.
[102] Hovannisian, *Armenia on the Road*, 191; Serge Afanasyan, *L'Arménie, l'Azerbaïdjan et la Géorgie: de l'indépendance à l'instauration du pouvoir soviétique 1917–1923* (Paris L'Harmattan, 1981), 57–58. Afanasyan and many other sources incorrectly give 28 May as the day the Armenian National Council declared independence. In fact,

lacked significant natural resources. The center of Armenian cultural, intellectual, and political life in the Caucasus had been Tiflis, but that city was now Georgia's capital. The Armenian National Council departed Tiflis for Yerevan, a provincial town that up until the middle of the nineteenth century had been predominantly Muslim and was located in a province where in 1914 Armenians were barely a majority.[103] Despite all the friction between Armenians and Azeris, the Azerbaijani National Council was not yet ready to rule out the possibility of joint federation with Armenia and in a gesture of good will voted to approve the Armenians' move to Yerevan.[104]

Although the reemergence of a regionally dominant Ottoman state ostensibly held promise for the Muslims of the Caucasus, Azerbaijan's "Act of Independence" was, like those of the Georgian and Armenian republics, subdued in tone. Indeed, the soon-to-be prime minister of the republic, Fathali Khan Khoiskii feared independence. He had advised the Azeri National Council to "refrain from declaring the independence of Azerbaijan and limit itself to the formation of a government with full rights for the conduct of peace talks with the powers,"[105] and when he had to read out Azerbaijan's act of independence he did so with an ashen face and trembling hands.[106] The act's text narrated Azerbaijan's emergence not as a positive act of will but as the unhappy consequence of war, Russia's collapse, and anarchy. It made no claim for a prior history of statehood and was devoid of any ethnonationalist, let alone pan-Turkist or pan-Islamic, sentiment. It made no reference to a titular or dominant nation, but defined the state in terms of territory and embraced the principle of neutrality with regard to nationality, religion, and sex. Its content demonstrated that the ideals of Russia's February Revolution and democratic socialism still retained a strong grip over the imagination of Azerbaijan's political elite.[107] With Baku under Bolshevik–Dashnak control, the Azeris chose Elisavetpol as their temporary capital.

Some Azeris did make their way to Batumi to float the idea of forming a federation between Azerbaijan and the Ottoman empire. The motives of these so-called annexationists (*ilhakçılar* or *ilkhagisty*) were rooted

the final decision for independence was made only on the evening of 29 May and the muted declaration issued the following day.

103 Armenians constituted 53.6 percent of the population of the Yerevan province (*guberniia*): Ishkhanian, *Narodnosti Kavkaza*, 25.
104 N. L. Näsibzadä, *Azärbaycan Demokratik Respublikası: Mägälär vä Sänädlär* (Baku: Elm, 1990), 45–46.
105 Aidyn Balaev, *Azerbaidzhanskoe natsional'noe dvizhenie v 1917–1918 gg.* (Baku: Elm, 1998), 209.
106 Michael G. Smith, "Anatomy of a Rumour: Murder Scandal, the Musavat Party, and Narratives of the Russian Revolution in Baku, 1917–1920," *Journal of Contemporary History*, 36, 2 (2001), 228.
107 Balaev, *Dvizhenie*, 204–05.

not so much in religious or ethnic sentiment but instead in fear of the domestic political agenda of the socialist Azerbaijani National Council. The annexationists reasoned that joining with Istanbul would stifle land redistribution and similar reforms. Accordingly, at Batumi they agitated against the National Council and sought to endear themselves to the Ottomans. They constituted, however, a minority voice. The Musavat, joined by the Muslim Socialist Bloc and the Himmet Party, rejected any union. As for the Ottomans, they dismissed the idea of union with Azerbaijan out of hand.[108]

A new architecture for the Caucasus

Istanbul promptly recognized the three fledgling republics, and on June 4 in Batumi Halil and Vehib concluded treaties of "peace and friendship" with Georgia and Armenia and treaties of "friendship" with Azerbaijan and the North Caucasus, as well as a number of supplementary agreements with all of them.[109] The treaties' contents reflected the inequality in relations between the signatories. They impinged on the sovereignty of Georgia and Armenia by, for example, reserving for the Ottomans the authority to limit the size of the Georgian and Armenian armies and granting to the Ottomans the right to use their railways so long as the war with Britain continued. Still, the treaties unequivocally recognized each signatory as an independent state and the relations the Ottomans established with each republic were in no way comparable to annexation. The national idea had triumphed, albeit to the regret of all the nations concerned.

When the Georgian and Ottoman delegations met, Halil scolded the Georgians for having brought misfortune upon themselves with their choice to fight the Ottoman empire. Georgian resistance to Ottoman demands, however, had paid off the night before, when Halil relented and agreed to let Georgia retain Ozurgeti and parts of Akhaltsikh and Akhalkalaki.[110] Despite the petitions Halil had received from Muslims of that area declaring their loyalty to the Ottoman empire, the fact was that, as Vehib had written earlier, their inclusion *in toto* into the empire

[108] Balaev, *Dvizhenie*, 207–08; Tedeusz Swietochowski, *Russia and Azerbaijan: A Borderland in Transition* (New York: Columbia University Press, 1995), 68. See also A. N. Kheifets, *Sovetskaia Rossiia i sopredel'nye strany vostoka v gody grazhdanskoi voiny (1918–1920)* (Moscow: Nauka, 1964), 53.
[109] The full texts of the treaties transliterated from Ottoman Turkish can be found in Şahin, *Trabzon* 700–50. The Russian version of the Ottoman–Georgian treaty can be found in Georgia, *Dokumenty i materialy*, 343–49.
[110] Georgia retained Abastuman and Askueri: Şahin, *Trabzon*, 616–17; Menteşe, *Anıları*, 229–30; Hovannisian, *Armenia on the Road*, 198.

was not a strategic necessity. Rather, as Halil emphasized in public to the Georgians, the formation of a solid and progressive state in the Caucasus was a vital interest of the Ottoman empire. Toward that end he also urged the Georgians to maintain good relations with the Muslims of the Caucasus.[111]

Whereas Georgia came out not too badly, Armenia's plight was pitiable. According to Khatisian's memoirs, at the signing Vehib spoke fantastically of how blood and faith ineluctably drew the Turks eastward.[112] If Khatisian's account is reliable, the fact that the Albanian Vehib was bluffing in order to intimidate Khatisian is readily evident from Vehib's track record of opposition to operations deep in the Caucasus. But if expansion to the east for the sake of blood and faith was not on the Ottoman agenda, crippling Armenia was. The Ottomans allowed the new state just over 10,000 km^2 cobbled from the district of Novo Baezit and portions of the districts of Yerevan, Echmiadzin, and Aleksandropol. As Khatisian complained, the land could not even sustain Armenia's present population, which included some 300,000 to 400,000 refugees. When Khatisian attempted to play the one card he had, the international one, by reminding Vehib that the Armenians had the great powers' attention, Vehib coolly turned the objection around, stating that precisely because the Armenian Question had been an international matter Istanbul had consented to the creation of an independent Armenian state. The creation of an Armenian state meant the end of the Armenian Question. Right after the signing, Vehib proposed that the Armenians now join the Ottomans to fight the British. Khatisian politely turned down the surreal offer by citing the Armenian people's exhaustion.[113]

Halil and Vehib met with the Azeris that same day and with the North Caucasians four days later to sign treaties of friendship with them. Here the term "friendship" had meaning. The Caucasian signatories were keen to obtain Ottoman assistance to liberate their territories from Bolshevik control, and immediately after the signings both invoked the prerogative specified in the treaties to request military assistance to "ensure internal order and security." With the end of the war approaching, however, time to secure the independence of the Caucasus was running out. The Ottomans and their Caucasian allies had a race to Baku.

Competition with Germany

The race was not a solo competition. The Germans and Bolsheviks, too, were scrambling to assert control over the Caucasus. The Germans in the

---

[111] Avalov, *Nezavisimost'*, 93.   [112] Hovannisian, *Armenia on the Road*, 195.
[113] Hovannisian, *Armenia on the Road*, 195.

spring had grown increasingly agitated over Ottoman policies and behavior in the region. They saw Enver as a "mad imperialist" and worried that Talât's animosity toward Armenians portended future massacres.[114] But what really exasperated the Germans was that the Ottomans were disrupting their plains to exploit the resources of the Caucasus. They were uncertain that the Ottomans would cooperate with them economically, and they feared that even if they did Ottoman incompetence would condemn the region's port and rail facilities to decrepitude.[115] As one German analysis complained, "during the war we invested millions to create a friendly Caucasian state which would help us to establish a bridge to Central Asia." Now the Ottomans were torpedoing their project.[116]

To counter this, the Germans' plan was to consolidate their hold on Georgia and use it as a base from which to extend their influence over the whole of the Caucasus, north and south. Immediately following Georgia's declaration of independence, mixed German–Georgian military units raced along the main Transcaucasian railway, occupying stations and planting Georgian flags along the way. The "German" soldiers were a mix of German POWs and Russian subjects of German descent who had settled in Georgia.[117] The pretense of dressing Russian settlers in German uniforms and calling them representatives of Germany bordered on the absurd, but the normative power of the national idea and its corollary that those settlers were bonded to Germany by their ethnicity was sufficient to make the tactic at least semi-legitimate. Meanwhile, Berlin ordered ground and air units from Ukraine and Crimea to Georgia.[118]

As Ottoman units pushed inside the Caucasus, Ottoman–German relations grew confrontational. On 8 and 9 June, Ludendorff and Chief of the German General Staff Paul von Hindenburg bluntly warned Enver to withdraw his forces in the Caucasus behind the borders established at Brest-Litovsk and divert them to Mesopotamia and northern Iran instead.[119] The Ottomans' discovery of German soldiers at the Karakilise train station following their capture of it from the Armenians seemingly confirmed Ottoman suspicions of German perfidy.[120] The crisis in Ottoman–German relations hit a peak on

---

[114] PA-AA, A23776, Notes of Meeting at the Reichskanzler, Rußland 11047, 3.6.1918.
[115] PA-AA, A21723, Letter of Wesendonk, Rußland 11045, 11.5.1918.
[116] PA-AA, A14195, Report on Russia, Rußland 11043, no date.
[117] Emekli Kaymakam Rüştü, *Askerî Mecmua'nin Tarih Kısmı: Büyük Harpte Bakû Yollarında. 5 Kafkas Piyade Fırkası* (Ankara: Askerî Matbaa, 1934), 4–5; Nâsır Yüceer, *Birinci Dünya Savaşı'nda Osmanlı Ordusu'nun Azerbaycan ve Dağıstan Harekâtı* (Ankara: Genelkurmay Basım Evi, 1996), 32.
[118] Allen and Muratoff, *Battlefields*, 477; Fischer, *Germany's Aims*, 506.
[119] Trumpener, *Germany*, 183–84.   [120] Çakmak, *Büyük Harpte*, 269.

10 June when Ottoman units moving to take control of the rail line encountered a German detachment, this time outside Aleksandropol. Vehib had authorized his men to use force against any German opposition, and so the Ottomans engaged the detachment in a firefight and took a number of prisoners. German headquarters responded by threatening to pull all of its personnel out of the Ottoman empire if the Ottomans did not immediately release the prisoners and halt the advance into Georgia.[121]

Enver responded to Hindenburg and Ludendorff by dismissing their complaints as groundless and threatening to resign. He then mollified Berlin by relieving Vehib and recalling him to Istanbul. Enver's tactics worked. The German High Command moderated its criticism and instructed General Hans von Seeckt in Batumi to work for reconciliation.[122] Tensions, however, remained. German encouragement of Georgian interference in the transportation of men and supplies along the Transcaucasian railroad, news of Germans conducting anti-Ottoman propaganda in Baku, and the discovery of maps showing plans to deploy German troops to Baku all reinforced Ottoman distrust of Germany.[123] Enver replaced Vehib as commander of the Eastern Armies Group with Halil Pasha and ordered him to take Baku, and then sweep south to envelop the British at Basra.[124]

Conclusion

Ottoman policy toward the Caucasus evolved according to the changing demands of the diplomatic and geopolitical environment. Initially wary that recognition of an independent Transcaucasus might lead them into a trap, the Ottomans later found themselves imploring the Transcaucasian Commissariat to declare independence and to participate in the peace talks at Brest-Litovsk. Although Transcaucasia's governing socialists rejected the Bolsheviks, they declined the invitation partly out of inertia and partly out of a lingering attachment to the ideal of a united and democratic Russia. This preference to remain part of Russia led them at the Trabzon peace talks to base their diplomacy on the incoherent assertion that they were an integral part of Russia yet not bound

[121] Allen and Muratoff, *Battlefields*, 478; Rüştü, *Bakû Yollarında*, 9, 17.
[122] Trumpener, *Germany*, 184.
[123] Süleyman İzzet, *Askerî Mecmua'nın Tarih Kısmı: Büyük Harpte 15. Piyade Tümeninin Azerbaycan ve Şimali Kafkasya'daki Hareket ve Muharebeleri* (Istanbul: Askerî Matbaa, 1936), 9.
[124] Halil Paşa, *Bitmeyen Savaş*, ed. M. Taylan Sorgun (Istanbul: Yaylacık Matbaası, 1972), 220.

by the Treaty of Brest-Litovsk. Transcaucasia's political elites revealed further inexperience when, against the desperate pleas of their foreign minister, they chose to go to war. In a matter of hours they lost Batumi and the war. Intent on punishing Tiflis for its defiance and concerned about the need to counter the British in Iran and liberate Baku from the Bolsheviks, the Ottomans made new demands regarding the Kars–Julfa railroad and the adjacent areas.

The political elites of Transcaucasia's three major peoples all found the idea of independence forbidding. Pressed by Ottoman demands and pulled by the lure of German patronage, however, the Georgians decided to break from the Transcaucasian Republic and declare independence. Armenia and Azerbaijan followed with their own declarations. Notably, all three republics regretted independence, but found that the collapse of the Russian empire gave them no choice but freedom. Although independence came as a bitter gift to the Transcaucasians, giving it represented a triumph of sorts for the Ottomans, who now had a belt of territory separating their empire from Russia. In order to consolidate that belt, however, they needed to expel the Bolsheviks from Azerbaijan and the North Caucasus before the end of war. The capture of Baku now became the number one objective of Ottoman policy in the Caucasus.

8   Racing against time

The Ottoman empire's leaders understood that Russia's collapse presented a historic window of opportunity to redraw the map of the Caucasus. They were convinced, however, that soon enough Russia would recover and reemerge as the dominant power in the region and shut that window. Ottoman diplomacy at Brest-Litovsk and Batumi had midwifed four new states that put space between the Ottoman empire and Russia, but with Azerbaijan and the North Caucasus under partial Bolshevik occupation, the achievement was fragile. If the diplomatic triumph were to endure, military intervention to expel the Bolsheviks was required. Adding to the sense of urgency were the expectation that a comprehensive peace settlement was imminent and the realization that the Germans and British were also rushing to fill the vacuum left by the collapse of tsarist power in the Caucasus. Thus, in the summer of 1918 the Ottomans endeavored to sweep the Caucasus of Bolshevik influence, put the fledgling republics of Azerbaijan and the North Caucasus on their feet, and block the Germans and British from penetrating further along their eastern marches. Far from being the irresponsible act of ethnic irredentism it has often been portrayed as, the Ottoman offensive into the Caucasus in 1918 was a calculated gamble to seize a critical moment to alter the region's geopolitics.

With the empire's Caucasian borders settled by the peace treaties with the three Transcaucasian republics (although technically the borders would not be fixed until the accession of Kars, Ardahan, and Batumi in August), the next objective of the Ottoman army was Baku, the prize of the Caucasus. Its oil was essential to Russian industry and coveted by the Germans, and the British wanted to deny it to both. As Azerbaijan's largest city and the only one with appreciable industry, Baku was essential to the viability of an independent Azerbaijan. By ejecting the Bolsheviks and putting the city under Azeri control the Ottomans would deprive their rivals of a key asset and impede their ability to operate in the region.[1]

---

[1] Halil Paşa, *Bitmeyen Savaş*, 220.

After taking Baku, Enver envisioned turning north to assist the embattled Mountaineer Republic in Dagestan and then sweeping southward to encircle the British in Mesopotamia and retake Baghdad.

The push to Baku and the Army of Islam

The Ottomans faced two constraints in their bid to liberate Baku. The first was that they had little manpower or resources to spare for an offensive. The other was that they would have to operate in the Caucasus without outside support. Not only could they expect resistance from Bolshevik Russia and Britain, but their nominal ally, Germany, also opposed the extension of their influence into the Caucasus. Such opposition did not have to be physical to be effective. The ultimate success of the Ottoman plan required that Azerbaijan and the North Caucasus emerge as viable independent states and this in turn would hinge significantly upon their recognition and acceptance into the community of states. The principle of "self-determination" had become the preferred criterion for entrance into that community. Entities created solely by force of Ottoman arms would be unlikely to gain international favor, but ones forged, at least in part, by their populations stood a chance.

Enver's remedy was to create a corps of Caucasian volunteers led by Ottoman officers called the "Caucasus Army of Islam." This force would overcome the manpower deficit by drawing on the Muslim population of the Caucasus for the bulk of its personnel. By embodying, or at least making the pretense to embody, the popular aspirations and will of the Muslims of the Caucasus, the Army of Islam also would present the appearance of a movement of self-determination, thereby strengthening the claims of those Muslims to statehood. This would also permit Istanbul to ascribe responsibility for the army's operations to indigenous Muslims acting independently and outside its control.

Whereas at the beginning of the war Enver had warned his commanders not to expect much assistance from the Muslims of the Caucasus, in 1918 he had reason to expect that substantial numbers of volunteers could be found there. During the summer of 1917, scattered delegations of Caucasian Muslims had begun making contact with Ottoman military personnel at the front. These Caucasians appealed for military aid and described the existence of populations back home eager to support the Ottomans and fight the Russians.[2] German and Austrian prisoners of war who had escaped from Russia via the Caucasus relayed to Enver and other

---

[2] Nâsır Yüceer, *Azerbaycan*, 41; Tuğaç, *Bir Neslin Dramı*, 192.

Ottoman officers their impressions of a Muslim Caucasus ripe for revolt.[3] Before the end of the year 1917, the Azeri magnate Isa Ashirbekov had raised a militia of nearly 5,000 men just outside Baku.[4] Ali Shikhlinskii, an Azeri and former tsarist general, had formed a "Tatar Regiment" from members of the Savage Division.[5] Similarly, some Ottoman prisoners of war had organized untrained locals into small militia groups. Enver and Vehib also received descriptions of vast stockpiles in the Caucasus of weapons and foodstuffs abandoned by the Russian army.[6]

Others, however, were skeptical of the possibilities for mobilizing the Muslims of the Caucasus. One Teşkilât-ı Mahsusa analyst, echoing the general analysis of Russia's Muslims as lacking a politicized consciousness and capacity for organization, cautioned that the only Muslim constituency inside Azerbaijan with a national consciousness were the intellectuals of Elisavetpol and Nagornyi Karabakh. Paradoxically, he observed, it was the same schooling that had "Russified" this class that had also introduced them to the ideas of national independence. The villagers, merchants, and others outside the educated class, by contrast, lacked a national consciousness and therefore, the analyst concluded, would be unlikely to join in a struggle for independence.[7]

Among Ottoman field commanders, Vehib was again the most critical. Where Enver saw enthusiastic volunteers, Vehib saw undisciplined and untrained men. Not least important, Vehib advised, sooner or later Russia would regain its strength, and when it did it would roll back whatever the Ottomans might achieve in the meantime.[8] Karabekir shared some of Vehib's doubts. When in February Enver had asked Karabekir if he would be willing to lead a force of native Caucasians into the North Caucasus, he declined the offer, telling Enver that the chances of success for such an operation were limited.[9] Karabekir's and Vehib's lack of enthusiasm was not unusual. The Azeri political leader Naki Keykurun records that in his meetings with Unionists in Istanbul only the triumvirs Enver, Talât,

---

[3] ATASE, Report on Conditions in the Caucasus, 3 Kanunusani 1334 [3.1.1918], K. 366, D. 739-1461, F. 13-3; Report on Conditions in Dagestan, 23 Teşrinievvel 1333 [23.10.1917], K. 502, D. 2040-502, F. 1, 1-1–1-3; Report on the Formation of the Army of Islam, K. 1, D. 1, F. 1–21, as cited in Mustafa Budak, "Nuri Paşa'nın Kafkas İslâm Ordusu Hakkındaki Raporu," *Kafkas Araştırmaları*, 4 (1998), 68. Cf. Nâsır Yüceer, *Azerbaycan*, 42.

[4] ATASE, Dispatch from the Muslim Committee of the Baku Prisoners' Society, 31 Kanunuevvel 1333 [31.12.1917], K. 1859, D. 88-142, F. 1-10.

[5] Budak, "Nuri Paşa'nın," 73–74.   [6] Tuğaç, *Bir Neslin Dramı*, 196, 210–13.

[7] ATASE, Report to the Directorate of Eastern Affairs of the Ministry of War, 28 Haziran to 28 Temmuz 1333 [28.6–28.7.1917], K. 1843, D. 129-67, F. 1-34-1-35.

[8] Nâsır Yüceer, *Azerbaycan*, 21.

[9] Karabekir, *Doğunun Kurtuluşu*, 102–03, 105; Sâbis, *Hatıralarım*, vol. IV, 189.

and Cemal favored an advance into the Caucasus. The rest opposed the idea.[10]

Enver intended to name the Circassian prince Ömer Faruk to lead the Army of Islam, but backed off when Keykurun, aghast at the prince's dissolute behavior, protested that Faruk drank and danced too much. Keykurun urged Enver instead to appoint his nephew Nuri, who had recently returned to Istanbul from Tripolitania, to lead the Caucasian offensive. He argued that Nuri's fame for his exploits in North Africa and his status as Enver's relative would energize Caucasian Muslims. Enver thought it over, and the next day informed Keykurun that Nuri would be commander of the army.[11]

Toward the end of March, Karabekir, fearing boredom and a lack of action on the rest of the front, reconsidered Enver's offer. He telegraphed Enver to ask if he could still participate in the Caucasian operation. Enver responded positively, and Karabekir readied to head to Sukhumi or Vladikavkaz with some of his staff to raise a native Caucasian force.[12] When in April he learned that he would have to serve under Nuri, however, he retracted his decision with a strongly worded telegram to Enver. Pointing out that Nuri's experience was limited to leading insurgent tribesmen in North Africa and that he had never commanded large units, Karabekir denounced Enver's recent promotion of his nephew from colonel to major general – conferring on him the honored title of "pasha" – as an insult to the military profession.[13]

Toward the end of February Nuri left Istanbul for Musul to begin preparations. There he assembled 149 officers and 488 soldiers to serve as the nucleus of his force and departed for Tabriz. On 5 April 1918 Enver signed a directive outlining the mission of the Army of Islam. The directive explained that the army was to be formed from Caucasians and would be used to train Caucasians and "establish in the Caucasus the interests of Islam and political and military ties with the Caliph of the Sacred Law and the Ottoman state."[14] This rhetoric notwithstanding, it would be a mistake to see the formation of the Army of Islam as an expression of authentic religious zeal. The Unionists, long tagged as "godless" for their disregard of religious values by many Muslims inside as well as outside the empire, during the war had only accelerated the secularization of the Ottoman state by nationalizing religious endowments and constricting the scope of Islamic law to family matters. The socialist Azeri leadership

---

[10] Keykurun, *Hatıralar*, 101.   [11] Keykurun, *Hatıralar*, 101–02.
[12] Karabekir, *Doğunun Kurtuluşu*, 272–73, 300.
[13] Karabekir, *Doğunun Kurtuluşu*, 300–02.
[14] Mehman Süleymanov, *Qafqaz İslam Ordusu vä Azärbaycan* (Baku: Härbi Näşriyyat, 1999), 104.

shared the Unionists' skepticism toward religion. When one Azeri *hoca* or religious authority sought to join the new formation, Keykurun rebuffed him. The Republic of Azerbaijan was a secular state and forbade *hocas* from involvement in worldly affairs. The Army of Islam, he explained, was no place for men of religion.[15] If *hocas* were not welcome in the Army of Islam, Christian military officers certainly were. By the summer, the native corps of the army counted 250 officers. Of these just twenty-three were Muslims, the rest being Christian former tsarist officers.[16] The presence of so many Christian officers did not unduly worry Nuri, who assured his fellow Ottoman commanders that the former tsarists were committed anti-Bolsheviks, reliable, and performing well.[17] By contrast, Ottoman officers serving in the North Caucasus later would express frustration over the native mountaineers' piousness, seeing their insistence on the performance of prayers and observance of religious holidays as a drag on operations.[18]

Nuri chose the city of Elisavetpol in western Azerbaijan as the staging ground for the Army of Islam. When he arrived there on 25 May from Tabriz, he received an enthusiastic reception from the population, who hailed him as if he were a savior "descended from the sky."[19] This was, perhaps, to be expected, given Elisavetpol's status as Azerbaijan's most politicized town and the center of its nationalist intelligentsia.[20] Amidst the enthusiasm, Nuri nonetheless noted some inauspicious signs. Natives were scarce in the local militias. Roughly one-half of the 1,000 militiamen were former Ottoman prisoners of war. Among the other half, ex-tsarist officers outnumbered the enlisted ranks. Nuri set to work undaunted, but soon it became clear that locals would not contribute significantly to the Army of Islam. As an abject Nuri wrote to Enver on 28 May, "Whereas 30,000 youths were expected to take up arms, instead only thirty-seven have." Three days later a frustrated Nuri reported, "The Muslims of the South Caucasus talk a lot but do little, they like comfort, and they have an inordinate love of money."[21] Even Shikhlinskii found himself

---

[15] Keykurun, *Hatıralar*, 103.
[16] ATASE, K. 1, D. 1, F. 1-119–1-120, as cited in Nâsır Yüceer, *Azerbaycan*, 73–74.
[17] ATASE, K. 3818, D. 4, F. 27, as cited in Süleymanov, *Qafqaz İslam Ordusu*, 154.
[18] İsmail Berkok, *Askerî Mecmua'nın Tarih Kısmı: Büyük Harpte Şimalî Kafkasya'daki Faaliyetlerimiz ve 15. Fırkanın Harekâtı ve Muharabeleri* (Ankara: Askerî Matbaa, 1934), 49.
[19] M. E. Resulzade, *Azerbaycan Cumhuriyeti: Keyfiyet-i Teşkili ve Şimdiki Vaziyeti* (Istanbul: Evkaf-ı İslâmiye Matbaası, 1341 [1925]), 59–60.
[20] Mehman Süleymanov, "Qafqaz İslam Ordusunun Quruluş, Hazırlıq vä Säfärbärlik Väziyyäti," in *Azärbaycan Xalq Cümhuriyyeti vä Qafqaz İslam Ordusu*, ed. Süleymanov and Mehmet Rıhtım (Baku: Qafkas Üniversiteti, 2008), 228–31.
[21] ATASE, K. 1, D. 1, F. 1-116, as cited in Nâsır Yüceer, *Azerbaycan*, 85.

unable to rouse the locals. While defending the village of Geokchai (Gökçay or Göyçay) from Bolshevik assault, he begged a crowd of villagers to help the soldiers fighting in the oppressive heat to save them. "If you cannot bear arms, then at least carry food and water to the soldiers," he pleaded. "Many of the officers and men fighting in this terrible heat have died from thirst." It was not an excessive request. Yet after hearing him out, his audience offered only polite applause before dispersing.[22]

Unable to recruit sufficient locals, Nuri at the beginning of June had little choice but to ask Enver and Vehib for more reinforcements, as well as extra supplies, arms, and ammunition. Enver understood that the demands of Nuri's mission exceeded the capacity of his force, and so ordered the 5th Caucasus Division transferred from Vehib's Eastern Armies Group to the Army of Islam. Vehib, however, modified the order by authorizing only one infantry and one cavalry regiment from that division to advance into Azerbaijan.[23] On 20 June Nuri again begged for reinforcements, warning Enver that the Bolsheviks were advancing on Elisavetpol, burning Muslim villages and killing those who could not flee. This time Enver replied that the Eastern Armies Group could not spare any men and ordered Nuri to use the forces at hand to engage the enemy.[24] Enver would in September commit more forces to Nuri, but the total amount of forces deployed to the Caucasus amounted to one and a half divisions, hardly an inordinate, let alone reckless, number.[25] Overall, the amount of resources the Ottomans assigned to operations in the Caucasus was limited. As early as May a lack of money hobbled Nuri's staff work,[26] while the lead Teşkilat-ı Mahsusa officer for the Caucasus and Turkistan desperately complained to headquarters in June 1918 that he had never received the fifteen hundred gold liras promised him more than a year ago and in the meantime had been forced to spend some sixteen hundred gold liras out of his own pocket.[27]

The Commune strikes out

While Nuri was struggling in Elisavetpol to raise and train the Army of Islam, the Baku Commune was readying to launch a strike to destroy

---

[22] Rüştü, *Bakû Yollarında*, 46–50.   [23] Rüştü, *Bakû Yollarında*, 7–8.

[24] Nâsır Yüceer, *Azerbaycan*, 76.

[25] Erickson, *Ordered*, 187–88; Genelkurmay Başkanlığı, *Üçüncü Ordu Harekâtı*, vol. II, charts 17–21.

[26] ATASE, Nuri Pasha to the Ottoman Army High Command, 11 Mayıs 1334 [11 May 1918], K. 1851, D. 64-111, F. 19.

[27] ATASE, Ruşeni to the Head of the Directorate of Eastern Affairs, 26 Haziran 1334 [26.6.1918], K. 1859, D. 88-142, F. 1-22.

his army and snuff out the fledgling Azeri government in the name of the revolution and a united Russia. At the end of May the Commune angrily denounced Transcaucasia's separation from "revolutionary Russia" and declared its resolution to fight the "Turco-German bands and their allies." On 10 June, the Commune's army set out to vanquish the Army of Islam in defense of the "Baku Democracy."[28]

The Commune, in fact, had little in common with democracy. It had been founded on fear. In the year following the fall of the tsar, the political situation in Baku had grown only more confused. The Bolshevik Revolution, civil war in Russia, the dissolution of the Transcaucasian Federation, the advance of the Ottoman army, the possibility of the British arriving from Iran – all these portended very different fates for the city and its inhabitants and made it exceedingly difficult for Baku's various factions to work together. A distrust of Baku's Muslim majority, however, united the Bolsheviks and Armenians. The former saw the "dark" Muslim masses as latent counterrevolutionaries, and the latter perceived them as a treacherous element all too likely to join the Ottomans. To Baku's Bolsheviks, the Armenians offered a disciplined military force they could use in defense of the revolution. To Baku's Armenians, the Bolsheviks represented not so much the revolutionary socialism of the future but the imagined Christian solidarity of the past.[29] That alliance of convenience had brought them to power following the March Events, but sharing the same enemies did not mean sharing the same preferences for allies. The likelihood of reinforcements arriving from Russia was slim to nonexistent, making the British the best bet for outside aid. Yet whereas the Armenians were more than willing to invite British forces into Baku, the Bolsheviks ardently opposed the idea. Their preference would be to let the Ottomans take the city. The Commune rested on a shaky coalition.

Between 60 and 70 percent of the Commune's army, which totaled up to 20,000, consisted of Armenians, many of whom were former soldiers who had ended up in Baku during the dissolution of the Caucasus Army. Most of the officers were Dashnaks. Many regarded Muslims by definition as the enemy. At the outset of the offensive, the Communards were confident they would rally the support of peasants and repel the ragtag Army of Islam.[30] The brutality the troops displayed toward the Muslim villagers they encountered, however, made a mockery of the Commune's claim to champion the cause of the exploited peasantry, Muslim and Christian alike. As one Armenian Bolshevik lamented about the

---

[28] Minets and Gorodetskii, eds., *Dokumenty*, vol. I, 285–86; Kazemzadeh, *Struggle*, 129–30.
[29] A. Iu. Bezugol'nyi, *Narody Kavkaza i Krasnaia armiia* (Moscow: Veche, 2007), 93.
[30] Suny, *Baku Commune*, 269–72.

Communards, their "hatred toward Muslims" motivated "requisitions, contemptuous treatment, and frequent shootings" and thereby unnecessarily alienated them.[31] Nonetheless, it would be a mistake to see the Commune as a purely sectarian affair. The Ottomans estimated that about 2,000 men, or one-tenth of the Commune's army, were Muslims, and reports from the battlefield confirm that some of these were fighting and dying for it.[32] In any event, the absence of support in the countryside combined with the relentless summer heat, lack of water, and sickness proved crippling to the Communards.[33] At the beginning of July just outside Geokchai their offensive sputtered and fell apart.

It was at this time that the famed half-Ossetian, half-Cossack Colonel Lazar Bicherakhov arrived at the front with his formidable Cossack brigade. His appearance boosted the spirits of the Communards. Although Bicherakhov was a fervent anti-Bolshevik, he was willing to swallow his enmity toward them in order to fight his wartime enemy, the Turks. An aggressive commander, Bicherakhov planned to punch through the Ottoman lines and revive the flagging offensive, but before he could move the Ottomans struck and took Kurdamir, sending the Communard forces reeling and forcing Bicherakhov to withdraw as well.[34]

As they retreated to Baku, the Communards implemented a scorched earth policy, destroying wells and tearing up train tracks to delay their opponents' advance. The tactics compounded the Army of Islam's logistical problems, which Vehib had already described as severe enough to throw into doubt the future of the 5th Division and the Azeri government alike.[35] The 5th Division alone demanded nearly 11,000 kilograms of provisions daily. Transporting such supplies was an immense challenge, in part because the Georgian and Armenian governments either refused or were unable to fulfill their treaty obligations regarding the use of the railroads. The hot climate and parched South Caucasian land meant that water, too, had to be shipped by rail, thus facilitating the spread of water-borne diseases like cholera.[36]

Encouraging Georgian intransigence were the Germans, who were still intent on keeping Baku's oil out of Ottoman hands. They were looking for ways to slow the Ottoman advance and even deploy their own

---

[31] Kazemzadeh, *Struggle*, 130–31.

[32] Genelkurmay Başkanlığı, *Üçüncü Ordu Harekâtı*, vol. II, 558; Rüştü, *Bakû Yollarında*, 66.

[33] İzzet, *15 Piyade Tümeni*, 40.

[34] Allen and Muratoff, *Battlefields*, 489; Rüştü, *Bakû Yollarında*, 87.

[35] ATASE, Dispatch from the Eastern Armies Group Commander, 5 Haziran 1334 [25.6.1918], K. 157, D. 409-695, F. 11-1.

[36] Rüştü, *Bakû Yollarında*, 33, 39, 42, 54, 62; Halil Paşa, *Bitmeyen Savaş*, 222.

forces to Baku.[37] The Bolsheviks similarly hoped to use the Georgians to impede the Ottomans, dispatching a six-man delegation to Tiflis. The emissaries obtained a promise from the Georgians to deny use of the Batumi–Tiflis–Elisavetpol railroad to the Ottomans, thereby compelling the Ottomans to switch to the Kars–Karakilise–Kazak route for transport into Azerbaijan.[38]

The Ottomans were not oblivious to the Germans' and the Bolsheviks' maneuvers. They had information that a German delegation had already flown into Baku under the pretext of prisoner exchange negotiations to coordinate efforts to keep the port out of Ottoman hands.[39] One Ottoman source reporting from inside Russia relayed information that the Germans were even working to arrange an alliance with the Armenians of Baku. Because they could pose as friends, the Germans, he cautioned, were a greater threat than the British.[40]

Despite these multiple obstacles, by the middle of July the Army of Islam stood just ninety kilometers from Baku. Enver instructed Nuri to seize Baku as soon as possible, writing that the current political situation demanded it. Intelligence reports claiming that British engineers had arrived in Baku to blow up the oil fields added further urgency.[41] By this time the Communard forces were few in number and all but thoroughly demoralized.[42] The way to Baku was seemingly open. Yet morale in the Army of Islam, too, was rather low, especially among the natives. Nuri had only some 8,000 men, of whom at least half were of doubtful utility in combat.[43] The men of the Army of Islam were advancing in a disorganized fashion, unable even to move forward in files or columns.[44]

Nonetheless, the advance upset the Germans, who were receiving updates from the Bolsheviks. Finally, after repeated warnings and protests, Bernstorff on 30 July extracted written pledges from Enver, Talât, and Nesimî that they had ordered Nuri to halt.[45] Enver duly issued orders to Nuri and Halil to bring the offensive to a halt. The Germans attached to the Ottoman General Staff knew the contents of these orders. What they did not know was that Enver had also issued secret orders restating the need to take Baku. He even authorized Nuri to use force against any German units that might be deployed to stop

[37] Trumpener, *Germany*, 186–87.   [38] Nâsır Yüceer, *Azerbaycan*, 86.
[39] Budak, "Nuri Paşa'nın," 76; Nâsır Yüceer, *Azerbaycan*, 86.
[40] ATASE, Report of a First Lieutenant to the War Ministry [spring of 1918, precise date unknown], K. 1854, D. 142-121, F. 2-32.
[41] ATASE, Report to the Third Army, 22 Temmuz 1334 [22.7.1918], K. 157, D. 409-695, F. 21.
[42] Suny, *Baku Commune*, 306.   [43] Allen and Muratoff, *Battlefields*, 489.
[44] Genelkurmay Başkanlığı, *Üçüncü Ordu Harekâtı*, vol. II, 571.
[45] Kurat, *Türkiye ve Rusya*, 544–46.

him. To further the deception Enver instructed that a German officer sent to the front to check Ottoman compliance be fooled into believing that the advance had ceased.[46]

Turmoil in Baku

The Baku Commune was in difficult straits. Its remaining units appeared insufficient to hold the city. The chairman of the Commune and Bolshevik extraordinary commissar Shaumian begged Lenin for help. The Red Army, however, was preoccupied with the revolt of the Czech Legion in the Volga–Ural region and was in no position to relieve Baku. The British were relatively close by in Iran, but Stalin, judging that it would be easier to expel the Ottomans than experienced British imperialists, categorically forbade Shaumian on 21 July to permit any British units to enter Baku. If Baku must fall, it should fall to the Ottomans. The non-Bolsheviks in Baku, however, could not relate so coolly to surrender and had no strong objections to the British. Thus when six days later advance units from the Army of Islam reached the hills overlooking Baku, a panicked Baku soviet overruled Shaumian and the Bolsheviks and voted to invite the British in.[47]

The tenuous anti-Ottoman alliance that had held together Baku's Dashnaks, Bolsheviks, Mensheviks, and Socialist Revolutionaries had frayed. Bicherakhov's men and the Dashnaks openly cheered news of the invitation while the Bolsheviks attempted to mount rallies against it. The British, however, were still far away and so a congress of Armenian leaders convoked by the Dashnaktsutiun decided that surrender to the Ottomans indeed was the best option. It sent a Muslim messenger to cross Ottoman lines and deliver a letter explaining the Armenians' readiness to negotiate and surrender if offered good terms. The Ottomans promised to treat Armenians well and agreed to parley. No response, however, followed.[48] Enver informed his subordinates that, if the Armenians were to surrender Baku and leave, they could be transported to Armenia. Believing the fall of the city to be imminent, Nuri told his commanders that in the event Baku surrendered they were to assert tight control and absolutely forbid any massacres or looting.[49]

[46] Rüştü, *Bakû Yollarında*, 107, 117; Bayur, *Türk İnkılâbı Tarihi*, vol. III, pt. 4, 222–23; Nâsır Yüceer, *Azerbaycan*, 93–96.

[47] Stalin to Lenin on the Situation in Baku, 21.7.1918, USSR, Ministerstvo inostrannykh del, *Dokumenty vneshnei politiki SSSR*, vol. I, 401–02; Shaumian to Lenin, 27.8.1918, USSR, Ministerstvo inostrannykh del, *Dokumenty vneshnei politiki SSSR*, vol. I, 411–12; Pipes, *Formation*, 160; Suny, *Baku Commune*, 306–15.

[48] Rüştü, *Bakû Yollarında*, 130; Süleymanov, *Qafqaz İslam Ordusu*, 267; Genelkurmay Başkanlığı, *Üçüncü Ordu Harekâtı*, vol. II, 575; Suny, *Baku Commune*, 315–18.

[49] Nâsır Yüceer, *Azerbaycan*, 102.

On 31 July the Army of Islam made a probing attack on the city. Wishing to avoid the ignominy of surrender, Shaumian moved his Bolshevik headquarters onto a steamer and set sail for Astrakhan. The warship *Ardahan*, manned by anti-Bolsheviks, intercepted the steamer almost immediately, however, and forced the Bolsheviks to return to the dock. Baku's Dashnaks, Mensheviks, and Socialist Revolutionaries formed a new government without the Bolsheviks, calling it the Central Caspian Dictatorship.[50] Meanwhile at the front, Bicherakhov executed a clever feint behind Ottoman lines and spooked them into pulling back. But then Bicherakhov, resentful of the indifference of Baku's socialists to the well-being of his men and fearing getting cut off from his native North Caucasus, suddenly quit Baku's defense and took his brigade north along the Caspian to Dagestan.[51]

Nuri sensed the moment was auspicious. On 5 August he gave the command for an all-out assault, and at 4:25 a.m. a thunderous artillery barrage fell on Baku. By mid morning Ottoman observers could witness city residents fleeing to boats in the harbor. Intercepted communications, including a report from a defending Muslim colonel to the Baku garrison commander, revealed that the city's defenses were disintegrating rapidly. Ottoman officers at the front expected the city to be theirs shortly.[52] Then suddenly a British detachment arrived, and Bolshevik artillery, newly authorized by Shaumian to join in the defense, opened fire. Their resolve stiffened; the defenders held – barely, but hold they did.[53] A now thoroughly exhausted Army of Islam withdrew, its morale spent. Due to combat losses, desertions, and disease it numbered barely 3,500.[54]

Nuri again begged Istanbul for 5,000 more trained men and more arms and ammunition. In response, Enver authorized the 1,200-man strong 107th regiment to transfer from the Ninth Army and leave for Baku on 9 August. In addition, he ordered the Ninth Army to threaten Enzeli and Hamadan in northern Iran so as to divert the British from Baku. It was something, but, once again, much less than what Nuri wanted.

From Corps to Republican Army

As units of the Army of Islam waited outside Baku, Nuri, still based in Elisavetpol, ordered the reorganization of the Army of Islam's native

---

[50] Kazemzadeh, *Struggle*, 138; Suny, *Baku Commune*, 318–21; A. N. Kheifets, *Sovetskaia Rossiia*, 55–56; A. I. Mikoian, *Dorogoi bor'by* (Moscow: Politizdat, 1971), 173, 176–77.
[51] Rüştü, *Bakû Yollarında*, 129; Allen and Muratoff, *Battlefields*, 490.
[52] Nâsır Yüceer, *Azerbaycan*, 103–04.
[53] Suny, *Baku Commune*, 326–27; Mikoian, *Dorogoi bor'by*, 179.
[54] Nâsır Yüceer, *Azerbaycan*, 105–06; Genelkurmay Başkanlığı, *Üçüncü Ordu Harekâtı*, vol. II, 581.

units, known as the Azerbaijani Corps. Enver wanted it transformed into an army fit for the republic Azerbaijan was to become. Nuri dismissed the Russian officers who had formed the largest part of the Azerbaijani officer corps and decreed that the official language of the army henceforth would be Turkish.[55] Russian would no longer be used. Officers and soldiers of the infantry were to wear Ottoman-style uniforms, while cavalrymen were to adopt Circassian-style uniforms.[56] The army would be composed of four regiments of three battalions each. Since trained native officers were in short supply, Ottoman officers were to fill the billets of regimental and battalion commanders with Azeris serving under them in a form of apprenticeship. The government of Azerbaijan was to bear the costs of maintaining these Ottoman officers.[57] Nuri, who was desperate for more officers than Istanbul could supply, enthusiastically backed a military academy project initiated by the Azeris. In June the academy took in its first class of 100 students for a six-month course. In August the Army of Islam established another school to train non-commissioned officers.[58] Back in Istanbul an Ottoman colonel began a program to prepare cadres of Azeri officers to staff a ministry of war for their republic by assigning Azeris to internships in the Ottoman Ministry of War.[59]

On 22 August Nuri completed a report on the progress of the Army of Islam. The delayed arrival in late July of staff officers had held up organizational matters, and he was still grappling with shortages of rifles, uniforms, and supplies. The local Muslims' lack of interest in serving in the Army of Islam continued to undermine the project. Nuri had ordered the forced conscription of local males between the ages of sixteen and sixty-five as well as the confiscation of weapons from locals to compensate for shortages.[60] Conscription, however, proved unpopular. Quality was as problematic as quantity. Ottoman officers judged the Azeri personnel as lacking sufficient "hardness" for combat.[61]

The growing presence of the British in the Caspian basin stoked fears in Ottoman headquarters that the British would concentrate forces in Baku

---

[55] ATASE, Report to the Eastern Armies Group Command, 22 Ağustos 1334 [22.8.1918], K. 3821, D. 16, F. 1-58.
[56] ATASE, Nuri Pasha on the Formation of the Army of the Republic of Azerbaijan, 13 Ağustos 1334 [13.8.1918], K. 3821, D. 1-30, F. 1-30; Süleymanov, *Qafqaz İslam Ordusu*, 130–31.
[57] ATASE, Nuri Pasha on the Reorganization of the Azerbaijani Corps, 6 Ağustos 1334 [6.8.1918], K. 3821, D. 16, F. 1-9.
[58] Süleymanov, *Qafqaz İslam Ordusu*, 143–44.
[59] Süleymanov, *Qafqaz İslam Ordusu*, 123–25; Budak, "Nuri Paşa'nın," 81–82.
[60] ATASE, Report to the Eastern Armies Group Command, 22 Ağustos 1334 [22.08.1918], K. 3821, D. 16, F. 1-58.
[61] ATASE, To the Chief of Staff, [undated], K. 3821, D. 16, F. 1-118.

and establish a greater Armenian state comprising most of Azerbaijan's territory and then use that state to threaten the Ottoman empire, Iran, and Georgia. To prevent further British reinforcements from reaching Baku, the Army of Islam actually requested a submarine, proposing that the vessel be disassembled and shipped over land and then reassembled on the shores of the Caspian. Seizing Baku sooner promised to be more effective, and so Enver toward the end of August ordered two more regiments and the headquarters of the 15th Infantry Division to Nuri.[62]

German–Bolshevik cooperation against the Ottomans

While the Army of Islam paused outside Baku, the Germans and Bolsheviks were stepping up their collaborative effort to keep the city out of Ottoman hands. Baku's oil was essential to Russia's economy, and the Bolsheviks were determined that the Caucasus would become part of Soviet Russia. Although the Germans in the long term envisioned extending their control over the whole of the Caucasus, including Baku, in the short term they were desperate to ensure that oil continued to flow to their war machine. Thus in July the former enemies agreed in principle that in exchange for oil Germany would compel the Ottomans to cease all operations beyond the borders set at Brest-Litovsk and would refrain from recognizing Armenia or Azerbaijan as independent states. Ludendorff on 4 August warned Enver that if the Ottomans assaulted Baku he would recall all German officers attached to the Ottoman high command.[63] The Germans continued to encourage Georgian intransigence on Ottoman use of Georgian railroads and territory and moved to block the transport of Ottoman soldiers and supplies by burning a bridge out of Georgia.[64] They pointedly declined to promise recognition of Baku as part of Azerbaijan despite Ottoman protests that an independent Azerbaijan could not survive without Baku. By mid August Enver had become aware that the Bolsheviks were delivering oil to Germany in exchange for German pressure against Istanbul.[65] He was willing to accommodate German economic interests in Baku and elsewhere in the Caucasus, but he remained prepared to engage the Germans in combat should they send any units to Baku. In order to obstruct the passage of any such German detachments Ottoman soldiers blew up a bridge and cut telegraph wires at the Georgian-Azeri border.[66]

---

[62] Genelkurmay Başkanlığı, *Üçüncü Ordu Harekâtı*, vol. II, 581–84.
[63] Trumpener, *Germany*, 188.   [64] Bayur, *Türk İnkılâbı Tarihi*, vol. III, pt. 4, 226.
[65] ATASE, Report from Gence to the Army High Command, 13 Ağustos 1334 [13.8.1918], K. 526, D. 2059-369, F. 16.
[66] Halil Paşa, *Bitmeyen Savaş*, 224.

In Moscow, Chicherin reprimanded Galip Kemalî Bey for the Caucasian advance, warning him that it violated the Treaty of Brest-Litovsk and was spoiling relations with Russia. Galip did not deny that the advance transgressed the peace treaty, but countered that the Bolsheviks had violated the treaty first when they failed to disarm the militias in the territories they occupied, thereby compelling the Ottomans to advance to protect Ottoman subjects and prisoners of war as well as the native Muslims. The argument failed to impress Chicherin, and their meeting concluded frostily. Another factor that made Galip feel unwelcome in Russia was the assassination of the German ambassador by a Socialist Revolutionary in Moscow earlier that summer. Galip knew that he had enemies among Muslim Bolsheviks and sympathizers, and feared for his life.[67] First and foremost among those enemies was Mustafa Suphi, an Ottoman subject, future founder of the Turkish Communist Party, and publisher of the Turkish-language socialist newspaper *Yeni Dünya* (New world). Galip had on several occasions complained to Chicherin about *Yeni Dünya*'s stridently anti-Unionist tone, but achieved only a momentary disruption of its publication. On 9 August he quit Moscow for Istanbul, leaving as the Ottoman empire's representative a single official who sat on a prisoner of war commission.[68]

Meanwhile, German and Soviet cooperation continued to deepen. On 27 August the Bolsheviks and Germans codified their agreement on Baku. In exchange for one-quarter of Baku's oil production, or a monthly minimum to be determined later, and effective acknowledgment of Georgia's independent status, Germany was to refrain from supporting any third party's military operations beyond Georgia or the provinces of Kars, Ardahan, or Batumi and was required to act to prevent any third party from crossing into a zone defined by a 65-km radius from Baku. Germany further agreed to supply the Soviet government with one-quarter of Georgia's manganese exports and promised not to intervene in Bolshevik–Ottoman clashes so long as the Bolsheviks did not violate Georgia's borders or cross the 1877 Russo-Ottoman border.[69]

When the next day the German ambassador to Istanbul disclosed the agreements, a firestorm erupted in the Ottoman press against German double-dealing.[70] The semi-official newspaper *Tanin*, however, reacted

---

[67] Yavuz Aslan, *Türkiye Komünist Fırkası'nın Kuruluşu ve Mustafa Suphi* (Ankara: Türk Tarih Kurumu, 1997), 35–41.

[68] Kurat, *Türkiye ve Rusya*, 545–48.

[69] Russo-German Supplemental Treaty, 27.8.1918, *Dokumenti vneshnei politiki SSSR*, vol. I, 443–44; Trumpener, *Germany*, 192–93; Bihl, *Die Kaukasus*, vol. II, 101.

[70] The publicity nonetheless did not stop one Ottoman "political and military agent" in Tiflis named Abdülkerim from boasting to the Ottoman General Staff on 22 September

coolly. It emphasized the Sublime State's vital interest in the establish-ment of Caucasian "buffer states" after enduring two and a half cen-turies of Russian enmity. Accordingly, it criticized the German–Bolshevik agreement's failure to recognize the independence of Azerbaijan and Armenia, but not before hailing the agreement's affirmation of Georgia's independence.[71] Talât, again revealing his view of Russia, reproached the Germans for cutting a deal with the "enemy of yesterday and the enemy of tomorrow."[72] Speaking for Azerbaijan, Mehmed Emin Resulzade assailed in private and in public the Germans' support for Russia's claim on Baku, charging that they had consented to see Azerbaijan become a headless body.[73]

Talât left for Berlin to discuss the crisis, but failed to effect any change in German policy. The German foreign minister Paul von Hintze plainly informed him that without Moscow's consent Germany would not recog-nize Armenia, Azerbaijan, or the North Caucasus. Talât tried to convince him that the Ottomans' objective in advancing on Baku was to block the British. It was a lame gambit, and one that Hintze exposed easily by proposing that the Ottomans pull back and let the Germans expel the British from Baku.[74]

The storming of Baku

The disclosure of German–Bolshevik collaboration only bolstered Enver's determination to seize Baku. The Ottomans' position was strengthening, whereas that of their opponents in Baku was eroding. When the city's defenders performed half-heartedly in fending off lim-ited Ottoman attacks, the disillusioned commander of the British detach-ment, Major Lionel Dunsterville, threatened to leave. The Central Caspian Dictatorship petulantly denied Dunsterville "permission" to leave, but then through the Georgians and the Armenian National Coun-cil in Tiflis quietly began seeking negotiations with the Ottomans.[75]

1918 that with "great sacrifices" he had obtained information that the Germans affirmed in a secret agreement that Baku belonged to Russia. A reader on the General Staff wrote on the copy of the report, "Apparently he did not read the newspapers!": ATASE, Dispatch from Tiflis to the General Staff, 22 Eylül 1334 [22.9.1918], K. 526, D. 2055-369, F. 16-1.

[71] As cited in Bayur, *Türk İnkılâbı Tarihi*, vol. III, pt. 4, 231–32.

[72] Trumpener, *Germany*, 193.

[73] Mirza Bala Mehmetzade, *Milli Azerbaycan Hareketi* (Ankara: Azerbaycan Kültür Merkezi, 1991), 96–98.

[74] Trumpener, *Germany*, 194–95.

[75] L. C. Dunsterville, *The Adventures of Dunsterforce* (London: E. Arnold, 1920), 283–85; Radio Communications of 22 August 1918, Radio Communications of 1–2 September 1918, Georgia, *Dokumenty i materialy*, 440–41; Suny, *Baku Commune*, 334–35.

Baku's fate, however, was sealed. On 8 September the latest Ottoman reinforcements, 5,632 men, reached the front. Two days later Nuri arrived to oversee the final operation. The assault opened at 1:00 a.m. on 14 September. Difficulties in bringing up artillery caused the attack to bog down by mid-afternoon just outside the city, but by evening it regained momentum as reserves swung into action. By nightfall Dunsterville concluded resistance was futile. He ordered his men to withdraw to the port, embark on ships, and sail away. The advancing Army of Islam encountered fierce resistance in some places but routed panicking defenders from others. In the morning the Ottomans could observe Baku's defenders shedding their uniforms and boarding boats in flight. Fighting now erupted inside the city between resident Armenians, Azeris, and Iranians.[76]

At 10:30 a.m. the chief of staff of the 5th Caucasus Division accepted a request for negotiations delivered by the Iranian consul on behalf of the Central Caspian Dictatorship and a group of foreign consuls. The Ottomans demanded an unconditional surrender and offered to guaranty the lives and property of the city's residents. At 3:00 p.m. the defenders began surrendering with white flags in hand.[77] Total Ottoman combat losses in men and officers from the beginning of August through the storming of Baku were 1,645. Two regiments, the 38th and the heavily Iraqi 107th, suffered the greatest losses.[78]

Nuri took the city in the name of the Republic of Azerbaijan. He barred his Ottoman regulars from entering the city immediately for the first day, but permitted his Azeris to enter. Nuri's guaranty of lives and property proved empty. The Azeri units, together with the city's Muslim residents, exacted vengeance for the March Events upon Baku's Armenians. Nearly half of the resident 70,000 Armenians fled by boat. Of those who remained, some 9,000 were slain, an astounding proportion. Nuri acknowledged that massacres had taken place in a report to Enver, but protested that the numbers of Armenians and Russians killed did not amount to 1 percent of the number of Muslims killed in March. He further suggested that Iranian workers in particular had been responsible for most of the looting and reported that the army had executed more than 100 looters for the purpose of maintaining order in the city.[79]

[76] Rüştü, *Bakû Yollarında*, 211–12; ATASE, K. 1, D. 1, F. 1-108, cited in Nâsır Yüceer, *Azerbaycan*, 122.
[77] Rüştü, *Bakû Yollarında*, 212–14; Genelkurmay Başkanlığı, *Üçüncü Ordu Harekâtı*, vol. II, 590–91.
[78] Nâsır Yüceer, *Azerbaycan*, 121–122.
[79] ATASE, BDH Koll., K. 3820, D. 12, F. 54, cited in Nâsır Yüceer, *Azerbaycan*, 124; Halil Paşa, *Bitmeyen Savaş*, 228–30.

After the initial bloodletting, Nuri appointed a commandant and assigned a regiment to keep order.[80] The municipal government was reestablished, shops were opened, and within several days the city began to function again. Prices for food fell sharply, and raisins, watermelons, and other fruits reappeared in the city markets for the first time since the beginning of Bolshevik rule.[81] Back in Istanbul, *Tanin* hailed Baku's capture as a triumph for the viability of the Azeri state. Notably, the newspaper downplayed the central role of the Ottoman army to contrast the way Azerbaijan achieved independence through the efforts of its own forces to the way Georgia effortlessly received independence through Germany and Russia.[82] The Germans continued to scheme about how to displace the Ottomans' influence in Baku with their own. They began encouraging Azerbaijan's neighbors to demand shares of Baku's oil, proposed making Baku an open city, and claimed a need to deploy a German contingent to protect German lives and property in the city. Enver would hear none of it.[83]

Rescuing the North Caucasus

Following the capture of Baku, Nuri turned his eyes northward to Dagestan. Combining in its name the Turkish word for "mountain" with the Persian word for "land," Dagestan arguably held little intrinsic value, consisting of a narrow strip of Caspian coast alongside a mountainous and difficult inland. It boasted no great natural resources and its population was poor, consisting predominantly of mountain shepherds and farmers. Its most famous export was religious scholars, and indeed Dagestan was known even in Arabia for producing experts in the Islamic sciences and Arabic. Dagestan interested the Ottomans in 1918 primarily for two reasons: first, because it held the invasion route from Russia to Azerbaijan and, second, because with its population of roughly 600,000 it was key to the future of the Union of Allied Mountaineers (UAM) of the North Caucasus. Together with the neighboring Chechens, the highlanders of Dagestan had provided the backbone of the Caucasian resistance to Russia in the Great Caucasian War of the nineteenth century.

Established in the spring of 1917, the UAM included representatives from all the mountain peoples of the North Caucasus. Like the

---

[80] Nâsır Yüceer, "Qafqaz İslam Ordusunun Bakı Şähärini Azad Etmäsi," in *Azärbaycan*, ed. Süleymanov and Rıhtım, 351–52.
[81] Kurat, *Türkiye ve Rusya*, 539; Süleymanov, *Qafqaz İslam Ordusu*, 364–65.
[82] Bayur, *Türk İnkılâbı Tarihi*, vol. III, pt. 4, 237–38.
[83] Genelkurmay Başkanlığı, *Üçüncü Ordu Harekâtı*, vol. II, 594–95; Şevket Süreyya Aydemir, *Enver Paşa*, vol. III, 425–26, n. 1.

Transcaucasians, the UAM's members disavowed separation from Russia in 1917. Although they recalled with pride the quarter-century-long struggle of Imam Shamil against the Russian empire and were deeply apprehensive about being demographically and culturally swamped by Russians, the UAM's members nonetheless understood that Russia offered to the mountain peoples their best, even sole, gateway to the economic and educational opportunities they needed to prosper in a rapidly changing world.

The ascent of the Bolsheviks and the Red Army's invasion of the North Caucasus in the winter of 1917–18, however, pushed the mountaineers to break from Russia and turn for help first to Tiflis. When the Transcaucasians could do nothing but dither, the UAM's leaders traveled to Istanbul, where on 11 May they declared independence.[84] Notably, the declaration staked the legitimacy of the North Caucasian state on its democratic origins by citing the North Caucasian peoples' election of a national assembly as the government's founding act.[85] The new state was defined as comprising the Dagestan, Kuban, Black Sea, Stavropol, and Terek provinces as well as Abkhazia. Although Abkhazia was technically in the Transcaucasus, because the Abkhaz belonged to the Circassian linguistic family they and their territory were considered constituent parts of the Mountaineer republic.[86]

North Caucasian emissaries and recent visitors to the region described to the Ottoman military in 1918 a land filled with fiery warriors in the mold of Shamil.[87] Ottoman intelligence analysts, however, were pessimistic. The mountaineer peoples had a "low cultural level," and were few in number, isolated from each other, and wedded to their own interests. Absent significant outside help, they had little chance to sustain independence.[88] Moreover, as one perceptive analyst observed, many of the mountaineer elite had been rewarded for service under the tsar and, like the Ottoman Kurdish regimental chiefs in 1908, actually desired the

---

[84] Michael A. Reynolds, "Native Sons: Post-Imperial Politics, Islam, and Identity in the North Caucasus, 1917–1918," *Jahrbücher für Geschichte Osteuropas*, 56 (March 2008), 232–37.

[85] For the declaration, see ATASE, K. 1857, D. 722, F. 1-27, as cited in Erşan, "Kuzey Kafkasya Siyaseti," 47. An imperfect English translation can be found in Haidar Bammate, *The Caucasus Problem* (Berne: n.p., 1919), 30–31.

[86] The coastal town of Ochamchira, however, was left to the Transcaucasians because its population was predominantly Georgian: "Şimalî Kafkasya Hükümetinin Teşekkülü," *Tasvir-i Efkâr*, 16.5.1918.

[87] ATASE, Report on Conditions in Dagestan, 23 Teşrinievvel 1333 [23.10.1917], K. 502, D. 2040-502, F. 1-2; Berkok, *Kafkasya'daki Faaliyetlerimiz*, 7.

[88] ATASE, Report to the Directorate of Eastern Affairs on Conditions in Russia, 28 Temmuz 1333 [28.7.1917], K. 1843, D. 129-67, F. 1-35; Zeki Pasha to Enver Pasha, 22 Kanunusani 1333 [22.12.1917], K. 530, D. 2070-928, F. 1-143.

preservation of the old system. This attachment to tsarism, the analyst suggested plausibly albeit incorrectly, explained the UAM's seemingly anomalous efforts to cooperate with the Cossacks, the Muslim mountaineers' erstwhile enemies.[89] The UAM, however, was determined to break from Bolshevik Russia, and this is what mattered. On 4 June, the day the Ottoman empire and the UAM concluded their Treaty of Friendship, an advance unit of 577 Ottoman soldiers and 74 officers arrived in the Dagestani town of Gunib.[90] In order to boost their prospects of rallying native support, the Ottomans had begun recruiting personnel of North Caucasian backgrounds from inside and outside the ranks of the army in February.[91] In April they selected an Ottoman Circassian, Major İsmail Hakkı (Berkok) Bey, to lead the expeditionary force, and in August they appointed another Circassian, Major General Yusuf İzzet Pasha, overall commander of forces in the North Caucasus and envoy to the North Caucasus.[92]

Berkok's mission was to raise and train a native force to drive out the Bolsheviks and restore the UAM government, while securing the northern flank of the Army of Islam as it marched on Baku. Upon his arrival, Berkok discovered the people of Dagestan "living in darkness, poverty, and need."[93] The mountaineers were indeed natural warriors, Berkok wrote, but their fierce individualism and tribal loyalties made them poor material for regular military discipline and training.[94] The lack of money, arms, supplies, and trained personnel, moreover, was crippling. The challenge of establishing a credible legion was formidable. Berkok and his men stuck doggedly to their training plan. By the middle of July they had assembled a force of sorts and were ready to move deeper into Dagestan.

---

[89] ATASE, Report to the Headquarters of the Directorate of Eastern Affairs, 23 Kanunuevvel 1334 [23.1.1918], K. 530, D. 2070-928, F. 1-151. Cf. Barasbi Baytugan, "Tarihi İnsanlar Yaratır," Şimalî Kafkasya–Severnyi Kavkaz, no. 41 (September 1937), 2–3. The reason for those overtures was the mountaineers' understanding that their self-interest would be best served by maintaining peace with their anti-Bolshevik neighbors: Reynolds, "Native Sons", 231.

[90] For the text of the treaty, see BOA, "Saltanat-ı Seniye-i Osmaniye ile Kafkasya Cibaliyun-u İttihadı Hükümeti Beyninde Münakid Muhadenet Muahedenamesi," HR.HMŞ.İŞO, D. 107, S. 10.

[91] ATASE, Dispatch from the Chief of Conscription, 30 Mart 1334 [30.3.1918], K. 1851, D. 64-111, F. 9.

[92] Bammatov to Chermoev, 31.7.1918, in M. D. Butaev, ed., Soiuz ob"edinennykh gortsev Severnogo Kavkaza i Dagestana (1917–1918 gg.), Gorskaia Respublika (1918–1920 gg.) (Makhachkala: Institut istorii, arkheologii i etnografii DNTs RAN, 1994) (hereafter SogSKiD) 144; Berkok, Kafkasya'daki Faaliyetlerimiz, 8.

[93] Berkok, Kafkasya'daki Faaliyetlerimiz, 20.

[94] Berkok, Kafkasya'daki Faaliyetlerimiz, 20–22, 37.

Islam was the most powerful unifying element in Dagestan. Given that Berkok and his men had come in the name of Islam to liberate the Caucasus from the Russians, it was perhaps ironic that their first major clash was with one of Dagestan's most influential men of religion, Najmuddin Gotsinskii. At the village of Khuntzakh, Gotsinskii ordered his followers to attack Berkok's men. Gotsinskii was a renowned Avar *'alim*, wealthy cattle baron, and son of one of Shamil's *naib*s, or deputies. Gotsinskii nurtured ambitions of restoring Shamil's imamate with himself as the new imam. The facts that Gotsinskii spoke Turkish, had met with Sultan Abdülhamid II, and had been known to the tsarist authorities as a dangerous Turcophile increased the irony.[95] Perhaps because of his familiarity with the Ottomans, Gotsinskii openly disparaged their practice of Islam.[96] Yet the real motive for his opposition was likely the calculation that the Ottomans' presence would block his ambition to become imam. When he witnessed the superior firepower of the Ottoman-led force, however, Gotsinskii submitted in the name of the sheikh ul-Islam in Istanbul.[97] The Ottomans found religion, and still less ideas of national liberation, to be of limited power in motivating and mobilizing the Dagestani populace. To compensate for this weakness, Berkok decreed the property of the Russians and of those sympathetic to the Russians to be fair plunder, and agreed to split the booty with the local raiders.[98] Like Nuri, Berkok grappled with a chronic lack of trained personnel and supplies and pled regularly for assistance. The drive on Baku had priority on scarce resources, and Berkok had no hope of receiving more until Baku was captured.

Ukraine: the pleasure of irony and the primacy of geopolitics

In April 1918, the Ukrainian Rada appointed as ambassador to the Ottoman empire one of its delegates to Brest-Litovsk, Mikola Levitskii. The newspaper *Tanin* hailed Levitskii's arrival as "the most vigorous and concrete proof of the greatest victory" the Ottomans had won against their "centuries-old" tsarist enemy. When the last tsarist ambassador departed Istanbul four years earlier, the newspaper taunted, he had probably anticipated a return as the city's new governor. Yet now Istanbul was greeting the representative of a new state recently rescued

---

[95] Khadzhi Murad Donogo, "Najmuddin Gotsinskii," *Voprosy istorii*, 6 (2005), 35–36.
[96] ATASE, To the Third Army Command, 31 Mart 1334 [31.3.1918], K. 2918, D. 496, F. 1-130.
[97] Berkok, *Kafkasya'daki Faaliyetlerimiz*, 31.
[98] Berkok, *Kafkasya'daki Faaliyetlerimiz*, 34, 43.

from tsarism. As *Tanin* noted with pleasure, Ukraine owed its existence in some measure to the Ottomans, who, by tenaciously defending the straits, had deepened Russia's economic crisis and helped precipitate the toppling of the tsarist regime. With Russia vanquished, Ukraine and the Ottoman empire could now look forward to a future of mutually beneficial relations.[99]

To be sure, the possession of a common enemy in Russia, a shared interest in stimulating Black Sea commerce, and the absence of shared borders offered a solid foundation for partnership. Nonetheless, there was a matter of potentially serious dispute between the two: Crimea. Once formally an autonomous region within the Ottoman empire, Crimea had been lost to Catherine the Great in 1783 and following that loss had witnessed expulsions of its Turkic Tatar population. The ritual of greetings that the Ottomans occasionally performed in Livadia for the arrival of the tsar to Crimea (such as that performed by Talât in May 1914) was a living reminder of the peninsula's Ottoman past. Periodic migrations of Crimean Tatars between the peninsula and the Ottoman empire continued throughout the nineteenth century and into the twentieth. The peninsula still retained a significant Muslim and Turkic minority in 1918.

Following the Russian Revolution, Tatar activists appealed to the Ottomans and wrote to Talât at Brest-Litovsk. Talât even speculated on the possibility of restoring a Muslim government to Crimea.[100] Nonetheless, the Ottomans made no effort to support the Crimean Tatar movement either diplomatically or materially at Brest-Litovsk[101] and received news of developments there largely through refugees.[102] When Ukraine's German-backed chief, General Pavlo Skoropadskii, asserted a claim to Crimea, two delegates from the Tatar National Administration managed to meet with Enver Pasha and succeeded in getting a note of protest published in the Istanbul press. That was the extent of the Crimeans' success. Talât brought up the issue in September in Berlin, but dropped it. Plaintive appeals from the Crimeans to the Teşkilât-ı Mahsusa went unanswered.[103] The Ottomans had no intention of permitting Crimea to harm their relations with either Ukraine or Germany.[104] Geopolitics, not blood or faith, determined their policy toward Crimea.

---

[99] "Siyaset: Türkiye–Ukrayna," *Tanin*, 20.4.1918.   [100] Kurat, *Türkiye ve Rusya*, 369.

[101] Fischer writes that at the end of March Enver promised to send Ottoman troops to Crimea, but that German opposition squelched it. To whom Enver made the promise is not stated: Fischer, *Germany's Aims*, 546.

[102] Kırımlı, "Relations," 204.   [103] Balcıoğlu, *Teşkilât-ı Mahsusa*, 128.

[104] Kırımlı, "Relations," 205–06.

Turkistan: "Our prayers are with you"

In the years leading up to World War I, Muslim intellectuals in the Ottoman empire and Central Asia developed a growing mutual interest. The collapse of tsarist authority and the possibility of autonomy or even independence in Central Asia further stimulated that interest. Although religious and linguistic ties nurtured the reciprocal curiosity, a strong sense of pragmatic self-interest on both sides also lay behind it. Thus the "Young Bukharans," self-styled progressives and advocates of the *usul ul-jadid* or "new style" of education pioneered by Russian Muslims, looked with favor upon the Ottoman empire not because it stood as the leader of an imagined Turkic community but because it represented a source of the sorts of cultural innovations that they desired to bring to Central Asia.[105] One Bukharan *komitacı* or activist in August 1918 got to the root of the dilemma in his essay "Does Russian or Ottoman Civilization Better Facilitate Bukhara's Progress?" Russian civilization, he argued, had shown itself a failure after nearly half a century of tsarist rule. Mutual distrust had kept the Russians and Bukharans separate. As a result, educational levels among Turkistan's Muslims were falling, not rising. The Ottoman empire, by contrast, offered enlightenment and education that Turkistanis could take advantage of by sending greater numbers of students to study in Istanbul.[106]

Indeed, it was precisely because the Ottoman system did represent dynamism that Bukhara's conservative *ulema* came to despise the native students who had studied in Istanbul, labeling them *kafirs*, unbelievers, and even declaring the spilling of their blood to be *helâl*, or religiously permissible. The mullahs in 1917 jailed many of the Young Bukharans, driving them into alliance with Russian socialists.[107] The fears of the conservative *ulema* were not groundless. The Ottomans represented the transformation, not the preservation, of old identities and ways. As an Ottoman appeal in 1918 to the Turkistanis proclaimed, "the aim of all Islam and Turkism" (*Bütün İslamiyet ve Türklüğün gayesi*) is to liberate ignorant and defenseless Muslims by modernizing their social life and destroying any obstacle on the road to civilization.[108]

---

[105] Adeeb Khalid, *The Politics of Muslim Cultural Reform: Jadidism in Central Asia* (Berkeley: University of California Press, 1998), 110.
[106] ATASE, "Does Russian or Ottoman Civilization Better Facilitate Bukhara's Progress?", 19 Ağustos 1334 [19.08.1918], K. 1854, D. 142-121, F. 2-19.
[107] İsrafil Kurtcephe, "Teşkilat-ı Mahsusa Belgelerine Göre 1917 Rus İhtilâli Sırasında Buhara Hanlığı," in *Beşinci Askerî Tarih Semineri Bildirileri I* (Ankara: Genelkurmay Basım Evi, 1996), 592–93.
[108] ATASE, Appeal to the Turkistanis, 22 Teşrinievvel 1334 [22.10.1918], K. 1854, D. 142-121, F. 12-1.

Upheaval in Russia stimulated some Russian Muslim expatriates inside the Ottoman empire to mobilize. In July 1917, for example, a group of students identifying themselves as representatives of the Kyrgyz–Kazak Turks wrote to the Ottoman War Ministry. They explained that they sought autonomy so that they might sedentarize their people, protect their lands, improve their education, raise their level of culture, and enable them to "preserve their existence." They envisioned sending more students to the Ottoman empire so they could more quickly disseminate Ottoman-style education at home.[109]

A native of Kazan and instructor at Istanbul's university, the Dar ül-fünun, named Halim Sabit (Şibay) wrote in 1918 a lengthy memorandum to Enver Pasha entitled, "Some Thoughts on the Historical Opportunity Created by the Defeat of Russia." Like the Kyrgyz–Kazak students and the North Caucasian mountaineers, he feared that Russia's Muslims were being overwhelmed economically, culturally, and demographically. Some, like the Chuvash of Siberia, had already succumbed.[110] Sabit urged the Ottomans in the short term to strengthen and coordinate the activities, including military ones, of Russia's Muslims and over the long term to raise their level of education by sponsoring academic exchanges and conferences, and offer scholarships to students from Russia to study in Istanbul.[111]

Just as Muslim delegates from the Caucasus and Crimea made contact with Ottoman officials, so, too, did others from elsewhere in Russia. In June 1918 Osman Tukumbet, the second in command of the İdil–Ural Military Council, arrived in Istanbul. Following the Bolsheviks' crushing of Kazan in the wake of Brest-Litovsk, he had contacted Galip Kemalî Bey, but then decided to go first to Berlin where he thought his chances of receiving support were better. The Germans disappointed him, however, and he departed for Istanbul.[112] Tukumbet's arrival attracted some press attention, and he and two compatriots gained an audience with Enver. What Enver may have offered them is unknown. Another group of three men claiming to represent the people of Turkistan arrived in Elisavetpol in August 1918 and told Nuri they wanted

[109] Mustafa Gül, "Bolşevik İhtilali Sırasında Kırgız–Kazak Öğrencilerin Osmanlı Hükümeti'ne Sundukları Bir Beyanname," *Atatürk Araştırma Merkezi Dergisi*, 11 (March 1995), 50–53.
[110] ATASE, "Some Thoughts on the Historical Opportunity Created by the Defeat of Russia," 12 Şubat 1334 [12.2.1918], K. 1857, D. 428-133, F. 1.
[111] ATASE, "Some Thoughts on the Historical Opportunity Created by the Defeat of Russia," 12 Şubat 1334 [12.2.1918], K. 1857, D. 428-133, F. 1–2.
[112] Kurat, *Türkiye ve Rusya*, 506.

to go to Istanbul to work alongside other Turkistanis with the Ottoman government.[113]

Later that month two more Turkistanis, Nureddin Bey Hudayarhan and Muhammad Gazi Yunus Bey, submitted a report on conditions in their homeland to the Ottoman War Ministry. They explained that a lack of "civilizational strength" and six decades of Russian repression had impaired the Turkistanis' ability to secure their own freedom. If, however, leadership were provided, they promised that the Turkistanis would be ready to spill "oceans of blood" for their freedom. In this case, "the Islamic world would win four million bayonets, bayonets as sharp as those of Anatolia," and Anatolia and Turkistan could save the whole of Islam.[114]

The Ottomans did attempt to assist the Turkistanis, although in terms of personnel and material resources the support was limited. When in July 1917 a group of twenty-five Central Asian Muslim prisoners freed from Austria expressed to the Teşkilât-ı Mahsusa their desire to return to their homeland and strengthen its ties to the Ottoman state in the name of Turan, they were lodged at the Uzbek Sufi lodge in Üsküdar, just across the Bosphorus from Istanbul proper. Dubbed "Ambassadors of Islam," they were later authorized to leave for Central Asia via Batumi.[115] In October 1918 the Teşkilât-ı Mahsusa requested that a similar group of sixty-three Turkistanis be supplied with travel documents so that they could proceed to Batumi and from there to Central Asia.[116]

Not long after arriving in the Caucasus, the Teşkilât-ı Mahsusa's regional point-man, Ruşenî Bey, sent a team of some twenty officers led by a former prisoner of war named Yusuf Ziya Bey to Tashkent. Their primary mission was to prevent British penetration. Yusuf Ziya Bey, however, decided that a team of just twenty could accomplish little and sent them back to Baku. On his own he continued to Samarkand, Bukhara, Ashkhabad, and Orenburg and then back to Tashkent.[117] From Tashkent Yusuf Ziya made contact with Galip Kemalî, who had advised Istanbul to dispatch five to ten officers to Central Asia following the fall of Baku. As Yusuf Ziya had already grasped, however, the fact was that three or four divisions, not a handful of officers, would be required if

[113] ATASE, Dispatch to the Ministry of War from the Political Affairs Department of the Caucasus Army of Islam, 20 Ağustos 1334 [20.8.1918], K. 1854, D. 142-121, F. 6.
[114] ATASE, Petition on the General Situation in Turkistan, 24 Ağustos 1334 [24.8.1918], K. 1854, D. 142-121, F. 2-6-2-9.
[115] ATASE, The Muslim Ambassadors Who Should Be Sent to Their Homelands by Way of Batumi [undated], K. 1854, D. 142-121, F. 1-19.
[116] ATASE, Dispatch to the Chief of the Second Intelligence Department of Headquarters, 13 Teşrinievvel 1334 [13.10.1918], K. 1854, D. 142-121, F. 1-20.
[117] Kurat, Türkiye ve Rusya, 512–13.

the Ottomans were to project any substantive influence into Central Asia. Yet the Ottoman state could barely support individual officers in the region. Yusuf Ziya had to live like a vagabond while traveling through Central Asia because of a lack of money. His impoverishment was not unusual. As noted earlier, the Teşkilât-ı Mahsusa's lack of funds forced Ruşenî Bey to spend from his own pocket, a situation that did not please him.[118] Needless to say, a state that had difficulty supporting individual officers was in no position to deploy divisions across the Caspian.

Thus, when in October 1918 a delegation of Turkistanis led by a certain Seyid Tahir met in Azerbaijan with Ottoman officers attached to the Caucasus Army of Islam, the Ottomans offered only advice and their best wishes and prayers. In an epistle for Tahir to take home they offered their best advice to the Turkistanis: to act without delay to take advantage of the "theories of nationality and union of peoples" (*ortaya atılan milliyet ve ittihad-ı akvam nazariyatı*) that were then current by declaring their independence. The changing global order offered the Turkistanis an opportunity to exploit. To do so effectively, however, they would have to speak as one and resist the "sweet voices" of their neighbors, i.e., the Bolsheviks with their seductive rhetoric of honoring self-determination. In the closing paragraph of the letter, the Ottomans assured the Central Asians that they would follow their efforts with great interest and would also pray for God to assist them.[119] The Ottoman message was clear: We wish you the best, but you are on your own.

The annexation of Elviye-i Selâse

At the same time that the Ottomans were fighting to install independent governments in Azerbaijan and the North Caucasus, they were busy reincorporating Kars, Ardahan, and Batumi back into their state. Article four of the Treaty of Brest-Litovsk did not assign the three provinces to the Ottoman empire. Rather, it recognized a right to self-determination for their populations and required Russia to withdraw all forces from them and also to refrain from interfering in the revision of the provinces' internal and international legal status. The population was then to establish a new order in accord with the wishes of neighboring states, and "especially" with the Ottoman state. All treaty signatories, however,

---

[118] Kurat, *Türkiye ve Rusya*, 514–16.
[119] ATASE, Dispatch to the Command of the Army of Islam, 22 Teşrinievvel 1334 [22.10.1918], K. 1854, D. 142-121, F. 12–12-1.

understood that the Ottomans would annex the provinces.[120] Once Georgia, Armenia, and Azerbaijan had ceded all claims to the territories in the treaties they concluded with the Ottoman empire, Istanbul ordered the army, the only branch of government functioning in the region, to begin organizing a plebiscite, and appointed a committee staffed by officials from the Interior Ministry and other civil servants to oversee it. Males nineteen and older were eligible to vote in the secret ballot and Russian records were used to create voter rolls. Local commissions distributed ballots reading "Yes" or "No," with each a different color.[121]

The results of the plebiscite were announced in August and published in the Ottoman press. The total adult male population of the three provinces was put at 161,908, of whom 138,582 were Muslim and 23,326 non-Muslim. There were 87,263 votes cast. Of these, 85,129 voted "yes" to the incorporation of the provinces, 441 voted "no," and 1,693 abstained.[122] A decree regulating the provinces' legal organization was prepared on 11 August. Four days later, a committee of some twenty representatives from locations throughout the provinces met with Sultan Mehmed VI Vahideddin to request that the three provinces be formally reincorporated into the Ottoman empire. That same day Vahideddin issued an imperial rescript to the "People of the Three Provinces" (*Elviye-i Selâse Ahâlîsine*). The rescript recalled the inclusion of the provinces into the Ottoman realm in the reigns of Sultans Selim the Grim and Süleyman the Law Giver and their surrender in 1878 as war reparations, recounted the Central Powers' diplomacy at Brest-Litovsk, and hailed the desire of the region's Muslims and non-Muslims to return to the "Divinely Protected Lands" of the Ottoman state.[123]

The lopsided nature of the voting makes clear that the plebiscite's outcome was predetermined. Nonetheless, the language of the rescript is noteworthy for several reasons. First, it highlighted the provinces' long history as Ottoman territories, their recent loss, and the manner of that loss. It thereby differentiated the provinces from those parts of the Caucasus that had never been part of the Ottoman empire or had been lost long ago to outright conquest. Second, the rescript drew attention

[120] Chicherin, for example, conceded on 14 March 1918 at the Fourth Congress of Soviets that the fourth article amounted to approval of Ottoman annexation of the region: Kurat, *Türkiye ve Rusya*, 489.
[121] BOA, The Annexation of Elviye-i Selâse, 29 Temmuz 1334 [29.7.1918], DH.İ.UM, D. 20-19, S. 13-13, F. 2; Hilmi Uran, *Hatıralarım* (Ankara: Ayyıldız Matbaası, 1959), 86, 90; Dayı, *Elviye-i Selâse'de*, 61; Kurat, *Türkiye ve Rusya*, 491.
[122] For a detailed breakdown of the voting, albeit with minor discrepancies, see Kurat, *Türkiye ve Rusya*, 491-92.
[123] BOA, The Annexation of Elviye-i Selâse, 15 Ağustos 1334 [15.8.1918], DH.İ.UM, D. 20-19, S. 13-41, F. 15.

to the legal ground of the annexation and the international legitimacy conferred at Brest-Litovsk by Germany, Austria-Hungary, and Bulgaria. Finally, and not least, the rescript's language portrayed the provinces' residents as the initiators of the process of annexation and the ultimate arbiters over that process. Neither the dictates of Islam nor those of ethnonationalism, nor the sultan's prerogative as a conquering warrior, were invoked to justify the annexation. The rescript joined two claims to sovereignty, the imperial and popular, but as the ritual of the plebiscite testified, the latter claim was the more contemporary and symbolically more powerful.

One month later the cabinet ministers of the Ottoman government issued a decree reorganizing the three provinces into the two districts of Batumi and Kars, which together formed the single province of Batumi.[124] Also in September the Ottomans initiated a census for the purposes of organizing conscription.[125] When some residents of Batumi attempted to form a "Batumi Russian National Council" for the sake of preserving the religious and national unity of Batumi's Slavs, the authorities moved to disband it in accord with the general law against political organizations formed along ethnic or tribal lines.[126] Just as Ottoman rhetoric, public and private, distinguished between the provinces of Kars, Ardahan, and Batumi and the rest of the Caucasus, referring to Elviye-i Selâse as "our provinces" and "our land," so did Ottoman behavior.

End game: diplomatic war and Ottoman withdrawal

Following the fall of Baku, Bolshevik concerns about the Ottomans began to dissipate. With the Germans in retreat in the west, the Bulgarians reeling, and the Ottomans vanquished in Palestine, it was clear that the Central Powers had lost the war. The Bolsheviks accordingly adopted a more aggressive stance. On 20 September the Soviet ambassador to Germany Adolf Ioffe delivered to his Ottoman counterpart in Berlin a note from Commissar for Foreign Affairs Chicherin. In it, Chicherin accused the Ottoman army of having "terrorized" the population of Kars, Ardahan, and Batumi, and declared the plebiscite to have been in violation of the Treaty of Brest-Litovsk and therefore invalid. Chicherin further blasted the Ottomans for teaming with bandits to occupy a "Soviet republic,"

---

[124] BOA, Decree on the Organization of the Province of Batumi by Uniting Batumi, Kars, and Ardahan, 14 Eylül 1334 [14.9.1918], DH.İ.UM, D. E-40, S. 30, F. 3.

[125] BOA, Minister of War to the Minister of the Interior Regarding the Conduct of a Census, 14 Eylül 1334 [14.9.1918], DH.İ.UM, D. 20-19, S. 13-48, F. 3.

[126] BOA, Legal Opinion of the Law Office, 19 Ağustos 1334 [19.8.1918], Charter of the Batumi Russian National Council, 1918, DH.İ.UM, D. 20-19, S. 13-26, F. 5-1, 7.

by which he meant Azerbaijan, and for seizing Baku in breach of their avowal not to. The Treaty of Brest-Litovsk was, he declared, now defunct between Soviet Russia and the Ottoman empire. [127] The commissar in turn informed Berlin grandiloquently that "Russian governmental circles and the Russian people" were disappointed with Germany's failure to restrain the Ottomans as agreed.[128] Simultaneously, the Bolshevik Karl Radek deployed his skills as a propagandist in the pages of the newspaper *Izvestiia* to attack the Ottomans for stealing Baku. Seeking to widen the rift between Berlin and Istanbul, he asserted that the Ottomans coveted Crimea and highlighted how poor an ally they were for the Germans, even raising the possibility that they might desire to switch sides to the Entente. He also made sure to draw attention to the fact that the Ottoman army, not any Azerbaijani force, had taken Baku.[129] Enver's Caucasus Army of Islam had obscured events and muddied perceptions, but in the end had fooled no one.

Talât and Nesimî met with Ioffe in Berlin on 21 and 22 September. The Soviet diplomat stipulated that the Ottomans withdraw all their forces behind the borders fixed at Brest-Litovsk, hand over all occupied territory including Baku to the Bolsheviks, and pay compensation for damages incurred. In the course of the discussion, Talât denied that regular Ottoman army units had participated in the assault on Baku and that Nuri had any official rank. He offered to pledge in writing that the Ottoman empire would not interfere in the internal affairs of the Caucasus. When two days later Ioffe reiterated his demands, Talât replied that the Ottomans lacked the authority to hand over any territory in the Caucasus.[130] Moreover, he stated, he could not in any event give a comprehensive answer without first consulting with other members of the Ottoman government.[131]

Talât in the meantime had met with Hintze to resolve differences between Berlin and Istanbul regarding the Caucasus, Crimea, Iran and Turkistan. Talât again asked that Germany recognize Armenia and Azerbaijan, stressing that the independence of these two states, like that of Georgia, was vital to the Ottoman empire. Although Hintze rejected the request, Talât in a secret protocol obtained a German commitment to establish *de facto* relations with the two republics as well as a promise

---

[127] Chicherin to the Turkish Foreign Ministry, 20.9.1918, USSR, Ministerstvo inostrannykh del, *Dokumenty vneshnei politiki SSSR*, vol. I, 490–92; A. N. Kheifets, *Sovetskaia Rossiia*, 68; Hovannisian, *Armenia on the Road*, 228.

[128] Chicherin to the German Consul, 21.9.1918, USSR, Ministerstvo inostrannykh del, *Dokumenty vneshnei politiki SSSR*, vol. I, 492–93.

[129] Viator, "Turtsiia," *Izvestiia*, 21.09.1918.   [130] Kurat, *Türkiye ve Rusya*, 554–55.

[131] A. N. Kheifets, *Sovetskaia Rossiia*, 70.

to soothe relations between Istanbul and Moscow should problems arise from Istanbul's recognition of the three Transcaucasian republics. In return, Istanbul was to withdraw its forces from Azerbaijan (qualified as "Caucasian Azerbaijan" to assuage Iranian concerns of territorial claims on Iran) and Armenia, after which Germany would work to obtain Russia's recognition of those republics. Germany expressed regret that it could not assist the Ottomans in establishing independent states in the North Caucasus and Turkistan but promised not to oppose such efforts. The Ottomans were to assist the Germans in obtaining Azeri consent to German administration of Baku's oilfields and the Baku–Batumi railroad and pipeline.[132]

On 3 October the Ottoman ambassador in Germany, Rifat Pasha, informed Ioffe that the Porte had ordered its forces to withdraw from the Caucasus and that those forces had in fact already begun pulling out. Rifat Pasha refused, however, to confirm whether this withdrawal applied to irregular forces. Still hoping to see a Transcaucasus free of Russian control, he balked also at Ioffe's demand that the Ottomans hand over the territory they were evacuating to the Russians. Ioffe thereupon declared the talks ended and formally presented Chicherin's note of protest.[133] Three days later the Ottoman foreign minister Nesimî Bey fired back and criticized Russia for its own violations of Brest-Litovsk. By not eliminating armed gangs attacking Muslims in Kars, Ardahan, and Batumi, Russia had failed to hand over the provinces in good order as the treaty required. Nesimî defended the plebiscite, pointing out that its outcome was natural given the region's Muslim majority and calling upon the Soviets to observe their own principle of self-determination in the Caucasus. Finally, Nesimî added, the Ottomans moved on Baku only because the British had established a presence there.[134]

Radek answered with an unoriginal but bald threat: "If Turkey does not agree to return Baku directly to our hands," it would encounter the "Armenian Question – moreover the question not only of Russian Armenians but the question of Turkish Armenia."[135] Chicherin in his official response implicitly dismissed Nesimî's citation of the principle of self-determination by denouncing the defunct Transcaucasian Republic as a

---

[132] Bayur, *Türk İnkılâbı Tarihi*, vol. III, pt. 4, 244–45; Trumpener, *Germany*, 196; Bihl, *Die Kaukasus*, vol. II, 123–24.

[133] Representative of the RSFSR in Germany to Rifat Pasha, 3.10.1918, USSR, Ministerstvo inostrannykh del, *Dokumenty vneshnei politiki SSSR*, vol. I, 509–10; A. N. Kheifets, *Sovetskaia Rossiia*, 70.

[134] Bayur, *Türk İnkılâbı Tarihi*, vol. III, pt. 4, 242–43. Bayur gives the date for this note as 24 September 1918.

[135] K. Radek, "Baku," *Izvestiia*, 9.10.1918.

government of mutineers, aided and abetted by the Ottomans, and lacking popular legitimacy. He made short shrift of Nesimî's other claims, pointing out, for example, that the Ottoman drive on Baku had started well before British troops entered the city. In short, "the political activity and military operations of the Turks throughout the Transcaucasus amounted to one huge violation of the Treaty of Brest-Litovsk." Istanbul, he restated, must surrender Baku and all territories outside Georgia and the borders delineated by that treaty.[136]

In the war's final weeks, Enver emphasized repeatedly to Nuri and Halil the importance of securing the independence of Azerbaijan and the North Caucasus. He ordered Nuri to contact the British and American consuls in Tehran and inform them that Germany intended to deploy a military force to Baku in the hopes that this would provoke London and Washington to recognize Azerbaijan.[137] Indeed, the changed geopolitical environment transformed Enver, like Talât, into an advocate of a strong and independent Armenia. Thus when in separate meetings in Istanbul with Talât, Nesimî Bey, and Minister of Justice Halil Bey, the special emissary of the Republic of Azerbaijan to the Ottoman empire, Alimardan Topchibashev, complained about the Armenians, all three Ottomans berated him and implored the Azeris to cooperate with the Armenians. The dissolution of tsarist Russia, Talât emphasized to Topchibashev, was the one positive achievement of the war, and to preserve this achievement it was imperative that the Azeris resolve their problems with the Armenians and live with them peacefully.[138]

Bulgaria's withdrawal from the war and the collapse of the Macedonian front prompted Enver to recall the 10th Division from Batumi and the 15th from Baku to protect Istanbul. Since the embarkation of the 10th Division would tie up Batumi's port facilities for several weeks, it was decided to send the 15th Division to Dagestan in the meantime rather than let it stand idle in the Transcaucasus. The liberation of Dagestan would both provide greater security for Baku and would give the government of the North Caucasian Mountaineer Republic a chance to establish itself and perhaps win recognition.[139]

---

[136] Commissariat of Foreign Affairs to Nesimi Bey, 10.10.1918, USSR, Ministerstvo inostrannykh del, *Dokumenty vneshnei politiki SSSR*, vol. I, 514–16; Kurat, *Türkiye ve Rusya*, 563; Hovannisian, *Armenia on the Road*, 228–29.
[137] Şevket Süreyya Aydemir, *Enver Paşa*, vol. III, 426–28.
[138] A. A. Topchibashev, *Diplomaticheskie besedy v Stambule, 1918–1919*, ed. Gasan Gasanov (Baku: Ergün, 1994), 9–15.
[139] Bayur, *Türk İnkılâbı Tarihi*, vol. III, pt. 4, 255.

Numbering just 2,200 men,[140] the 15th Division under the Ottoman Circassian colonel Süleyman İzzet[141] marched north along the Caspian coast to link up with Berkok's mixed force of Ottoman volunteers and Dagestani irregulars. The ancient city of Derbent, defended by a mishmash of Russian and Armenian soldiers, fell on 6 October. One week later Yusuf İzzet Pasha and UAM officials held a ceremony to celebrate the restoration of the UAM government to the North Caucasus. Pan-Islamic and pan-Turanic themes were absent. Indeed, the North Caucasian president, Tapa Chermoev, emphasized in his first decrees the political, not fraternal, nature of the UAM–Ottoman relationship and compared it to Germany's assistance to Ukraine and Georgia. He stressed the liberal principles of the republic and its recognition of the rights of all regardless of ethnicity or religion.[142] To underscore the theme of ecumenicism, at the Ottomans' and North Caucasians' behest Georgian and Russian Orthodox priests and a Jewish rabbi participated in the ceremony.[143]

Chermoev had reason to stress the instrumental nature of Ottoman–North Caucasian ties. Writing from Istanbul in July, Bammate had warned him, "in the council of ministers there was no program or even the slightest reliable sympathy for us." With the exception of Enver, he explained, the Unionists were indifferent or even hostile to the North Caucasians.[144] Like the Azeri Keykurun, Bammate had found the Ottoman political elite rather cool toward the Muslims of the Caucasus, and in part for that reason Bammate gave priority to courting Germany.[145]

When on 2 October Enver learned of Germany's decision to approach the United States to arrange a peace settlement and end the war, he wired Nuri, telling him "we have lost the game." "In our condition," he went on, "securing Azerbaijan's independence is extremely important." Toward that end, he impressed upon Nuri and Halil Pashas that the Azeris must get along with the Armenians and deal directly with the Americans and British.[146] He predicted a peace settlement would soon be worked out and would be based on the principle of ethnic self-determination. He instructed that the 5th Division, now deployed in Nagornyi Karabakh, be put last in the order of withdrawal in the expectation that peace would be concluded before it could be moved, thereby enabling Ottoman

[140] Kadircan Kaflı, *Şimalî Kafkasya* (Istanbul: Vakit Matbaası, 1942), 139.
[141] İzzet Aydemir, *Muhaceretteki Çerkes Aydınları* (Ankara: n.p., 1991), 101.
[142] Decree of Chermoev, 14.10.1918, *SogSKiD*, 162–63.
[143] İzzet, *15 Piyade Tümeni*, 147; Berkok, *Kafkasya'daki Faaliyetlerimiz*, 73.
[144] Bammatov to Chermoev, 31.7.1918, *SogSKiD*, 145.
[145] Bammatov to Chermoev, 31.8.1918, *SogSKiD*, 152.
[146] Şevket Süreyya Aydemir, *Enver Paşa*, vol. III, 443.

personnel there to continue training the Azeri army. He urged that some personnel volunteer to take local citizenship so that they could legally remain and thereby continue their training mission, and ordered that more arms for the Azeris and North Caucasians be sent while it was still possible.[147] Recognizing that Azerbaijan's development required more than a potent army, he told Halil also to dispatch legal, educational, and other experts there.[148]

In the face of inevitable defeat, Talât concluded that he and his cabinet must resign. The war after all, had been their project. Over the objections of Justice Minister Halil (Menteşe), Education Minister Nâzım Bey, and Enver, all of whom wished first to see what terms the Entente might offer, Talât made the decision for the cabinet to resign on 8 October.[149] Even so, Enver's mind continued to spin in search of a way to maintain the independence of the Caucasus. The next day he wrote the Ottoman representative in Switzerland, the Egyptian Fuad Selim, to tell him to look into the possibility of Azerbaijan and the North Caucasus cutting a deal with the British, perhaps trading access to natural resources for a guaranty of independence. Enver even flirted with the idea of relocating to Azerbaijan and continuing the war. He had made contingency plans for the establishment of a resistance movement in Eastern Anatolia and the Transcaucasus against the Entente if the war should go badly.[150] Halil, however, advised Enver against coming to Azerbaijan. He was skeptical of Azerbaijan's prospects as a viable state. Moreover, he cautioned, "as soon as the influence of other powerful states is felt here tomorrow, these people who today embrace us claiming to share the same origins will drop us as soon as possible."[151] His prophecy would be borne out soon enough.

Petrovsk: victory in vain?

On 27 October, a delegation led by Rauf Bey opened ceasefire talks with the British on the warship *Agamemnon*, anchored in the port of Mudros

---

[147] Şevket Süreyya Aydemir, *Enver Paşa*, vol. III, 440, 445; Bayur, *Türk İnkılâbı Tarihi*, vol. III, pt. 4, 255; Halil Bal, "Kuzey Kafkasya'nın İstiklali ve Türkiye'nin Askeri Yardımı (1914–1918)," *Kafkas Araştırmaları*, 3 (1997), 87.

[148] Genelkurmay Başkanlığı, *Üçüncü Ordu Harekâtı*, vol. II, 601; Şevket Süreyya Aydemir, *Enver Paşa*, vol. III, 445; Bayur, *Türk İnkılâbı Tarihi*, vol. III, pt. 4, 258. The date of Enver's order is given as 5–6 October in Genelkurmay Başkanlığı, *Üçüncü Ordu Harekâtı*, vol. I, whereas Bayur writes 15 October.

[149] Celal Bayar, *Ben de Yazdım*, vol. 1 (Istanbul: Baha Matbaası, 1965), 21.

[150] Ali Fuat Cebesoy, *Milli Mücadele Hatıraları* (Istanbul: Vatan Neşriyatı, 1953), 42–43. Although Cebesoy writes that the movement was to be based in Baku, Kurat (*Türkiye ve Rusya*, 572–73) suggests that this is a mistake and that Kars was the more likely choice for the base. Kurat's suggestion does make more sense.

[151] Şevket Süreyya Aydemir, *Enver Paşa*, vol. III, 440–48.

on the Aegean island of Limnos. Three days later the two sides signed an armistice. The war had ended, yet the Ottomans and North Caucasians fighting in the cold, mud, and autumn rain outside Dagestan's administrative capital, Port Petrovsk, had no idea. Indeed, on the same day that the armistice was signed Chermoev and Yusuf İzzet Pasha met to plan their final assault on the Caspian port. The climactic battle for Petrovsk was fought on the night of 5 November through the following morning. Water and food were in short supply, and cold, wind, and rain lashed those fighting. The wounded suffered indescribable torment as they were carried down the slippery and rocky slopes, bouncing on the shoulders of their bearers. Wounded in the left foot, exhausted from a lack of sleep, shivering from exposure to the cold and rain, and suffering from a recurrent malaria attack, the commander of the 15th Division, Colonel Süleyman İzzet, rallied his junior officers with his grim determination and pushed them forward. On 8 November, a mixed delegation of Muslims and Christians from Petrovsk came forth to announce the city's surrender. The exhausted Ottomans marched victoriously into the port and there learned of the armistice and its requirement for an immediate Ottoman withdrawal from the Caucasus. İzzet had lost in the battle two of his best and most courageous company commanders, Aziz Efendi and Sabri Efendi, the latter to a Russian artillery shell. They had fought at the Dardanelles, in Romania, and at Baku, only to meet their end outside Petrovsk in a battle fought after the war had already ended.[152]

The campaign in Dagestan had, if nothing else, demonstrated the extraordinary tenacity of the Ottoman officer corps. Their state had been the least developed and least capable of the Great War's major participants, yet against expectations they had held together through four years of total warfare. Nonetheless, it appeared that their struggle and sacrifice had, like the deaths of Aziz and Sabri Efendi, been in vain. Appearances, however, sometimes deceive.

---

[152] İzzet, *15. Piyade Tümeni* 203–06, 222–23; Genelkurmay Başkanlığı, *Üçüncü Ordu Harekâtı*, vol. II, 615.

Epilogue

By entering the war, the Unionist leadership had gambled and had lost everything. Their one achievement in the war had been to outlast the Russian empire and oversee the emergence of a Caucasian buffer zone for their empire. The Mudros Armistice reversed that achievement and laid the groundwork for their empire's final dissolution. The armistice terms required the Ottoman army to withdraw all personnel from the Caucasus and Iran to behind the empire's prewar eastern borders and to surrender all garrisons in the Hijaz, Asir, the Yemen, Syria, Cilicia, and Iraq and all personnel and ports in Tripolitania and Cyrenaica. It recognized the right of the Allies to occupy the Dardanelles and Bosphorus, as well as Batumi, and forbade the Ottomans from raising objections to the occupation of Baku. The armistice also awarded to the Allies the prerogative to occupy the six Eastern Anatolian provinces claimed by Armenians, i.e., Van, Erzurum, Bitlis, Diyar-ı Bekir, Mamuret ül-Aziz, and Sivas, in the event of disorder there, and to occupy any point inside the empire in the event of any threat to their own security. The Unionist leadership fled Istanbul in disgrace. The triumvirs Talât, Cemal, and Enver all later fell to bullets: Talât in Berlin to an Armenian assassin exacting vengeance for the horrors inflicted on his people, Cemal in Tiflis to a Bolshevik or Armenian assassin, and Enver in Central Asia while fighting alongside a dwindling band of tribesmen after having doublecrossed his Bolshevik sponsors.

The victorious Entente powers proceeded to dismantle the Ottoman empire. The British had started the final process in 1916 when they presented the rebellion of some Bedouin tribes they sponsored as a "Great Arab Revolt." They followed through after the war, invoking Arab ethnic difference and the national idea to strip the Arab lands from the Ottoman dynasty. They occupied Istanbul, and Britain deployed troops throughout the Transcaucasus, filling the vacuum left there by Russia's collapse. Worse was to follow.

Even more than the loss of the empire, the prospect of Anatolia's partition had haunted the Unionists. In August 1920 the Entente powers resolved the details of that partition. Meeting in the French town of Sèvres, they concluded a treaty that left the Ottoman sultan in control of a rump "Turkish" territory in the north-central section of Anatolia. Istanbul would become an open city and the straits a demilitarized zone. Britain, France, and Italy were to assume formal "zones of influence" in Anatolia. Greece was to assume possession of not just Edirne and most of Thrace but also Izmir and its environs in Western Anatolia and the Aegean islands commanding the Dardanelles. In Eastern Anatolia, an expansive Armenian Republic was to stretch from Nagornyi Karabakh in the southeast across Van all the way to Trabzon in the northwest. To the south of Armenia the treaty placed Kurdistan, an autonomous entity expected eventually to acquire full sovereign statehood. The Treaty of Sèvres represented the Unionists' ultimate nightmare, and they had paved the road right to it.

As counterproductive as the Unionists' policies appeared to have been, the tsarist regime's quest for security on Russia's southern borders proved no less ruinous. The regime's desire to assert control over Eastern Anatolia and the straits in the name of shielding Russia's underbelly had helped create the conditions that brought about its own downfall. The wartime blockade of the Black Sea Straits had disrupted the best supply route to Russia, further straining an already burdened Russian war economy. Sazonov's commitment to a two-front war and disregard for Yudenich's warnings to seek peace with the Ottomans had overstretched Russia.[1] Although it is impossible to know with certainty whether a less aggressive policy toward the Ottoman empire before the war would have caused Istanbul to maintain neutrality or whether Russia later might have induced Istanbul to leave the war, the outcome of tsarist foreign policy could not have been worse. Before the end of 1917, the tsarist regime had been toppled, Russia had been engulfed by civil war, and the borderlands of the empire were seceding or being cleaved off.

Chaos to order

At the end of 1918, the former spaces of the Ottoman, Russian, and Austro-Hungarian empires were in disarray. Creating a new framework for order in the vast territories of the Middle East, Eurasia, and Eastern Europe was one of the challenges facing the victorious Entente powers. Shortly after the Bolsheviks had announced national self-determination as their formula for the postimperial order, President Woodrow Wilson of the United States embraced it in a bid to undercut Bolshevism, thereby

---

[1] Bobroff, *Roads*, 150–53.

ensuring that it would become a foundational principle of the postwar order. Such, perhaps, was Wilson's idealism that he believed that popular and democratic sovereignty would determine the shape of the postwar settlement. His British and French allies were decidedly less enthusiastic about the principle, but their endorsement of it was not a matter of mere rhetoric or a fraudulent pose. It heralded the emergence of a definitively different interstate system, one clearly "focused on populations and an ideal of state sovereignty rooted in national homogeneity."[2] Diplomacy and international relations were never the same afterward.

Nonetheless, states continued the competitive pursuit of interests under, and even through, the new architecture of global order. The powerful accommodated the principle of national self-determination when it served their interests and bent it when it did not. Thus during the post-Great War scramble for territory in Eastern Europe, Poland managed to extend its borders beyond those suggested by ethnography, acquiring a population that was fully one-third non-Polish thanks to its powerful army and the backing of Britain and France, who were keen to oversee the creation of barriers to the revival of German and Russian power.[3]

Neutralizing their continental rivals this way allowed Britain and France to devote greater attention to their empires overseas, including in the Middle East. In the Arab lands, they could project superior power and dominate the local societies with relative ease. Britain, concerned to enhance the security of its lines of communication to India, assumed control over Iraq and Palestine while France took Syria and Lebanon. The principle of self-determination notionally prevented the assertion of imperial ambition, but Britain and France reconciled the contradiction between that principle and their actions by inventing the concept of "mandate," whereby the newly founded League of Nations approved outside rule of a population as a form of tutelage until such time as the population was capable of self-rule.

Elsewhere in the postwar Ottoman and Romanov spheres, however, the imperial powers found it much harder to influence outcomes. The heartlands of Russia and Anatolia were comparatively remote and contained organized armed movements determined to defy the emerging world order. Indeed, the possibility that these movements might join in a grand revolutionary alliance stirred anxiety among Western policymakers. The worries were not unfounded.

---

[2] Weitz, "From the Vienna to the Paris System," 1314.
[3] Aviel Roshwald, *Ethnic Nationalism and the Fall of Empires: Central Europe, Russia, and the Middle East, 1914–1923* (New York: Routledge, 2001), 162, 164; Mark Mazower, *Dark Continent: Europe's Twentieth Century* (New York: Vintage Books, 2000), 42.

The geopolitics of inverted alliances

Sitting in Moscow in the spring of 1919, Lenin was following the course
of events to his south attentively, even as his embattled Bolshevik government waged civil war on multiple fronts. The same imperial powers seeking to snuff out his government were attempting to tame the
Near East, and so he recognized a potential ally in an embryonic Anatolian resistance movement. The leader of that movement was the unusually talented Mustafa Kemal Pasha. Unlike the sultan who was willing
to accommodate the Western powers in order to salvage the Ottoman
dynasty, Mustafa Kemal was resolute to defy them and declared his
determination to do so upon arriving in the Black Sea town of Samsun
in May 1919. He was no less perceptive than Lenin of transregional
geopolitics, and one of his very first acts as leader of Anatolia's "national
forces" (*Kuva-yı Milliye*) was to contact the Bolsheviks. By that summer,
the two were cooperating. Kemal and his followers, all but destitute and
operating in a war-ravaged land, needed guns and money. Motorboats
began picking up supplies from Odessa and other Black Sea ports, running the British naval blockade to deliver their loads to Anatolian shores.[4]
In exchange for their assistance, the Bolsheviks wanted the Caucasus.

The reversal of the geopolitical dynamics could not have been any
more stunning. In less than two years' time, Russia had metamorphosed
from the greatest threat to the Ottoman empire to the best hope for
Muslim sovereignty in Anatolia. Whereas in 1918 the Ottomans had
rejoiced at Russia's collapse and sent their army into the Caucasus to
establish anti-Russian buffer states, now the remnants of that army were
scrambling to hand those same lands over to Bolshevik Russia. The fact
that Mustafa Kemal, a self-consciously nationalist Turk, would subvert
the independence of another Turkic people, the Azeris, only heightened
the irony.

Mustafa Kemal had assumed command of the resistance movement,
but it was the Unionists who had created it. Before the end of World
War I, Enver had ordered that arms be stockpiled and cadres organized for a war of popular resistance.[5] By December 1918, organizations
with names such as the "Society for the Defense of National Rights"
(Müdafaa-i Hukuk-ı Milliye Cemiyeti) began popping up from Thrace

---

[4] Erol Mütercimler, *Denizden Gelen Destek: Sovyetler Birliğinden Alınan Yardım ve Kuva-yı
Milliye Donanması* (Ankara: Yaprak Yayınları, 1992). A list of the amount and types of
aid supplied can be found in Saime Yüceer, *Milli Mücadele Yıllarında Ankara–Moskova
İlişkileri* (Bursa: Motif Matbaası, 1997), 292–96.
[5] Erik Jan Zürcher, *The Unionist Factor: The Rôle of the Committee of Union and Progress in
the Turkish National Movement, 1905–1926* (Leiden: E. J. Brill, 1984), 68–105.

across Anatolia to Kars. These organizations took their rhetorical cues from the global discourse of nationhood and self-determination. They asserted the demographic and historical claims of Muslims to Anatolia and neighboring lands. Their use of the words *millet* and *milli*, translated typically as "nation" and "national," did not yet signal a clear ethnonational agenda. They would acquire an explicitly ethnic connotation only after the establishment of the Turkish Republic.[6] Rather, what bound the national forces together during what the Turkish Republic would come to call its "War of Independence" was not Turkish ethnic identity so much as the corporate ties of the military officers and state officials who formed the movements' cadres and the common Muslim identity that linked those cadres to the majority population of Anatolia. Fear of the dismal fate for Muslims portended by foreign rule motivated most of Anatolia's Muslim Turks, Kurds, Circassians, and multiple other ethnicities to support Mustafa Kemal's forces.[7]

The most immediate threats to Muslim sovereignty in Anatolia came from the Armenians in the east and the Greeks in the west. The two states sent their armies to claim large chunks of Anatolia. Mustafa Kemal focused first on securing his rear. Caucasia was in flux. Georgia and Armenia were clashing over border regions, including Kars, where a third group, local Muslims, had proclaimed a Government of Southwest Caucasia. Armenian forces drove Muslims from the Armenian Republic's new heartland around Yerevan, and fought Azeri formations for control of the provinces of Nagornyi Karabakh, Zangezur, and Nakhichevan. Meanwhile, the British had taken the key terminals of Batumi and Baku under control. The battle between the Red Army and anti-Bolshevik General Anton Denikin's Volunteer Army for the fate of Russia consumed the North Caucasus, eclipsing the mountaineers' struggle to maintain statehood.

The victorious Allies had lent their diplomatic approval to a "Greater Armenia" but extended little military support to the tiny Armenian army. Mustafa Kemal's main forces handily beat it back from Eastern Anatolia. Meanwhile, the Red Army, assisted by former Ottoman army personnel who urged the native Muslims not to resist, took the lowlands of Dagestan in 1919.[8] On orders from Lenin, the commander of Bolshevik armies in

[6] Erik Jan Zürcher, "The Vocabulary of Muslim Nationalism," *International Journal of the Sociology of Language*, 137 (1999), 81–92.

[7] This is a generalization. Significant groups of Muslims did pursue other agendas. See, for example, Ryan Gingeras, *Sorrowful Shores: Violence, Ethnicity, and the End of the Ottoman Empire, 1912–1923* (New York: Oxford University Press, 2009).

[8] Bülent Gökay, *A Clash of Empires: Turkey Between Russian Bolshevism and British Imperialism* (London: Tauris Academic Studies, 1997), 75.

the Caucasus, a former tsarist general, prepared to subjugate the Trans-caucasus while a special "Caucasian Bureau" under the Georgian Bol-shevik Sergo Ordzhonikidze planned how to reintegrate it politically.[9] In April 1920, responding to staged appeals for help from the Azerbaijani Communist Party and again with assistance from former Ottomans, the Red Army rolled into Baku. That same month, Mustafa Kemal and his supporters convened what they called the "Grand National Assembly" in the sleepy but remote and strategically secure Anatolian town of Ankara. When the Red Army swept into the province of Nakhichevan, Azeris accused Mustafa Kemal's men of having sold them out to the Rus-sians in order to save themselves.[10] The charge was not baseless. Indeed, the Turks' support for the Bolsheviks extended beyond the Caucasus. When in March 1921 on the island of Kronstadt the formerly staunch pro-Bolshevik sailors of the Baltic Fleet accused Lenin's government of betraying the revolution and rose in rebellion, General Ali Fuat (Cebe-soy), then serving as ambassador to Russia, intervened by appealing to two divisions of Muslim Tatars to help suppress the rebellion and thereby helped the Bolshevik regime survive one of its most critical moments.[11]

After Azerbaijan it was Armenia's turn to fall to Bolshevism. War on the Polish frontier in the spring of 1920 caused the Bolsheviks to post-pone their invasion until the fall. In October, with Turkish armies serving as the anvil and the Red Army as a hammer poised to strike, the Bol-sheviks compelled Yerevan's isolated Dashnak government to capitulate and Armenia to accept Bolshevik rule. Georgia was left standing alone. The Bolsheviks weakened the already faltering Georgian republic from within, fomenting tensions between Tiflis and Georgia's minority Osse-tians by infiltrating saboteurs into Ossetia and ordering Georgia's Bol-shevik Party to conduct strikes and destabilize the government. Then, in February 1921, the Red Army attacked, again taking advantage of Turk-ish military pressure to overwhelm the Caucasians.[12] The triumphant Reds installed pro-Bolshevik puppet governments in the three republics and converted them into nominally independent Soviet republics. Offi-cials of the republics met with representatives of Ankara on 13 October 1921 in Kars where they signed a treaty confirming an agreement the Turkish nationalists and Bolsheviks had concluded in March in Moscow. Batumi went to the Soviets, while Kars and Ardahan now belonged to

[9] Pipes, *Formation*, 224.
[10] Veysel Ünüvar, *Kurtuluş Savaşına Bolşeviklerle Sekiz Ay, 1920–1921* (Istanbul: Şirket-i Mürettebiye Basımevi, 1948), 24.
[11] Ivar Spector, "General Ali Fuat Cebesoy and the Kronstadt Revolt (1921): A Footnote to History," *International Journal of Middle East Studies*, 3, 4 (October 1972), 491–93.
[12] Figes, *Peoples' Tragedy*, 714–15.

the Turks. Due in part to Turkish lobbying, the Bolsheviks assigned the enclave of Nakhichevan not to Armenia but to Azerbaijan. They left the contested but predominantly Armenian province of Nagornyi Karabakh inside Azerbaijan, but assigned it autonomous status. The treaty squared its endorsement of self-determination with its rapid rearrangement of borders by granting the affected populations the temporary right to emigrate from one state to the other.

With his rear in the Caucasus secured, Mustafa Kemal turned toward the west. He compelled the French to withdraw from Anatolia southward into Syria and the British and Italians to relinquish their pretensions to influence in Anatolia. Unlike the Armenians, the Greeks did receive meaningful aid from the Allies. Nonetheless, Mustafa Kemal in 1922 managed to drive the Greek army out of Anatolia back to Greece, sending hundreds of thousands of Orthodox Christian Anatolians in train. The following January Turkey and Greece finalized an "exchange" of populations that formalized the transfer of approximately 1.2 million Christians to Greece and nearly 400,000 Muslims to Turkey.[13] These measures, combined with the earlier massacres and ethnic cleansing of Armenians and Assyrians, transformed Anatolia's population into an overwhelmingly Muslim, if not yet wholly Turkish, one.

Mustafa Kemal's achievement of military dominance over Anatolia nullified the Treaty of Sèvres, compelling the great powers to sit with his representatives in Lausanne, Switzerland, in 1923 and conclude a new treaty that acknowledged the territorial integrity and full sovereignty of the new Anatolian hegemon, the Republic of Turkey. The capitulations and compromised statehood of the Ottomans were no more. During the same period, the Bolshevik state consolidated its control over virtually all of the former Russian Empire except for Poland, Finland, Bessarabia and what became the Baltic states of Lithuania, Latvia, and Estonia. Initially regarded as a rogue or outcast state, by the middle of the 1920s the Soviet Union had won recognition from most of the great powers.

The fact that Mustafa Kemal and Lenin worked together did not mean that their relationship lacked a competitive dimension. The Bolsheviks nurtured ambitions of cultivating influence throughout the Muslim world, including Anatolia. Toward that end, they hosted the First Congress of the Peoples of the East in Baku in September 1920. Among the participants were Enver Pasha, who through Karl Radek had come to Moscow with the hope that the Bolsheviks would relaunch his career inside Anatolia, and Mustafa Suphi, who founded the Turkish Communist Party right after the congress. Mustafa Kemal, however,

[13] Onur Yıldırım, *Diplomacy and Displacement: Reconsidering the Turco-Greek Exchange of Populations, 1922–1934* (New York: Routledge, 2006).

parried the Bolsheviks by blocking Enver's return and establishing a rival communist party under his control.[14] The Kemalist regime's unyielding pursuit of centralization, Turkification, and secularization stirred some Kurds to revolt, and, in the middle of the 1920s, the Soviet Union attempted to revive its influence in Anatolia by lending support to Kurdish exiles plotting rebellion. The Kemalist regime's determination and coercive capabilities, however, were greater than those of its Unionist predecessor, and it handily suppressed this and other challenges to its rule in Eastern Anatolia.[15]

The Soviets found more opportunities next door inside chaotic postwar Iran. In 1920 a Shi'i cleric named Muhammad Khiyabani, who had picked up socialist ideas during several years spent in Russia's Caucasus, established inside Iran a socialist state of sorts called Azadistan, or "Freedom Land." On Iran's Caspian shore, Red Army units fresh from the recapture of Baku helped the Iranian revolutionary Mirza Kuchuk Khan found a "Soviet Republic of Gilan." When, however, Moscow concluded a treaty of friendship with Tehran in 1921, it withdrew support, and both the Gilan Republic and Azadistan fell to Tehran's army.

Parallels in postimperial paths

Just as the dynamic of interstate competition pushed Ankara and Moscow to adopt complementary foreign policies, it also elicited parallels in domestic policies. Whereas the origins of the Turkish Republic lay in a project to adapt to the interstate order, the Soviet state was born in defiance of that order, but in a matter of years it too would conform. As heirs to defeated empires, the Kemalist and Soviet elites came to share the conviction that the survival of their respective states demanded comprehensive and radical reform not just of the institutions of state but also of society, economy, and culture as a whole. The centrality of the motif of revolution to the Bolsheviks needs no elaboration. Less well known is that the Kemalists dubbed their program of radical reform the "Turkish Revolution" (*Türk İnkılâbı*), and that they even drew some inspiration from the Soviet model of state-led development.[16]

The geopolitical imperative for modernization was from the beginning foremost for the Unionists' successors, the Kemalists. Experience had seared into them the lesson that poorly educated and technologically backward populations suffered. This was the meaning of modernity. As

---

[14] Unlike Enver, Suphi managed to enter Anatolia, but was murdered at sea outside Trabzon in January 1921 under unclear circumstances. On Suphi, see Aslan, *Türkiye Komünist Fırkası'nın Kuruluşu ve Mustafa Suphi.*

[15] McDowall, *Kurds*, 192–207.   [16] Lewis, *Emergence*, 470–71.

Mustafa Kemal put it, "Uncivilized people are doomed to be trodden under the feet of civilized people."[17] The Bolsheviks initially gave little thought to the geopolitical imperatives of modernization, expecting world revolution to sweep the interstate system away along with capitalism. Yet, as Orlando Figes has observed, among those who threw their weight behind the Bolsheviks during the Russian Civil War was a small but critical constituency of military officers and bureaucrats who believed that Russia needed the sort of rapid modernization the Bolsheviks promised.[18] As hopes for world revolution faded and the Bolsheviks resigned themselves to building "socialism in one country," the geopolitical imperative of modernization grew in importance until it became a leitmotif under Stalin. Addressing an audience of workers in 1931 during his campaign for breakneck industrialization, Stalin famously recounted Russia's defeats over the prior centuries to warn, "those who fall behind get beaten . . . We are fifty or a hundred years behind the advanced countries. We must make good this distance in ten years. Either we do it, or they crush us."[19]

The Kemalist and Soviet elites saw themselves as strong-willed, elite vanguards of progressive change, uniquely capable of imposing the necessary if often resented modernizing reforms upon their as yet unenlightened populations. They both judged religion to be a source of superstitious ignorance and an impediment to the propagation of positive science, a *sine qua non* for modernization. They also saw religion as subversive of the state because of its association with the old regime and because it advanced rival claims to truth. Militant secularism therefore was another key common component of their worldviews and policies, although the Turkish Republic never dared turn its campaign against religion into an outright assault as the Soviet Union did.

One area where the two regimes diverged, however, was in their policies on ethnonational identity. Aside from the minority identities of Orthodox Greek, Armenian, and Jew specified in the Treaty of Lausanne, the Turkish Republic recognized just one identity, that of "Turk." Existing in perpetual dread of a new Sèvres, the republican elites regarded assertions of identities other than that of Sunni Turk as inherently destabilizing and subversive, and suppressed them vigorously. They imposed a rigorous program of linguistic and cultural Turkification, seeking to

[17] Mango, *Atatürk*, 438.
[18] Figes, *People's Tragedy*, 591. Former tsarist officers serving in the Red Army numbered 75,000 and constituted three-quarters of its senior leadership: A. G. Kavtaradze, *Voennye spetsialisty na sluzhbe Respubliki Sovetov, 1917–1920 gg.* (Moscow: Nauka, 1988), 221–23.
[19] Joseph Stalin, "The Breakneck Speed of Industrialization," in *Stalin and Stalinism*, ed. Martin McCauley (London: Longman, 1995), 92–93.

transform Anatolia's Muslims into a homogeneous and indivisible nation. The assimilation of the multiple but scattered and small communities of non-Turkish Muslims proved remarkably successful over time. The great exception, however, was the Kurds, who by virtue of their large numbers – between 10 and 20 percent of Turkey's population – and compact settlement in Eastern Anatolia proved resistant to assimilation.[20]

Turkey's adoption of an aggressively nationalist ideology was by no means unusual, and in fact adhered to a general pattern followed by its neighbors in the Balkans and Middle East. The Soviet Union, by contrast, implemented an exceptional approach toward national identity. Like the Kemalists, the Bolsheviks conceived of national identity as a component of modernization. Yet whereas the Kemalists saw the creation of a national identity as the ultimate end of their revolution, the Bolsheviks understood national identity to be a necessary but temporary stage toward the emergence of a universal class identity. Far from suppressing ethnic identities, the Bolsheviks required every Soviet subject to acquire one. The Soviet Union recognized well over 100 national identities, codifying each according to a standard template to ensure that every nation had a defined territory, distinct language, national poet, costume, flag, etc. With this process, they stamped clear ethnonational identities upon populations that had lacked them, such as Central Asian Muslims. The point was not to give expression to national sentiment for its own sake but to develop and channel it toward the ends of socialism and the Soviet state.[21] The Communist Party controlled all manifestations of nationalism and made sure to restrain and at times repress even Russian identity.[22]

Notably, the Soviet state's embrace of ethnic pluralism did not prevent it from looking with suspicion upon border populations. Whereas during the early 1920s Moscow had imagined it might exploit its populations' crossborder ethnic ties to subvert neighboring states, by the 1930s it had come to fear precisely the opposite process. Thus between 1935 and 1938, the Soviet authorities deported, arrested, or executed approximately 800,000 individuals in ethnic cleansing operations. Ethnic chauvinism played no role in these actions. Instead, anxieties about state security drove them.[23]

[20] Soner Çağaptay, *Islam, Secularism, and Nationalism: Who is a Turk?* (New York: Routledge, 2006), 11–40.

[21] The standard work on Soviet nationalities policy is Martin, *Affirmative Action Empire.* See also Francine Hirsch, *Empire of Nations: Ethnographic Knowledge and the Making of the Soviet Union* (Ithaca: Cornell University Press, 2005).

[22] Geoffrey Hosking, *Rulers and Victims: The Russians in the Soviet Union* (Cambridge, MA: Belknap Press of Harvard University Press, 2006), 70–89.

[23] Terry Martin, "The Origins of Soviet Ethnic Cleansing," *Journal of Modern History,* 70, 4 (December 1998), 858.

Population politics returned with a fury to the old Russo-Ottoman borderlands when in 1944 Stalin ordered the mass deportation of the Chechens, Ingush, Balkars, Kalmyks, Meskhetian Turks, and Crimean Tatars from their homelands to Central Asia and Siberia with horrific losses.[24] Although the Soviet authorities justified the deportations with accusations of collaboration with the invading Germans, the fact that they conducted the deportations after the German threat had been turned back suggests the real motive was likely related to demands Stalin made the following year for Turkey to surrender Kars and Ardahan and permit Soviet naval bases in the Black Sea Straits. As Stalin and his foreign minister Viacheslav Molotov explained to US president Harry Truman and British prime minister Winston Churchill in the summer of 1945, Kars and Ardahan properly belonged to Soviet Armenia and Georgia, not Turkey. Poland, Stalin pointed out, had just reconsidered the injustice of its expansion in 1921 and adjusted its borders with the Soviet Union. He suggested Turkey might do the same.[25]

Stalin was rejoining the struggle for Anatolia and the Caucasus. He was already active in Iran, where in 1941 the Soviets in conjunction with the British had invaded and occupied the country to ensure that in this war against Germany supply lines to Russia stayed open. Alongside the Soviet army returned the cadres of Iranians who had fled to the Soviet Union following the collapse of the Azadistan and Gilan Republics. These exiles had assimilated Soviet conceptions of national identity, and together with Iranian Azeris and Iranian and Iraqi Kurds they invoked ethnicity to establish inside Iran Azerbaijani and Kurdish governments. Interstate dynamics, however, proved decisive. Stalin's challenges to the territorial integrity of Turkey and Iran had alarmed the United States. Relenting under Washington's pressure in some of the Cold War's first scuffles, Stalin withdrew his demands regarding Kars and Ardahan and the straits as well as his support for the nascent Iranian Azerbaijani and Kurdish governments, sealing their fate. The Iranian army made short work of them at the end of 1946.[26]

---

[24] A. M. Nekrich, *The Punished Peoples: The Deportation and Fate of Soviet Minorities at the End of the Second World War*, tr. George Saunders (New York: Norton, 1978).

[25] *Sovetskii soiuz na mezhdunarodnykh konferentsiiakh perioda Velikoi otechestvennoi voiny 1941–1945*, vol. VI, *Berlinskaia (Potsdamskaia) konferentsiia rukovoditelei trekh soiuznykh derzhav – SSSR, SShA Velikobritaniia (17 iiulia–2 avgusta 1945 g.)*, ed. A. A. Gromyko et al. (Moscow: Izdatel'stvo politicheskoi literatury, 1980), 40–41, 145, 158.

[26] Jamil Hasanli, *At the Dawn of the Cold War: The Soviet–American Crisis over Iranian Azerbaijan, 1941–1946* (New York: Rowman and Littlefield, 2006); Louise L'Estrange Fawcett, *Iran and the Cold War: The Azerbaijan Crisis of 1946* (New York: Cambridge University Press, 1992); William Eagleton, *The Kurdish Republic of 1946* (London: Oxford University Press, 1963).

A balance sheet

Turks sometimes refer to the period from the beginning of the Balkan Wars in 1912 to the conclusion of the Turkish War of Independence as a single conflict, the Ten Years War.[27] There is a good case to be made for such a classification. As we have seen, contemporary observers believed the Balkan Wars signaled the imminent end of the Ottoman empire. In order to forestall that outcome and win some breathing space, the Unionists joined with Germany in 1914 and entered World War I. During that war, Russia and its allies resolved the question of how to partition the Ottoman Empire. The death warrant for the Ottoman empire had been signed, and Russia could claim its share, the straits and Eastern Anatolia.

That plan to divide the Ottoman empire fell apart in 1917 when Russia succumbed to revolution and civil war. Istanbul sought to exploit Russia's moment of disarray to establish a belt of one or more buffer states in the Caucasus. The war, however, ended not with the anticipated negotiated settlement but instead with the Central Powers' capitulation. Defeat caused the Unionist leadership to flee. The organizational structure that they left behind, however, endured and made possible the victory of Mustafa Kemal's national forces in 1922. The land over which the national forces consolidated control in 1922 was ravaged, destitute, and in ruins, but it was indisputably theirs. They had driven out the European powers and their local Armenian and Greek allies and then at Lausanne won the powers' acceptance of the new Turkish Republic as a sovereign equal. The Unionists' efforts had ultimately paid off with the achievement of these two long-term objectives.

The Unionists had managed to salvage an independent state from their unraveling empire despite the long odds against them because they had understood the changing nature of world order and had prepared for it. The Ottoman empire's prolonged experience of defeat had conditioned the Unionists' worldview, attuning them to the unsentimental dynamics of power politics and teaching them an acute sense of their own limits as well as those of their opponents. The looming prospect of foreign domination had spurred them to organize while in opposition and braced them for protracted struggles while in power. Their achievement of an independent state was a rare feat in the non-Western world at this time.

The Romanov regime, by contrast, disappeared along with its empire. Russia's state institutions had never faced incentives to reform as dire or

---

[27] Fahrettin Altay, *10 Yıl Savaş, 1912–1922 ve Sonrası* (Istanbul: İnsel Yayınları, 1970).

persistent as those the Ottomans faced. Consequently, they never produced a constituency for reform as radical or determined as the CUP.
Nonetheless, a considerable number of tsarist officials had been harboring anxieties over the regime's archaic nature and comparative weakness
and went on to assist the Bolsheviks in virtually recreating the Romanov
empire in territorial terms and making the Soviet Union a new great
power. One might suggest that, because the Bolsheviks went on to forge
an industrial and technologically proficient state that prevailed in World
War II and emerged as a global superpower, their rise and rule were
ultimately salutary for Russia. So bloody and destructive was Soviet
communism, however, that the case for Bolshevism as a prophylactic
is unconvincing. It is difficult to regard the Russian experience between
1908 and 1918 as anything other than a tragedy.

If Russia's fate was tragic in the sense that Russia's own actions brought
upon it the very calamity it had been seeking to avoid, the fate of the
Armenians was the cruelest irony. One might have expected that among
the peoples of Anatolia and the Caucasus the Armenians stood to benefit the most from the changing politics and economics of the twentieth
century. They possessed the highest rates of literacy and, arguably, the
strongest – if yet very far from homogeneous – collective identity. Positioned between two imperial states, they had multiple options to advance
their interests. They could maintain neutrality and sit passively, align with
one empire against the other, or appeal to outside powers. In reality, however, none of their options were good. Despite the strength of their identity, the national idea fit the Armenians' situation poorly, converting them
into threats to their neighbors and objects of the power politics of outsiders whether they wanted to be or not. Because they were settled thinly
throughout Eastern Anatolia and the Caucasus, claims of theirs to territorial sovereignty were weak and provocative and available for manipulation
against one or other empire, or both. At the same time, the instability
and economic and political conditions in Eastern Anatolia made passive
acceptance of the status quo unbearable for Ottoman Armenians. The
Armenian reform program of February 1914 had promised a step toward
a resolution of sorts. It also, however, constituted a direct challenge to
Ottoman sovereignty and the future of Eastern Anatolia's Muslims. The
outbreak of war in August effectively deprived the Armenians of options.
The Unionists, acting in concert with local tribes in Anatolia, effectively
destroyed the Armenian community, expunging them from the greater
part of what had been their historical homeland. True, an Armenian
Republic had been established and would guaranty the preservation of
Armenian language and culture, but it amounted to a rump of historical
Armenia and fell to Moscow's control.

The Kurds too suffered horrendously yet, arguably, had even less to show for it than the Armenians. Prior to 1914 most of them had inhabited a unified space in the Ottoman empire. Sunni Kurds could claim equality as subjects and possessed a tie to the Ottoman caliph. After 1922, however, they found themselves divided among three new states – Turkey, Syria, and Iraq – as well as Iran and the Soviet Union. All these states embraced ethnic identity as a political category. Although only Turkey actually forbade Kurdish identity, none was sympathetic to expressions of Kurdishness, and the Kurds found the new national regimes more intrusive and repressive than the older imperial ones.

Elsewhere in the Transcaucasus, the outcomes were more favorable. The Georgians overall had risked relatively little, and, albeit still under Moscow's political and economic domination, they could now claim cultural primacy within the territory demarcated as the Georgian Republic. Georgia's minorities, and in particular the Abkhaz and Ossetians, were in a less enviable position, but they too were recognized as nations and had Moscow to keep Tiflis in check. In 1936, Moscow abolished the Transcaucasian Soviet Federated Socialist Republic and bestowed upon Georgia, Armenia and Azerbaijan privileged status as soviet republics, the highest administrative division of the Union of Soviet Socialist Republics. This elevation in status was particularly advantageous to the Azeris, who had a comparatively weak sense of national identity.

The Muslim mountaineers of the North Caucasians had fewer reasons to be sanguine. Their desperate resistance against the Bolsheviks had failed, and Bolshevik repression was harsh. Collectivization would inflict misery here as elsewhere in the Soviet Union, and geopolitics would revisit havoc on the North Caucasus with the deportations of 1944. Those who in 1918 had striven to create a united Mountaineer state saw their efforts dashed when the Soviets divided their lands according to ethnicity, with the exception of polyethnic Dagestan. Yet at the same time, the creation of different autonomous regions and the recognition of multiple ethnicities was a boon to some local cadres and groups.

While surveying the aftermath of the collapse of imperial order in Europe, Eurasia, and the Middle East after World War I, an analyst observed:

The present political structure of Europe is the result of the violent resolution, into what are in theory uni-national states of the modern type, of the great supranational empires which (in whole up to a century ago and for the greater part up to 1914) had divided between them the belt of mixed population . . . Well treated or not, the submerged nationalities had come, with hardly an exception, to entertain as their true and ultimate ambition the ideal of complete independence . . . The desires of the subject nationalities for freedom enjoyed considerable sympathy among liberal opinion in western Europe, which saw in them a struggle of democracy against tyranny.[28]

The expectation had been that the shattering of empires would liberate nations, bring freedom, and improve the lives of their individual members. In short, good would triumph over evil. The results, however, were mixed at best. The same analyst continued:

The result of the Peace Settlement was that every state in the belt of mixed population, with [a] few modifications . . . now looked upon itself as a national state. But the facts were against them. Not one of these states was, in fact, uni-national, just as there was not, on the other hand, one nation all of whose members lived in a single state.[29]

The national idea had triumphed in form, but not in content. The empires, or at least the defeated ones, were gone. Nation-states had been created, but some twenty-five to thirty million people, or nearly one-quarter of the states' populations, were now officially minorities.[30] The nations, too, had been shattered, first by warring empires and states and then by peacemaking ones.

The "belt of mixed population" extended from Europe into Eurasia and the Near East. Earlier generations of historians tended to see developments inside Europe and those on its periphery as largely separate, with autonomous dynamics shaped by regional patterns of culture and civilization. Today it has become more common to acknowledge the parallels and interconnections in the upheavals that shook all these lands in the nineteenth and twentieth centuries. Calling the Eastern Question "Europe's continuous calamity," one such interpretation argues that the ethnic passions and conflicts that brought down the empires along Europe's periphery ultimately penetrated and destabilized Europe's center.[31] This study, by contrast, has focused on the institutions and actors that prosecute conflict rather than on the identities and passions generated by conflict. It has contended that the export from Europe of a new form of global order centered on the national idea better explains the transformation of conflicts in Europe's periphery and beyond into ethnonational ones. As interstate competition undermined and destroyed empires, the global order gave increasing valence to a form of political legitimacy tied to ethnicity. As movements and actors emerging from the ruins of empire struggled for statehood, they complied with and then embraced

[28] C. A. Macartney, *National States and National Minorities* (London: Oxford University Press, 1934), 179.
[29] Macartney, *National States*, 210.   [30] Macartney, *National States*, 211.
[31] Dan Diner, *Cataclysms: A History of the Twentieth Century from Europe's Edge*, tr. William Temple and Joel Golb (Madison: University of Wisconsin Press, 2008), 7–8.

the national idea, ensuring the proliferation of the nation-state or, as in the Russian case, its imitation in the form of Soviet republics.

This study at the outset questioned the veracity of certain lessons of history, and in particular the lesson of the anachronism of empire in an age of nationalism. Yet it would endorse one lesson as old as Thucydides' history of the Peloponnesian War: The quest for absolute security is the road to ruin. Security can be no more absolute than the future can be knowable. Anxiety is the permanent human condition. The potential threat by its nature is omnipresent and impossible to vanquish. To chase it means to provoke reactions, setting off chains of events beyond one's control. Inevitably, some of those chains will lead to adverse consequences. The severity of those consequences will vary, and some will be negligible. Sooner or later, however, some will prove catastrophic.

Select bibliography

ARCHIVES

GENELKURMAY ASKERÎ TARİH VE STRATEJİC ETÜT BAŞKANLIĞI ARŞİVİ
Balkan Harbi
Birinci Dünya Harbi
İstiklâl Harbi

BAŞBAKANLIK OSMANLI ARŞİVİ (ISTANBUL)
Bab-ı Alî Evrak Odası
Harbiye Gelen-Giden
Harbiye Takrir
Hariciye Gelen-Giden
Hariciye Müteferrikası

Dahiliye Nezareti
İdarî Kısım (DH.İD)
İdâre-i Umumiye (DH.İUM)
Kalem-i Mahsûs Müdûriyeti (DH.KMS)
Muhaberât-ı Umumiye İdaresi (DH.MUİ)
Şifre Kalemi (DH.ŞFR)
Siyasî Kısım (DH.SYS)

Hariciye Nezareti
Hukuk Müşavirliği İstişare Odası (HR.HMŞ.İSO)

Meclis-i Vükelâ Mazbataları

TÜRK TARİH KURUMU (ANKARA)
Enver Paşa Arşivi
Kâzım Orbay Arşivi

GOSUDARSTVENNYI ARKHIV ROSSIISKII FEDERATSII (MOSCOW)
Ministerstvo iustitsii (fond 124)

Biuro zaveduiushchego zagranichnoi agenturoi Departamenta
politsii v Konstantinopole (fond 529)

ROSSIISKII GOSUDARSTVENNYI ARKHIV VNESHNEI POLITIKI
ROSSIISKOI IMPERII (MOSCOW)

Turetskii stol (fond 129)
Arkhiv "Voina" (fond 134)
Osobyi politicheskii otdel (fond 135)
Sekretnyi arkhiv ministra (fond 138)
Persidskii stol (fond 144)
Politicheskii arkhiv (fond 151)
Aziatskii departament (fond 161/4)
Posol'stvo v Konstantinopole (fond 180)
Diplomaticheskaia kantseliariia pri Stavke (fond 323)

ROSSIISKII GOSUDARSTVENNYI VOENNO-ISTORICHESKII ARKHIV
(MOSCOW)

Turtsiia (fond 450)
Shtab Kavkazskoi armii (fond 2168)
Upravlenie inspektora opolchenskikh chastei Kavkazskoi armii
(fond 2169)
Pervyi Kavkazskii kavaleriiskii korpus (fond 2320)
Tret'aia Kubanskaia plastunskaia brigada (fond 15243)
Tylovoi sud Kavkazskoi armii (fond 15244)
Dagestanskii konnyi polk g. Temir-Khan-Shura (fond 15568)

POLITISCHES ARCHIV DES AUSWÄRTIGES AMTES (BERLIN)

Rußland

HOUGHTON LIBRARY, HARVARD UNIVERSITY (CAMBRIDGE, MA)

Georgian Archive

OFFICIAL PUBLICATIONS AND COLLECTIONS OF DOCUMENTS

Adamov, E.A., ed. *Konstaninopl' i prolivy po sekretnym dokumentam byvshego ministerstva inostrannykh del.* 2 vols. Moscow: Litizdat NKID, 1925–26.
  ed. *Razdel Aziatskoi Turtsii po sekretnym dokumentam byvshego Ministerstva inostrannykh del.* Moscow: Litizdat NKID, 1924.
Alikberov, G. A., ed. *Bor'ba za ustanovlenie Sovetskoi vlasti v Dagestane, 1917–1921 gg: sbornik dokumentov i materialov.* Moscow: Izdatel'stvo Akademii nauk SSSR, 1958.

Arkomed, S. T., ed. *Materialy po istorii otpadeniia Zakavkaz'ia ot Rossii*. Tiflis: Gosizdat Gruzii, 1931.

Bardakçı, Murat, ed. *Talât Paşa'nın Evrak-ı Metrûkesi*. İstanbul: Everest Yayınları, 2008.

Binark, İsmet, ed. *Osmanlı Belgelerinde Ermeniler*. 2nd edn. Ankara: T. C. Başbakanlık Devlet Arşivleri Genel Müdürlüğü, 1994.

Burdett, Anita L. P., ed. *Armenia: Political and Ethnic Boundaries*. Slough, UK: Archive Editions, 1998.

Butaev, M. D., ed. *Soiuz ob"edinennykh gortsev Severnogo Kavkaza i Dagestana (1917–1918 gg.), Gorskaia Respublika (1918–1920 gg.)*. Makhachkala: Institut istorii, arkheologii i etnografii DNTs RAN, 1994.

Degras, Jane, ed. *Soviet Documents on Foreign Policy*. Vol. I. New York: Oxford University Press, 1951.

Dimanshtein, S. M., ed. *Revoliutsiia i natsional'nyi vopros: dokumenty i materialy po istorii natsional'nogo voprosa v Rossii i SSSR v XX veke*. Vol. III. Moscow: Kommunisticheskaia akademiia, 1930.

Dugdale, E. T. S., ed. *German Diplomatic Documents, 1871–1914, vol. IV, The Descent to the Abyss, 1911–1914*. New York: Harper and Brothers, 1931.

Gal'perina, B. D., ed. *Sovet ministrov Rossiiskoi imperii v gody pervoi mirovoi voiny: bumagi A. N. Iakhontova*. St. Petersburg: Dmitrii Bulanin, 1999.

Genelkurmay Askeri Tarih ve Stratejik Etüt Başkanlığı. *Askerî Tarih Belgeleri Dergisi*, 31, 81 (December 1982).

Georgia, Republic of. *Dokumenty i materialy po vneshnei politike Zakavkaz'ia i Gruzii*. Tiflis: Tipografiia pravitel'stva Gruzinskoi respubliki, 1919.

Hurewitz, J. C. *Diplomacy in the Middle East: A Documentary Record, 1535–1956*. 2 vols. Reprint, Gerrards Cross, UK: Archive Editions, 1987.

Institut des langues orientales (Russia). *Sbornik diplomaticheskikh dokumentov: reformy v Armenii, 26 noiabria 1912 goda–10 maia 1914 goda*. Petrograd: Gosudarstvennaia tipografiia, 1915.

Kliuchnikov, Iu. V. and Andrei Sabanin, eds. *Mezhdunarodnaia politika noveishego vremeni v dogovorakh, notakh, i deklaratsiiakh*. Moscow: Litizdat NKID, 1925.

Kommissia po izdaniiu dokumentov epokhi imperializma. *Mezhdunarodnye otnosheniia v epokhu imperializma*. Moscow and Leningrad: Gosudarstvennoe sotsial'no-ekonomicheskoe izdatel'stvo, 1931–40.

Lenin, V. I. *Leninskii sbornik*. Vol. XXXVI. Moscow: Institut Marksizma-Leninizma pri KPSS, 1959.

Minets, I. and E. Gorodetskii, eds. *Dokumenty po istorii grazhdanskoi voiny v SSSR*. Vol. I. Moscow: Politizdat, 1941.

Münir Süreyya Bey. *Ermeni Meselesinin Siyasî Tarihçesi (1877–1914)*. Ed. Uğurhan Demirbaş, et al. Ankara: Başbakanlık Basımevi, 2001.

Pokrovskii, M. N. "Stavka i ministerstvo inostrannykh del." *Krasnyi arkhiv: istoricheskii zhurnal*, 26 (1928), i–50; 27 (1928), 3–57; 28 (1928), 3–58; 29 (1928), 3–54; 30 (1928), 5–45.

Popov, A. "Turetskaia revoliutsiia – 1908–1909." *Krasnyi arkhiv: istoricheskii zhurnal*, 43 (1930), 3–54; 44 (1931), 3–39; 45 (1931), 27–52.

Russia, Ministerstvo inostrannykh del. *Sbornik diplomaticheskikh dokumentov kasaiushchikhsia sobytii v Persii. Vypusk VII (s 1 iiulia po 31 dekabria 1911 g.)*. St. Peterburg: Gosudarstvennaia tipografiia, 1913.

Rustamova-Togidi, Solmaz, ed. *Mart 1918 g. Baku: azerbaidzhanskie pogromy v dokumentakh*. Baku: n.p., 2009.

Sovetskii soiuz na mezhdunarodnykh konferentsiiakh perioda Velikoi otechestvennoi voiny 1941–1945, vol. VI, *Berlinskaia (Potsdamskaia) konferentsiia rukovoditelei trekh soiuznykh derzhav – SSSR, SShA i Velikobritaniia (17 iiulia–2 avgusta 1945 g.)*. Ed. A. A. Gromyko, *et al.* (Moscow: Izdatel'stvo politicheskoi literatury, 1980).

Turkey, Prime Ministry. *Documents on Ottoman Armenians*. Vol. III. Ankara: Directorate of Press and Information, 1986.

Türkiye Büyük Millet Meclisi. *Meclis-i Mebusan Zabıt Ceridesi*. Ankara: TBMM Basımevi, 1991.

United States, Department of State. *Proceedings of the Brest-Litovsk Peace Conference: The Peace Negotiations Between Russia and the Central Powers, 21 November 1917–3 March 1918* (Washington, DC: Government Printing Office, 1918).

USSR (Union of Soviet Socialist Republics), Ministerstvo inostrannykh del. *Dokumenty vneshnei politiki SSSR*. Vol. I. Moscow: Politizdat, 1959.

Zhordaniia, Noi. *Za dva goda: doklady i rechi*. Tiflis: Istoricheskaia kommissia Ispolnitel'nogo komiteta soveta rabochikh deputatov, 1919.

NEWSPAPERS AND PERIODICALS

İkdam (Istanbul)
Izvestiia (Moscow)
The Orient (Istanbul)
Sabah (Istanbul)
Servet-i Fünun (Istanbul)
Tanin (Istanbul)
Tasvir-i Efkâr (Istanbul)
Vakit (Istanbul)
Voennyi sbornik (St. Petersburg)

FIRST-HAND ACCOUNTS AND MEMOIRS

Avalov, Zurab. *Nezavisimost' Gruzii v mezhdunarodnoi politike, 1918–1921 gg.* New York: Chalidze Publications, [1924] 1982.

Aydemir, Şevket Süreyya. *Suyu Arayan Adam*. Istanbul: Ramzi Kitabevi, 1995.

Balakian, Grigoris. *Armenian Golgotha*, tr. and ed. Peter Balakian and Aris Sevag. New York: Alfred Knopf, 2009.

Bammate, Haidar. *The Caucasus Problem*. Berne: n.p., 1919.

Bayar, Celal. *Ben de Yazdım*. Vol. I. Istanbul: Baha Matbaası, 1965.

Bedirhan, Abdurrezak. *Otobiyografya (1910–1916)*. Tr. Hasan Cunî. Ankara: Perî Yayınları, 2000.

Bekguliants, R. *Po Turetskoi Armenii*. Rostov on Don: Tipografiia Ia. M. Iskidarova, 1914.

Berkok, İsmail. *Askerî Mecmua'nın Tarih Kısmı: Büyük Harpte Şimali Kafkasya'daki Faaliyetlerimiz ve 15. Fırkanın Harekâtı ve Muharabeleri*. Ankara: Askerî Matbaa, 1934.

Beury, Charles E. *Russia After the Revolution*. Philadelphia: George W. Jacobs & Company, 1918.

Butbay, Mustafa. *Kafkasya Hatıraları*. Ankara: Türk Tarih Kurumu, 1992.

Cebesoy, Ali Fuat. *Milli Mücadele Hatıraları*. Istanbul: Vatan Neşriyatı, 1953.

Cemal Paşa. *Hatıralar ve Vesikalar*, vol. II, *Harp Kabinelerinin İsticvabı* Istanbul: Vakit, 1933.

Hatırat. Ed. Metin Martı. Istanbul: Arma Yayınları, [1920] 1996.

Czernin, Ottokar. *In the World War*. New York: Harper and Brothers Publishers, 1920.

Edib Adıvar, Halidé. *Memoirs of Halide Edib*. London: Century Co., 1926.

Eliseev, F. I. *Kazaki na Kavkazskom fronte*. Moscow: Voenizdat, 2001.

Emirî, Ali. *Osmanlı Vilâyât-ı Şarkiyesi*. Dar ul-Hilafete al-Aliye: Evkaf-ı İslâmiye Matbaası, 1334 [1918].

Erdoğan, Fahrettin. *Türk Ellerinde Hatıralarım*. Ankara: T. C. Kültür Bakanlığı, 1998.

Ertürk, Hüsamettin. *İki Devrin Perde Arkası*. Ed. Samih Nafiz Tansu. Istanbul: Sebil Yayınevi, 1996.

Guinness, Walter. "Impressions of Armenia and Kurdistan." *National Review*, 62 (September 1913–February 1914), 789–801.

Halil Paşa. *Bitmeyen Savaş*. Ed. M. Taylan Sorgun, Istanbul: Yaylacık Matbaası, 1972.

Heazell, F. N. and Mrs. Margoliouth, eds. *Kurds and Christians*. London: Wells Gardner, Darton and Co., 1913.

Hoffmann, Max. *War Diaries and Other Papers*. Vol. II. Tr. Eric Sutton. London: Martin Secker Ltd., 1929.

Iakhontov, A. N., *Prologue to Revolution: Notes of A. N. Iakhontov on the Secret Meetings of the Council of Ministers 1915*. Ed. Michael Cherniavsky. Englewood Cliffs, NJ: Prentice Hall, 1967.

İlden, Köprülü Şerif. *Sarıkamış: Birinci Dünya Savaşı Başlangıcında Üçüncü Ordu Kuşatma Manevrası ve Meydan Savaşı*. Ed. Sami Önal. Istanbul: Türkiye İş Bankası Kültür Yayınları, 1998.

İlter, Aziz Samih. *Büyük Harpte Kafkas Cephesi Hatıraları: Zivinden Peterice*. Ankara: Büyük Erkân-ı Harbiye Matbaası, 1934.

İzzet, Süleyman. *Askerî Mecmua'nın Tarih Kısmı: Büyük Harpte 15. Piyade Tümeninin Azerbaycan ve Şimalî Kafkasya'daki Hareket ve Muharebeleri*. Istanbul: Askerî Matbaa, 1936.

Kalmykow, Andrew D. *Memoirs of a Russian Diplomat: Outposts of the Empire, 1893–1917*. New Haven: Yale University Press, 1971.

Karabekir, Kâzım. *Doğunun Kurtuluşu: Erzincan ve Erzurum'un Kurtuluşu. Sarıkamış, Kars, ve Ötesi*. Erzurum: Erzurum Ticaret ve Sanayi Odası, 1990.

Keykurun, Naki. *Azerbaycan İstiklâl Mücadelesinden Hatıralar (1905–1920)*. Ankara: İlke Kitabevi, 1998.

Kühlmann, Richard von. *Thoughts on Germany*. Tr. Eric Sutton. London: Macmillan & Co. Ltd., 1932.

Lermioğlu, Muzaffer. *Akçaabat: Akçaabat Tarihi ve Birinci Genel Savaşı: Hicret Hatıraları*. Istanbul: Kardeşler Basımevi, 1949.

Liman von Sanders, Otto Viktor Karl. *Five Years in Turkey*. Berlin: August Scherl, 1920. Reprint, Annapolis, MD: United States Naval Institute, 1927.

Mehmetzade, Mirza Bala. *Milli Azerbaycan Hareketi*. Ed. Ahmet Karaca. Ankara: Azerbaycan Kültür Merkezi, 1991.

Menteşe, Halil. *Osmanlı Mebusan Meclisi Reisi Halil Menteşe'nin Anıları*. Istanbul: Hürriyet Vakfı Yayınları, 1986.

Mikoian, A. I. *Dorogoi bor'by*. Moscow: Politizdat, 1971.

Nogales, Rafael de. *Four Years Beneath the Crescent*. Tr. Muna Lee. New York: Charles Scribner's Sons, 1926.

Ordzhonikidze, Sergo. *Stat'i i rechi*. Vol. I. Moscow: Gosizdat politicheskoi literatury, 1956.

Polivanov, A. A. *Iz dnevnikov i vospominanii po dolzhnosti voennogo ministra i ego pomoshchnika 1907–1916 gg.* Ed. A. M. Zaionchkovskii. Moscow: Vyshii voennyi redaktsionnyi sovet, 1924.

Pomiankowski, Joseph. *Osmanlı İmparatorluğu'nun Çöküşü*. Tr. Kemal Turan. 2nd edn. Istanbul: Kayıhan Yayınları, [1928] 1997.

Price, M. Philips. *War and Revolution in Asiatic Russia*. London: G. Allen and Unwin, 1918.

Refik, Ahmed. *Kafkas Yollarında*. Istanbul: Kütübhane-i Askerî ve İslâm, 1919.

Resulzade, M. E. *Azerbaycan Cumhuriyeti: Keyfiyet-i Teşkili ve Şimdiki Vaziyeti*. Istanbul: Evkaf-i İslâmiye Matbaası, 1341 [1925].

Rusya'yı Tanıyan Bir Zat Tarafından Rapor. Dersaadet: Matbaa-ı Askeriye, 1333 [1917].

Rüştü, Emekli Kaymakam. *Askerî Mecmua'nın Tarih Kısmı: Büyük Harpte Bakû Yollarında. 5 Kafkas Piyade Fırkası*. Ankara: Askerî Matbaa, 1934.

Sâbis, Ali İhsan. *Harp Hatıralarım*. 4 vols. Istanbul: Nehir Yayınları, 1990.

Sazonov, S. D. *Vospominaniia*. Moscow: Mezhdunarodnye otnosheniia, [1927] 1991.

Shklovskii, Viktor. *Sentimental'noe puteshestvie*. Moscow: Novosti, 1990.

Soane, E. B. *To Mesopotamia and Kurdistan in Disguise*. London: J. Murray, 1912.

Söylemezoğlu, Galip Kemalî. *Hariciye Hizmetinde Otuz Sene*. 4 vols. Istanbul: Şaka Matbaası, 1949–55.

Talât Paşa. *Talât Paşa Anıları*. Ed. Alpay Kabacalı. Istanbul: Türkiye'nin İş Bankası Kültür Yayınları, 2000.

Topchibashev, A. A. *Diplomaticheskie besedy v Stambule, 1918–1919*. Ed. Gasan Gasanov. Baku: Ergün, 1994.

Trotskii, Lev. *Moia zhizn'*. Moscow: Vagrius, 2001.

Tuğaç, Hüsamettin. *Bir Neslin Dramı: Kafkas Cephesinden, Çarlık Rusyasında Tutsaklıktam Anılar*. Istanbul: Çağdaş Yayınları, 1975.

Türkgeldi, Ali Fuad. *Görüp İşittiklerim*. 3rd edn. Ankara: Türk Tarih Kurumu, 1984.

Ünüvar, Veysel. *Kurtuluş Savaşına Bolşeviklerle Sekiz Ay, 1920–1921*. Istanbul: Şirketi Murettebiye Basımevi, 1948.

Uran, Hilmi. *Hatıralarım*. Ankara: Ayyıldız Matbaası, 1959.

Waugh, Telford. *Turkey: Yesterday, Today, and Tomorrow*. London: Chapman and Hall, 1930.

Whitman, Sidney. *Turkish Memories*. New York: Chas. Scribner's Sons, 1914.

Wilson, Arnold T. *Loyalties: Mesopotamia 1914–1917*. London: Oxford University Press, 1930.

SECONDARY SOURCES

Afanasyan, Serge. *L'Arménie, l'Azerbaidjan et la Géorgie de l'indépendance à l'instauration du pouvoir soviétique 1917–1923*. Paris: L'Harmattan, 1981.

Ahmad, Feroz. "The Agrarian Policy of the Young Turks, 1908–1918." In *Économie et sociétés dans l'Empire ottoman (fin du XVIIIe–début du XXe siècle)*. Ed. Jean-Louis Bacqué-Grammont and Paul Dumont, 275–84. Paris: Éditions du Centre national de la recherche scientifique, 1983.

The Making of Modern Turkey. London and New York: Routledge, 1993.

"Unionist Relations with the Greek, Armenian, and Jewish Communities of the Ottoman Empire, 1908–1914." In *Christians and Jews in the Ottoman Empire*. Vol. I. Ed. Benjamin Braude and Bernard Lewis, 401–34. New York: Holmes and Meier Publishers, 1982.

The Young Turks: The Committee of Union and Progress in Turkish Politics, 1908–1914. Oxford: Clarendon Press, 1969.

Ahmad, Kamal Madhar. *Kurdistan During the First World War*. Tr. Ali Masher Ibrahim. London: Saqi Books, 1994.

Akbay, Cemal. *Birinci Dünya Harbi'nde Türk Harbi: Osmanlı İmparatorluğu'nun Siyasi ve Askeri Hazırlıkları ve Harbe Girişi*. Ankara: Genelkurmay Basım Evi, 1991.

Akçam, Taner. *Ermeni Meselesi Hallolunmuştur: Osmanlı Belgelerine Göre Savaş Yıllarında Ermenilere Yönelik Politikalar*. Istanbul: İletişim Yayınları, 2008.

From Empire to Republic: Turkish Nationalism and the Armenian Genocide. New York: Zed Books, 2004.

A Shameful Act: The Armenian Genocide and the Question of Turkish Responsibility. New York: Metropolitan Books, 2006.

Akgül, Suat. "Rusya'nın Doğu Anadolu Politikası." Ph.D. Dissertation, Hacettepe University, 1995.

"Rusya'nın Yürüttüğü Doğu Anadolu Politikası İçinde İrşad ve Cihandani Cemiyetlerinin Rolü." In *Prof. Abdurrahman Çaycı'ya Armağan*. Ed. Abdurrahman Çayci, 25–32. Ankara: Hacettepe Üniversitesi Atatürk İlkeleri ve İnkılâp Enstitüsü, 1995.

Aknouni, E. *Political Persecution: Armenian Prisoners of the Caucasus*. New York: n. p., 1911.

Aksakal, Mustafa. "Not 'by those old books of international law, but only by war': Ottoman Intellectuals on the Eve of the Great War." *Diplomacy and Statecraft*, 15, 3 (2004), 507–44.

The Ottoman Road to War in 1914: The Ottoman Empire and the First World War. New York: Cambridge University Press, 2008.

Aktar, Ayhan and Abdülhamit Kırmızı. "'Bon Pour l'Orient': Fuat Dündar'ın Kitabını Deşifre Ederken . . ." *Tarih ve Toplum Yeni Yaklaşımlar,* 8 (Spring 2009), 157–86.

Albertini, Luigi. *The Origins of the War of 1914.* Vol. III. New York: Oxford University Press, 1957.

Allen, W. E. D. and Paul Muratoff. *Caucasian Battlefields: A History of the Wars on the Turco-Caucasian Border, 1828–1921.* Cambridge: Cambridge University Press, 1953.

Altay, Fahrettin. *10 Yıl Savaş, 1912–1922 ve Sonrası.* Istanbul: İnsel Yayınları, 1970.

Altstadt, Audrey L. *The Azerbaijani Turks: Power and Identity Under Russian Rule.* Stanford: Hoover Institution Press, 1992.

Amirkhanian, M. D., ed. *Genotsid Armian i russkaia publitsistika.* Yerevan: Muzei-Institut genotsida armian, 1998.

Anderson, Benedict. *Imagined Communities.* 2nd edn. New York: Verso, 1991.

Anderson, M. S. *The Eastern Question, 1774–1923: A Study in International Relations.* London: Macmillan, 1966.

Angell, Norman. *The Great Illusion: A Study of the Relation of Military Power in Nations to Their Economic and Social Advantage.* London: G. P. Putnam's Sons, 1911.

Antonius, George. *The Arab Awakening: The Story of the Arab National Movement.* Safety Harbor, FL: Simon Publications, [1939] 2001.

Arai, Masami. *Turkish Nationalism in the Young Turk Era.* Leiden: E. J. Brill, 1992.

Aron, Raymond. *Peace and War: A Theory of International Relations.* Tr. Richard Howard and Annette Baker Fox. Garden City, NY: Doubleday, 1966.

Arsharuni, A. and Kh. Gabidullin. *Ocherki panislamizma i pantiurkizma v Rossii.* London: Society for Central Asian Studies, [1931] 1990.

Arutiunian, A. O. *Kavkazskii front, 1914–1917 gg.* Yerevan: Aiastan, 1971.

Aslan, Yavuz. *Türkiye Komünist Fırkası'nın Kuruluşu ve Mustafa Suphi.* Ankara: Türk Tarih Kurumu, 1997.

Atamian, Sarkis. *The Armenian Community: The Historical Development of a Social and Ideological Conflict.* New York: Philosophical Library, 1955.

Aver'ianov, P. I. *Etnograficheskii i voenno-politicheskii obzor aziatskikh vladenii Ottomanskoi imperii.* St. Petersburg: Voennaia tipografiia, 1912.

Kurdy v voinakh Rossii s Persiei i Turtsiei v techenie XIX stoletiia. Sovremennoe politicheskoe polozhenie turetskikh, persidskikh i russkikh kurdov. Istoricheskii ocherk. Tiflis: Izdatel'stvo otdela General'nago Shtaba pri Shtabe Kavkazsk-ago voennago okruga, 1900.

Aydemir, İzzet. *Muhaceretteki Çerkes Aydınları.* Ankara: n.p., 1991.

Aydemir, Şevket Süreyya. *Makedonya'dan Orta Asya'ya. Enver Paşa.* 3 vols. Istanbul: Remzi Kitabevi, 1992.

Aydoğan, Erdal. *İttihat ve Terakki'nin Doğu Politikası.* Istanbul: Ötüken Neşriyat, 2005.

Baberowski, Jörg. *Der Feind ist überall: Stalinismus im Kaukasus.* Munich: Deutsche Verlags Anstalt, 2003.

Bal, Halil. "Kuzey Kafkasya'nın İstiklali ve Türkiye'nin Askeri Yardımı (1914–1918)." *Kafkas Araştırmaları,* 3 (1997), 29–92.

Balaev, Aidyn. *Azerbaidzhanskoe natsional'noe dvizhenie v 1917–1918 gg.* Baku: Elm, 1998.

Balcıoğlu, Mustafa. *Teşkilat-ı Mahsusa'dan Cumhuriyete.* 2nd edn. Ankara: Asil Yayın Dağıtım, 2004.

Baron, Nick and Peter Gatrell, eds. *Homelands: War, Population, and Statehood in Eastern Europe and Russia.* London: Anthem Press, 2004.

Baytugan, Barasbi. "Tarihi İnsanlar Yaratır," *Şimalî Kafkasya–Severnyi Kavkaz,* no. 41 (September 1937), 2–5.

Bayur, Yusuf Hikmet. "Birinci Genel Savaştan Sonra Yapılan Barış ve Anlaşmalarımız," *Belleten,* 29, 115 (1965), 499–516.

Türk İnkılâbı Tarihi. 4 vols. Ankara: Türk Tarih Kurumu, 1940.

Bedickian, S. V. *The Red Sultan's Soliloquy.* Tr. Alice Stone Blackwell. Boston: Sherman, French, and Co., 1912.

Beissinger, Mark R. "The Persisting Ambiguity of Empire." *Post-Soviet Affairs,* 11, 2 (1995), 149–84.

Belen, Fahri. *Birinci Cihan Harbinde Türk Harbi.* Vols. III–V. Ankara: Genelkurmay Basımevi, 1965–67.

Berberian, Houri. *Armenians and the Iranian Constitutional Revolution, 1905–1911.* Boulder: Westview, 2001.

Berlin, Isaiah. *Against the Current.* Ed. Henry Hardy. London: Pimlico, 1997.

The Crooked Timber of Humanity. Ed. Henry Hardy. Princeton: Princeton University Press, 1990.

The Magus of the North: J. G. Hamann and the Rise of Modern Irrationalism. Ed. Henry Hardy. New York: Farrar, Straus and Giroux, 1994.

Bestuzhev, I. V. *Bor'ba v Rossii po voprosam vneshnei politiki, 1906–1910.* Moscow: Akademiia nauk SSSR, 1961.

"Russian Foreign Policy, February–June 1914." *Journal of Contemporary History,* 1, 3 (July 1966), 93–112.

Beylerian, Arthur, ed. *Les Grandes puissances, l'Empire ottoman et les Arméniens dans les archives françaises (1914–1918).* Paris: Université de Paris I, Panthéon, Sorbonne, 1983.

Bezugol'nyi, A. Iu. *Narody Kavkaza i Krasnaia armiia.* Moscow: Veche, 2007.

Bihl, Wolfdieter. *Die Kaukasus-Politik der Mittelmächte.* 2 vols. Vienna: Hermann Böhlaus Nachf., 1975.

Birinci, Ali. *Hürriyet ve İtilâf: II. Meşrutiyet Devrinde İttihat ve Terraki'ye Karşı Çıkanlar.* Istanbul: Dergâh Yayınları, 1990.

Bloxham, David. "The Armenian Genocide of 1915–1916: Cumulative Radicalization and the Development of a Destruction Policy." *Past and Present,* 181 (November 2003), 141–92.

The Great Game of Genocide: Imperialism, Nationalism, and the Destruction of the Ottoman Armenians. Oxford: Oxford University Press, 2005.

Bobroff, Ronald. *Roads to Glory: Late Imperial Russia and the Turkish Straits.* New York: I. B. Tauris, 2006.

Borian, B. A. *Armeniia, mezhdunarodnaia diplomatiia i SSSR.* 2 vols. Moscow: Gosizdat, 1928.

Breuilly, John. *Nationalism and the State.* 2nd edn. Chicago: University of Chicago Press, [1982] 1993.

Brower, Daniel and Edward J. Lazzerini, eds. *Russia's Orient: Imperial Borderlands and Peoples, 1700–1917.* Bloomington: Indiana University Press, 1997.

Brubaker, Rogers. *Nationalism Reframed: Nationhood and the National Question in the New Europe.* New York: Cambridge University Press, 1996.

Bruinessen, Martin van. *Agha, Shaikh, and State: The Social and Political Structures of Kurdistan.* London: Zed Books, 1992.

"Kurdish Tribes and the State of Iran: The Case of Simko's Revolt." In *The Conflict of Tribe and State in Iran and Afghanistan.* Ed. Richard Tapper, 364–400. New York: St. Martin's Press, 1983.

Budak, Mustafa. "Nuri Paşa'nın Kafkas İslâm Ordusu Hakkındaki Raporu." *Kafkas Araştırmaları,* 4 (1998), 61–106.

Bull, Hedley. *The Anarchical Society: A Study of Order in World Politics.* 3rd edn. New York: Columbia University Press. [1977] 2002.

Bury, G. W. *Pan-Islam.* London: Macmillan, 1919.

Buxton, Noel and the Rev. Harold Buxton. *Travels and Politics in Armenia.* New York: Macmillan, 1914.

Cabağı, Wassan-Giray. *Kafkas-Rus Çatışması.* Istanbul: Flaş Ajans, 1967.

Cabağı, Wassan-Giray [Vassan-Giray Jabagi]. "Revolution and Civil War in the North Caucasus – End of the 19th–Beginning of the 20th Century." *Central Asian Survey,* 10, 1–2 (1991), 119–32.

Çağaptay, Soner. *Islam, Secularism, and Nationalism: Who Is a Turk?* New York: Routledge, 2006.

Çakmak, Fevzi. *Büyük Harpte Şark Cephesi Hareketleri: Şark Vilâyetlerimizde, Kafkasyada ve İranda.* Ankara: Genelkurmay Matbaası, 1936.

Campbell, Elena. "The Muslim Question in Late Imperial Russia." In *Russian Empire: Space, People, Power, 1700–1930.* Ed. Jane Burbank, Mark von Hagen, Anatolyi Remner, 320–47. Bloomington: Indiana University Press, 2007.

Carrère d'Encausse, Hélène. *The Great Challenge: Nationalities and the Bolshevik State.* Tr. Nancy Festinger. New York: Holmes and Meier, 1992.

Çelebyan, Antranik [Antranig Chalabian]. *Antranik Paşa.* Tr. Mariam Arpi and Nairi Arek. Istanbul: Perî Yayınları, 2003.

Cemil, Arif. *Birinci Dünya Savaşinda Teşkilat-ı Mahsusa.* Istanbul: Arba Yayınları, 1997.

Chalabian, Antranig. *Revolutionary Figures: Mihran Damadian, Hambardzum Boyadjian, Serob Aghibur, Hrair-Dzhoghk, Gevorg Chavush, Sebastatsi Murad, Nikol Duman.* Tr. Arra S. Avakian. USA [sic]: A. Chalabian, 1994.

Çolak, Mustafa. *Alman İmparatorluğu'nun Doğu Siyaseti Çerçevesinde Kafkasya Politikası (1914–1918).* Ankara: Türk Tarih Kurumu, 2006.

Enver Paşa: Osmanlı–Alman İttifakı. Istanbul: Yeditepe Yayınevi, 2008.

Dadrian, Vahakn. *The History of the Armenian Genocide: Ethnic Conflict from the Balkans to Anatolia to the Caucasus.* Providence, RI: Berghahn Books, 1995.

Dasnabedian, Hratch. *History of the Armenian Revolutionary Federation Dashnaktsutiun 1890/1924.* Milan: Oemme edizioni, 1990.

Davison, Roderic. "The Armenian Crisis, 1912–1914." *American Historical Review,* 53, 3 (April 1948), 481–505.

Dawisha, A. I. *Arab Nationalism in the Twentieth Century: From Triumph to Despair.* Princeton: Princeton University Press, 2003.

Dayı, S. Esin. *Elviye-i Selâse'de (Kars, Ardahan, Batum) Millî Teşkilâtlanma.* Erzurum: Kültür Eğitim Vakfı Yayınları, 1997.

Deringil, Selim. "'The Armenian Question Is Finally Closed': Mass Conversions of Armenians in Anatolia During the Hamidian Massacres of 1895–1897." *Comparative Studies in Society and History,* 51, 2 (2009), 344–71.

The Ottomans, the Turks, and World Power Politics: Collected Essays. Istanbul: Isis Press, 2000.

The Well-Protected Domains: Ideology and the Legitimation of Power in the Ottoman Empire, 1876–1909. London: I. B. Tauris, 1998.

Devlet, Nadir. *1917 Ekim İhtilâli ve Türk–Tatar Millet Meclisi.* Istanbul: Ötüken Neşriyat, 1998.

İsmail Bey Gaspıralı, 1851–1914. Ankara: Kültür ve Turizm Bakanlığı, 1988.

Diakin, V. S. *Natsional'nyi vopros vo vnutrennei politike tsarizma (XIX–nachalo XX vv.).* S. Petersburg: LISS, 1998.

Dickinson, G. Lowes. *The European Anarchy.* London: George Allen and Unwin Ltd., 1916.

The International Anarchy, 1904–1914. New York: The Century Co., 1926.

Diner, Dan. *Cataclysms: A History of the Twentieth Century from Europe's Edge.* Tr. William Temple and Joel Golb. Madison: University of Wisconsin Press, 2008.

Donogo, Khadzhi Murad. "Nazhmuddin Gotsinskii." *Voprosy istorii,* 6 (2005), 34–57.

Duguid, Stephen. "The Politics of Unity: Hamidian Policy in Eastern Anatolia." *Middle Eastern Studies,* 9 (1973), 145–55.

Dunsterville, L. C. *The Adventures of Dunsterforce.* London: E. Arnold, 1920.

Duran, Tülay. "I. Dünya Savaşı Sonunda Türk Diplomasisinin İlk Başarısı: Brest-Litovsk Hazırlıkları." Parts 1–3. *Belgelerle Türk Tarihi Dergisi,* 12, no. 67–68 (April–May 1973), 43–49; 12, no. 69 (June 1973), 22–26; 12, no. 70 (July 1973), 31–34.

Dündar, Fuat. *Crime of Numbers: The Role of Statistics in the Armenian Question (1878–1918).* New Brunswick: Transaction Publishers, 2010.

"'Ermeni Meselesi Hallolunmuş' Mudur? Taner Akçam'ı Son Kitabı Vesilesiyle '% 10 Katliam' Meselesi." *Toplumsal Tarih,* 174 (June 2008), 79–83.

İttihat ve Terakki'nin Müslümanları İskân Politikası (1913–1918). Istanbul: İletişim Yayınları, 2001.

Modern Türkiye'nin Şifresi: İttihat ve Terakki'nin Etnisite Mühendisliği, 1913–1918. Istanbul: İletişim, 2008.

"Pouring a People into the Desert: The 'Definitive Solution' to the Armenian Question." In *A Question of Genocide.* Ed. Ronald Grigor Suny. Oxford: Oxford University Press, forthcoming.

Dzhalil, Dzhalile. *Iz istorii obshchestvenno-politicheskoi zhizni Kurdov v kontse XIX nachale XX vv.* St. Petersburg: Nauka, 1997.

"Pervye kurdskie obshchestvennye politicheskie organizatsii." *Tiurkologicheskii sbornik, 1973,* 172–86. Moscow: Nauka, 1975.

Eagleton, William. *The Kurdish Republic of 1946*. London: Oxford University Press, 1963.

Eley, Geoff and Ronald Grigor Suny, eds. *Becoming National: A Reader*. New York: Oxford University Press, 1996.

Emirî, Ali. *Osmanlı Vilâyât-ı Şarkiyesi*. Istanbul: Evkaf-ı İslâmiye Matbaası, 1918.

Eraslan, Cezmi. *II. Abdülhamid ve İslam Birliği*. Istanbul: Ötüken, 1992.

Erat, Muhammet. "Kâzım Karabekir'in Nahçıvan ve Çevresindeki Faaliyetleri." *Kafkas Araştırmaları* 4. 39–59. Istanbul: Acar Yayinlar, 1998.

Erickson, Edward J. "Bayonets on Musa Dagh: Ottoman Counterinsurgency Operations – 1915," *Journal of Strategic Studies*, 28, 3 (June 2005), 529–48.

Ordered to Die: A History of the Ottoman Army in the First World War. Westport, CT: Greenwood Press, 2001.

Erşan, Mesut. "Birinci Dünya Harbinde Osmanlı Devletinin Kuzey Kafkasya Siyaseti." Ph.D. Dissertation, Atatürk University, 1995.

Fawcett, Louise L'Estrange. *Iran and the Cold War: The Azerbaijan Crisis of 1946*. New York: Cambridge University Press, 1992.

Figes, Orlando. *A People's Tragedy: The Russian Revolution, 1891–1924*. London: Jonathan Cape, 1996.

Findley, Carter. *Ottoman Civil Officialdom*. Princeton: Princeton University Press, 1989.

Fink, Carole. *Defending the Rights of Others*. Cambridge: Cambridge University Press, 2004.

Fischer, Fritz. *Germany's Aims in the First World War*. New York: W. W. Norton and Company, 1967.

Fromkin, David. *A Peace to End All Peace: Creating the Modern Middle East, 1914–1922*. New York: Henry Holt and Company, 1989.

Fuller, William C. "The Russian Empire." In *Knowing One's Enemies: Intelligence Assessment Before the Two World Wars*. Ed. Ernest R. May, 98–126. Princeton: Princeton University Press, 1984.

Strategy and Power in Russia, 1600–1914. New York: Free Press, 1992.

Gatrell, Peter. *Government, Industry, and Rearmament in Russia, 1900–1914: The Last Argument of Tsarism*. New York: Cambridge University Press, 1994.

Gaunt, David. *Massacres, Resistance, Protectors: Muslim–Christian Relations in Eastern Anatolia During World War I*. Piscataway, NJ: Gorgias Press, 2006.

Gellner, Ernest. *Encounters with Nationalism*. Cambridge, MA: Blackwell, 1994.

Nations and Nationalism. Ithaca: Cornell University Press, 1983.

Gelvin, James. *Divided Loyalties: Nationalism and Mass Politics in Syria at the Close of Empire*. Berkeley: University of California Press, 1998.

Genelkurmay Başkanlığı. *Birinci Dünya Harbinde Türk Harbi Kafkas Cephesi Üçüncü Ordu Harekâtı*. 2 vols. Ankara: Genelkurmay Basımevi, 1993.

Genis, Vladimir. *Vitse-konsul Vvedenskii: sluzhba v Persii i Bukharskom khanstve (1906–1920 gg.)*. Moscow: Mysl', 2003.

Georgeon, François. *Abdülhamid II: le sultan calife, 1876–1909*. Paris: Fayard, 2003.

Aux origines du nationalisme turc: Yusuf Akçura (1876–1935). Paris: ADPF, 1980.

Geraci, Robert. "Russian Orientalism at an Impasse: Tsarist Education Policy and the 1910 Conference on Islam." In *Russia's Orient*. Ed. Brower and Lazzerini, 138–62.

Window on the East: National and Imperial Identities in Late Tsarist Russia. Ithaca: Cornell University Press, 2001.

Gilbert, Martin. *The First World War: A Complete History*. New York: Henry Holt and Company, 1994.

Gilensen, V. M. "'Osinye gnezda' pod konsul'skoi kryshei." *Voenno-istoricheskii zhurnal* (September–October 1997), 49–59.

Gingeras, Ryan. *Sorrowful Shores: Violence, Ethnicity, and the End of the Ottoman Empire, 1912–1923*. New York: Oxford University Press, 2009.

Ginio, Eyal. "Mobilizing the Ottoman Nation During the Balkan Wars (1912–1913): Awakening from the Ottoman Dream." *War and History*, 12, 2 (2005), 156–77.

Gökay, Bülent. *A Clash of Empires: Turkey Between Russian Bolshevism and British Imperialism*. London: Tauris Academic Studies, 1997.

Gökdemir, Ahmet Ender. *Cenûb-i Garbî Kafkas Hükûmeti*. Ankara: Atatürk Araştırma Merkezi, 1998.

Gordlevskii, V. A. *Izbrannye sochineniia*. 4 vols. Moscow: Izdatel'stvo vostochnoi literatury, 1962.

Gorganian, Gabriel. "Armenian Participation in World War I on the Caucasus Front." *Armenian Review*, 20, 3 (Autumn 1967), 3–21; 20, 4 (Winter 1967), 66–80; 21, 2 (Summer 1968), 66–80; 21, 4 (Winter 1968), 69–74; 22, 1 (Spring 1969), 71–77; 22, 4 (Winter 1970), 68–71; 23, 1 (Spring 1970), 72–79; 24, 2 (Summer 1970), 45–65.

Gül, Mustafa. "Bolşevik İhtilali Sırasında Kırgız–Kazak Öğrencilerin Osmanlı Hükümeti'ne Sundukları Bir Beyanname." *Atatürk Araştırma Merkezi Dergisi*, 11 (March 1995), 49–54.

Guse, Felix. *Die Kaukasusfront im Weltkrieg bis zum Frieden von Brest*. Leipzig: Koehler Amelang, 1940.

Hagopian, J. Michael. "Hyphenated Nationalism: The Spirit of the Revolutionary Movement in Asia Minor and the Caucasus, 1896–1910." Ph.D. dissertation, Harvard University, 1942.

Hale, Charles D. "The Desperate Ottoman: Enver Pasha and the Ottoman Empire," Parts 1–2. *Middle Eastern Studies*, 30, 1 (January 1994), 1–51; 30, 2 (April 1994), 224–51.

Hall, Richard C. *The Balkan Wars, 1912–1913: Prelude to the First World War*. London: Routledge, 2000.

Hanioğlu, M. Şükrü. *Bir Siyasal Düşünür Olarak Doktor Abdullah Cevdet ve Dönemi*. Istanbul: Üçdal Neşriyatı, 1981.

A Brief History of the Ottoman Empire. Princeton: Princeton University Press, 2008.

Kendi Mektuplarında Enver Paşa. Istanbul: Der Yayınları, 1989.

Preparation for a Revolution: The Young Turks, 1902–1908. New York: Oxford University Press, 2001.

The Young Turks in Opposition. New York: Oxford University Press, 1995.

Hasanli, Jamil. *At the Dawn of the Cold War: The Soviet–American Crisis over Iranian Azerbaijan, 1941–1946.* New York: Rowman and Littlefield, 2006.

Hechter, Michael. *Containing Nationalism.* New York: Oxford University Press, 2000.

Heyd, Uriel. *Foundations of Turkish Nationalism: The Life and Teachings of Ziya Gökalp.* London: Luzac, 1950.

Hirsch, Francine. *Empire of Nations: Ethnographic Knowledge and the Making of the Soviet Union.* Ithaca: Cornell University Press, 2005.

Hobsbawm, Eric. *Nations and Nationalism Since 1780: Programme, Myth, and Reality.* New York: Cambridge University Press, 1990.

Hoffman, Tessa and Gerayer Koutcharian. "The History of Armenian–Kurdish Relations in the Ottoman Empire." *Armenian Review*, 30, 4 (Winter 1986), 1–44.

Holquist, Peter. "Armenian Occupation." In *A Question of Genocide.* Ed. Suny.

"To Count, to Extract, and to Exterminate: Population Statistics and Population Politics in Late Imperial and Soviet Russia." In *A State of Nations.* Ed. Suny and Martin, 111–44.

Hosking, Geoffrey. *Rulers and Victims: The Russians in the Soviet Union.* Cambridge, MA: Belknap Press of Harvard University Press, 2006.

Hovannisian, Richard G. *Armenia on the Road to Independence, 1918.* Berkeley: University of California Press, 1967.

ed. *The Armenian Genocide: History, Politics, and Ethics.* Houndmills, UK: Macmillan, 1992.

ed. *The Armenian People from Ancient to Modern Times.* New York: St. Martin's Press, 1997.

"The Armenian Question in the Ottoman Empire." *East European Quarterly*, 6, 1 (March 1972), 1–26.

ed. *Armenian Tsopk/Kharpert.* Costa Mesa, CA: Mazda Publishers, 2002.

The Republic of Armenia. 4 vols. Berkeley: University of California Press, 1971.

Howard, Harry N. *The Partition of Turkey: A Diplomatic History, 1913–1923.* Norman: University of Oklahoma Press, 1931.

Howard, Michael. "The First World War Reconsidered." In *The Great War and the Twentieth Century.* Ed. Jay Winter, Geoffrey Parker, and Mary R. Habeck, 13–29. New Haven: Yale University Press, 2000.

Huri, Pol. *Türkiye Nasıl Paylaşıldı?* Istanbul: Kitaphane-yi İslam ve Askerî, 1329 [1913].

Ieshke, G. [Gotthard Jäschke] "Poraboshchennye Rossiei narody na Lozanskom kongresse 1916 goda." *Şimalî Kafkasya–Severnyi Kavkaz*, no. 42–43 (October–November 1937).

Ishkhanian, Bakshi. *Narodnosti Kavkaza: sostav naseleniia, professional'naia gruppirovka i obshchestvennoe razsloenie Kavkazskikh narodnostei.* Petrograd: M. V. Popov, 1916.

Iuzbashian, K. N. *Akademik Iosif Abgarovich Orbeli (1887–1961).* Moscow: Nauka, 1986.

Jäschke, Gotthard. "Der Turanismus der Jungtürken. Zur Osmanischen Aussen-politik im Weltkriege." *Die Welt des Islams*, 23, 1–2 (1941), 1–53.

Jedlicki, Jerzy. *A Suburb of Europe: Nineteenth-Century Polish Approaches to Western Civilization*. Budapest: CEU Press [1988] 1999.

Jelavich, Barbara. *A Century of Russian Foreign Policy, 1814–1914*. Philadelphia: Lippincott, 1964.

Russia's Balkan Entanglements, 1806–1914. Cambridge: Cambridge University Press, 1991.

Jervis, Robert. "Cooperation Under the Security Dilemma." *World Politics*, 30, 2 (January 1978), 167–214.

System Effects: Complexity in Political and Social Life. Princeton: Princeton University Press, 1997.

Jones, Stephen F. *Socialism in Georgian Colors: The European Road to Social Democracy, 1883–1917*. Cambridge, MA: Harvard University Press, 2005.

Joseph, John. *The Modern Assyrians of the Middle East: Encounters with Western Christian Missions, Archeologists, and Colonial Powers*. Leiden: Brill, 2000.

The Nestorians and Their Muslim Neighbors: A Study of Western Influence on Their Relations. Princeton: Princeton University Press, 1961.

Jwaideh, Wadie. *The Kurdish National Movement: Its Origins and Development*. Syracuse: Syracuse University Press, 2006.

Kaflı, Kadircan. *Şimalî Kafkasya*. Istanbul: Vakıt Matbaası, 1942.

Kaligian, Dikran Mesrob. *Armenian Organization and Ideology Under Ottoman Rule, 1908–1914*. New Brunswick: Transaction Publishers, 2009.

Kappeler, Andreas. *The Russian Empire: A Multiethnic History*. Tr. Alfred Clayton. New York: Longman, 2001.

Karpat, Kemal. "The Memoirs of N. Batzaria: The Young Turks and Nationalism." *International Journal of Middle East Studies*, 6, 3 (1975), 276–99.

Ottoman Population in Anatolia. Madison: University of Wisconsin Press, 1985.

The Politicization of Islam: Reconstructing Identity, State, Faith, and Community in the Late Ottoman State. New York: Oxford University Press, 2001.

Studies on Ottoman Social and Political History. Leiden: Brill, 2002.

Kavtaradze, A. G. *Voennye spetsialisty na sluzhbe Respubliki Sovetov, 1917–1920 gg.* Moscow: Nauka, 1988.

Kayalı, Hasan. *Arabs and Young Turks: Ottomanism, Arabism, and Islamism in the Ottoman Empire, 1908–1918*. Berkeley: University of California Press, 1997.

Kayaloff, Jacques. *The Battle of Sardarabad*. The Hague: Mouton, 1973.

Kazemzadeh, Firuz. *The Struggle for Transcaucasia*. New York: Philosophical Library, 1951.

Kedourie, Elie. *Nationalism*. 4th edn. Oxford: Blackwell, [1966] 1993.

Kedourie, Sylvia, ed. *Turkey Before and After Ataturk: Internal and External Affairs*. London: Frank Cass, 1999.

Keleşyılmaz, Vahdet. "Kafkas Harekâtının Perde Arkası." *Ankara Üniversitesi Osmanlı Tarihi Araştırma Merkezi Dergisi*, 11 (2001), 277–304.

Kenez, Peter. *Civil War in South Russia, 1918*. Berkeley: University of California Press, 1971.

Kent, Marian, ed. *The Great Powers and the End of the Ottoman Empire*. 2nd edn. London: Frank Cass, 1996.

Kerner, R. J. "The Mission of Liman von Sanders." *Slavonic Review*, 6, 16 (1927), 12–27; 6, 17 (1927), 344–63; 6, 18 (1928), 543–60; 7, 19 (1928), 90–112.

Khalid, Adeeb. "Pan-Islamism in Practice: The Rhetoric of Muslim Unity and Its Uses." In *Late Ottoman Society: The Intellectual Legacy*. Ed. Elisabeth Özdalga, 201–24. London: RoutledgeCurzon, 2005.

The Politics of Muslim Cultural Reform: Jadidism in Central Asia. Berkeley: University of California Press, 1998.

Khalidi, Rashid. "Ottomanism and Arabism in Syria Before 1914: A Reassessment." In *The Origins of Arab Nationalism*. Ed. Rashid Khalidi, Lisa Anderson, Muhammad Muslih, and Reeva S. Simon, 50–72. New York: Columbia University Press, 1991.

Palestinian Identity: The Construction of Modern National Consciousness. New York: Columbia University Press, 1997.

Kheifets, A. N. *Sovetskaia Rossiia i sopredel'nye strany vostoka v gody grazhdanskoi voiny (1918–1920)*. Moscow: Nauka, 1964.

Kheifets, S. Ia. "Zakavkaz'e v pervuiu polovinu 1918 g. i Zakavkazskii Seim." *Byloe*, no. 21 (1923), 298–310.

Kieser, Hans-Lukas. *Der verpasste Friede: Mission, Etnie und Staat in den Ostprovinzen der Türkei, 1838–1938*. Zurich: Chronos, 2000.

Vorkämpfer der "Neuen Türkei": revolutionäre Bildungseliten am Genfersee (1870–1939). Zurich: Chronos, 2005.

Kılıç, Selami. *Türk–Sovyet İlişkilerinin Doğuşu*. Istanbul: Dergâh Yayınları, 1998.

Kinnane, Derk. *The Kurds and Kurdistan*. London: Oxford University Press, 1964.

Kırımlı, Hakan. *National Movements and National Identity Among the Crimean Tatars, 1905–1916*. Leiden: E. J. Brill, 1996.

Klein, Janet. "Power in the Periphery." Ph.D. Dissertation, Princeton University, 2003.

Kodaman, Bayram. *Sultan II. Abdulhamid Devri Doğu Anadolu Politikası*. Ankara: Türk Kültürünü Araştirma Enstitüsü, 1987.

Koloğlu, Orhan. *Abdülhamit Gerçeği*. Istanbul: Gür Yayınları, 1987.

Korsun, N. G. *Sarykamyshkaia operatsiia*. Moscow: Voenizdat, 1937.

Krasner, Stephen D. *Sovereignty: Organized Hypocrisy*. Princeton: Princeton University Press, 1999.

Kurat, Akdes Nimet. *Birinci Dünya Savaşı Sırasında Türkiye'de Bulunan Alman Generallerinin Raporları*. Ankara: Türk Kültürünü Araştırımı Ensitüsü, 1966.

Türkiye ve Rusya: XVIII Yüzyıl Sonundan Kurtuluş Savaşına Kadar Türk–Rus İlişkileri (1798–1919). Ankara: Ankara University Press, 1970.

Kurtcephe, İsrafil. "Teşkilât-ı Mahsusa Belgelerine Göre 1917 Rus İhtilâli Sırasında Buhara Hanlığı." In *Beşinci Askeri Tarih Semineri Bildirileri I*, 588–95. Ankara: Genelkurmay Basım Evi, 1996.

Kushner, David. *The Rise of Turkish Nationalism, 1876–1908*. London: Cass, 1977.

Kutlay, Naci. *İttihat-Terakki ve Kürtler*. Istanbul: Fırat Yayınları, 1991.

Landau, Jacob M. *Pan-Turkism: From Irredentism to Cooperation.* 2nd edn. London: Hurst and Company, 1995.

The Politics of Pan-Islam. 2nd edn. New York: Oxford University Press, 1994.

Lang, David Marshall. *A Modern History of Soviet Georgia.* Westport, CT: Greenwood Press, 1962.

Larcher, Maurice. *La Guerre Turque dans la Guerre mondiale.* Paris: E. Chiron, 1926.

Lattimore, Owen. *Studies in Frontier History.* New York: Oxford University Press, 1962.

Lazarev, M. S. *Kurdskii vopros (1881–1917).* Moscow: Nauka, 1972.

Lazzerini, Edward. "Ismail Bey Gasprinskii and Muslim Modernism in Russia, 1878–1914." Ph.D. Dissertation, University of Washington, 1973.

Levene, Mark. *Genocide in the Age of the Nation-State,* vol. II, *The Rise of the West and the Coming of Genocide.* New York: I. B. Tauris, 2005.

Lewis, Bernard. *The Emergence of Modern Turkey.* 2nd edn. London: Oxford University Press, 1968.

Libaridian, Gerard. *Modern Armenia: People, Nation, State.* New Brunswick: Transaction Publishers, 2004.

"Revolution and Liberation in the 1892 and 1907 Programs of the Dashnaktsutiun." In *Transcaucasia.* Ed. Suny, 185–96.

Lieven, Dominic. *Empire: The Russian Empire and Its Rivals.* New Haven: Yale University Press, 2000.

Russia and the Origins of the First World War. New York: St. Martin's Press, 1983.

Liulevicius, Vegas G. *War Land on the Eastern Front: Culture, National Identity, and German Occupation in World War I.* New York: Cambridge University Press, 2000.

Llobera, Josep R. *The God of Modernity: The Development of Nationalism in Western Europe.* Providence, RI: Berg Publishers, 1994.

Lohr, Eric. *Nationalizing the Russian Empire: The Campaign Against Enemy Aliens During World War I.* Cambridge, MA: Harvard University Press, 2003.

Lorei, German. *Operatsii germano-turestskikh morskikh sil v 1914–1918 gg.* Moscow: Gosudarstvennoe voennoe izdatel'stvo, 1934.

Macartney, C. A. *National States and National Minorities.* London: Oxford University Press, 1934.

Magnes, Judah L. *Russia and Germany at Brest-Litovsk.* New York: Rand School of Social Science, 1919.

Manela, Erez. *The Wilsonian Moment: Self-Determination and the International Origins of Anticolonial Nationalism.* New York: Oxford University Press, 2007.

Mango, Andrew. *Atatürk: The Biography of the Founder of Modern Turkey.* Woodstock, NY: Overlook Press, 2001.

Mann, Michael. *The Dark Side of Democracy: Explaining Ethnic Cleansing.* New York: Cambridge University Press, 2005.

Martin, Terry. *The Affirmative Action Empire: Nations and Nationalism in the Soviet Union, 1923–1939.* Ithaca: Cornell University Press, 2001.

"The Origins of Soviet Ethnic Cleansing." *Journal of Modern History,* 70, 4 (September 1998), 813–61.

Maslovskii, E. V. *Mirovaia voina na Kavkazskom fronte, 1914–1917*. Paris: Vozrozhdenie, 1933.

May, Ernest R., ed. *Knowing One's Enemies: Intelligence Assessment Before the Two World Wars*. Princeton: Princeton University Press, 1984.

Mazower, Mark. *The Balkans: A Short History*. New York: Random House, 2000.

Dark Continent: Europe's Twentieth Century. New York: Vintage Books, 2000.

Salonica, City of Ghosts: Christians, Muslims, and Jews, 1430–1950. London: Harper Collins, 2004.

McCarthy, Justin. *Death and Exile: The Ethnic Cleansing of Ottoman Muslims, 1821–1922*. Princeton: Darwin Press, 1995.

Muslims and Minorities: The Population of Ottoman Anatolia and the End of the Empire. New York: New York University Press, 1983.

McCarthy, Justin Esat Arslan, Cemalettin Taşkiran, and Ömer Turan. *The Armenian Rebellion at Van*. Salt Lake City: University of Utah Press, 2006.

McCauley, Martin, ed. *Stalin and Stalinism*. London: Longman, 1995.

McDonald, David MacLaren. *United Government and Foreign Policy in Russia, 1900–1914*. Cambridge, MA: Harvard University Press, 1992.

McDowall, David. *A Modern History of the Kurds*. 2nd edn. New York: I. B. Tauris, 2000.

McKale, Donald. *War by Revolution: Germany and Great Britain in the Middle East in the Era of World War I*. Kent, OH: Kent State University Press, 1998.

McMeekin, Sean. *The Berlin–Baghdad Express: The Ottoman Empire and Germany's Bid for World Power*. Cambridge, MA: Harvard University Press, 2010.

McNeill, William H. *Polyethnicity and National Unity in World History*. Toronto: University of Toronto Press, 1986.

Mearsheimer, John J. *The Tragedy of Great Power Politics*. New York: Norton, 2001.

Mehmetzade, Mirza Bala. *Milli Azerbaycan Hareketi*. Ankara: Azerbaycan Kültür Merkezi, 1991.

Meyer, James. "Immigration, Return, and the Politics of Citizenship: Russian Muslims in the Ottoman Empire, 1860–1914." *International Journal of Middle East Studies*, 39 (2007), 15–32.

"Turkic Worlds: Community Representation and Collective Identity Formation in the Russian and Ottoman Empires, 1870–1914." Ph.D. Dissertation, Brown University, 2007.

Mikaelian, Vargdes. *Armianskii vopros i genotsid Armian v Turtsii (1913–1919)*. Yerevan: Akademiia nauk Armianskoi respubliki, 1995.

Miliukov, Pavel. *Balkanskii krizis i politika A. P. Izvol'skogo*. St. Petersburg: Obshchestvennaia pol'za, 1909.

Miller, Geoffrey. *Straits: British Policy Towards the Ottoman Empire and the Origins of the Dardanelles Campaign*. Hull: University of Hull Press, 1997.

Mol, Jons. *Londra Konferansındaki Meselelerden: Türkiye Anadolu'da Yaşayacak mı? Yaşamayacak mı?* Tr. Hâbil Âdem. Dersaadet, 1910.

Mukhammetdinov, R. F. *Zarozhdenie i evoliutsiia Tiurkizma*. Kazan: Zaman, 1996.

Munro, Henry F. *The Berlin Congress*. Washington, DC: US Government Printing Office, 1918.

Musa, İsmayıl. "Azerbaycan–Osmanlı Siyasi–Askeri İlişkileri (1917–1918)." *Belleten*, 64, 240 (August 2000), 508–21.

Mütercimler, Erol. *Denizden Gelen Destek: Sovyetler Birliğinden Alınan Yardım ve Kuva-yı Milliye Donanması*. Ankara: Yaprak Yayınları, 1992.

Muthu, Sankar. *Enlightenment Against Empire*. Princeton: Princeton University Press, 2003.

Naganawa, Norihiro. "Letters from Istanbul: The Ottoman Empire and the First Balkan War Observed by a Tatar Intellectual." Paper presented at the American Association for the Advancement of Slavic Studies, 39th annual conference, 15.11.2007.

Naimark, Norman. *Fires of Hatred: Ethnic Cleansing in Twentieth-Century Europe*. Cambridge, MA: Harvard University Press, 2001.

Nairn, Tom. *The Break-Up of Britain: Crisis and Neo-Nationalism*. London: NLB, 1977.

Nalbandian, Louise. *The Armenian Revolutionary Movement: The Development of Armenian Political Parties Through the Nineteenth Century*. Berkeley: University of California Press, 1963.

Näsibzadä, N. L. *Azärbaycan Demokratik Respublikası: Mägälär vä Sänädlär*. Baku: Elm, 1990.

Nekrich, A. M. *The Punished Peoples: The Deportation and Fate of Soviet Minorities at the End of the Second World War*. Tr. George Saunders. New York: Norton, 1978.

Nikitin, V. P. *Kurdy*. Translated from the French. Moscow: Progress, 1964.

Ortaylı, İlber. *Osmanlı İmparatorluğunda İktisadî ve Sosyal Değişim*. Ankara: Turhan Kitabevi, 2000.

Özoğlu, Hakan. *Kurdish Notables and the Ottoman State: Evolving Identities, Competing Loyalties, and Shifting Boundaries*. Albany: State University of New York Press, 2004.

Palmer, Alan. *The Decline and Fall of the Ottoman Empire*. London: John Murray, 1992.

Panossian, Razmik. *The Armenians: From Kings and Priests to Merchants and Commissars*. London: Hurst and Company, 2006.

Petrov, M. *Podgotovka Rossii k mirovoi voine na more*. Leningrad: Voenizdat, 1926.

Pinson, Mark. "Demographic Warfare: An Aspect of Ottoman and Russian Policy, 1854–1866." Ph.D. Dissertation, Harvard University, 1970.

Pipes, Richard. *The Formation of the Soviet Union: Communism and Nationalism*. Rev. edn. Cambridge, MA: Harvard University Press, [1954] 1997.

Posen, Barry. "Nationalism, the Mass Army, and Military Power." *International Security*, 18, 2 (Fall 1993), 80–124.

"The Security Dilemma and Ethnic Conflict." *Survival*, 35, 1 (Spring 1993), 27–47.

Quataert, Donald. *Social Disintegration and Popular Resistance in the Ottoman Empire, 1881–1908: Reactions to European Economic Penetration*. New York: New York University Press, 1983.

Reynolds, Michael A. "Native Sons: Post-Imperial Politics, Islam, and Identity in the North Caucasus, 1917–1918." *Jahrbücher für Geschichte Osteuropas,* 56 (March 2008), 232–37.

Rieber, Alfred. "Persistent Factors in Russian Foreign Policy: An Interpretive Essay." In *Imperial Russian Foreign Policy.* Ed. Hugh Ragsdale, 315–59. New York: Cambridge University Press, 1993.

Roldakarabilis, N. *Rusya'nın Şark Siyaseti ve Vilayet-i Şarkiye Meselesi.* Tr. Halil Adım. Dersaadet: Matbaa-ı Şems, 1332 [1914].

Rooney, Chris B. "The International Significance of British Naval Missions to the Ottoman Empire, 1908–1914." *Middle Eastern Studies,* 34 (1998), 1–29.

Rorlich, Azade-Ayşe. *The Volga Tatars: A Profile in National Resilience.* Stanford: Hoover Institution Press, 1986.

Roshwald, Aviel. *Ethnic Nationalism and the Fall of Empires: Central Europe, Russia, and the Middle East, 1914–1923.* New York: Routledge, 2001.

Rossos, Andrew. *Russia and the Balkans: Inter-Balkan Rivalries and Russian Foreign Policy.* Toronto: University of Toronto Press, 1981.

Safrastian, Arshak. *Kurds and Kurdistan.* London: Harvill Press, 1948.

Şahin, Enis. *Trabzon ve Batum Konferansları ve Anlaşmaları (1917–1918).* Ankara: Türk Tarih Kurumu, 2002.

Sait, Baha. *İttihat ve Terakki'nin Alevilik Bektaşilik Araştırması.* Ed. Nejat Birdoğan. Istanbul: Berfin Yayınları, 1994.

Sakal, Fahri. *Ağaoğlu Ahmed Bey.* Ankara: Türk Tarih Kurumu, 1999.

Sanborn, Josh. *Drafting the Russian Nation: Military Conscription, Total War, and Mass Politics, 1905–1925.* DeKalb: Northern Illinois University Press, 2003.

Sargizov, L. M. *Assiriitsy stran Blizhnego i Srednego Vostoka.* Yerevan: Aiastan, 1979.

Sarısaman, Sadık. "Birinci Dünya Savaşı Sırasında İran Elçiliğimiz ile İrtibatlı Bazı Teşkilat-ı Mahsusa Faaliyetleri." *Ankara Üniversitesi Osmanlı Tarihi Araştırma ve Uygulama Merkezi Dergisi,* 7 (1996), 209–14.

"Birinci Dünya Savaşı'nda Osmanlı Devleti'nin Bahtiyari Politikası." *Ankara Üniversitesi Osmanlı Tarihi Araştırma ve Uygulama Merkezi Dergisi,* 8 (1997), 296–318.

Birinci Dünya Savaşı'nda Türk Cephelerinde Beyannemelerle Psikolojik Harp. Ankara: Genelkurmay Basım Evi, 1999.

Sarkisian, E. K. *Ekspansionistskaia politika Osmanskoi imperii v Zakavkaz'e nakanune i v gody pervoi mirovoi voiny.* Yerevan: Akademiia nauk Armianskoi respubliki, 1962.

Sasuni, Garo. *Kürt Ulusal Hareketleri ve 15. Yüzyıldan Günümüze Ermeni–Kürt İlişkileri.* Istanbul: Med Yayınevi, 1992.

Schmitt, Bernadotte E. and Harold C. Vedeler. *The World in a Crucible, 1914–1919.* New York: Harper and Row, 1984.

Selçuk, İlhan. *Yüzbaşı Selahattin'in Romanı.* Istanbul: Remzi Kitabevi, 1973.

Seton-Watson, Hugh. *Nations and States: An Enquiry into the Origins of Nations and the Politics of Nationalism.* Boulder: Westview, 1977.

Shatsillo, K. F. *Russkii imperializm i razvitie flota nakanune pervoi mirovoi voiny (1906–1914).* Moscow: Nauka, 1968.

Shaw, Stanford. *From Empire to Republic: The Turkish War of National Liberation.* 5 vols. Ankara: Türk Tarih Kurumu, 2000.

Shaw, Stanford and Ezel Kural Shaw. *History of the Ottoman Empire and Modern Turkey,* vol. II, *Reform, Revolution, and Republic: The Rise of Modern Turkey, 1808–1975.* New York: Cambridge University Press, 1977.

Shissler, Holly A. *Between Two Empires: Ahmet Ağaoğlu and the New Turkey.* London: I. B. Tauris, 2002.

Slezkine, Yuri. "The USSR as a Communal Apartment, or How a Socialist State Promoted Ethnic Particularism." *Slavic Review,* 53, 2 (Summer 1994), 414–52.

Smal-Stocki, Roman. "Actions of 'Union for the Liberation of Ukraine' During World War I." *Ukrainian Quarterly,* 15, 2 (June 1959), 169–74.

Smith, C. Jay. *The Russian Struggle for Power, 1914–1917: A Study of Russian Foreign Policy During the First World War.* New York: Philosophical Library, 1956.

Smith, Michael G. "Anatomy of a Rumour: Murder Scandal, the Musavat Party, and Narratives of the Russian Revolution in Baku, 1917–1920." *Journal of Contemporary History,* 36, 2 (2001), 211–40.

"The Russian Revolution as a National Revolution: Tragic Deaths and Rituals of Remembrance in Muslim Azerbaijan (1907–1920)." *Jahrbücher für Geschichte Osteuropas,* 49, 3 (2001) 363–88.

Snyder, Jack. *The Ideology of the Offensive: Military Decision Making and the Disasters of 1914.* Ithaca: Cornell University Press, 1984.

Sohrabi, Nader. "Historicizing Revolutions: Constitutional Revolutions in the Ottoman Empire, Iran and Russia, 1905–1908." *American Journal of Sociology,* 100, 6 (May 1995), 1383–1447.

Sokol'nikov, G. Ia. *Brestskii mir.* Moscow: Gosudarstvennoe izdatel'stvo, 1920.

Somakian, Manoug Joseph. *Empires in Conflict: Armenia and the Great Powers, 1895–1920.* London: I. B. Tauris, 1995.

Spector, Ivar. "General Ali Fuat Cebesoy and the Kronstadt Revolt (1921): A Footnote to History." *International Journal of Middle East Studies,* 3, 4 (October 1972), 491–93.

Spring, D. W. "Russian Foreign Policy, Economic Interests and the Straits Question, 1905–1914." In *New Perspectives in Modern Russian History.* Ed. Robert B. McKean, 203–21. New York: St. Martin's Press, 1992.

Stoddard, Philip Hendrick. "The Ottoman Government and the Arabs: A Preliminary Study of the Teşkilat-ı Mahsusa." Ph.D. Dissertation, Princeton University, 1966.

Stone, Norman. *The Eastern Front, 1914–1917.* London: Hodder and Stoughton, 1975.

Strachan, Hew. *The First World War,* vol. I, *Call to Arms.* New York: Oxford University Press, 2001.

Süleymanov, Mehman. *Qafqaz İslam Ordusu vä Azärbaycan.* Baku: Härbi Näşriyyat, 1999.

Süleymanov, Mehman and Mehmet Rıhtım, eds. *Azärbaycan Xalq Cümhuriyyeti vä Qafqaz İslam Ordusu.* Baku: Qafkas Üniversiteti, 2008.

Sumner, B. H. *Russia and the Balkans, 1870–1880.* Oxford: Clarendon Press, 1937.

Suny, Ronald Grigor. *The Baku Commune, 1917–1918: Class and Nationality in the Russian Revolution.* Princeton: Princeton University Press, 1972.
"Eastern Armenians Under Tsarist Rule." In *Armenian People.* Ed. Hovannisian, 109–37.
Looking Toward Ararat: Armenia in Modern History. Bloomington: Indiana University Press, 1993.
The Making of the Georgian Nation. Bloomington: Indiana University Press, 1994.
ed. *A Question of Genocide.* Oxford: Oxford University Press, forthcoming.
ed. *Transcaucasia: Nationalism and Social Change: Essays in the History of Armenia, Azerbaijan, and Georgia.* Ann Arbor: University of Michigan Press, 1983.
Suny, Ronald Grigor and Terry Martin, eds. *A State of Nations: Empire and Nation-Making in the Age of Lenin and Stalin.* New York: Oxford University Press, 2001.
Swanson, Glen W. "Enver Pasha: The Formative Years." *Middle Eastern Studies,* 16, 3 (1980), 193–99.
Swietochowski, Tadeusz. *Russia and Azerbaijan: A Borderland in Transition.* New York: Columbia University Press, 1995.
Russian Azerbaijan, 1905–1920. Cambridge: Cambridge University Press, 1985.
Sykes, Mark. "The Kurdish Tribes of the Ottoman Empire." *Journal of the Royal Anthropological Institute of Great Britain and Ireland,* 38 (July–December 1908), 451–86.
Ter Minassian, Anahide. *Nationalism and Socialism in the Armenian Revolutionary Movement (1887–1912).* Tr. A. M. Barrett. Cambridge, MA: Zoryan Institute, 1984.
"Van 1915." In *Armenian Van/Vaspurakan.* Ed. Richard G. Hovannisian, 209–44. Costa Mesa, CA: Mazda, 2000.
Tilly, Charles. *Coercion, Capital, and European States AD 990–1992.* Cambridge, MA: Blackwell, 1992.
"Reflections on the History of European State-Making." In *The Formation of National States in Western Europe.* Ed. Charles Tilly, 13–84. Princeton: Princeton University Press, 1975.
"War Making and State Making as Organized Crime." In *Bringing the State Back In.* Ed. Peter B. Evans, Dietrich Rueschemeyer, and Theda Skocpol, 169–91. New York: Cambridge University Press, 1985.
Toprak, Zafer. "İttihat ve Terakki Fırkası 1332 Senesi Kongre Raporu." *Tarih ve Toplum,* 22 (June 1986), 133–38.
Türkiye'de Millî İktisat 1908–1918. Ankara: Yurt Yayınları, 1982.
Trumpener, Ulrich. *Germany and the Ottoman Empire, 1914–1918.* Princeton: Princeton University Press, 1968.
"Liman von Sanders and the German–Ottoman Alliance." *Journal of Contemporary History,* 1, 4 (October 1966), 179–92.
"Suez, Baku, Gallipoli: The Military Dimensions of the German–Ottoman Coalition." In *East Central European Society in World War I.* Ed. Bela Kiraly and Nandor F. Dreisziger, 381–400. Boulder: Social Science Monographs, 1985.

Tunaya, Tarık Zafer. *Türkiye'de Siyasal Partiler*. Vol. I. Istanbul: İletişim Yayınları, 1998.

Turan, Ömer. "Bolşevik İhtilalini Takip Eden Günlerde Kuzey Kafkasya'da Bağımsızlık Hareketleri ve Yusuf Ercan'ın Sohum Müfrezesi Hatıraları." *Askeri Tarih Bülteni*, 21, 40 (February 1996), 136–164.

Turfan, M. Naim. *Rise of the Young Turks: Politics, the Military, and Ottoman Collapse*. New York: St. Martin's Press, 2000.

Türkgeldi, Emin Ali. "Brest-Litowsk Konferansı Hatıraları." *Belgelerle Türk Tarihi Dergisi*, 3, 13 (March 1986), 46–53.

Türkmen, Zekeriya. *Vilayât-ı Şarkiye (Doğu Anadolu Vilayetleri) Islahat Müfettişliği 1913–1914*. Ankara: Türk Tarih Kurumu, 2006.

Türkoğlu, İsmail. *Sibiryalı Meşhur Seyyah Abdürreşid İbrahim*. Ankara: Diyanet Vakfı, 1997.

Üngör, Uğur Ü. "'A Reign of Terror': CUP Rule in Diyarbekir Province, 1913–1918." M. A. Thesis, University of Amsterdam, 2005.

Validov, Dzhamaliutdin. *Ocherk istorii obrazovannosti i literatury Tatar*. Kazan: Iman, 1998.

Vanly, Ismet Cheriff. "The Kurds in the Soviet Union." In *The Kurds: A Contemporary Overview*. Ed. Philip G. Kreyenbroek and Stefan Sperl, 193–218. London: Routledge, 1992.

Vigasin, A. A., A. N. Khokhlov, and P. M. Shastitko, eds. *Istoriia otechestvennogo vostokovedeniia s serediny XIX veka do 1917 goda*. Moscow: Vostochnaia literatura, 1997.

Von Hagen, Mark. "The Great War and the Mobilization of Ethnicity in the Russian Empire." In *Post-Soviet Political Order: Conflict and State Building*. Ed. Jack Snyder and Barnett Rubin, 34–57. New York: Routledge, 1998.

Walker, Christopher. *Armenia: The Survival of a Nation* 2nd edn. London: Routledge, 1990.

Waltz, Kenneth. *Theory of International Politics*. New York: McGraw-Hill, 1979.

Watenpaugh, Keith David. *Being Modern in the Middle East: Revolution, Nationalism, Colonialism, and the Arab Middle Class*. Princeton: Princeton University Press, 2006.

Weber, Frank G. *Eagles on the Crescent: Germany, Austria, and the Diplomacy of the Turkish Alliance, 1914–1918*. Ithaca: Cornell University Press, 1970.

Weeks, Theodore. *Nation and State in Late Imperial Russia: Nationalism and Russification on the Western Frontier, 1863–1914*. DeKalb: Northern Illinois University Press, 1996.

Weitz, Eric D. "From the Vienna to the Paris System: International Politics and the Entangled Histories of Human Rights, Forced Deportations, and Civilizing Missions." *American Historical Review* (December 2008), 1314–43.

Wendt, Alexander. "Anarchy Is What States Make of It: The Social Construction of Power Politics." *International Organization*, 46, 2 (Spring 1992), 391–425.

Wheeler-Bennett, John W. *Brest-Litovsk, the Forgotten Peace, March, 1918*. London: Macmillan, 1938.

Wigram, W. A., and Edgar T. A. Wigram. *The Cradle of Mankind: Life in Eastern Kurdistan*. London: Adam and Charles Black, 1914.

Wildman, Allan K. *The End of the Russian Imperial Army*. Vol. I. Princeton: Princeton University Press, 1980.

Williamson, Samuel R. Jr. *Austria-Hungary and the Origins of the First World War*. New York: Macmillan, 1991.

Wohlforth, William C. "The Perception of Power: Russia in the Pre-1914 Balance." *World Politics*, 39, 3 (April 1987), 353–81.

Wolfers, Arnold. *Discord and Collaboration: Essays on International Politics*. Baltimore: Johns Hopkins University Press, [1962] 1991.

Wortman, Richard S. *Scenarios of Power: Myth and Ceremony in Russian Monarchy*. Abridged edn. Princeton: Princeton University Press, 2006.

Yalman, Ahmed Emin. *Turkey in the World War*. New Haven: Yale University Press, 1930.

Yamauchi, Masayuki. *The Green Crescent Under the Red Star: Enver Pasha in Soviet Russia, 1919–1922*. Tokyo: Institute for the Study of Languages and Cultures, 1991.

Yasamee, F. A. K. "Colmar Freiherr von der Goltz and the Rebirth of the Ottoman Empire." *Diplomacy and Statecraft*, 9, 2 (July 1998), 91–128.

"Ottoman Empire." In *Decisions for War*. Ed. Keith Wilson, 229–68. London: UCL Press, 1995.

Yerasimos, Stefanos. *Türk–Sovyet İlişkileri Ekim Devriminden "Milli Mücadele"ye*. İstanbul: Gözlem Yayınları, 1979.

Yıldırım, Onur. *Diplomacy and Displacement: Reconsidering the Turco-Greek Exchange of Populations, 1922–1934*. New York: Routledge, 2006.

Yosmaoğlu, İpek. "Counting Bodies, Shaping Souls: The 1903 Census and National Identity in Ottoman Macedonia." *International Journal of Middle East Studies*, 38, 1 (2006), 55–77.

Yüceer, Nâsır. *Birinci Dünya Savaşı'nda Osmanlı Ordusu'nun Azerbaycan ve Dağıstan Harekâtı*. Ankara: Genelkurmay Basım Evi, 1996.

Yüceer, Saime. *Milli Mücadele Yıllarında Ankara–Moskova İlişkileri*. Bursa: Motif Matbaası, 1997.

Zaionchkovskii, A. M. *Podgotovka Rossii k imperialisticheskoi voine: ocherki voennoi podgotovki i pervonachal'nykh planov. Po arkhivnym dokumentam*. Moscow: Voennoe izdatel'stvo, 1926.

Podgotovka Rossii k mirovoi voine v mezhdunarodnom otnoshenii. Leningrad: Voennaia tipografiia, 1926.

Zakher, Ia. "Konstantinopl' i prolivy." *Krasnyi arkhiv: istoricheskii zhurnal*, 6 (1924), 48–76; 7 (1924), 32–54.

Zaya, Joseph. "General Agha Petros: Biographical Notes." Tr. S. Osipov. *Meltha: Proceedings of the Assyrian Public and Political Bulletin of the Assyrian National Club of Intellectuals*. Nos. 1–10 (1994–2000), 89–95.

Zeman, Z. A. B. and W. B. Scharlau. *The Merchant of Revolution: The Life of Alexander Israel Helphand (Parvus), 1867–1924*. New York: Oxford University Press, 1965.

Zenkovsky, Serge A. *Pan-Turkism and Islam in Russia*. Cambridge, MA: Harvard University Press, 1960.

Zürcher, Erik Jan. "Ottoman Conscription in Theory and Practice." In *Arming the State: Military Conscription in the Middle East and Central Asia, 1775–1925.* Ed. Zürcher, 79–94. London: I.B. Tauris, 1999.

Turkey: A Modern History. New York: I. B. Tauris, 1993.

The Unionist Factor: The Rôle of the Committee of Union and Progress in the Turkish National Movement, 1905–1926. Leiden: E. J. Brill, 1984.

"The Vocabulary of Muslim Nationalism." *International Journal of the Sociology of Language,* 137 (1999), 81–92.

"The Young Turks: Children of the Borderlands?" *International Journal of Turkish Studies,* 9, 1–2 (Summer 2003), 275–85.

Index

Russian empire, 26
  and Balkan Wars, 35–37
  and Kurland, 137
  Armenian massacres of 1894–96 and,
    54, 71–72, 98–102, 140, 157
  see also Russian empire: dilemmas of rule
    in Eastern Anatolia
  as potential Ottoman ally, 108
  backing for Armenian, Assyrian,
    and Kurdish revolts in 1914,
    115–16
  breakdown of imperial authority in
    occupied areas precipitates Christian
    attacks on Muslims, 194–95
  concerns about pan-Islam, 89–93
  covert activities in the Ottoman empire,
    63–64, 72, 73, 80, 94–98, 137
  deportations of Muslims, 144,
    147
  dilemmas of rule in Eastern Anatolia,
    142, 156–65
  diplomacy towards Ottoman empire on
    eve of World War I, 114–15
  see also Girs and Sazonov
  experience between 1908 and 1918 as
    tragic, 263
  February Revolution, 167–68
  flow of deserters and defectors to and
    from Ottoman empire, 103–06
  initial war plans, 123
  Kurdish policies of, 56–61, 63–70,
    77–78, 115–19, 141–42, 146
  see also Russian empire: dilemmas of rule
    in Eastern Anatolia
  legal scholars coin phrse "crimes
    against humanity and civilization",
    148
  Muslim emigres, 89–90
  Muslim population of, 82
  Muslims' ambivalence toward
    Ottomans, 91, 92
  Muslims rally to support empire in war,
    123
  occupation of Eastern Anatolia and
    Istanbul anticipated, 76
  overstretched, 253
  prewar security concerns of, 28, 40–41,
    57
  Provisional Government's pro-Armenian
    stance, 162, 195
  relations with Pontic Greeks,
    163–65
  relative power of, 2–3, 26, 27–28
  war with Ottomans as "War of
    Liberation," 141–42

Russian navy,
  expansion of in Black Sea, 36, 41
  Naval Ministry covets Trabzon and
    Sinop, 140, 141
  plans for expansion in Black Sea, 31–32
Russo-Ottoman War of 1877–78, 17,
  49–50

Sabahaddin Bey, Prince, 83, 97
Said Halim Pasha (grand vizier), 43, 44,
  76, 112, 113
  extracts better alliance terms from
    Germany, 111
  meets with Ukrainians, 134
  signs secret treaty with Germany, 109
Said Pasha, 33, 63
Şakir Niyazi, 97
Salonica, 30, 157
San Stefano peace talks, 14
Sazonov, Sergei, Plate 2, 29, 33, 35, 36,
  40, 41, 42, 44, 45, 61, 69, 73, 86,
  108, 141, 142, 148, 160, 253
  and Kurdish school in Khoy, 69
  approves arming Armenians, 117
  assists CUP opponents' operations, 98
  cautions of retribution against
    Armenians, Assyrians, and Kurds,
    142
  doubts on legal guaranties, 36
  indifference to Ottoman hostility, 110
  meeting with Talât, 43–44
  on Caucasus as turbulent region, 141
  on dangers of Ottoman disintegration,
    36–37
  on Kurds as potential force, 77
  on need to unite Kurds, 72
  on use of Kurds, Armenians, and
    Assyrians, 115
  orders more consulates opened in
    Eastern Anatolia, 73
  rejects peace talks with Ottomans, 137
  seeks Ottoman neutrality, 111–12
  threatens Ottomans with military
    intervention, 76
Serbia, 13, 14, 31, 34, 38, 107, 120, 172,
  174
Sèvres, Treaty of, 253, 258
Seyid Ali, 60
Shahtahtinskii, Ali, 92, 94
Shakhovskoi, Boris, 158
  accused of forming anti-Russian front
    with Kurds and Yezidis, 161–62
Shamil, Imam, 130, 236
Shaumian, Stepan, 179, 228, 229
Shikhlinskii, Ali, 223